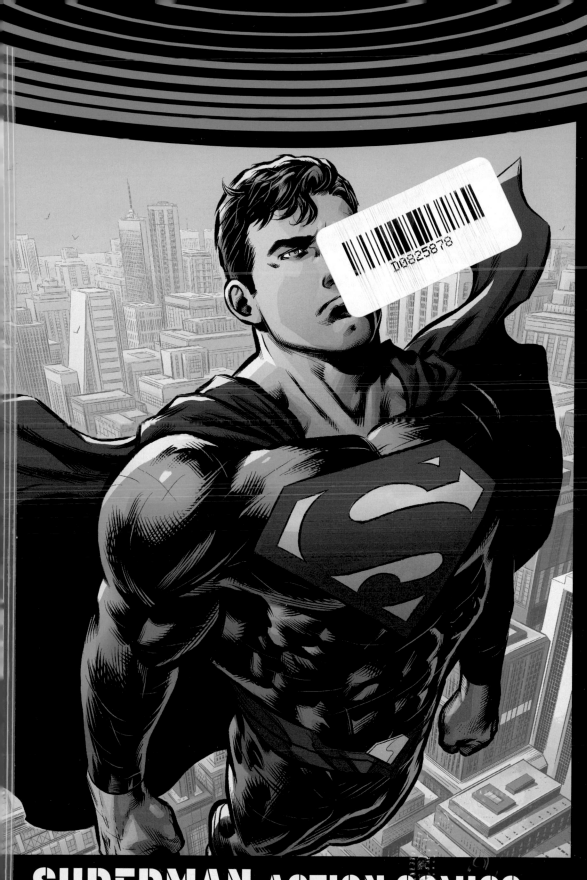

SUPERMAN ACTION COMICS
VOL.4 THE NEW WORLD

D0825878

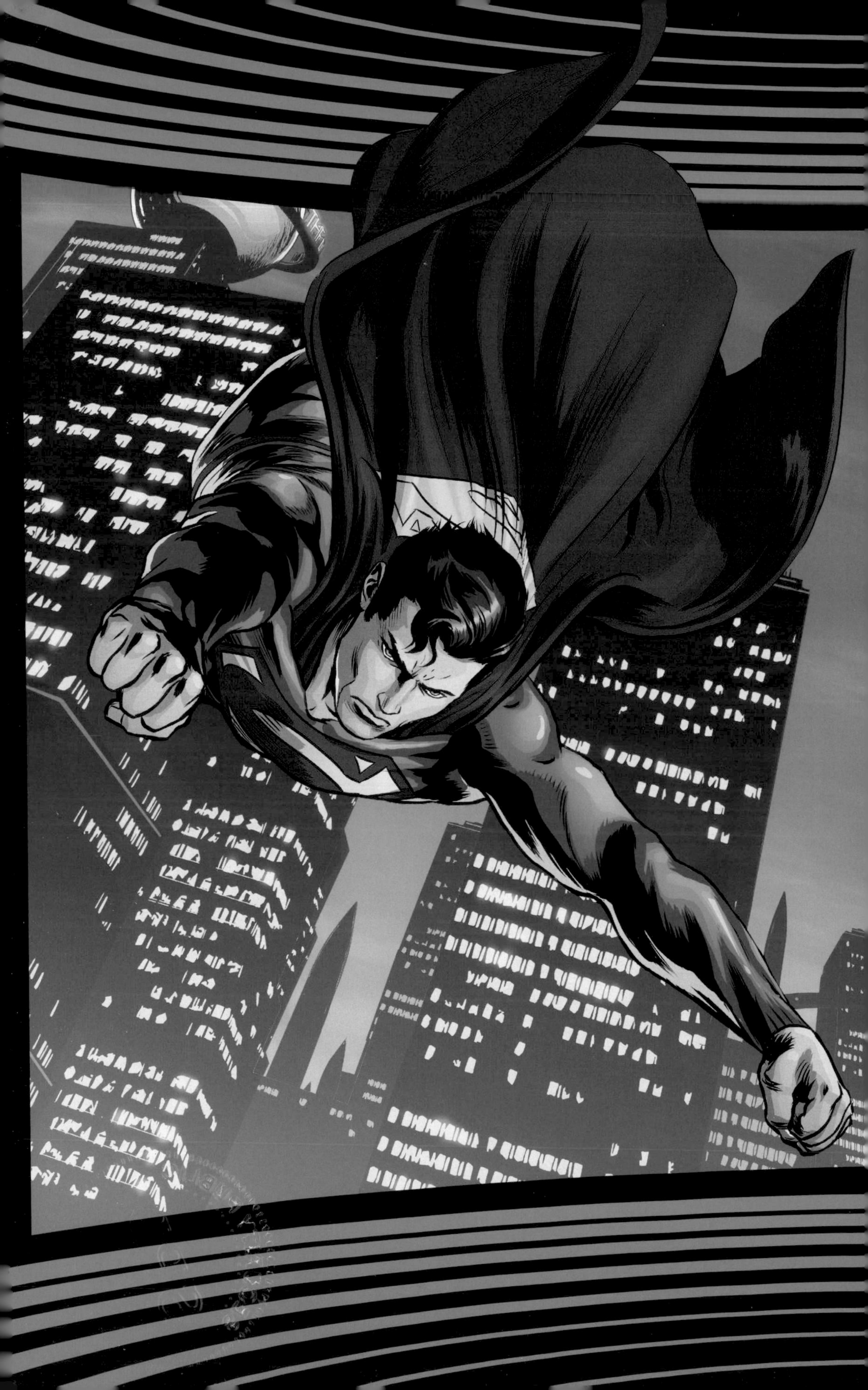

SUPERMAN ACTION COMICS
VOL.4 THE NEW WORLD

DAN JURGENS
writer

PATCH ZIRCHER * **IAN CHURCHILL** * **CARLO BARBERI**
MATT SANTORELLI * **JACK HERBERT** * **JOSE LUIS**
RAY MCCARTHY * **VIKTOR BOGDANOVIC** * **JONATHAN GLAPION**
artists

HI-FI * **MIKE SPICER**
colorists

ROB LEIGH
letterer

ANDY KUBERT and BRAD ANDERSON
collection cover artists

SUPERMAN created by **JERRY SIEGEL** and **JOE SHUSTER**
By special arrangement with the Jerry Siegel family

MIKE COTTON Editor - Original Series ✳ PAUL KAMINSKI Associate Editor - Original Series
JEB WOODARD Group Editor - Collected Editions ✳ PAUL SANTOS Editor - Collected Edition
STEVE COOK Design Director - Books ✳ SHANNON STEWART Publication Design

BOB HARRAS Senior VP - Editor-in-Chief, DC Comics
PAT McCALLUM Executive Editor, DC Comics

DIANE NELSON President ✳ DAN DiDIO Publisher ✳ JIM LEE Publisher ✳ GEOFF JOHNS President & Chief Creative Officer
AMIT DESAI Executive VP - Business & Marketing Strategy, Direct to Consumer & Global Franchise Management
SAM ADES Senior VP & General Manager, Digital Services ✳ BOBBIE CHASE VP & Executive Editor, Young Reader & Talent Development
MARK CHIARELLO Senior VP - Art, Design & Collected Editions ✳ JOHN CUNNINGHAM Senior VP - Sales & Trade Marketing
ANNE DePIES Senior VP - Business Strategy, Finance & Administration ✳ DON FALLETTI VP - Manufacturing Operations
LAWRENCE GANEM VP - Editorial Administration & Talent Relations ✳ ALISON GILL Senior VP - Manufacturing & Operations
HANK KANALZ Senior VP - Editorial Strategy & Administration ✳ JAY KOGAN VP - Legal Affairs ✳ JACK MAHAN VP - Business Affairs
NICK J. NAPOLITANO VP - Manufacturing Administration ✳ EDDIE SCANNELL VP - Consumer Marketing
COURTNEY SIMMONS Senior VP - Publicity & Communications ✳ JIM (SKI) SOKOLOWSKI VP - Comic Book Specialty Sales & Trade Marketing
NANCY SPEARS VP - Mass, Book, Digital Sales & Trade Marketing ✳ MICHELE R. WELLS VP - Content Strategy

SUPERMAN: ACTION COMICS VOL. 4 — THE NEW WORLD

Published by DC Comics. Compilation and all new material Copyright © 2017 DC Comics. All Rights Reserved.
Originally published in single magazine form in ACTION COMICS 977-984. Copyright © 2017 DC Comics. All Rights Reserved.
All characters, their distinctive likenesses and related elements featured in this publication are trademarks of DC Comics.
The stories, characters and incidents featured in this publication are entirely fictional.
DC Comics does not read or accept unsolicited submissions of ideas, stories or artwork.

DC Comics, 2900 West Alameda Ave., Burbank, CA 91505.
Printed by LSC Communications, Kendallville, IN, USA. 9/29/17. First Printing
ISBN: 978-1-4012-7440-5

Library of Congress Cataloging-in-Publication Data is available.

PEFC Certified

Printed on paper from
sustainably managed
forests, controlled
sources

PEFC/29-31-337   www.pefc.org

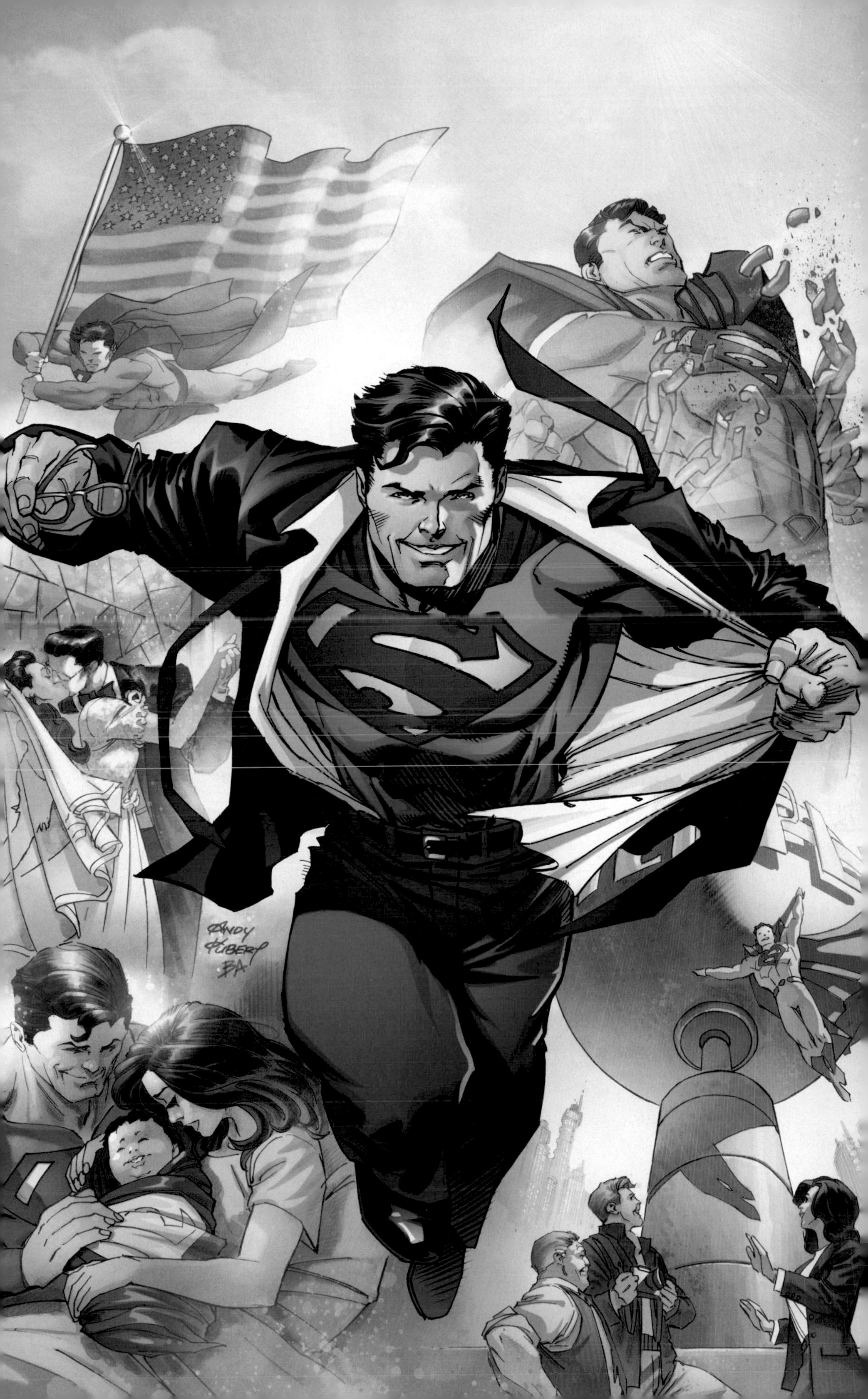
ANDY
KUBERT
BA

THE NEW WORLD PART 1

IAN CHURCHILL artist * HI-FI colorist

ANDY KUBERT BRAD ANDERSON cover artists

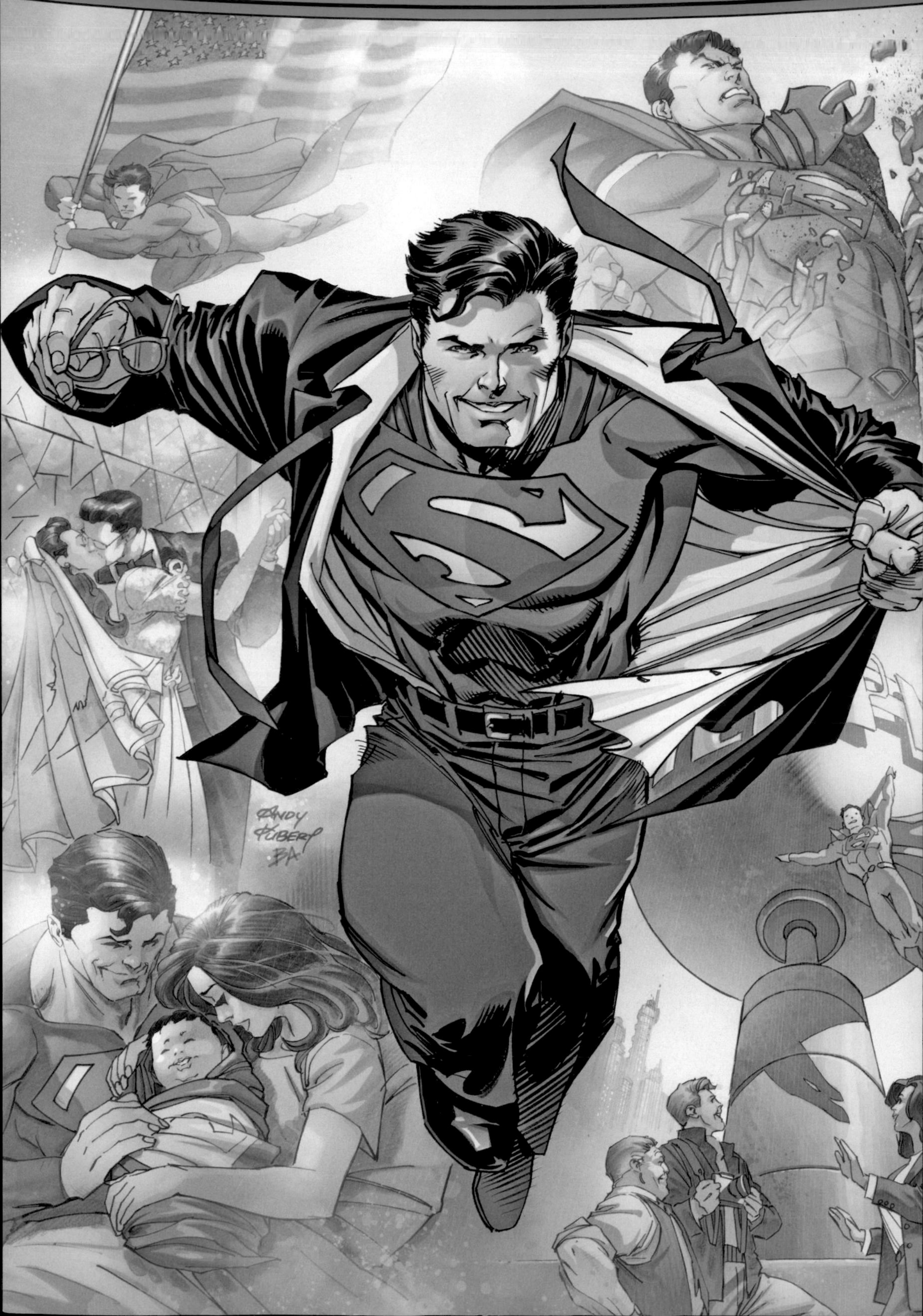
ANDY KUBERT BA

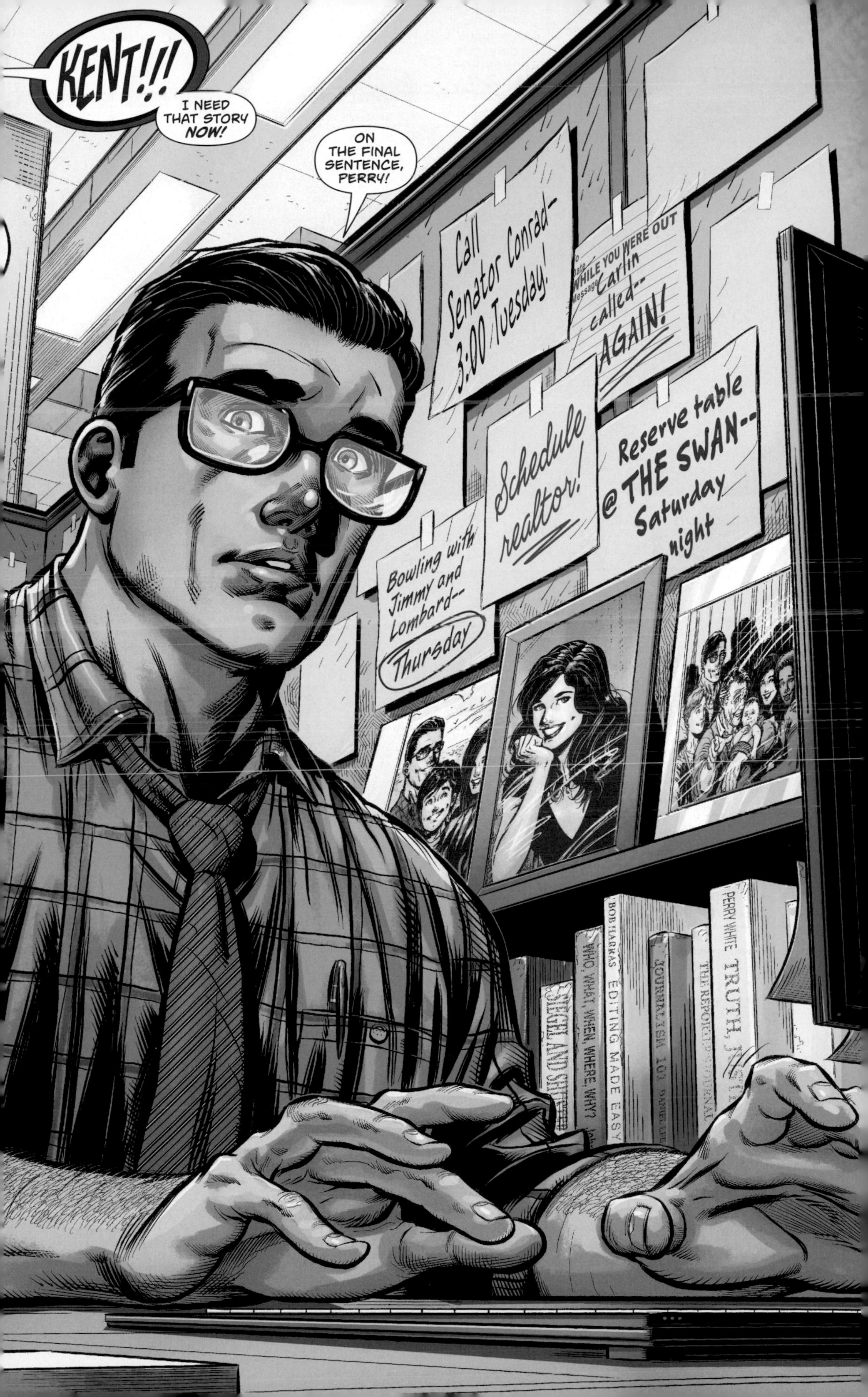
KENT!!!
I NEED THAT STORY NOW!
ON THE FINAL SENTENCE, PERRY!
Call Senator Conrad-- 3:00 Tuesday!
WHILE YOU WERE OUT
To
Date
Message Carlin called-- AGAIN!
Schedule realtor!
Reserve table @ THE SWAN-- Saturday night
Bowling with Jimmy and Lombard-- Thursday
BOB HARRAS EDITING MADE EASY
WHO, WHAT, WHEN, WHERE, WHY?
JOURNALISM 101
PERRY WHITE TRUTH, JU
THE REPORTER'S JOURNAL

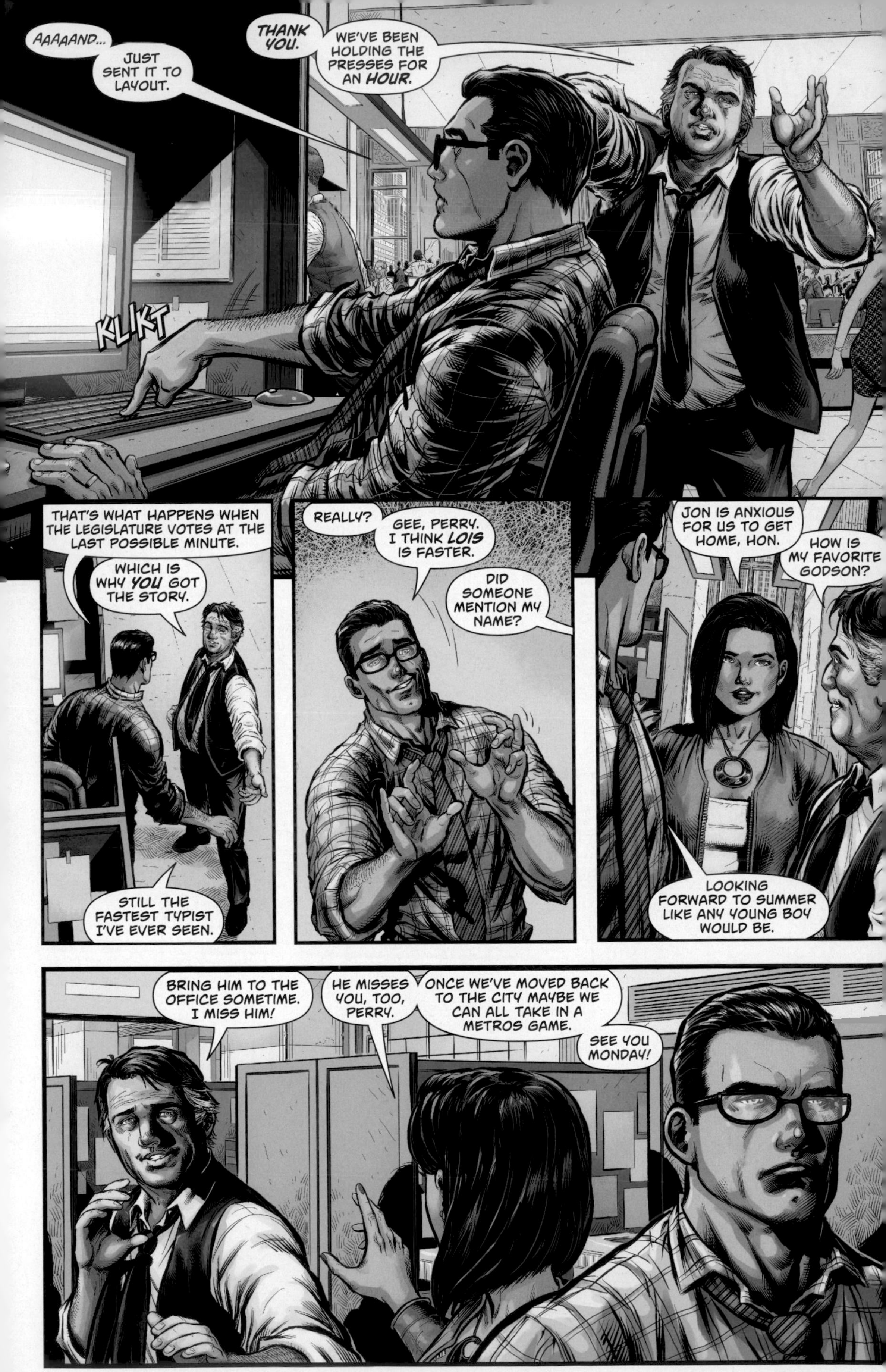
AAAAAND...
JUST SENT IT TO LAYOUT.
KLIKT
THANK YOU.
WE'VE BEEN HOLDING THE PRESSES FOR AN HOUR.
THAT'S WHAT HAPPENS WHEN THE LEGISLATURE VOTES AT THE LAST POSSIBLE MINUTE.
WHICH IS WHY YOU GOT THE STORY.
STILL THE FASTEST TYPIST I'VE EVER SEEN.
REALLY?
GEE, PERRY. I THINK LOIS IS FASTER.
DID SOMEONE MENTION MY NAME?
JON IS ANXIOUS FOR US TO GET HOME, HON.
HOW IS MY FAVORITE GODSON?
LOOKING FORWARD TO SUMMER LIKE ANY YOUNG BOY WOULD BE.
BRING HIM TO THE OFFICE SOMETIME. I MISS HIM!
HE MISSES YOU, TOO, PERRY.
ONCE WE'VE MOVED BACK TO THE CITY MAYBE WE CAN ALL TAKE IN A METROS GAME.
SEE YOU MONDAY!

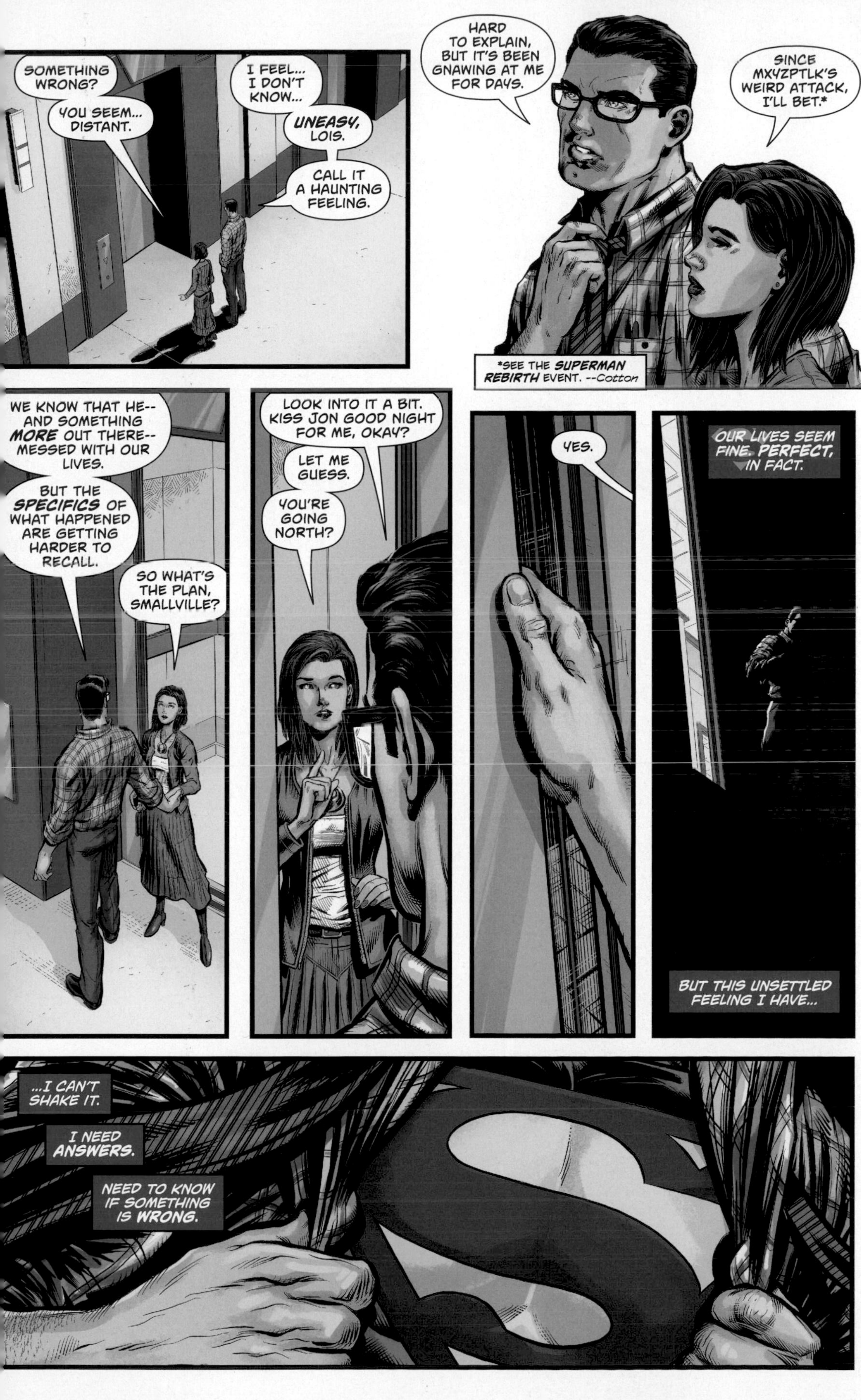
SOMETHING WRONG?
YOU SEEM... DISTANT.
I FEEL... I DON'T KNOW...
UNEASY, LOIS.
CALL IT A HAUNTING FEELING.
HARD TO EXPLAIN, BUT IT'S BEEN GNAWING AT ME FOR DAYS.
SINCE MXYZPTLK'S WEIRD ATTACK, I'LL BET.*
*SEE THE SUPERMAN REBIRTH EVENT. --Cotton
WE KNOW THAT HE--AND SOMETHING MORE OUT THERE--MESSED WITH OUR LIVES.
BUT THE SPECIFICS OF WHAT HAPPENED ARE GETTING HARDER TO RECALL.
SO WHAT'S THE PLAN, SMALLVILLE?
LOOK INTO IT A BIT. KISS JON GOOD NIGHT FOR ME, OKAY?
LET ME GUESS.
YOU'RE GOING NORTH?
YES.
OUR LIVES SEEM FINE. PERFECT, IN FACT.
BUT THIS UNSETTLED FEELING I HAVE...
...I CAN'T SHAKE IT.
I NEED ANSWERS.
NEED TO KNOW IF SOMETHING IS WRONG.

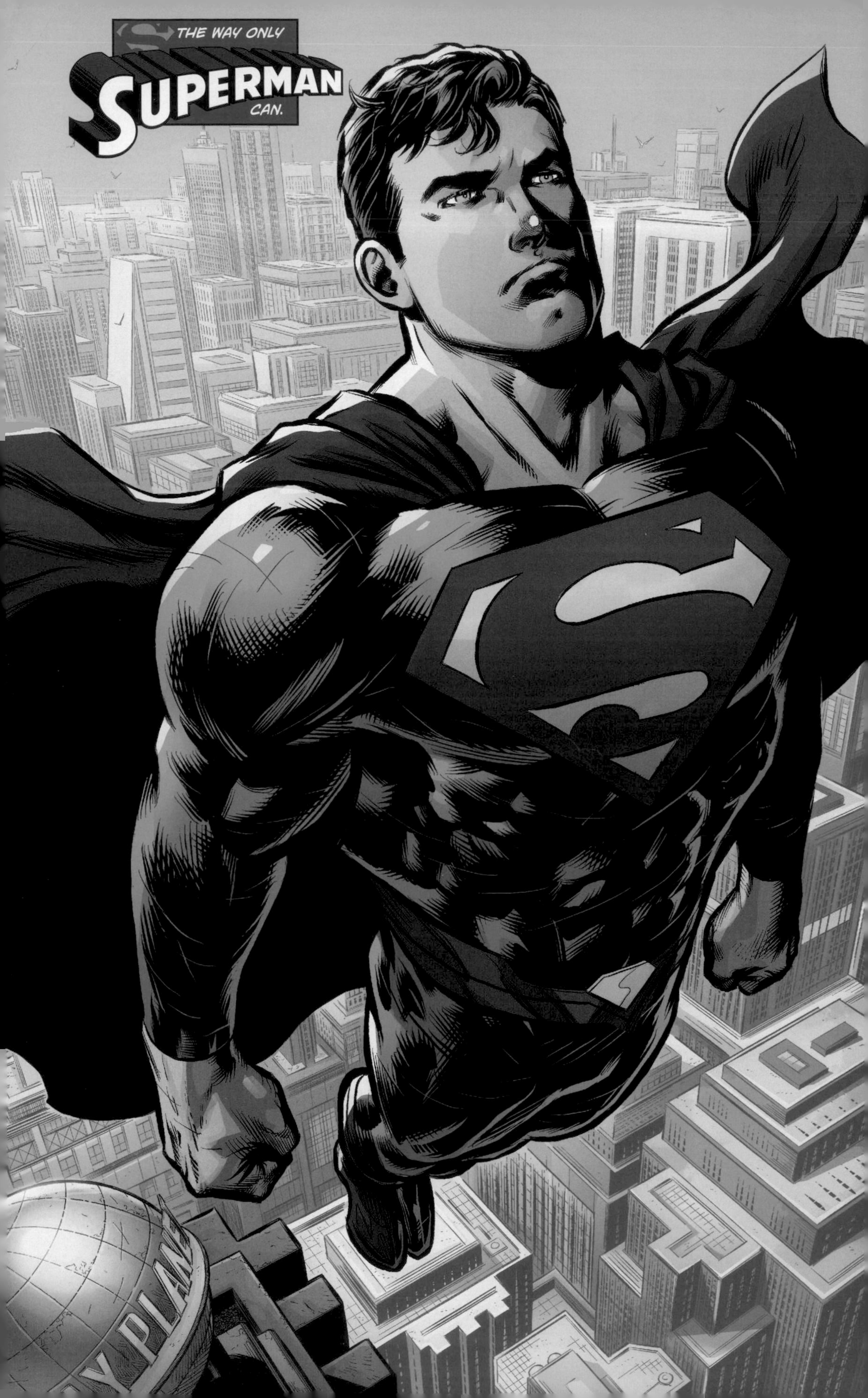
THE WAY ONLY
SUPERMAN
CAN.

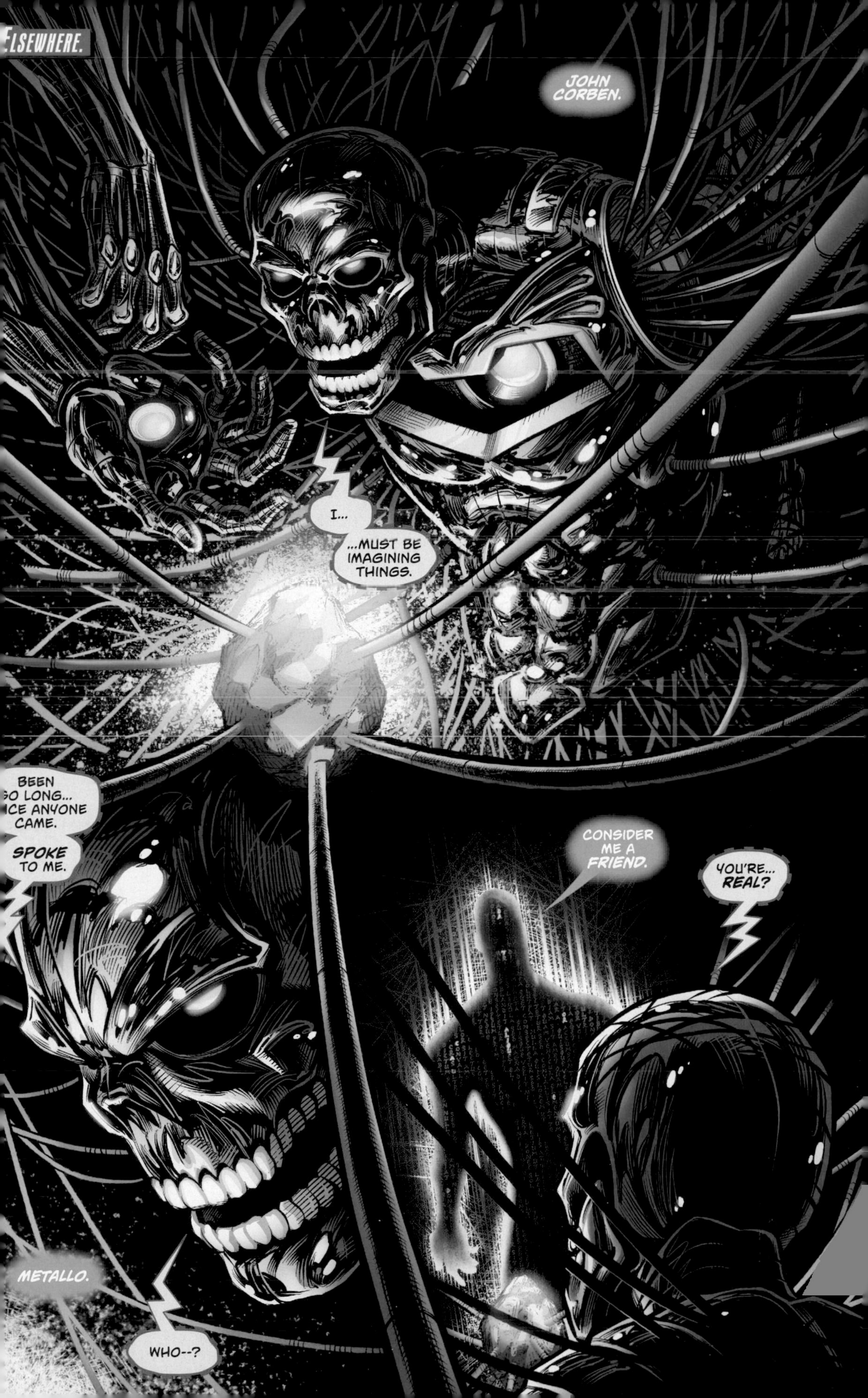
ELSEWHERE.
JOHN CORBEN.
I...
...MUST BE IMAGINING THINGS.
BEEN SO LONG... SINCE ANYONE CAME.
SPOKE TO ME.
CONSIDER ME A FRIEND.
YOU'RE... REAL?
METALLO.
WHO--?

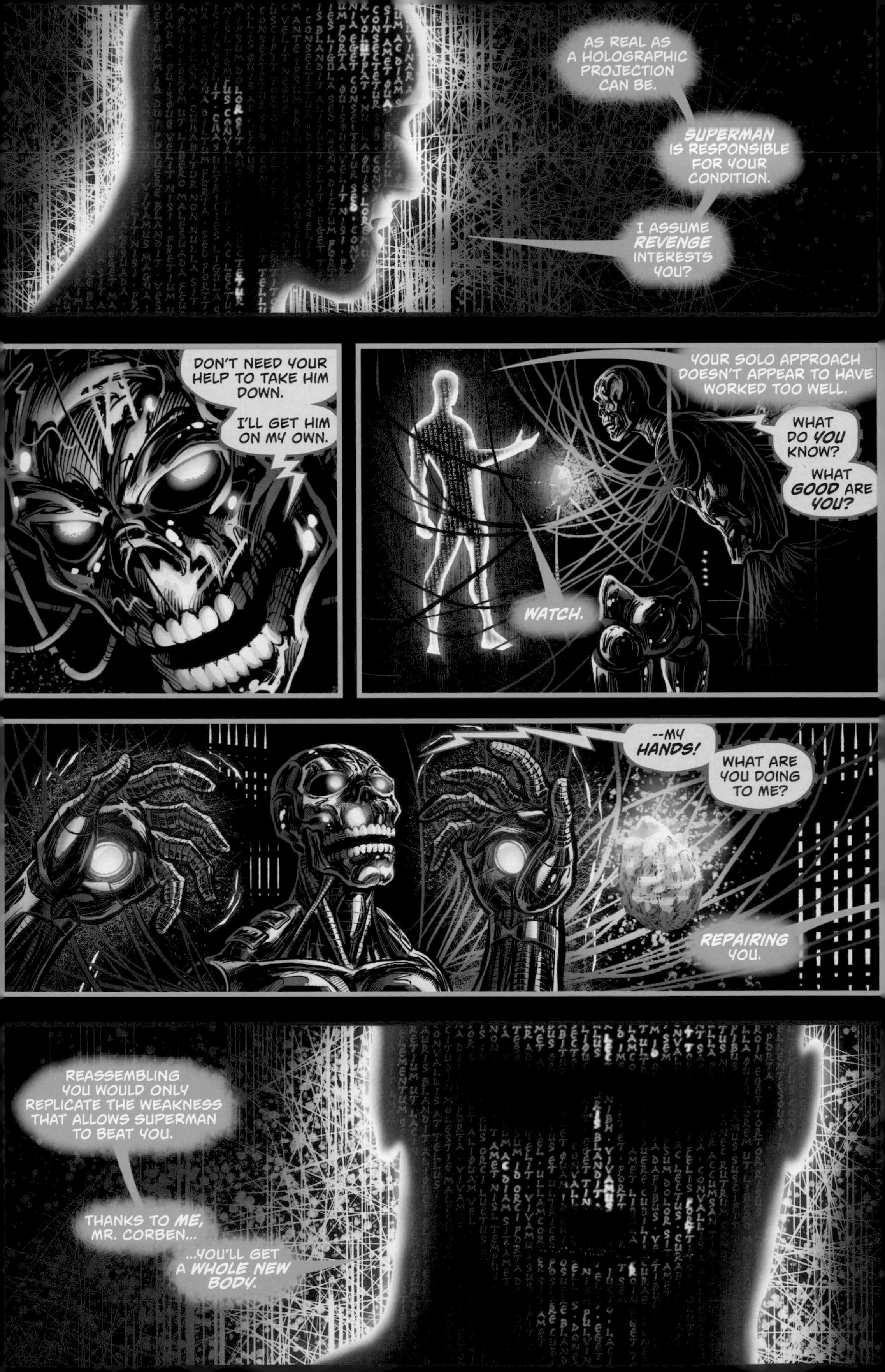

AS REAL AS A HOLOGRAPHIC PROJECTION CAN BE.
SUPERMAN IS RESPONSIBLE FOR YOUR CONDITION.
I ASSUME REVENGE INTERESTS YOU?
DON'T NEED YOUR HELP TO TAKE HIM DOWN.
I'LL GET HIM ON MY OWN.
YOUR SOLO APPROACH DOESN'T APPEAR TO HAVE WORKED TOO WELL.
WHAT DO YOU KNOW?
WHAT GOOD ARE YOU?
WATCH.
--MY HANDS!
WHAT ARE YOU DOING TO ME?
REPAIRING YOU.
REASSEMBLING YOU WOULD ONLY REPLICATE THE WEAKNESS THAT ALLOWS SUPERMAN TO BEAT YOU.
THANKS TO ME, MR. CORBEN...
...YOU'LL GET A WHOLE NEW BODY.

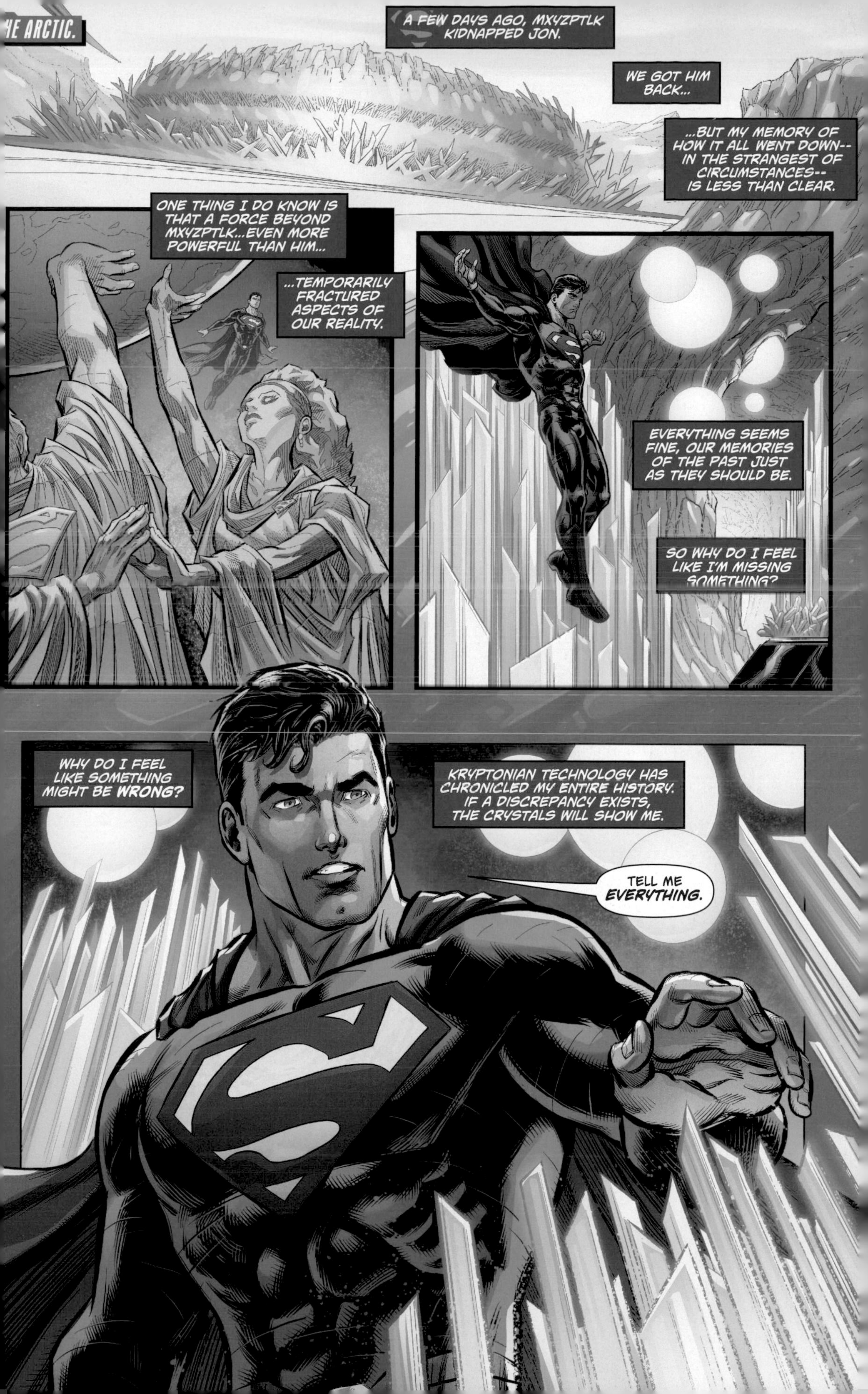

HE ARCTIC.
A FEW DAYS AGO, MXYZPTLK KIDNAPPED JON.
WE GOT HIM BACK...
...BUT MY MEMORY OF HOW IT ALL WENT DOWN-- IN THE STRANGEST OF CIRCUMSTANCES-- IS LESS THAN CLEAR.
ONE THING I DO KNOW IS THAT A FORCE BEYOND MXYZPTLK...EVEN MORE POWERFUL THAN HIM...
...TEMPORARILY FRACTURED ASPECTS OF OUR REALITY.
EVERYTHING SEEMS FINE, OUR MEMORIES OF THE PAST JUST AS THEY SHOULD BE.
SO WHY DO I FEEL LIKE I'M MISSING SOMETHING?
WHY DO I FEEL LIKE SOMETHING MIGHT BE WRONG?
KRYPTONIAN TECHNOLOGY HAS CHRONICLED MY ENTIRE HISTORY. IF A DISCREPANCY EXISTS, THE CRYSTALS WILL SHOW ME.
TELL ME EVERYTHING.

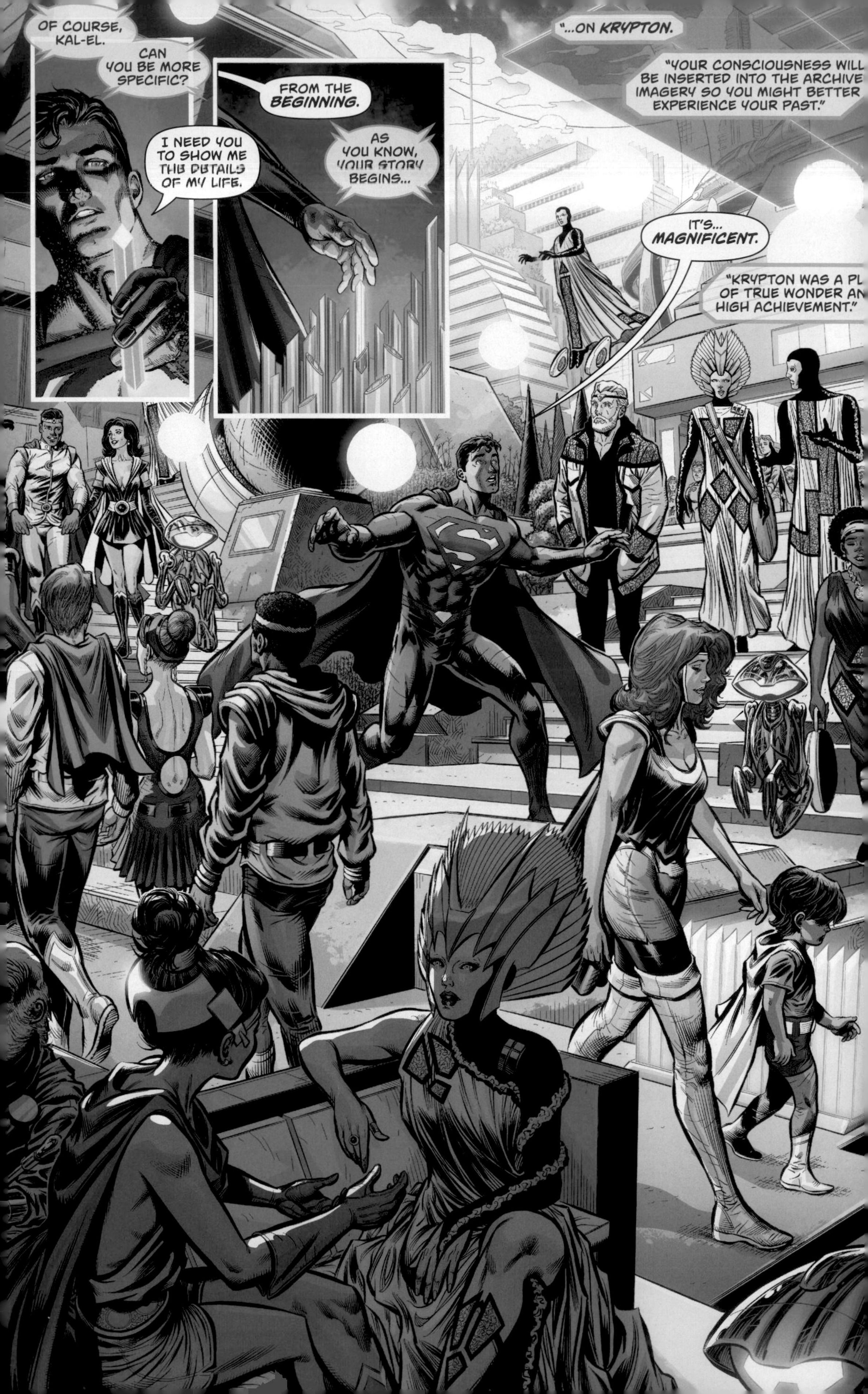
OF COURSE, KAL-EL.
CAN YOU BE MORE SPECIFIC?
I NEED YOU TO SHOW ME THE DETAILS OF MY LIFE.
FROM THE BEGINNING.
AS YOU KNOW, YOUR STORY BEGINS...
"...ON KRYPTON.
"YOUR CONSCIOUSNESS WILL BE INSERTED INTO THE ARCHIVE IMAGERY SO YOU MIGHT BETTER EXPERIENCE YOUR PAST."
IT'S... MAGNIFICENT.
"KRYPTON WAS A PL OF TRUE WONDER AN HIGH ACHIEVEMENT."

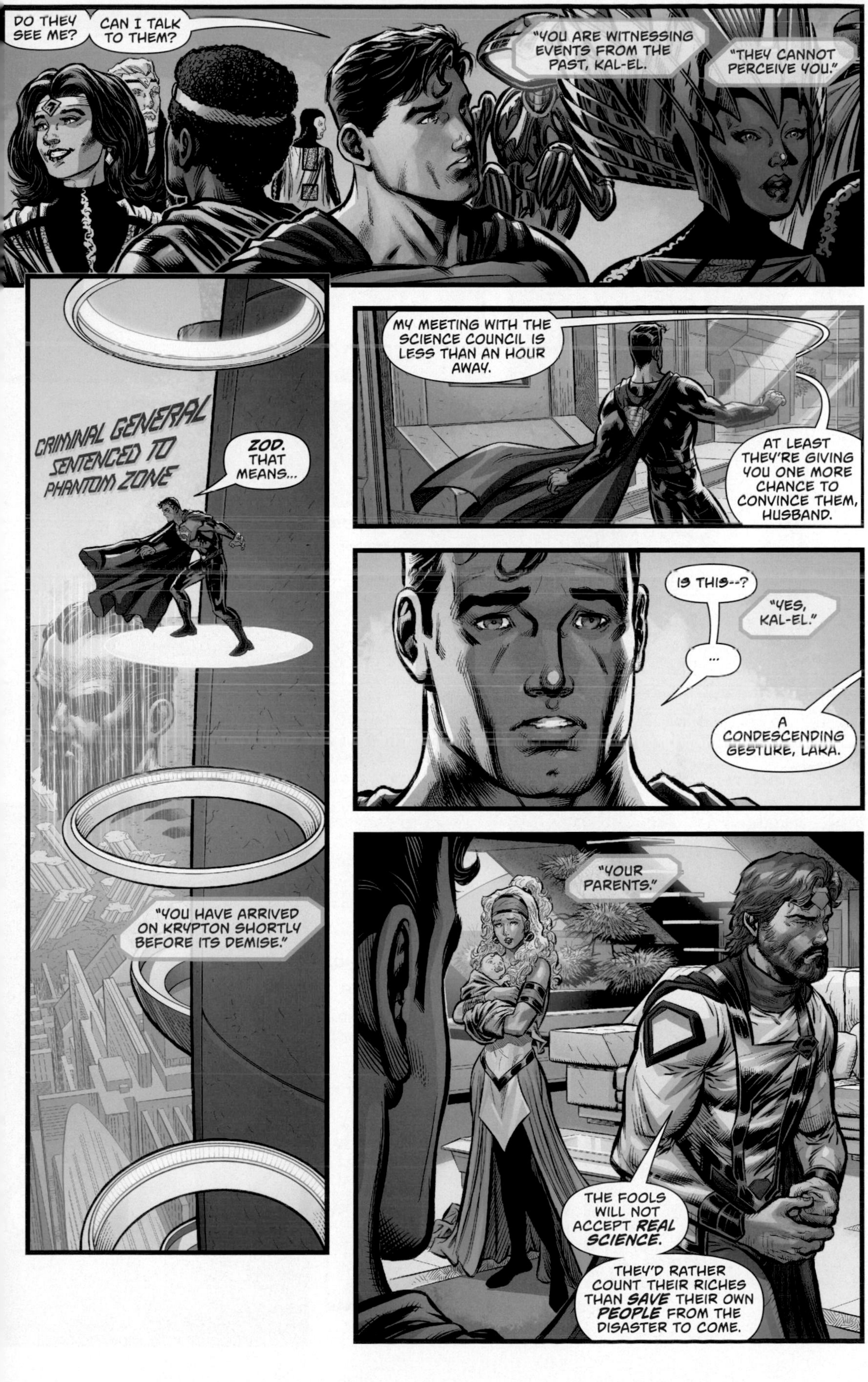
DO THEY SEE ME?
CAN I TALK TO THEM?
"YOU ARE WITNESSING EVENTS FROM THE PAST, KAL-EL.
"THEY CANNOT PERCEIVE YOU."
CRIMINAL GENERAL SENTENCED TO PHANTOM ZONE
ZOD. THAT MEANS...
"YOU HAVE ARRIVED ON KRYPTON SHORTLY BEFORE ITS DEMISE."
MY MEETING WITH THE SCIENCE COUNCIL IS LESS THAN AN HOUR AWAY.
AT LEAST THEY'RE GIVING YOU ONE MORE CHANCE TO CONVINCE THEM, HUSBAND.
IS THIS--?
"YES, KAL-EL."
...
A CONDESCENDING GESTURE, LARA.
"YOUR PARENTS."
THE FOOLS WILL NOT ACCEPT REAL SCIENCE.
THEY'D RATHER COUNT THEIR RICHES THAN SAVE THEIR OWN PEOPLE FROM THE DISASTER TO COME.

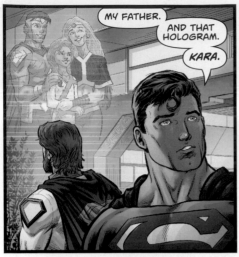

MY FATHER.

AND THAT HOLOGRAM.

KARA.

YOU MUST CONVINCE THEM, JOR. WE CANNOT LOSE OUR FUTURE--OUR *CHILD*--TO THEIR *IGNORANCE*.

MOTHER...

JOR--?

BRRMMMMM

EARTHQUAKE.

THE THIRD ONE TODAY.

MAYBE *THIS* WILL BE ENOUGH TO CONVINCE THE COUNCIL THAT KRYPTON IS *DOOMED*.

THAT WE HAVE TO BUILD AN EVACUATION *FLEET* AS QUICKLY AS POSSIBLE!

WHY DIDN'T THEY *LISTEN*?

"THEY THOUGHT YOUR FATHER AN ALARMIST, KAL-EL. THAT THEY HAD YEARS TO CORRECT THE PROBLEM."

RAO BE WITH YOU, HUSBAND.

HOW COULD THEY CONDEMN THEIR WORLD... THEIR OWN *PEOPLE* TO *OBLIVION*?

DADDY WILL CONVINCE THEM, KAL.

HE *MUST*.

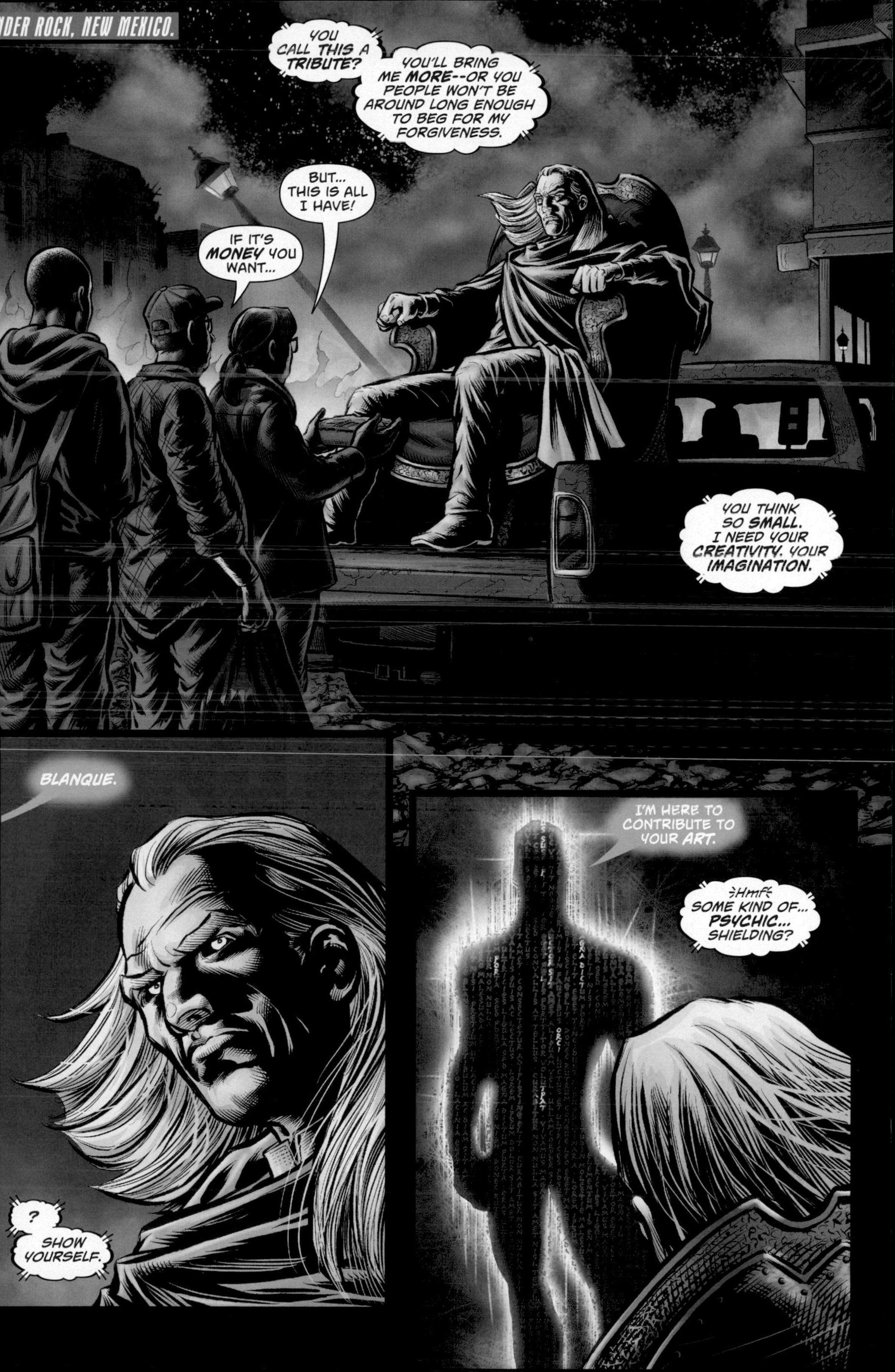

NDER ROCK, NEW MEXICO.
YOU CALL THIS A TRIBUTE?
YOU'LL BRING ME MORE--OR YOU PEOPLE WON'T BE AROUND LONG ENOUGH TO BEG FOR MY FORGIVENESS.
BUT... THIS IS ALL I HAVE!
IF IT'S MONEY YOU WANT...
YOU THINK SO SMALL. I NEED YOUR CREATIVITY. YOUR IMAGINATION.
BLANQUE.
?
SHOW YOURSELF.
I'M HERE TO CONTRIBUTE TO YOUR ART.
Hmf
SOME KIND OF... PSYCHIC... SHIELDING?

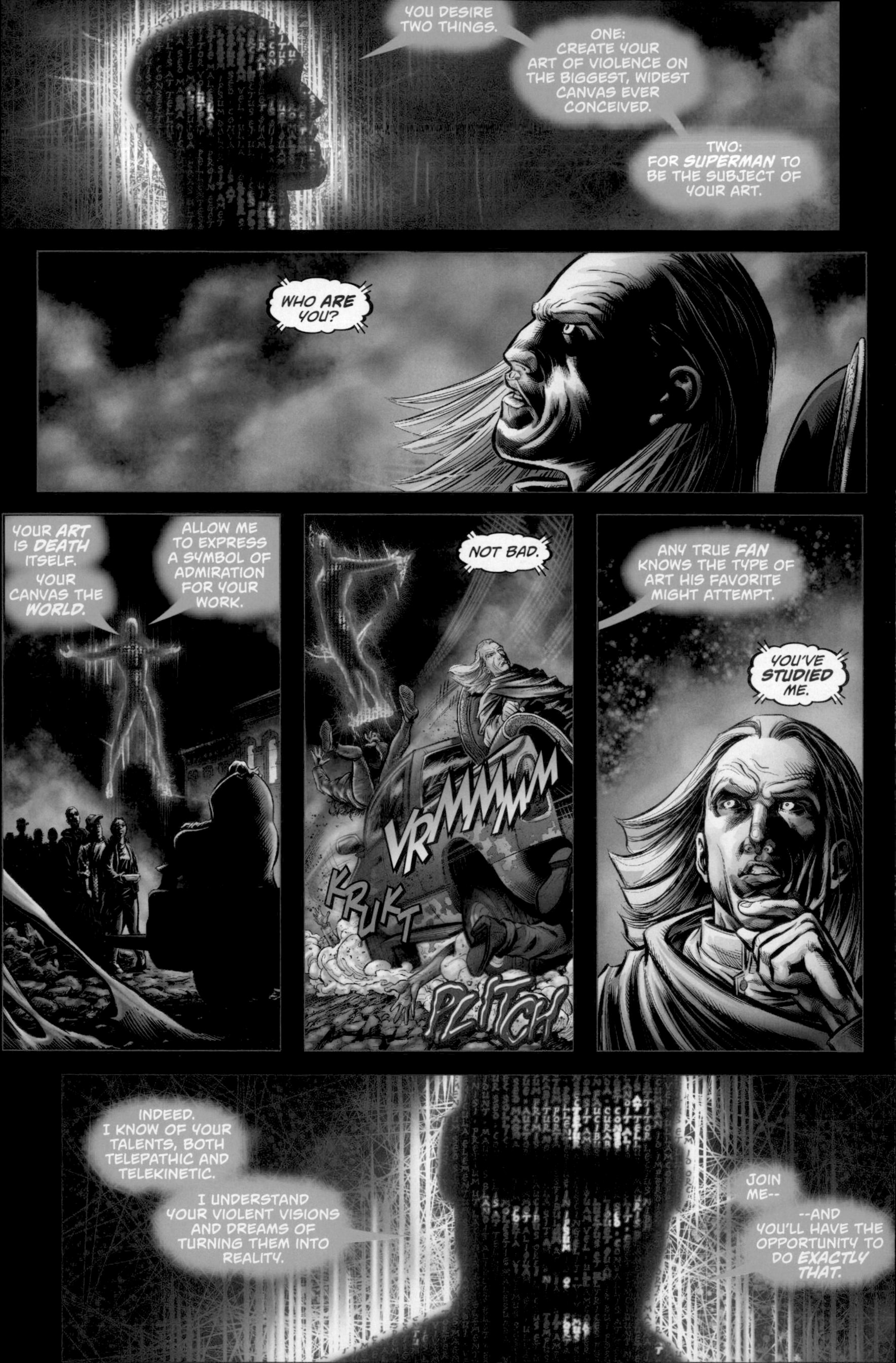
YOU DESIRE TWO THINGS.
ONE: CREATE YOUR ART OF VIOLENCE ON THE BIGGEST, WIDEST CANVAS EVER CONCEIVED.
TWO: FOR *SUPERMAN* TO BE THE SUBJECT OF YOUR ART.
WHO *ARE* YOU?
YOUR *ART* IS *DEATH* ITSELF.
YOUR CANVAS THE *WORLD.*
ALLOW ME TO EXPRESS A SYMBOL OF ADMIRATION FOR YOUR WORK.
NOT BAD.
VRMMMM
KRUKT
PLTCH
ANY TRUE *FAN* KNOWS THE TYPE OF ART HIS FAVORITE MIGHT ATTEMPT.
YOU'VE *STUDIED* ME.
INDEED. I KNOW OF YOUR TALENTS, BOTH TELEPATHIC AND TELEKINETIC.
I UNDERSTAND YOUR VIOLENT VISIONS AND DREAMS OF TURNING THEM INTO REALITY.
JOIN ME--
--AND YOU'LL HAVE THE OPPORTUNITY TO DO *EXACTLY THAT.*

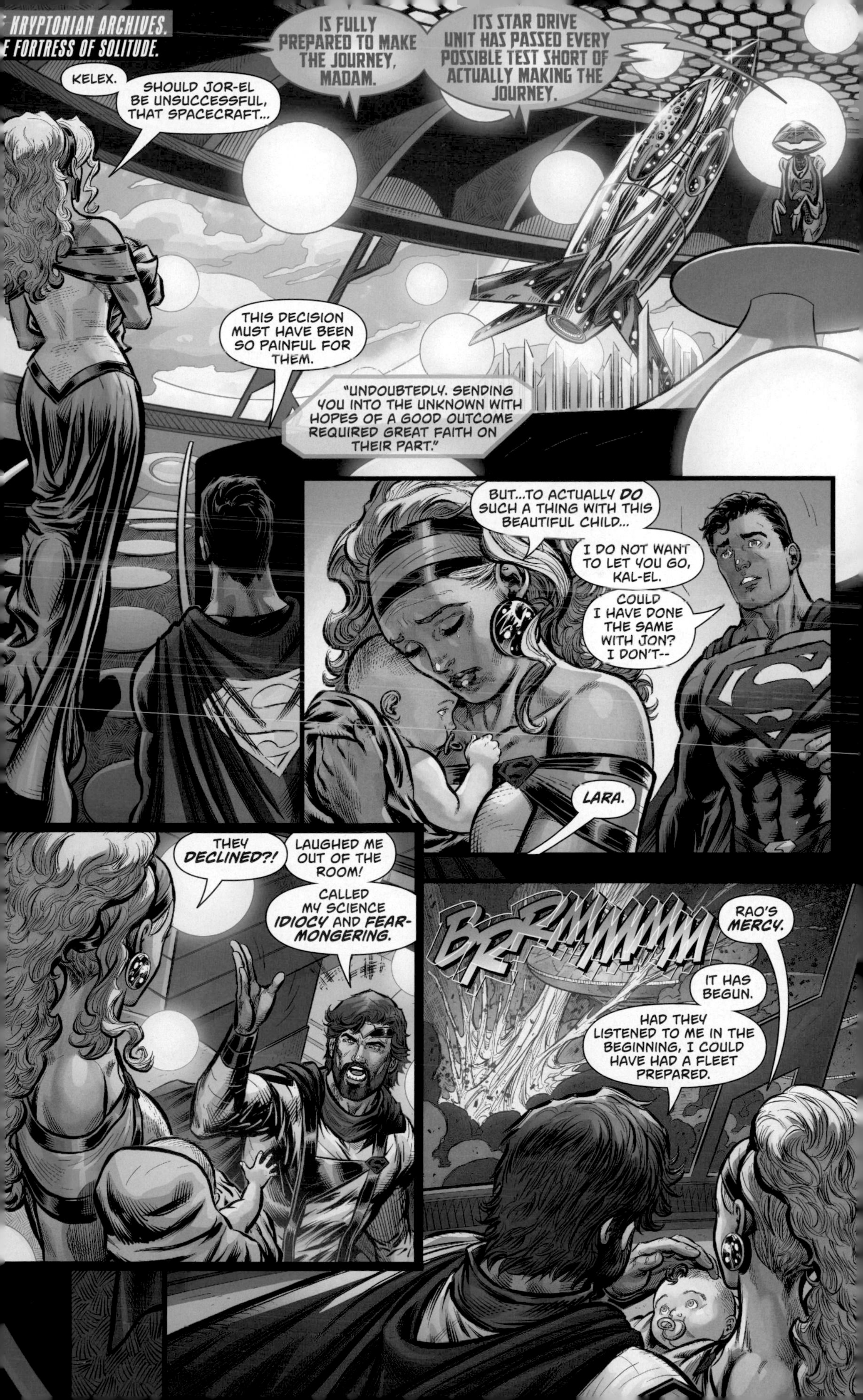

KRYPTONIAN ARCHIVES.
FORTRESS OF SOLITUDE.
KELEX.
SHOULD JOR-EL BE UNSUCCESSFUL, THAT SPACECRAFT...
IS FULLY PREPARED TO MAKE THE JOURNEY, MADAM.
ITS STAR DRIVE UNIT HAS PASSED EVERY POSSIBLE TEST SHORT OF ACTUALLY MAKING THE JOURNEY.
THIS DECISION MUST HAVE BEEN SO PAINFUL FOR THEM.
"UNDOUBTEDLY. SENDING YOU INTO THE UNKNOWN WITH HOPES OF A GOOD OUTCOME REQUIRED GREAT FAITH ON THEIR PART."
BUT...TO ACTUALLY DO SUCH A THING WITH THIS BEAUTIFUL CHILD...
I DO NOT WANT TO LET YOU GO, KAL-EL.
COULD I HAVE DONE THE SAME WITH JON? I DON'T--
LARA.
THEY DECLINED?!
LAUGHED ME OUT OF THE ROOM!
CALLED MY SCIENCE IDIOCY AND FEAR-MONGERING.
BRRMMMMM
RAO'S MERCY.
IT HAS BEGUN.
HAD THEY LISTENED TO ME IN THE BEGINNING, I COULD HAVE HAD A FLEET PREPARED.

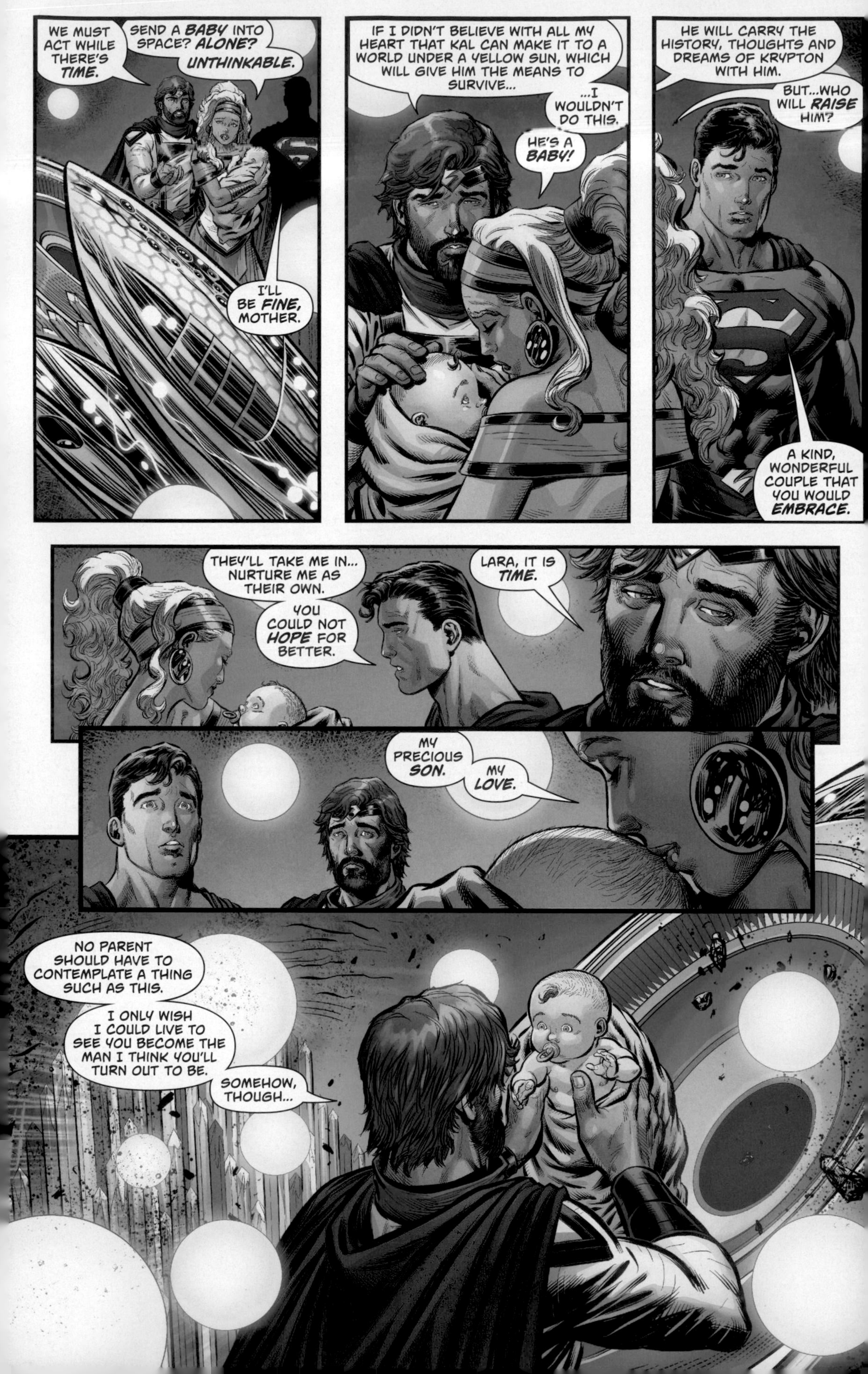
WE MUST ACT WHILE THERE'S *TIME.*
SEND A *BABY* INTO SPACE? *ALONE?* *UNTHINKABLE.*
I'LL BE *FINE,* MOTHER.
IF I DIDN'T BELIEVE WITH ALL MY HEART THAT KAL CAN MAKE IT TO A WORLD UNDER A YELLOW SUN, WHICH WILL GIVE HIM THE MEANS TO SURVIVE...
...I WOULDN'T DO THIS.
HE'S A *BABY!*
HE WILL CARRY THE HISTORY, THOUGHTS AND DREAMS OF KRYPTON WITH HIM.
BUT...WHO WILL *RAISE* HIM?
A KIND, WONDERFUL COUPLE THAT YOU WOULD *EMBRACE.*
THEY'LL TAKE ME IN... NURTURE ME AS THEIR OWN.
YOU COULD NOT *HOPE* FOR BETTER.
LARA, IT IS *TIME.*
MY PRECIOUS *SON.*
MY *LOVE.*
NO PARENT SHOULD HAVE TO CONTEMPLATE A THING SUCH AS THIS.
I ONLY WISH I COULD LIVE TO SEE YOU BECOME THE MAN I THINK YOU'LL TURN OUT TO BE.
SOMEHOW, THOUGH...

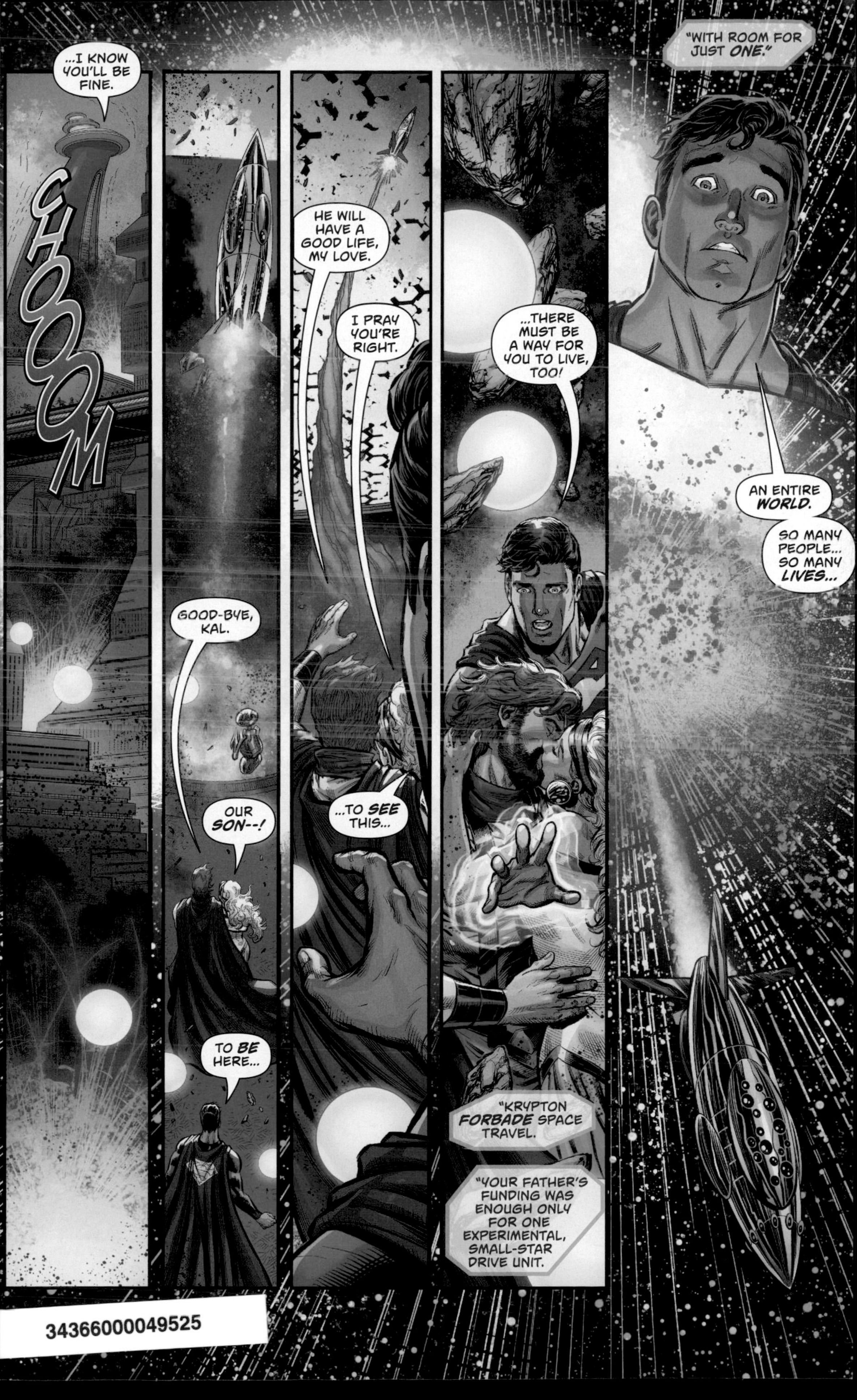

...I KNOW YOU'LL BE FINE.
CHOOOM
GOOD-BYE, KAL.
OUR SON--!
TO BE HERE...
HE WILL HAVE A GOOD LIFE, MY LOVE.
I PRAY YOU'RE RIGHT.
...TO SEE THIS...
...THERE MUST BE A WAY FOR YOU TO LIVE, TOO!
"KRYPTON FORBADE SPACE TRAVEL.
"YOUR FATHER'S FUNDING WAS ENOUGH ONLY FOR ONE EXPERIMENTAL, SMALL-STAR DRIVE UNIT.
"WITH ROOM FOR JUST ONE."
AN ENTIRE WORLD.
SO MANY PEOPLE... SO MANY LIVES...

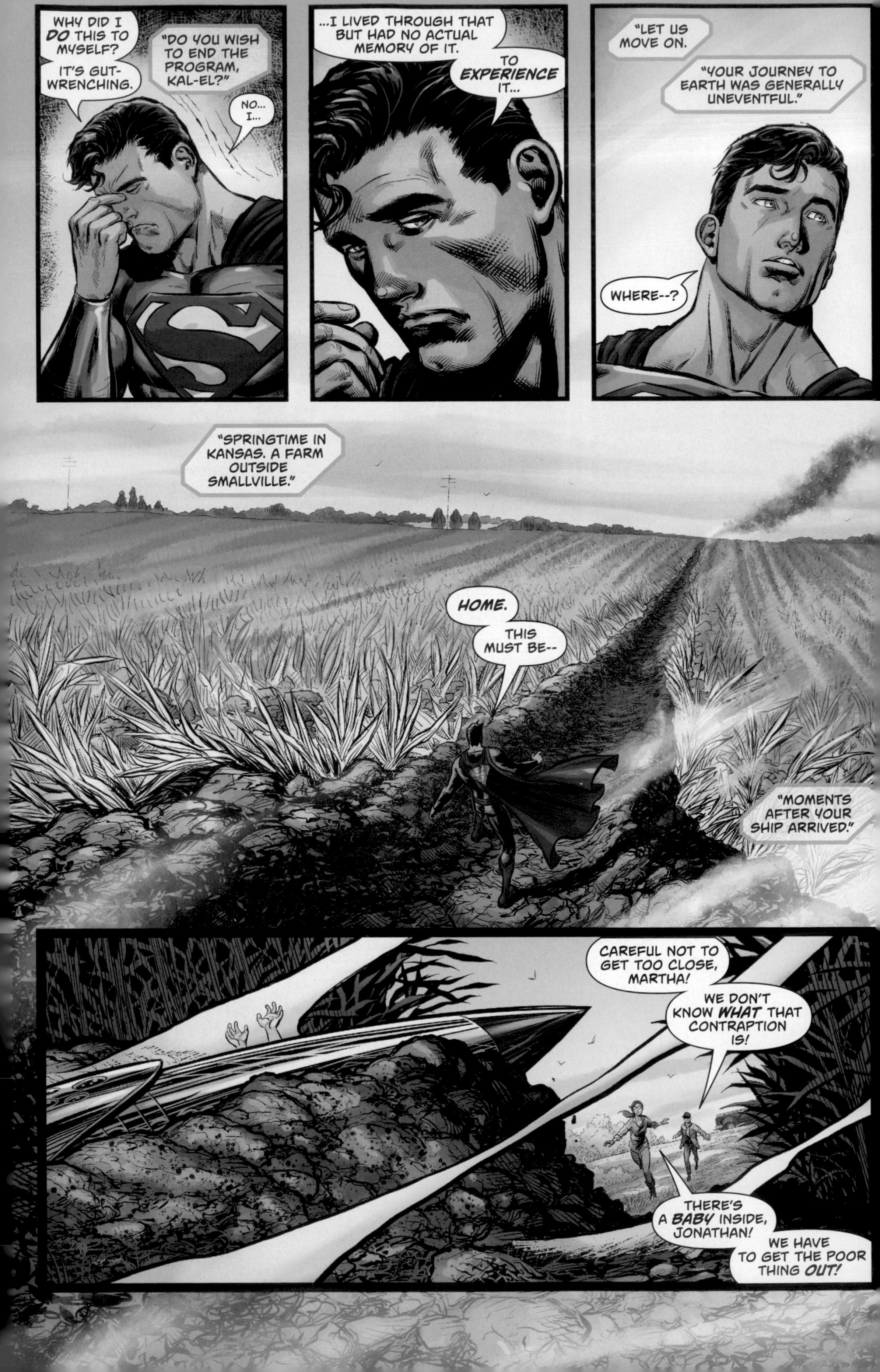
WHY DID I DO THIS TO MYSELF?
IT'S GUT-WRENCHING.
"DO YOU WISH TO END THE PROGRAM, KAL-EL?"
NO... I...
...I LIVED THROUGH THAT BUT HAD NO ACTUAL MEMORY OF IT.
TO EXPERIENCE IT...
"LET US MOVE ON.
"YOUR JOURNEY TO EARTH WAS GENERALLY UNEVENTFUL."
WHERE--?
"SPRINGTIME IN KANSAS. A FARM OUTSIDE SMALLVILLE."
HOME.
THIS MUST BE--
"MOMENTS AFTER YOUR SHIP ARRIVED."
CAREFUL NOT TO GET TOO CLOSE, MARTHA!
WE DON'T KNOW WHAT THAT CONTRAPTION IS!
THERE'S A BABY INSIDE, JONATHAN!
WE HAVE TO GET THE POOR THING OUT!

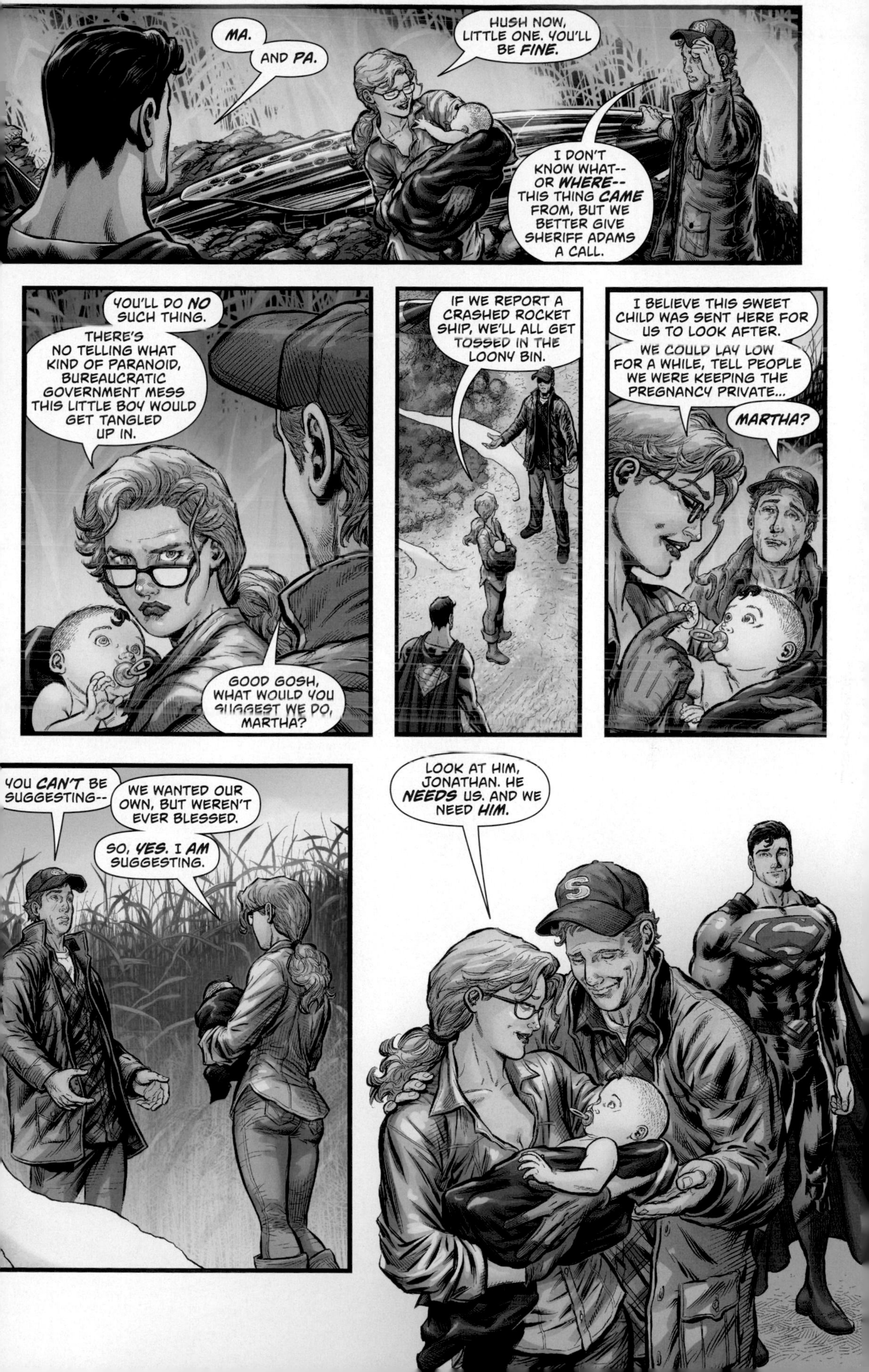
MA.
AND PA.
HUSH NOW, LITTLE ONE. YOU'LL BE FINE.
I DON'T KNOW WHAT-- OR WHERE-- THIS THING CAME FROM, BUT WE BETTER GIVE SHERIFF ADAMS A CALL.
YOU'LL DO NO SUCH THING.
THERE'S NO TELLING WHAT KIND OF PARANOID, BUREAUCRATIC GOVERNMENT MESS THIS LITTLE BOY WOULD GET TANGLED UP IN.
GOOD GOSH, WHAT WOULD YOU SUGGEST WE DO, MARTHA?
IF WE REPORT A CRASHED ROCKET SHIP, WE'LL ALL GET TOSSED IN THE LOONY BIN.
I BELIEVE THIS SWEET CHILD WAS SENT HERE FOR US TO LOOK AFTER.
WE COULD LAY LOW FOR A WHILE, TELL PEOPLE WE WERE KEEPING THE PREGNANCY PRIVATE...
MARTHA?
YOU CAN'T BE SUGGESTING--
WE WANTED OUR OWN, BUT WEREN'T EVER BLESSED.
SO, YES. I AM SUGGESTING.
LOOK AT HIM, JONATHAN. HE NEEDS US. AND WE NEED HIM.

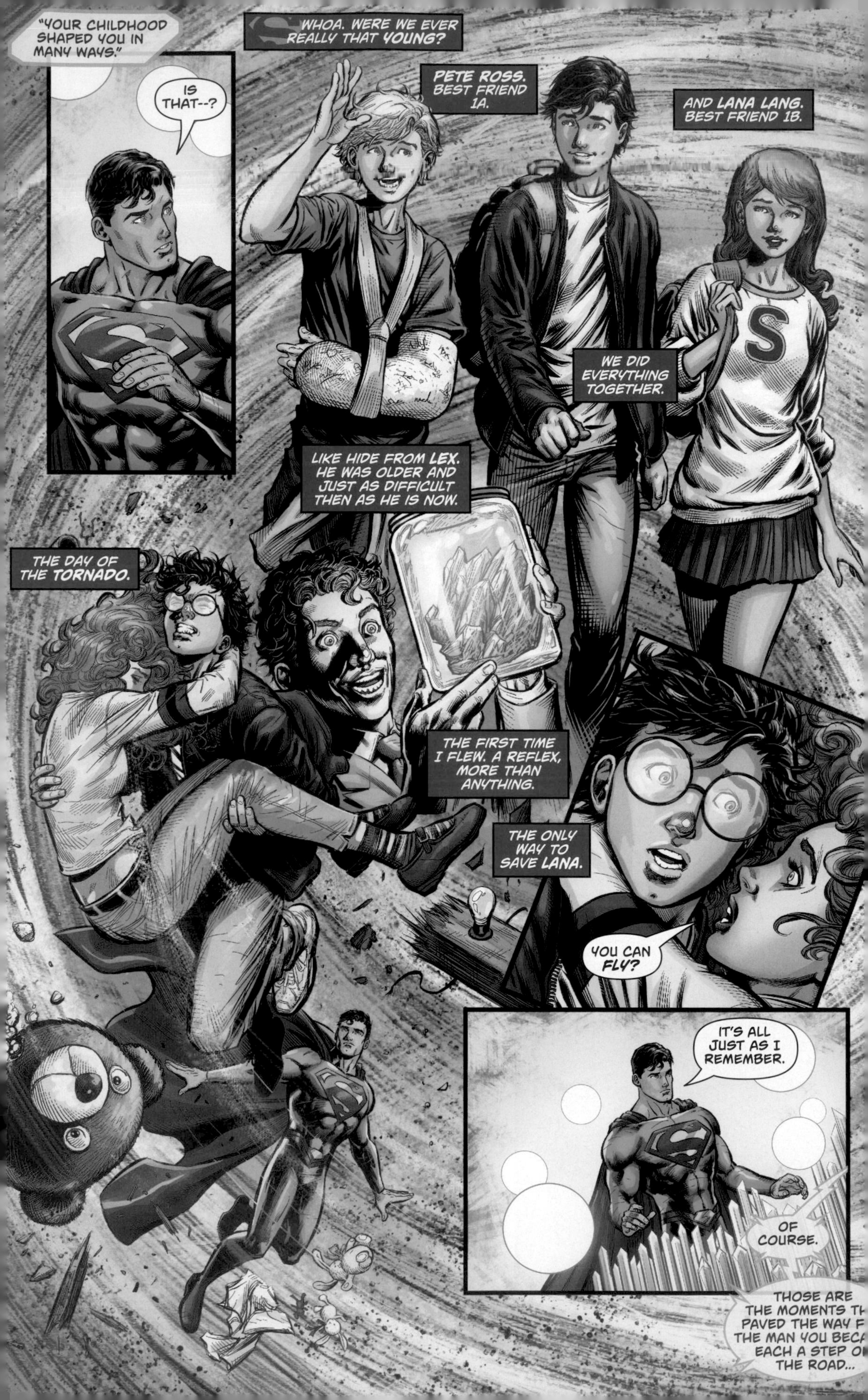
"YOUR CHILDHOOD SHAPED YOU IN MANY WAYS."
WHOA. WERE WE EVER REALLY THAT YOUNG?
IS THAT--?
PETE ROSS. BEST FRIEND 1A.
AND LANA LANG. BEST FRIEND 1B.
WE DID EVERYTHING TOGETHER.
LIKE HIDE FROM LEX. HE WAS OLDER AND JUST AS DIFFICULT THEN AS HE IS NOW.
THE DAY OF THE TORNADO.
THE FIRST TIME I FLEW. A REFLEX, MORE THAN ANYTHING.
THE ONLY WAY TO SAVE LANA.
YOU CAN FLY?
IT'S ALL JUST AS I REMEMBER.
OF COURSE.
THOSE ARE THE MOMENTS TH PAVED THE WAY F THE MAN YOU BECA EACH A STEP O THE ROAD...

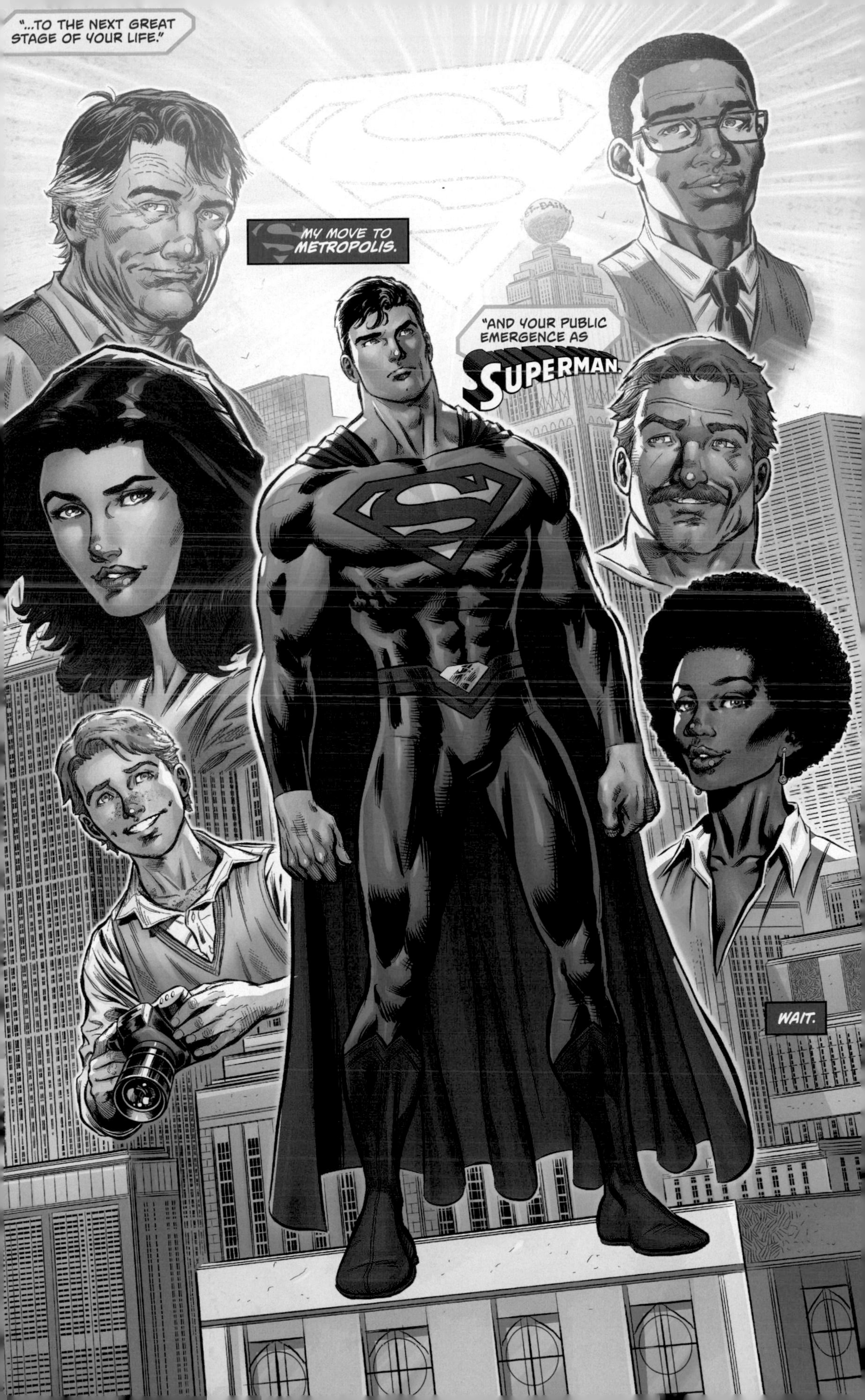
"...TO THE NEXT GREAT STAGE OF YOUR LIFE."
MY MOVE TO METROPOLIS.
"AND YOUR PUBLIC EMERGENCE AS SUPERMAN.
WAIT.

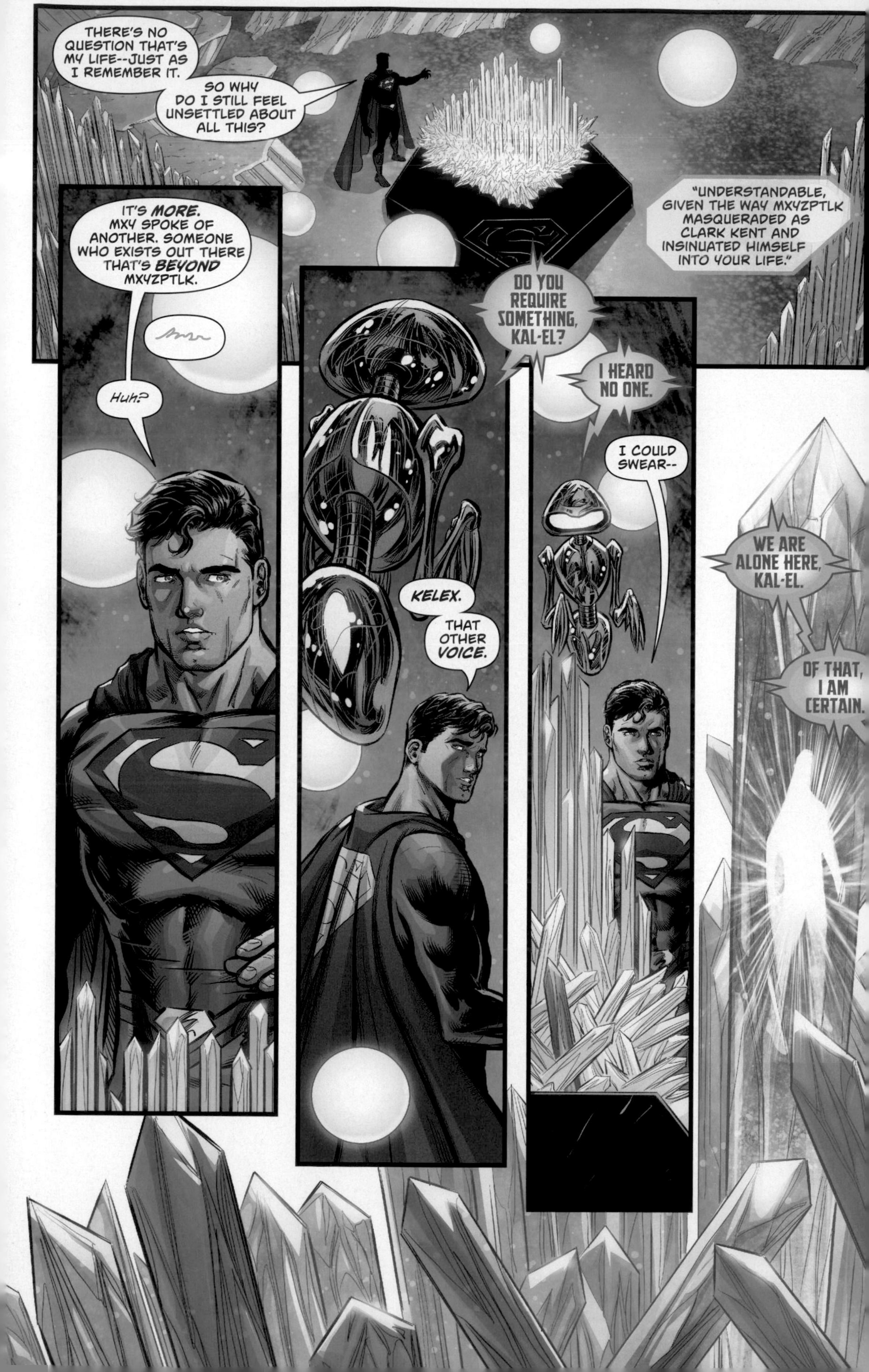
THERE'S NO QUESTION THAT'S MY LIFE--JUST AS I REMEMBER IT.
SO WHY DO I STILL FEEL UNSETTLED ABOUT ALL THIS?
"UNDERSTANDABLE, GIVEN THE WAY MXYZPTLK MASQUERADED AS CLARK KENT AND INSINUATED HIMSELF INTO YOUR LIFE."
IT'S MORE. MXY SPOKE OF ANOTHER. SOMEONE WHO EXISTS OUT THERE THAT'S BEYOND MXYZPTLK.
Huh?
DO YOU REQUIRE SOMETHING, KAL-EL?
KELEX.
THAT OTHER VOICE.
I HEARD NO ONE.
I COULD SWEAR--
WE ARE ALONE HERE, KAL-EL.
OF THAT, I AM CERTAIN.

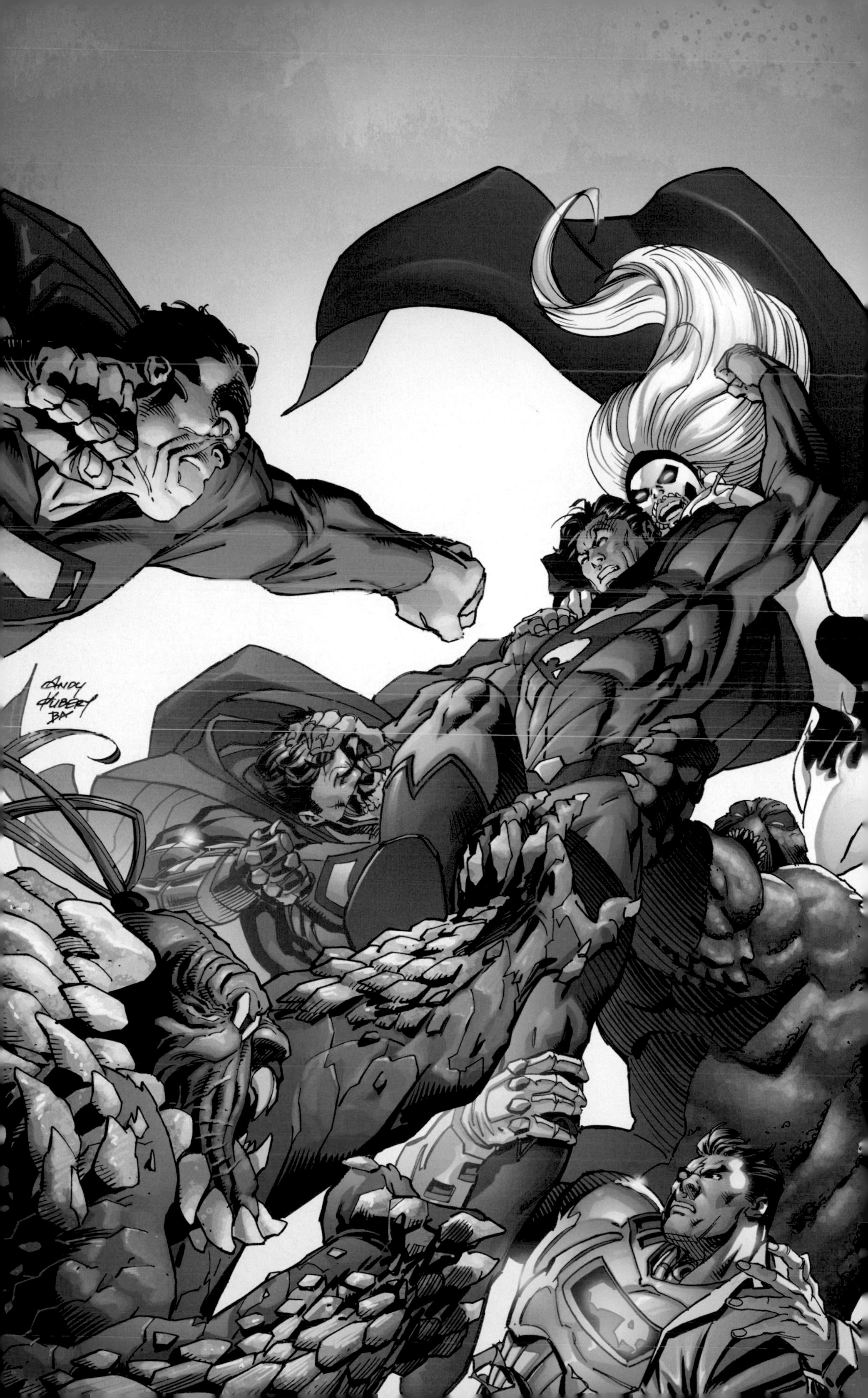
ANDY KUBERT BA

THE NEW WORLD PART 2

CARLO BARBERI penciller * MATT SANTORELLI inker * HI-FI colorist
ANDY KUBERT BRAD ANDERSON cover artists

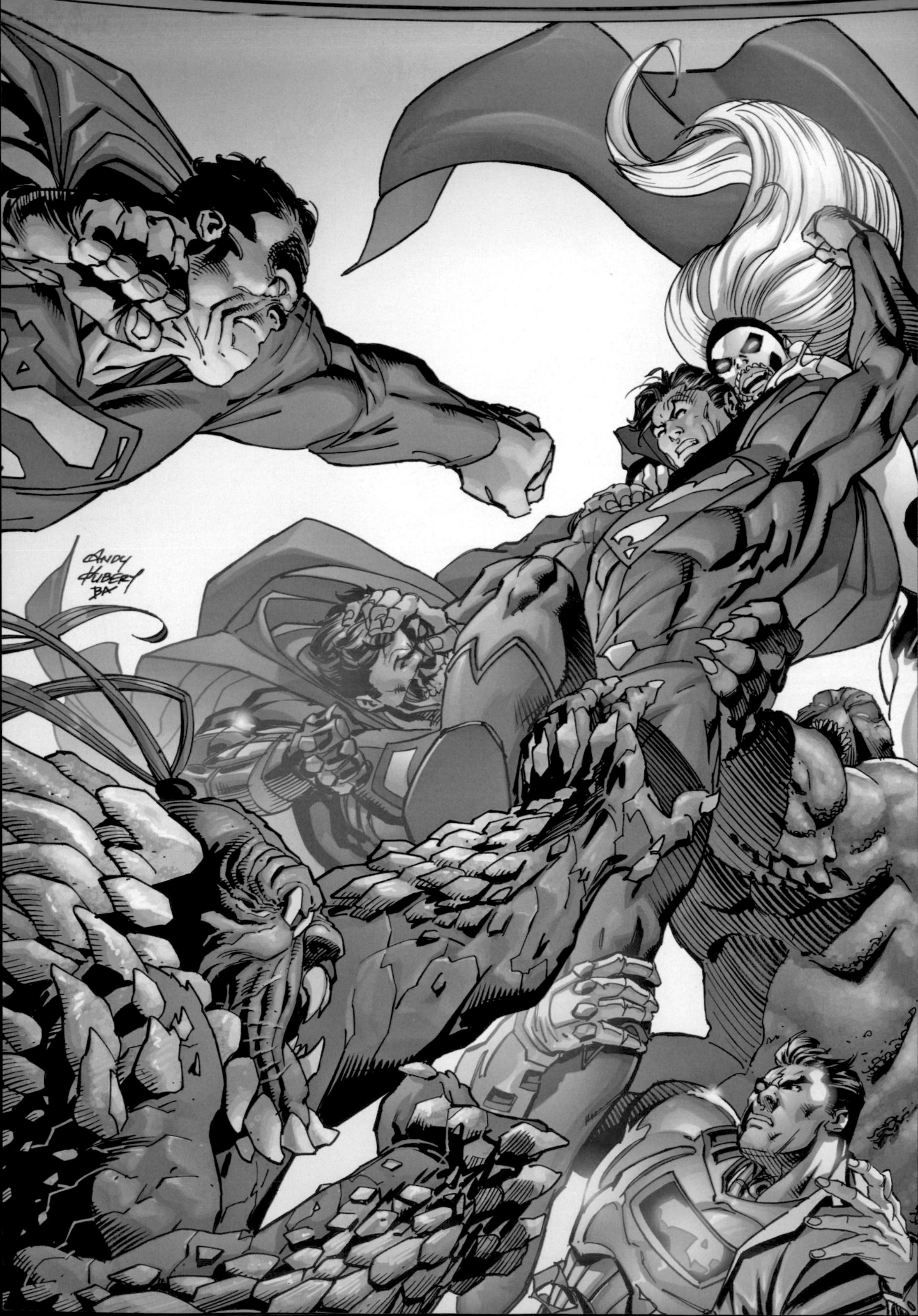

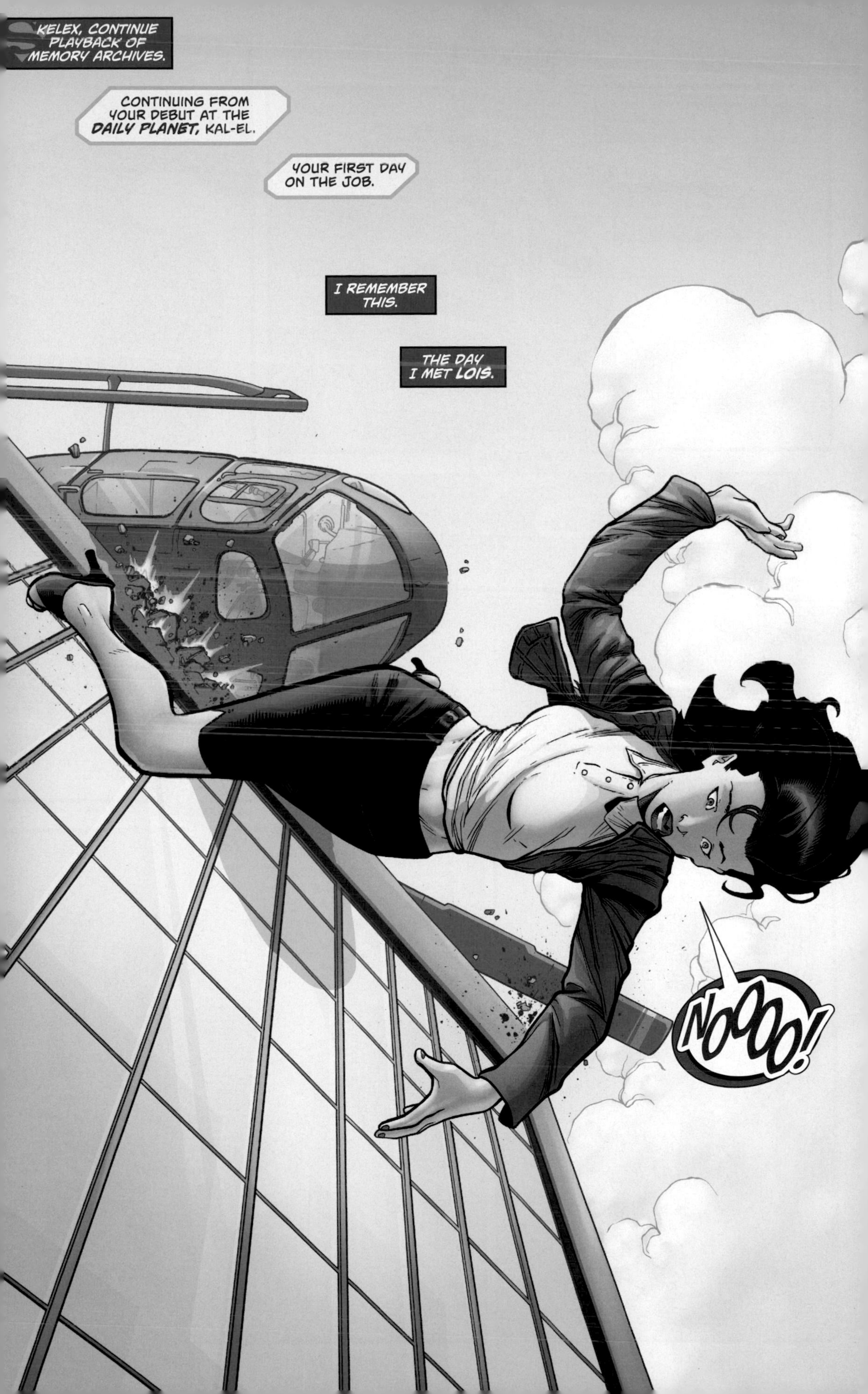
KELEX, CONTINUE PLAYBACK OF MEMORY ARCHIVES.
CONTINUING FROM YOUR DEBUT AT THE DAILY PLANET, KAL-EL.
YOUR FIRST DAY ON THE JOB.
I REMEMBER THIS.
THE DAY I MET LOIS.
NOOOO!

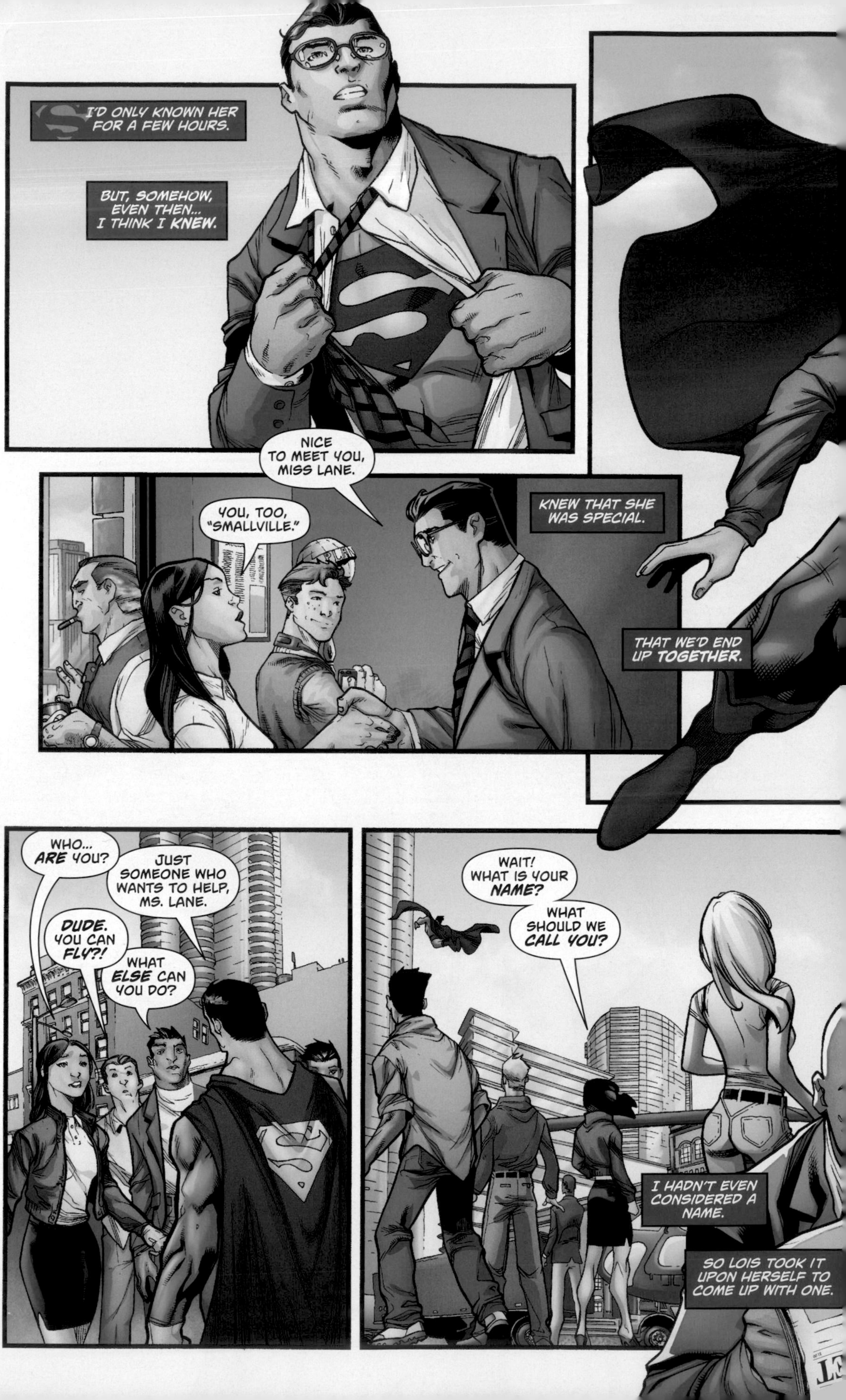
I'D ONLY KNOWN HER FOR A FEW HOURS.
BUT, SOMEHOW, EVEN THEN... I THINK I KNEW.
NICE TO MEET YOU, MISS LANE.
YOU, TOO, "SMALLVILLE."
KNEW THAT SHE WAS SPECIAL.
THAT WE'D END UP TOGETHER.
WHO... ARE YOU?
JUST SOMEONE WHO WANTS TO HELP, MS. LANE.
DUDE. YOU CAN FLY?!
WHAT ELSE CAN YOU DO?
WAIT! WHAT IS YOUR NAME?
WHAT SHOULD WE CALL YOU?
I HADN'T EVEN CONSIDERED A NAME.
SO LOIS TOOK IT UPON HERSELF TO COME UP WITH ONE.

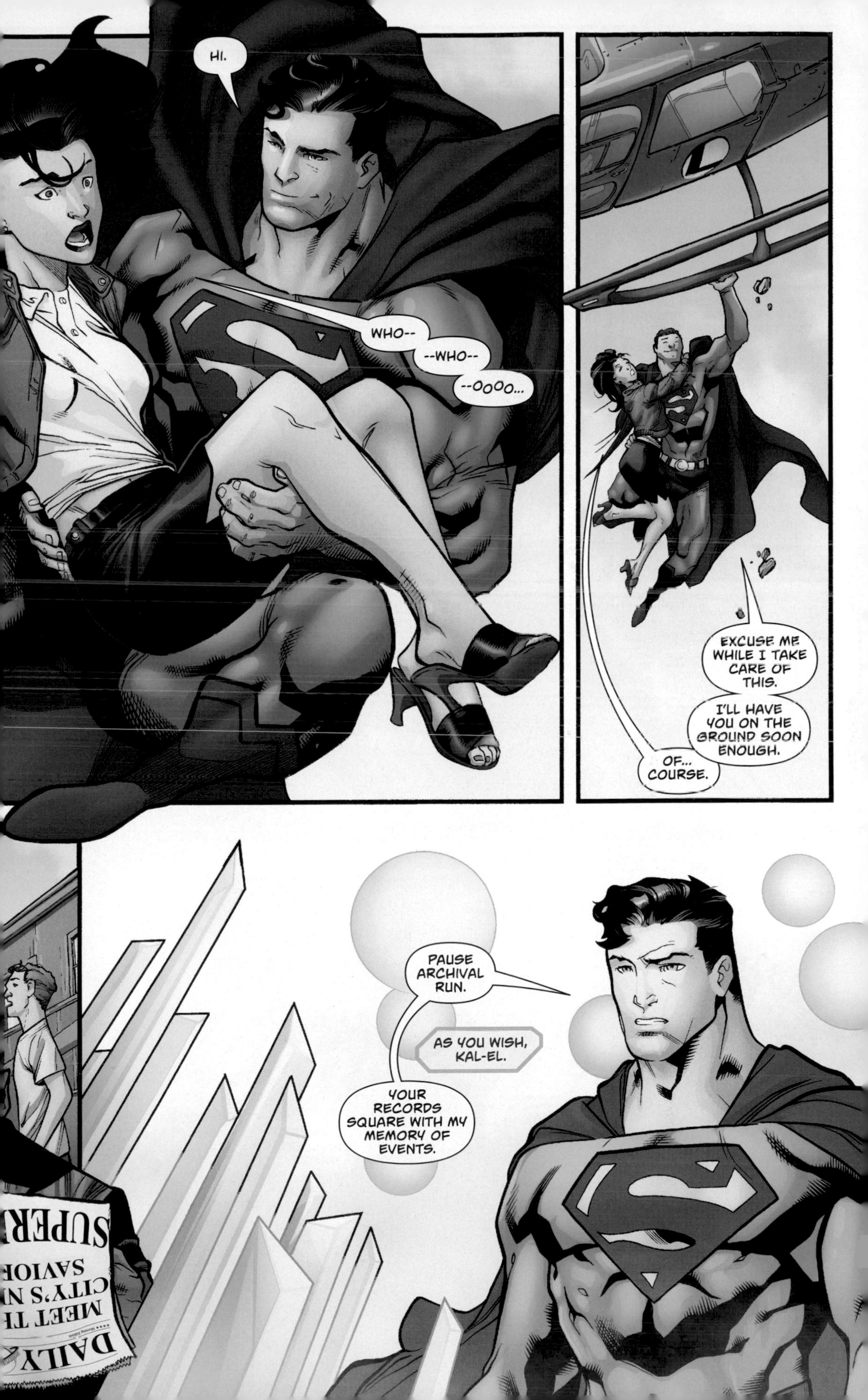
HI.
WHO--
--WHO--
--OOOO...
EXCUSE ME WHILE I TAKE CARE OF THIS.
I'LL HAVE YOU ON THE GROUND SOON ENOUGH.
OF... COURSE.
PAUSE ARCHIVAL RUN.
AS YOU WISH, KAL-EL.
YOUR RECORDS SQUARE WITH MY MEMORY OF EVENTS.

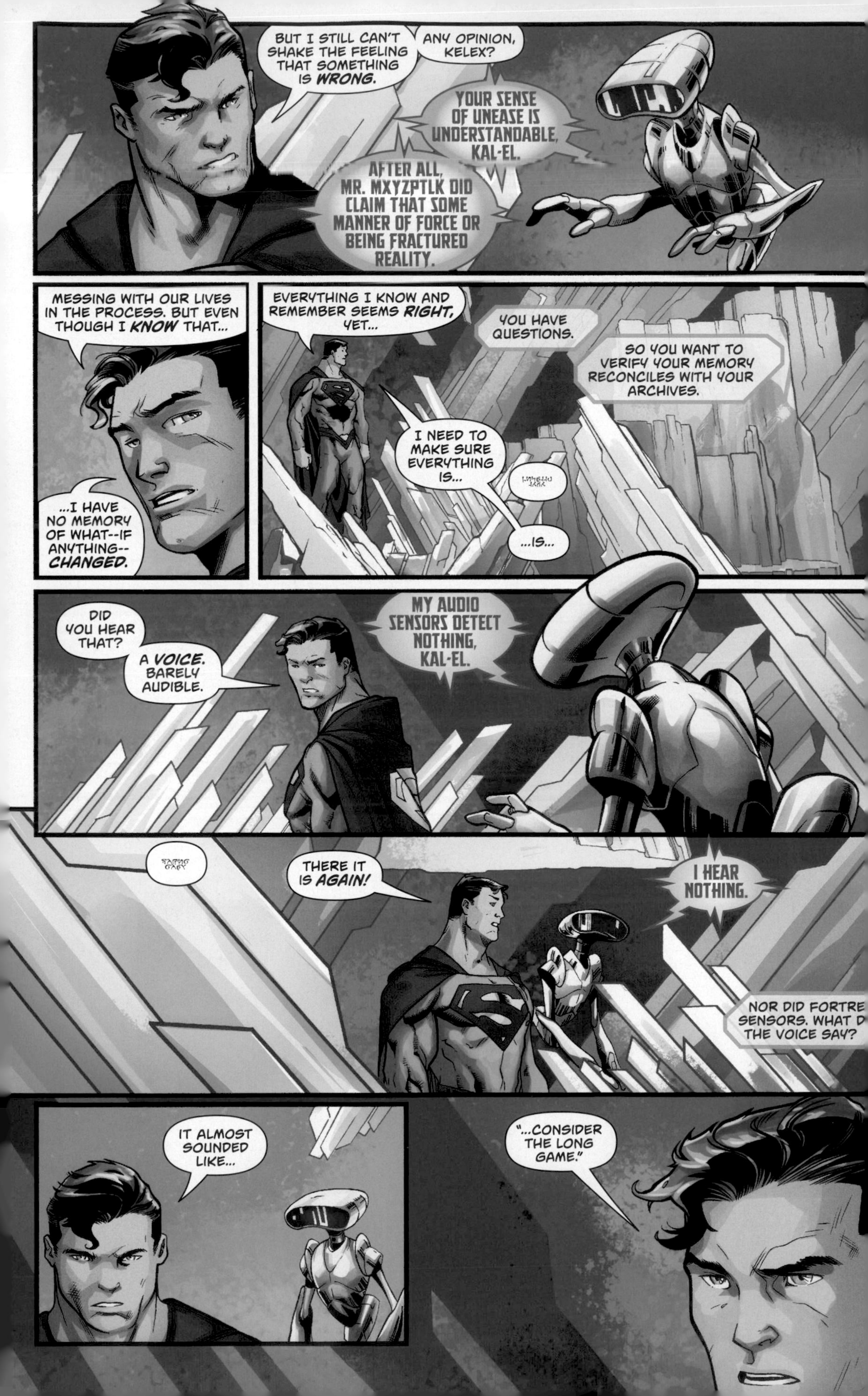
BUT I STILL CAN'T SHAKE THE FEELING THAT SOMETHING IS WRONG.
ANY OPINION, KELEX?
YOUR SENSE OF UNEASE IS UNDERSTANDABLE, KAL-EL.
AFTER ALL, MR. MXYZPTLK DID CLAIM THAT SOME MANNER OF FORCE OR BEING FRACTURED REALITY.
MESSING WITH OUR LIVES IN THE PROCESS. BUT EVEN THOUGH I KNOW THAT...
...I HAVE NO MEMORY OF WHAT--IF ANYTHING--CHANGED.
EVERYTHING I KNOW AND REMEMBER SEEMS RIGHT, YET...
YOU HAVE QUESTIONS.
SO YOU WANT TO VERIFY YOUR MEMORY RECONCILES WITH YOUR ARCHIVES.
I NEED TO MAKE SURE EVERYTHING IS...
...IS...
DID YOU HEAR THAT?
A VOICE. BARELY AUDIBLE.
MY AUDIO SENSORS DETECT NOTHING, KAL-EL.
THERE IT IS AGAIN!
I HEAR NOTHING.
NOR DID FORTRE SENSORS. WHAT D THE VOICE SAY?
IT ALMOST SOUNDED LIKE...
"...CONSIDER THE LONG GAME."

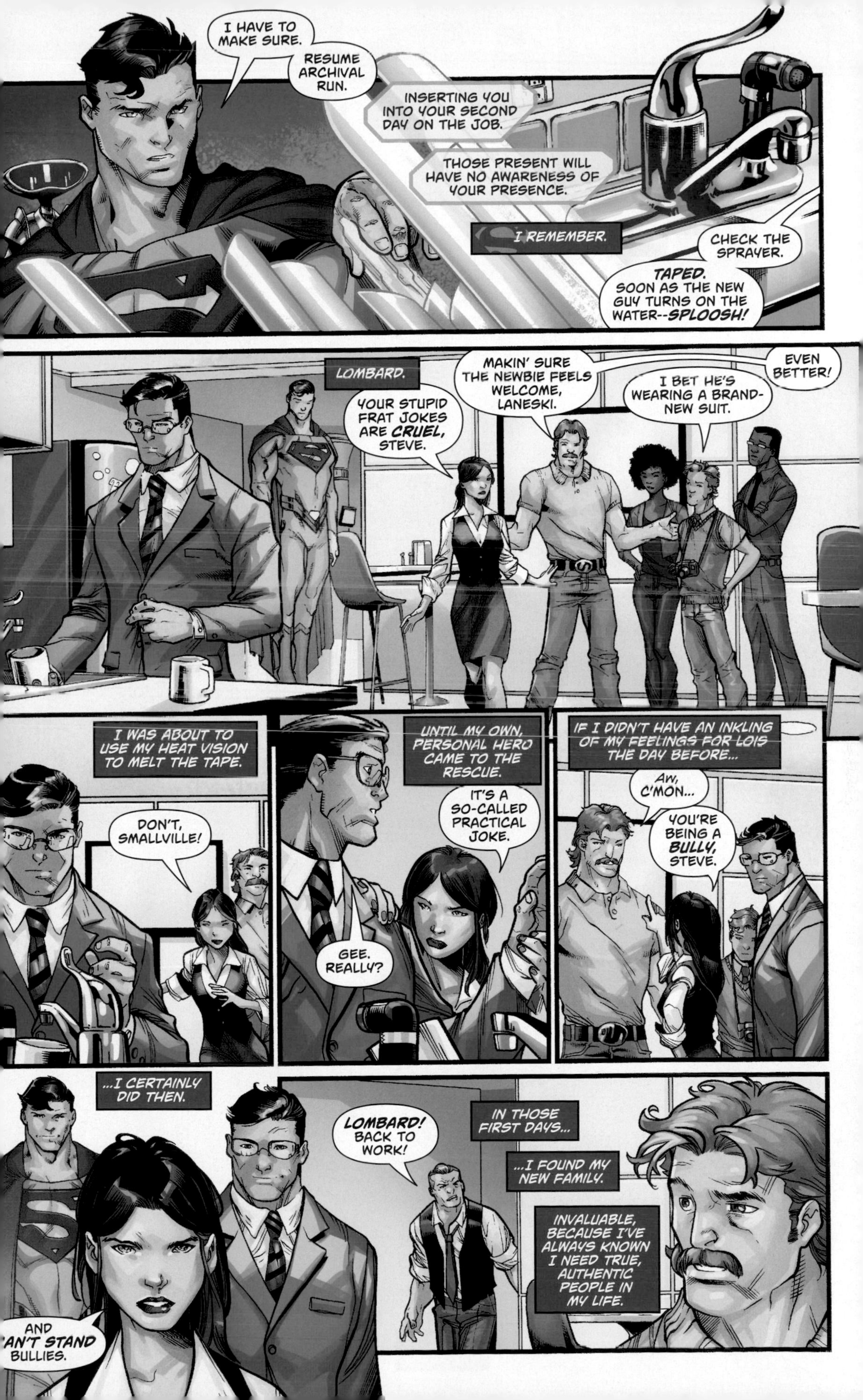
I HAVE TO MAKE SURE.
RESUME ARCHIVAL RUN.
INSERTING YOU INTO YOUR SECOND DAY ON THE JOB.
THOSE PRESENT WILL HAVE NO AWARENESS OF YOUR PRESENCE.
I REMEMBER.
CHECK THE SPRAYER.
TAPED. SOON AS THE NEW GUY TURNS ON THE WATER--SPLOOSH!
LOMBARD.
YOUR STUPID FRAT JOKES ARE CRUEL, STEVE.
MAKIN' SURE THE NEWBIE FEELS WELCOME, LANESKI.
EVEN BETTER!
I BET HE'S WEARING A BRAND-NEW SUIT.
I WAS ABOUT TO USE MY HEAT VISION TO MELT THE TAPE.
DON'T, SMALLVILLE!
UNTIL MY OWN, PERSONAL HERO CAME TO THE RESCUE.
IT'S A SO-CALLED PRACTICAL JOKE.
GEE. REALLY?
IF I DIDN'T HAVE AN INKLING OF MY FEELINGS FOR LOIS THE DAY BEFORE...
AW, C'MON...
YOU'RE BEING A BULLY, STEVE.
...I CERTAINLY DID THEN.
AND 'AN'T STAND BULLIES.
LOMBARD! BACK TO WORK!
IN THOSE FIRST DAYS...
...I FOUND MY NEW FAMILY.
INVALUABLE, BECAUSE I'VE ALWAYS KNOWN I NEED TRUE, AUTHENTIC PEOPLE IN MY LIFE.

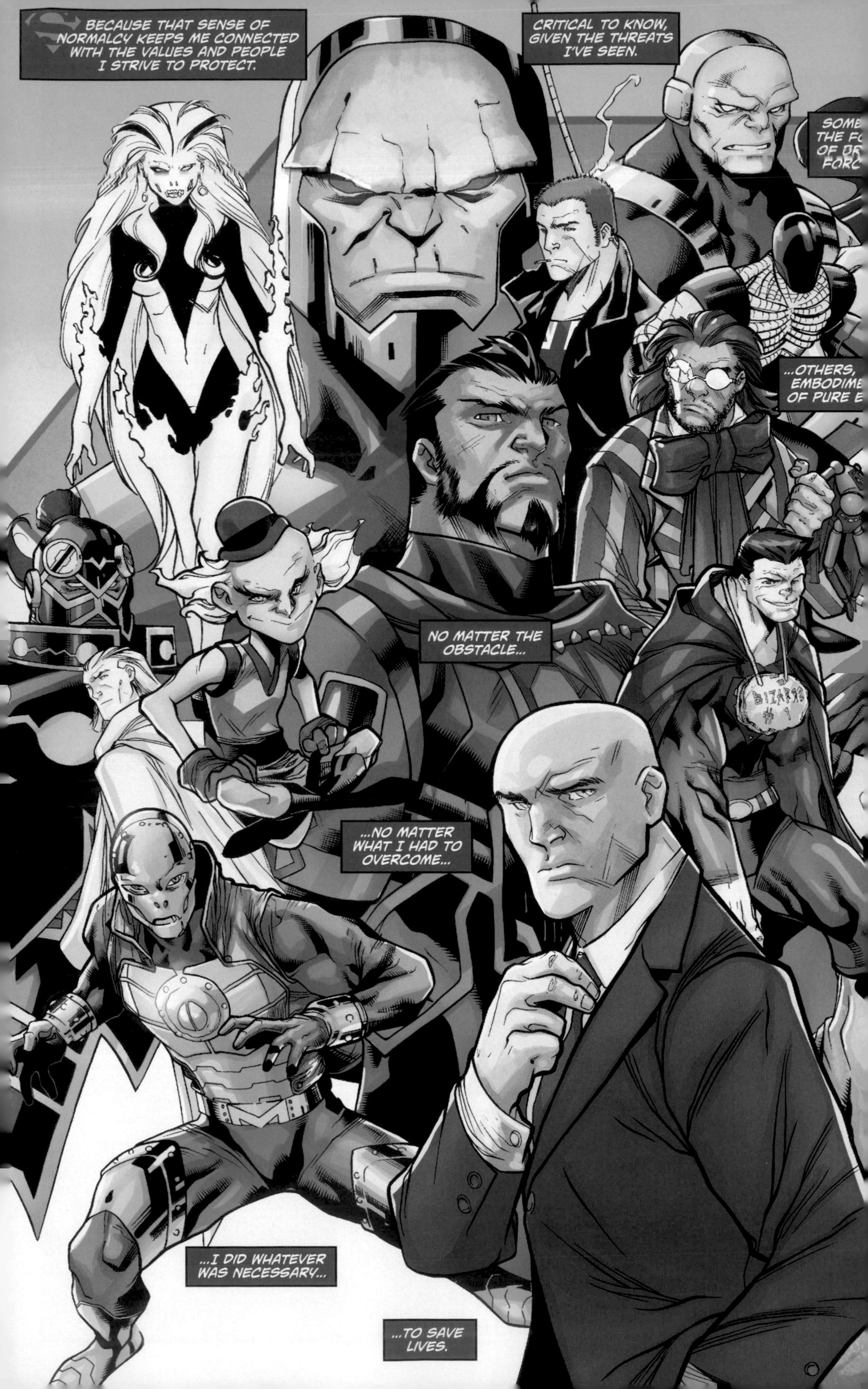
BECAUSE THAT SENSE OF NORMALCY KEEPS ME CONNECTED WITH THE VALUES AND PEOPLE I STRIVE TO PROTECT.
CRITICAL TO KNOW, GIVEN THE THREATS I'VE SEEN.
...OTHERS,
NO MATTER THE OBSTACLE...
BIZARRO #1
...NO MATTER WHAT I HAD TO OVERCOME...
...I DID WHATEVER WAS NECESSARY...
...TO SAVE LIVES.

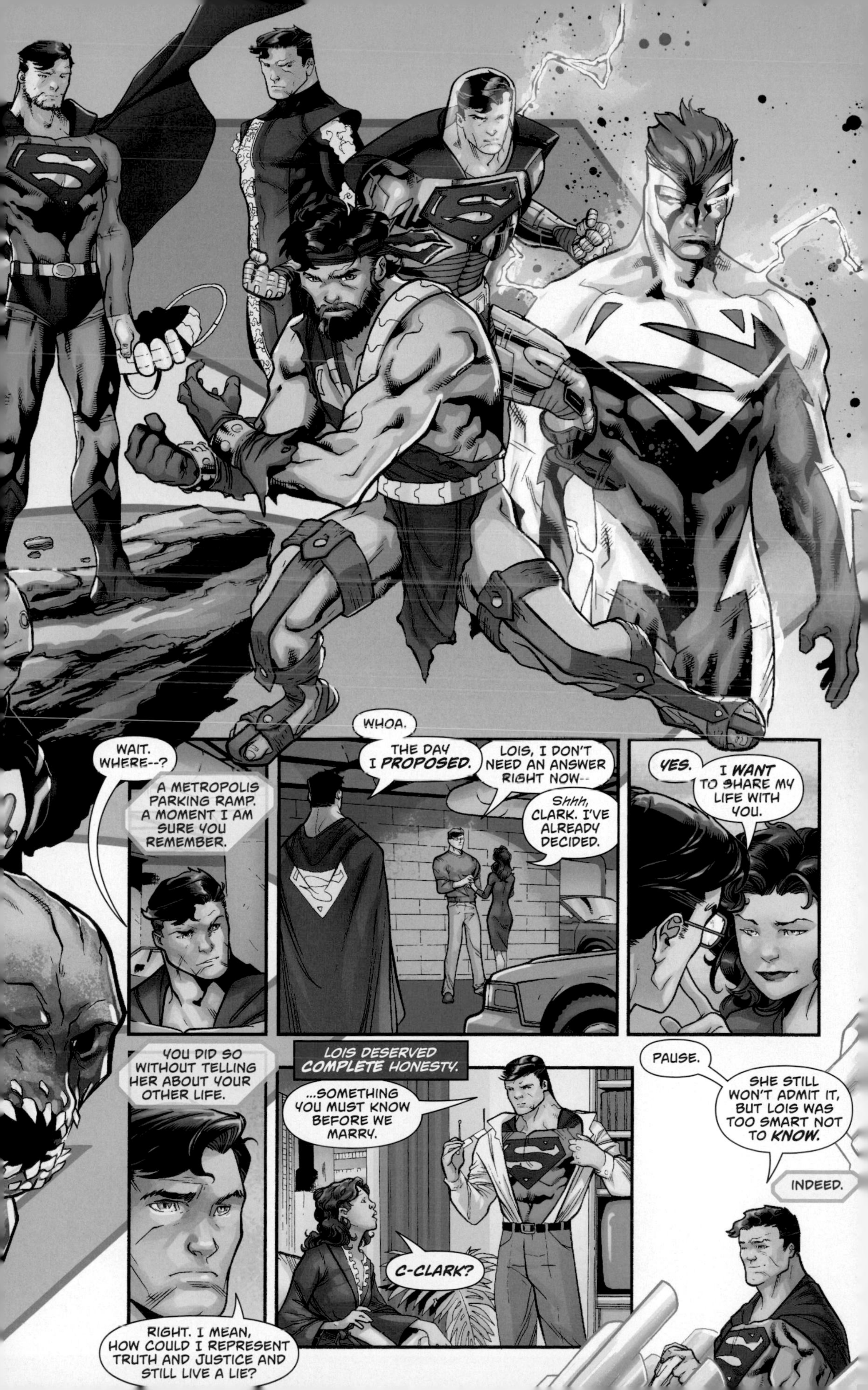
WHOA.
WAIT. WHERE--?
A METROPOLIS PARKING RAMP. A MOMENT I AM SURE YOU REMEMBER.
THE DAY I PROPOSED.
LOIS, I DON'T NEED AN ANSWER RIGHT NOW--
Shhh, CLARK. I'VE ALREADY DECIDED.
YES.
I WANT TO SHARE MY LIFE WITH YOU.
YOU DID SO WITHOUT TELLING HER ABOUT YOUR OTHER LIFE.
RIGHT. I MEAN, HOW COULD I REPRESENT TRUTH AND JUSTICE AND STILL LIVE A LIE?
LOIS DESERVED COMPLETE HONESTY.
...SOMETHING YOU MUST KNOW BEFORE WE MARRY.
C-CLARK?
PAUSE.
SHE STILL WON'T ADMIT IT, BUT LOIS WAS TOO SMART NOT TO KNOW.
INDEED.

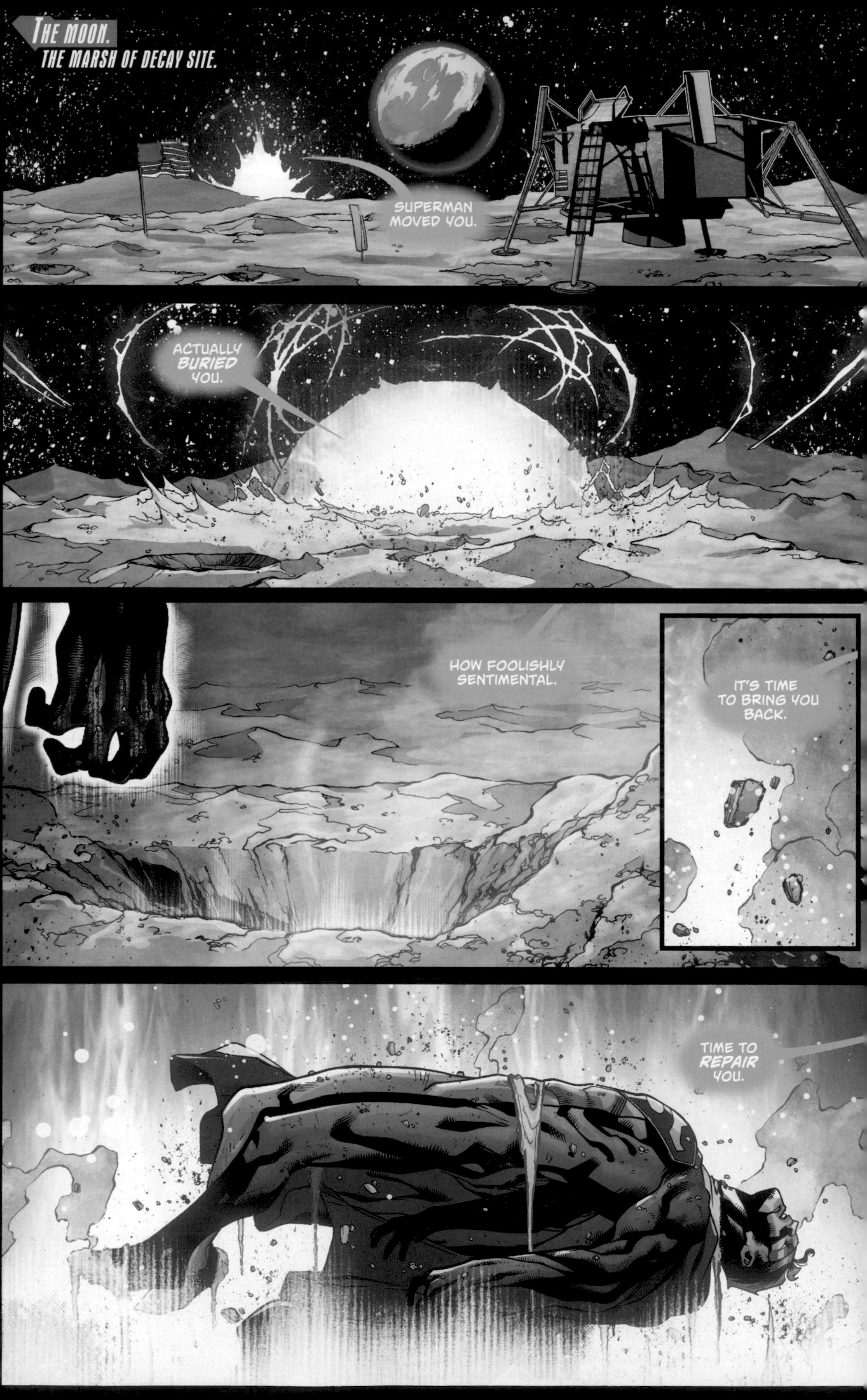
THE MOON.
THE MARSH OF DECAY SITE.
SUPERMAN MOVED YOU.
ACTUALLY BURIED YOU.
HOW FOOLISHLY SENTIMENTAL.
IT'S TIME TO BRING YOU BACK.
TIME TO REPAIR YOU.

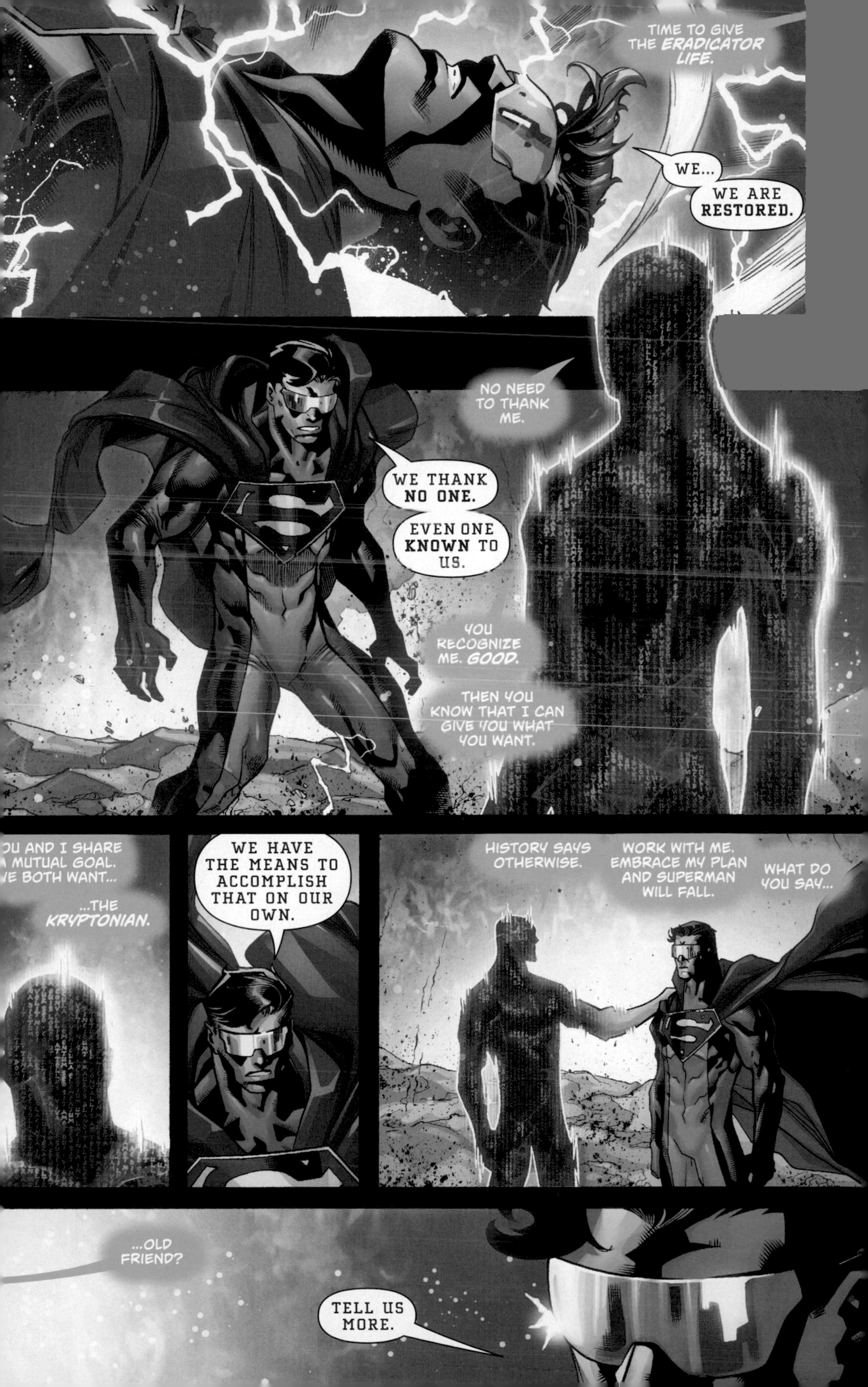
TIME TO GIVE THE ERADICATOR LIFE.
WE... WE ARE RESTORED.
NO NEED TO THANK ME.
WE THANK NO ONE.
EVEN ONE KNOWN TO US.
YOU RECOGNIZE ME. GOOD.
THEN YOU KNOW THAT I CAN GIVE YOU WHAT YOU WANT.
OU AND I SHARE A MUTUAL GOAL. WE BOTH WANT...
...THE KRYPTONIAN.
WE HAVE THE MEANS TO ACCOMPLISH THAT ON OUR OWN.
HISTORY SAYS OTHERWISE.
WORK WITH ME. EMBRACE MY PLAN AND SUPERMAN WILL FALL.
WHAT DO YOU SAY...
...OLD FRIEND?
TELL US MORE.

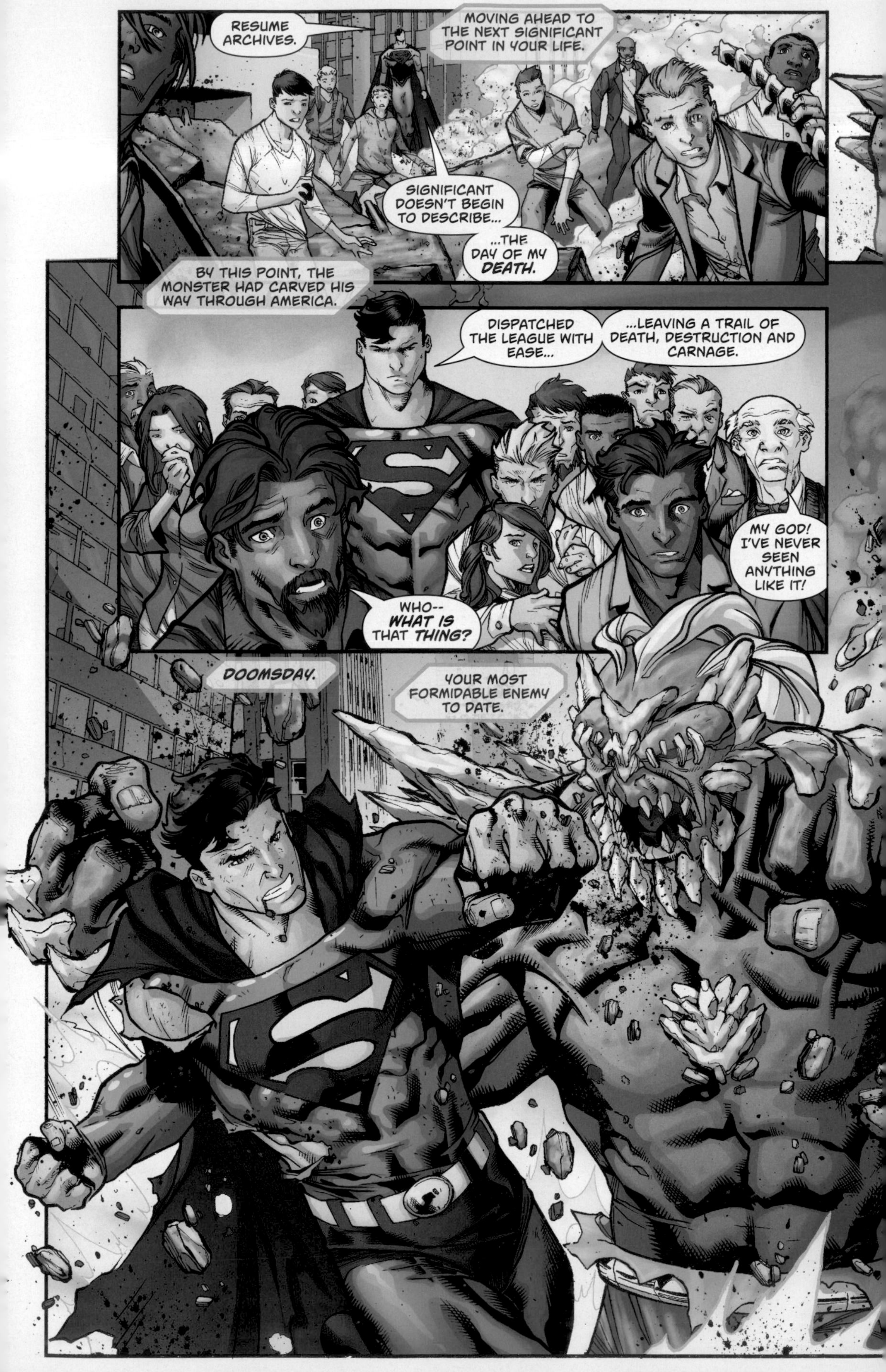
RESUME ARCHIVES.
MOVING AHEAD TO THE NEXT SIGNIFICANT POINT IN YOUR LIFE.
SIGNIFICANT DOESN'T BEGIN TO DESCRIBE...
...THE DAY OF MY DEATH.
BY THIS POINT, THE MONSTER HAD CARVED HIS WAY THROUGH AMERICA.
DISPATCHED THE LEAGUE WITH EASE...
...LEAVING A TRAIL OF DEATH, DESTRUCTION AND CARNAGE.
MY GOD! I'VE NEVER SEEN ANYTHING LIKE IT!
WHO-- WHAT IS THAT THING?
DOOMSDAY.
YOUR MOST FORMIDABLE ENEMY TO DATE.

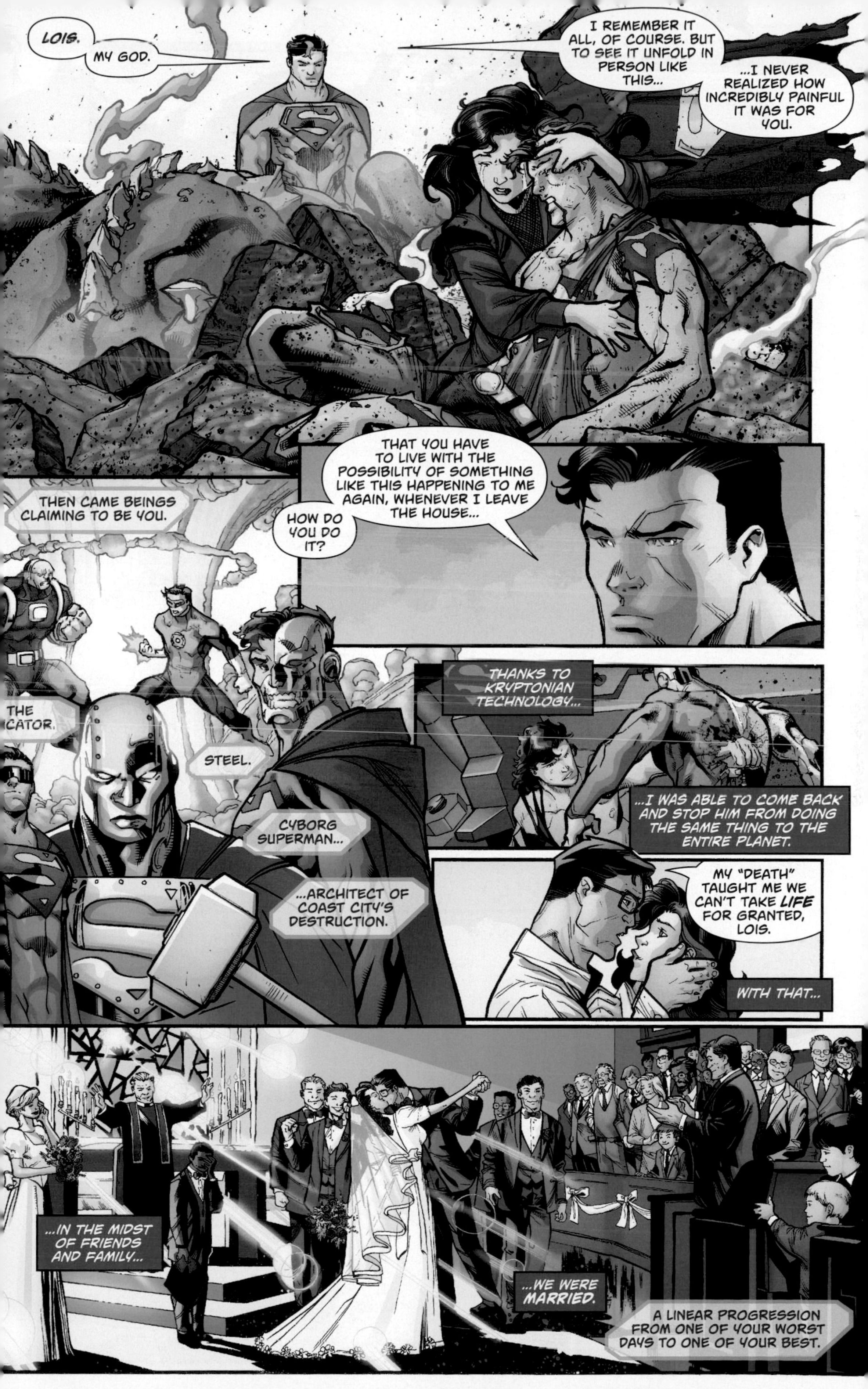
LOIS.
MY GOD.
I REMEMBER IT ALL, OF COURSE. BUT TO SEE IT UNFOLD IN PERSON LIKE THIS...
...I NEVER REALIZED HOW INCREDIBLY PAINFUL IT WAS FOR YOU.
THAT YOU HAVE TO LIVE WITH THE POSSIBILITY OF SOMETHING LIKE THIS HAPPENING TO ME AGAIN, WHENEVER I LEAVE THE HOUSE...
HOW DO YOU DO IT?
THEN CAME BEINGS CLAIMING TO BE YOU.
THE CATOR.
STEEL.
CYBORG SUPERMAN...
...ARCHITECT OF COAST CITY'S DESTRUCTION.
THANKS TO KRYPTONIAN TECHNOLOGY...
...I WAS ABLE TO COME BACK AND STOP HIM FROM DOING THE SAME THING TO THE ENTIRE PLANET.
MY "DEATH" TAUGHT ME WE CAN'T TAKE LIFE FOR GRANTED, LOIS.
WITH THAT...
...IN THE MIDST OF FRIENDS AND FAMILY...
...WE WERE MARRIED.
A LINEAR PROGRESSION FROM ONE OF YOUR WORST DAYS TO ONE OF YOUR BEST.

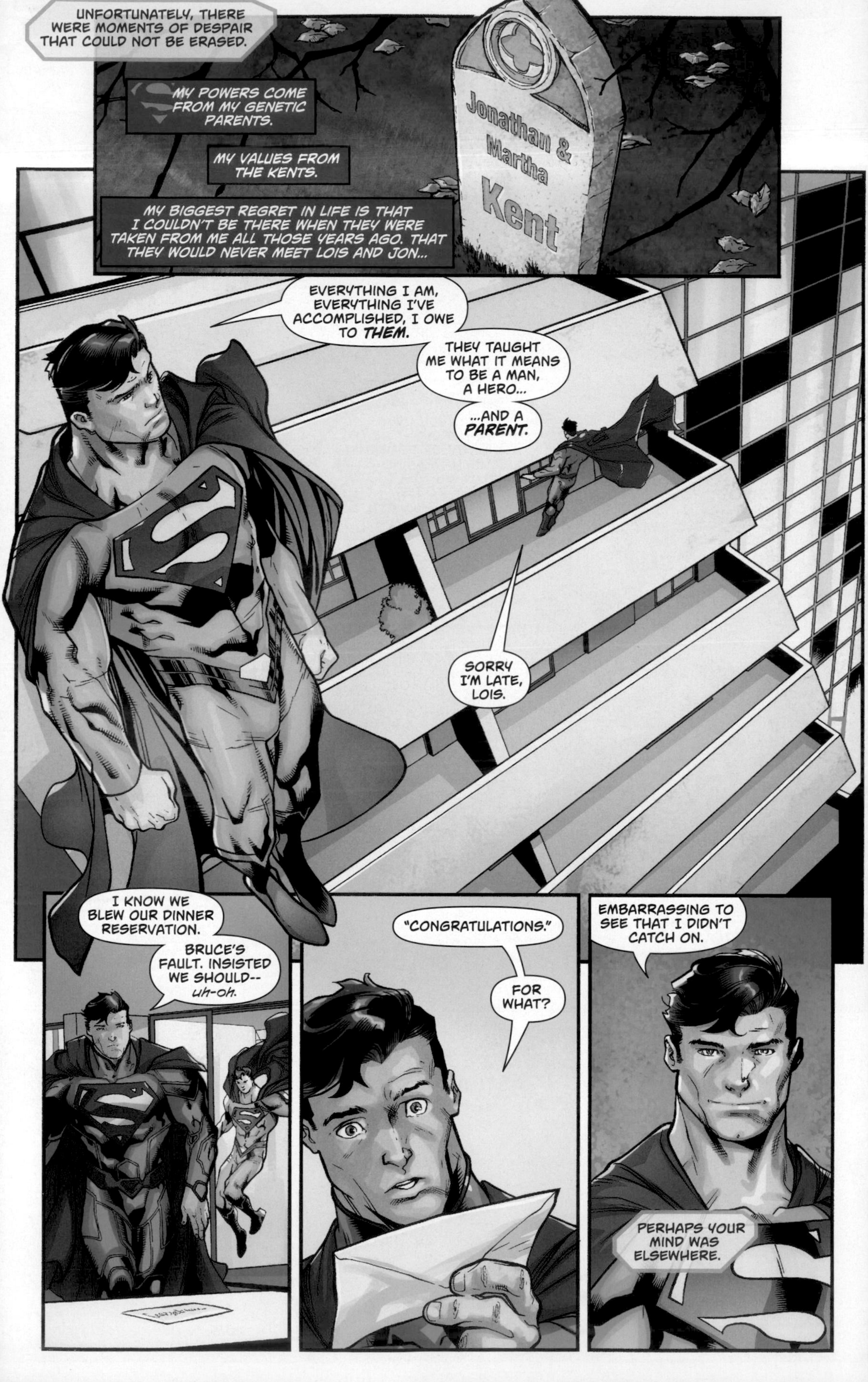
UNFORTUNATELY, THERE WERE MOMENTS OF DESPAIR THAT COULD NOT BE ERASED.
MY POWERS COME FROM MY GENETIC PARENTS.
MY VALUES FROM THE KENTS.
MY BIGGEST REGRET IN LIFE IS THAT I COULDN'T BE THERE WHEN THEY WERE TAKEN FROM ME ALL THOSE YEARS AGO. THAT THEY WOULD NEVER MEET LOIS AND JON...
Jonathan & Martha Kent
EVERYTHING I AM, EVERYTHING I'VE ACCOMPLISHED, I OWE TO THEM.
THEY TAUGHT ME WHAT IT MEANS TO BE A MAN, A HERO...
...AND A PARENT.
SORRY I'M LATE, LOIS.
I KNOW WE BLEW OUR DINNER RESERVATION.
BRUCE'S FAULT. INSISTED WE SHOULD-- uh-oh.
"CONGRATULATIONS."
FOR WHAT?
EMBARRASSING TO SEE THAT I DIDN'T CATCH ON.
PERHAPS YOUR MIND WAS ELSEWHERE.

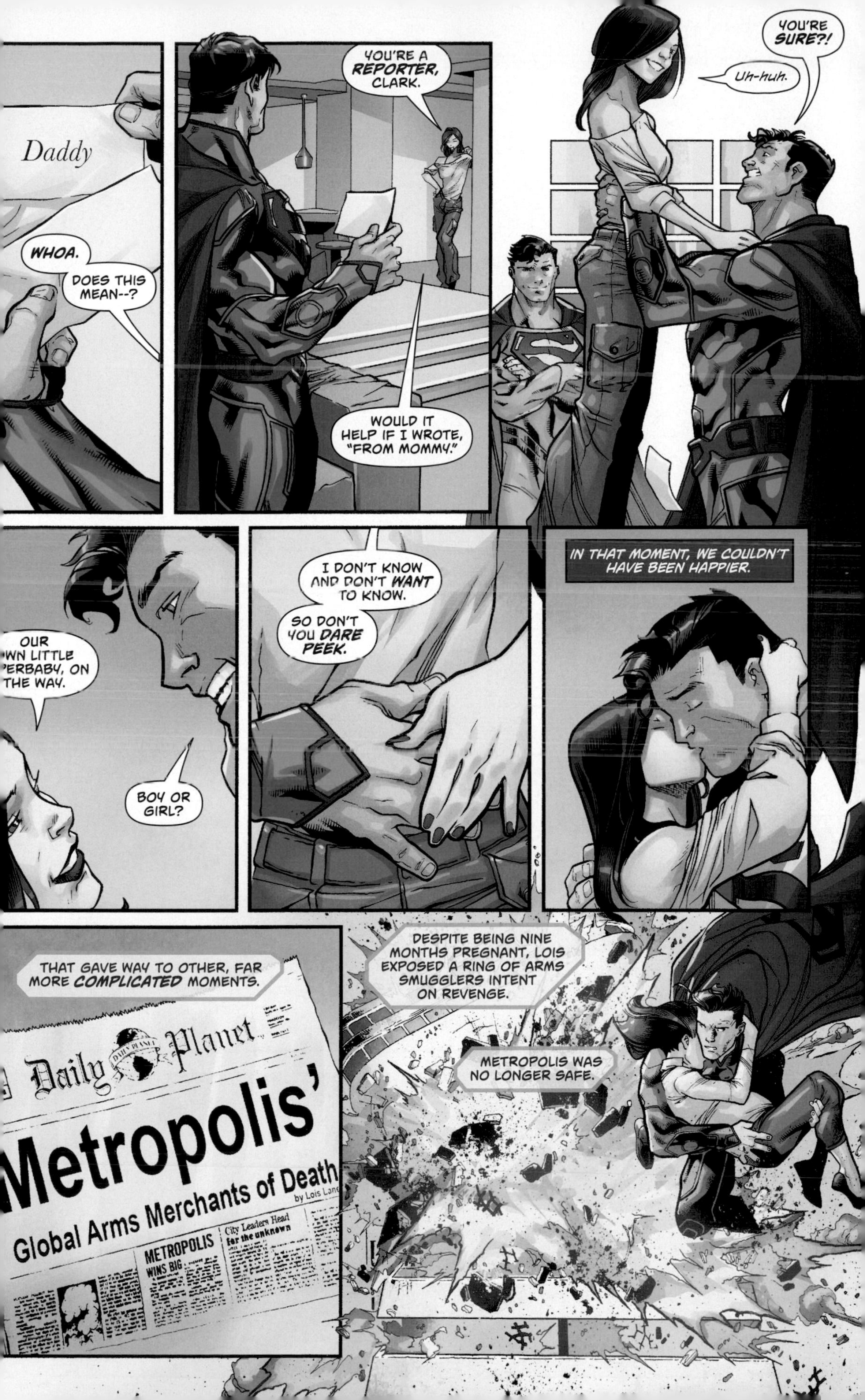

Daddy
WHOA.
DOES THIS MEAN--?
YOU'RE A REPORTER, CLARK.
WOULD IT HELP IF I WROTE, "FROM MOMMY."
YOU'RE SURE?!
Uh-huh.
OUR OWN LITTLE SUPERBABY, ON THE WAY.
BOY OR GIRL?
I DON'T KNOW AND DON'T WANT TO KNOW.
SO DON'T YOU DARE PEEK.
IN THAT MOMENT, WE COULDN'T HAVE BEEN HAPPIER.
THAT GAVE WAY TO OTHER, FAR MORE COMPLICATED MOMENTS.
Daily Planet
Metropolis'
Global Arms Merchants of Death
by Lois Lane
City Leaders Head for the unknown
METROPOLIS WINS BIG
DESPITE BEING NINE MONTHS PREGNANT, LOIS EXPOSED A RING OF ARMS SMUGGLERS INTENT ON REVENGE.
METROPOLIS WAS NO LONGER SAFE.

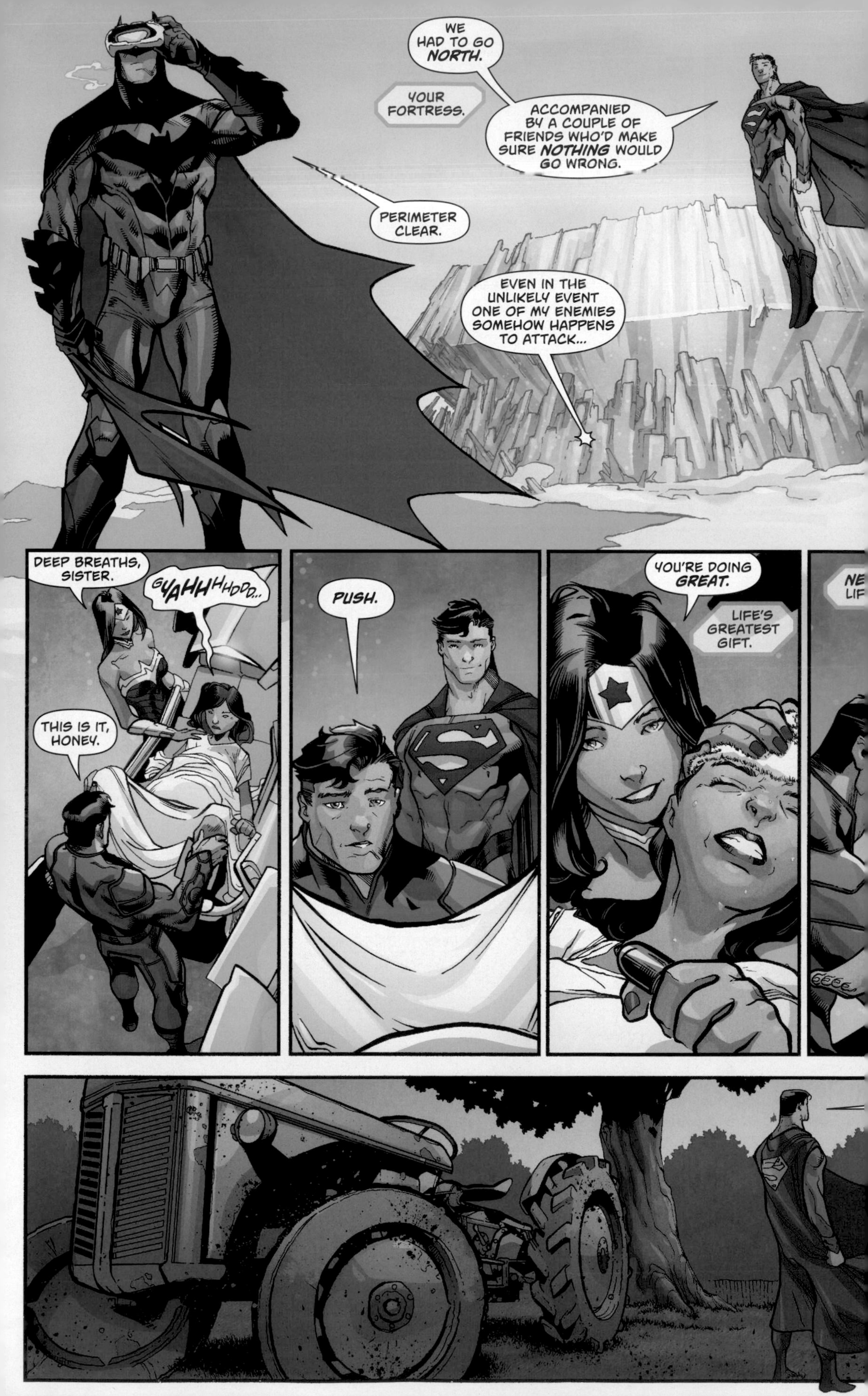
WE HAD TO GO NORTH.
YOUR FORTRESS.
ACCOMPANIED BY A COUPLE OF FRIENDS WHO'D MAKE SURE NOTHING WOULD GO WRONG.
PERIMETER CLEAR.
EVEN IN THE UNLIKELY EVENT ONE OF MY ENEMIES SOMEHOW HAPPENS TO ATTACK...
DEEP BREATHS, SISTER.
GYAHHHHDDD...
THIS IS IT, HONEY.
PUSH.
YOU'RE DOING GREAT.
LIFE'S GREATEST GIFT.

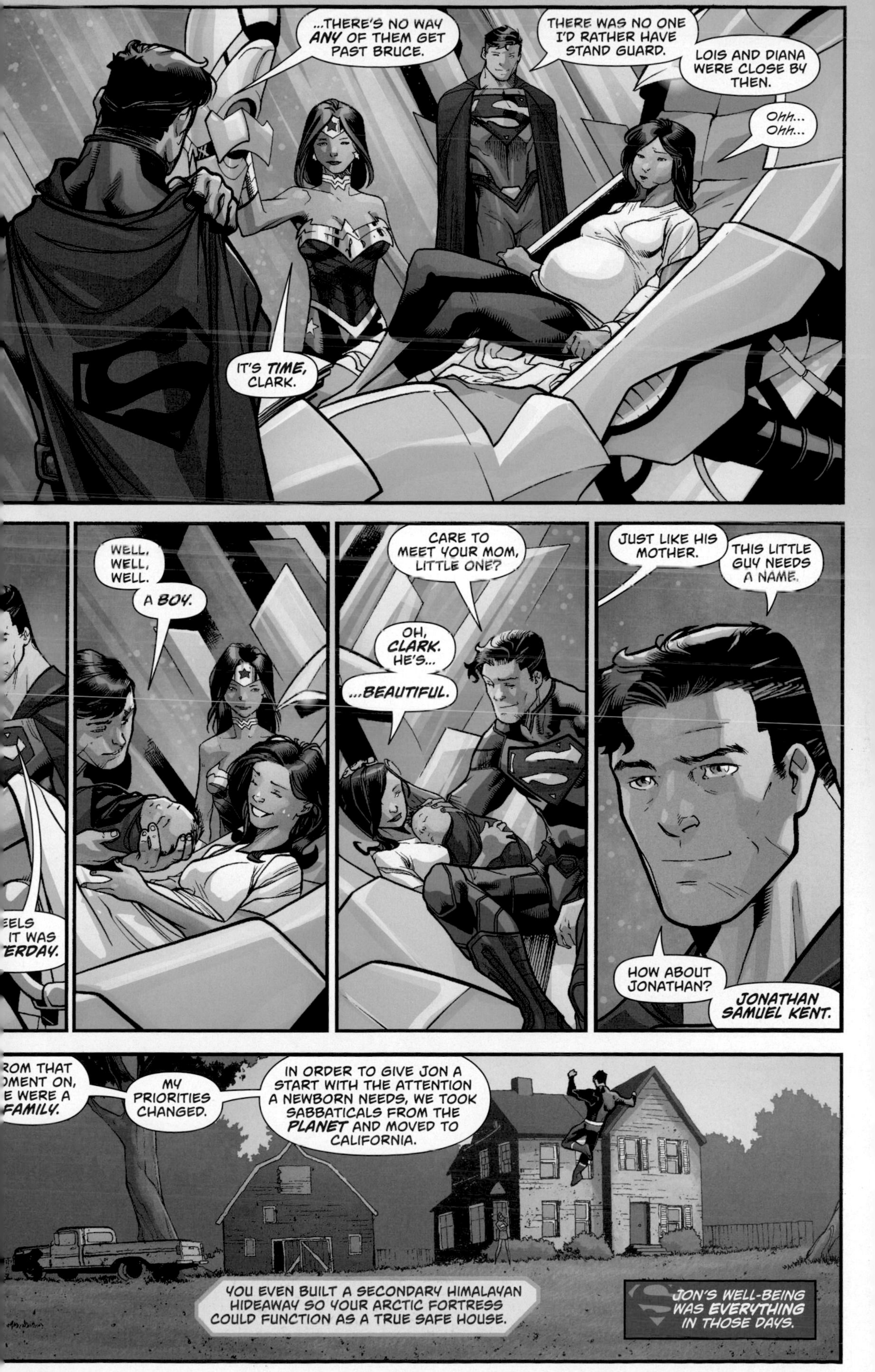
...THERE'S NO WAY ANY OF THEM GET PAST BRUCE.
THERE WAS NO ONE I'D RATHER HAVE STAND GUARD.
LOIS AND DIANA WERE CLOSE BY THEN.
Ohh... Ohh...
IT'S TIME, CLARK.
EELS
IT WAS
ERDAY.
WELL, WELL, WELL.
A BOY.
CARE TO MEET YOUR MOM, LITTLE ONE?
OH, CLARK. HE'S...
...BEAUTIFUL.
JUST LIKE HIS MOTHER.
THIS LITTLE GUY NEEDS A NAME.
HOW ABOUT JONATHAN?
JONATHAN SAMUEL KENT.
ROM THAT
OMENT ON,
E WERE A
FAMILY.
MY PRIORITIES CHANGED.
IN ORDER TO GIVE JON A START WITH THE ATTENTION A NEWBORN NEEDS, WE TOOK SABBATICALS FROM THE PLANET AND MOVED TO CALIFORNIA.
YOU EVEN BUILT A SECONDARY HIMALAYAN HIDEAWAY SO YOUR ARCTIC FORTRESS COULD FUNCTION AS A TRUE SAFE HOUSE.
JON'S WELL-BEING WAS EVERYTHING IN THOSE DAYS.

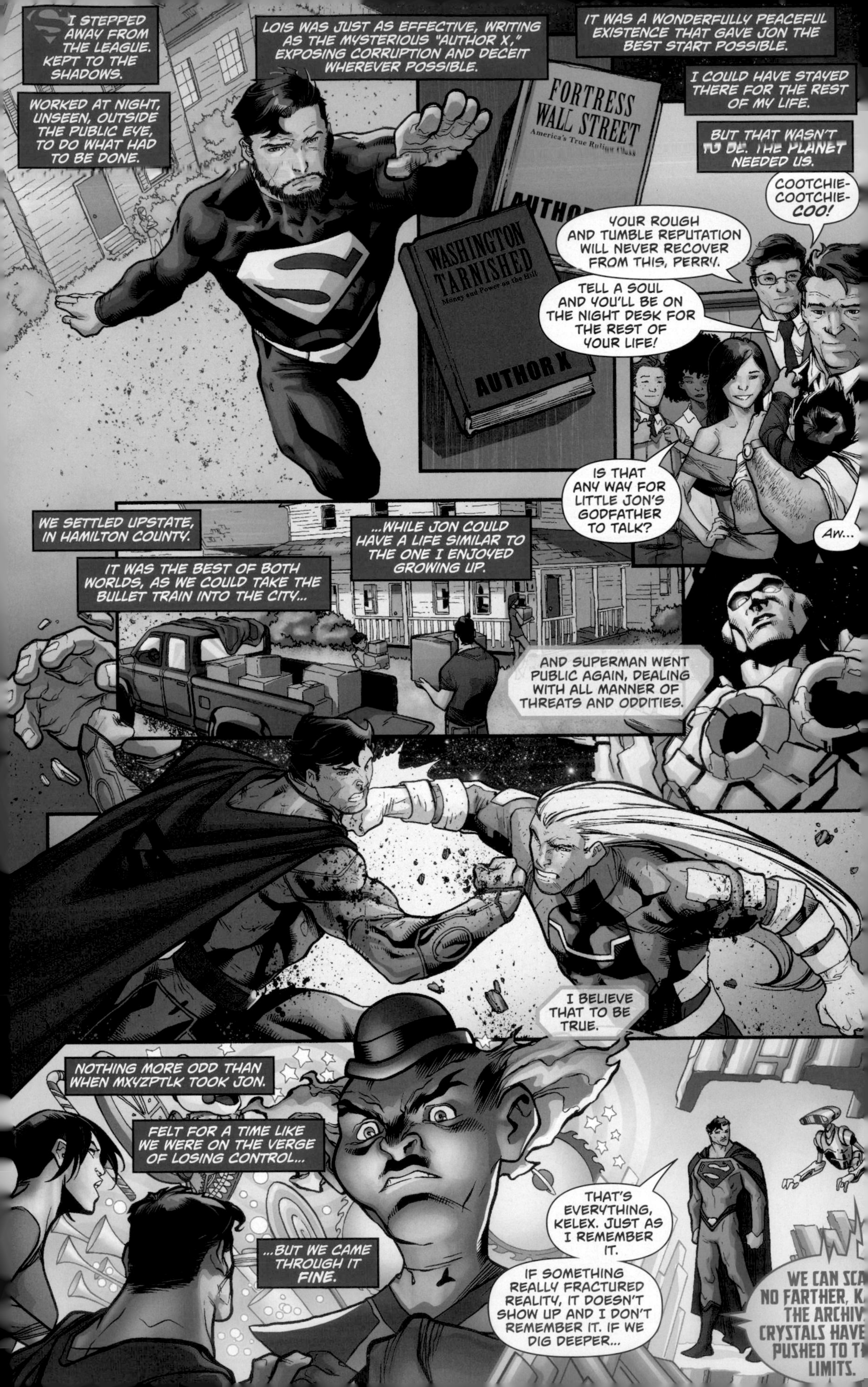
I STEPPED AWAY FROM THE LEAGUE. KEPT TO THE SHADOWS.
WORKED AT NIGHT, UNSEEN, OUTSIDE THE PUBLIC EYE, TO DO WHAT HAD TO BE DONE.
LOIS WAS JUST AS EFFECTIVE, WRITING AS THE MYSTERIOUS "AUTHOR X," EXPOSING CORRUPTION AND DECEIT WHEREVER POSSIBLE.
FORTRESS WALL STREET
America's True Ruling Class
WASHINGTON TARNISHED
Money and Power on the Hill
AUTHOR X
IT WAS A WONDERFULLY PEACEFUL EXISTENCE THAT GAVE JON THE BEST START POSSIBLE.
I COULD HAVE STAYED THERE FOR THE REST OF MY LIFE.
BUT THAT WASN'T TO BE. THE PLANET NEEDED US.
COOTCHIE-COOTCHIE-COO!
YOUR ROUGH AND TUMBLE REPUTATION WILL NEVER RECOVER FROM THIS, PERRY.
TELL A SOUL AND YOU'LL BE ON THE NIGHT DESK FOR THE REST OF YOUR LIFE!
IS THAT ANY WAY FOR LITTLE JON'S GODFATHER TO TALK?
AW...
WE SETTLED UPSTATE, IN HAMILTON COUNTY.
IT WAS THE BEST OF BOTH WORLDS, AS WE COULD TAKE THE BULLET TRAIN INTO THE CITY...
...WHILE JON COULD HAVE A LIFE SIMILAR TO THE ONE I ENJOYED GROWING UP.
AND SUPERMAN WENT PUBLIC AGAIN, DEALING WITH ALL MANNER OF THREATS AND ODDITIES.
I BELIEVE THAT TO BE TRUE.
NOTHING MORE ODD THAN WHEN MXYZPTLK TOOK JON.
FELT FOR A TIME LIKE WE WERE ON THE VERGE OF LOSING CONTROL...
...BUT WE CAME THROUGH IT FINE.
THAT'S EVERYTHING, KELEX. JUST AS I REMEMBER IT.
IF SOMETHING REALLY FRACTURED REALITY, IT DOESN'T SHOW UP AND I DON'T REMEMBER IT. IF WE DIG DEEPER...
WE CAN SCA NO FARTHER, K THE ARCHIV CRYSTALS HAVE PUSHED TO T LIMITS.

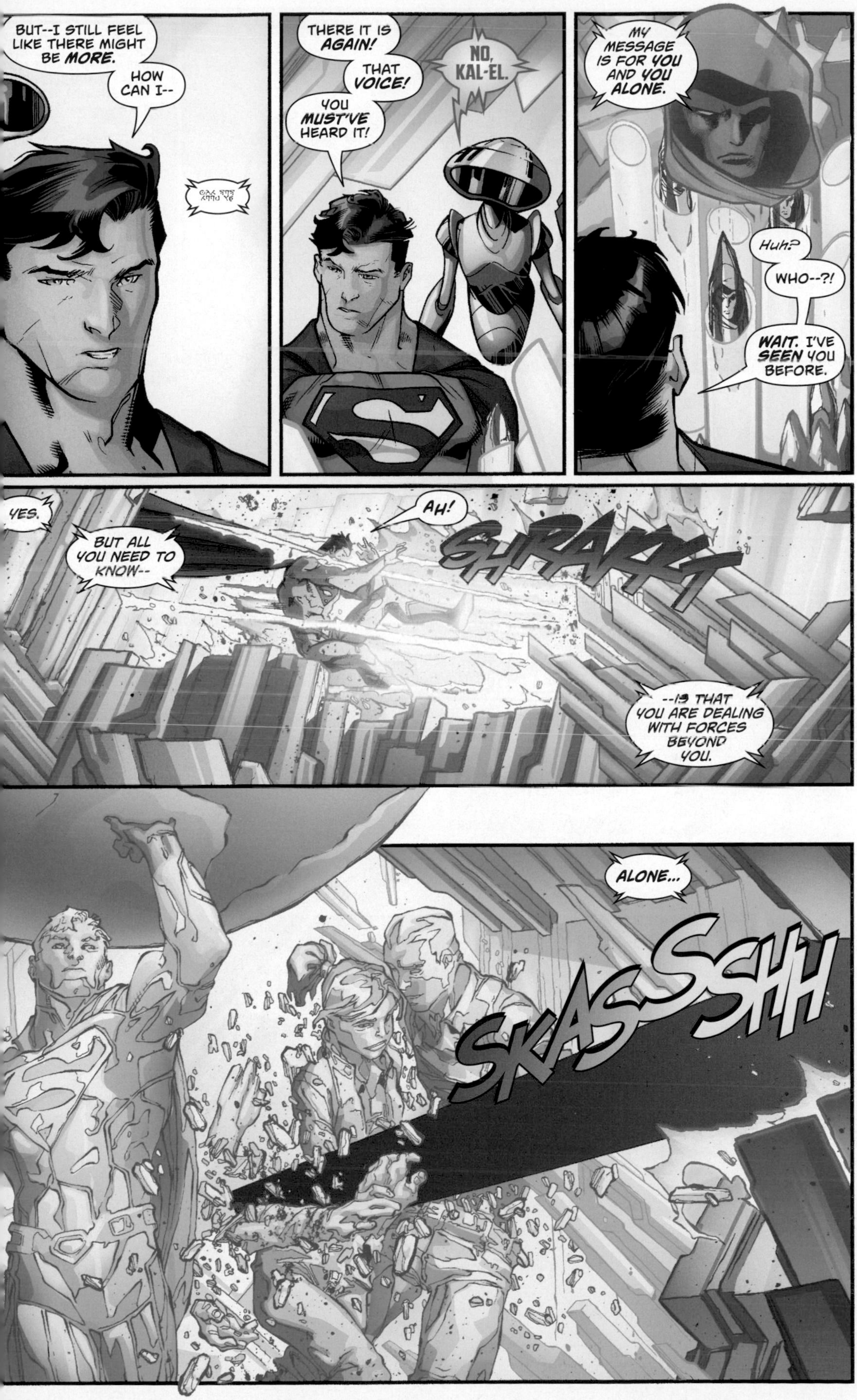
BUT--I STILL FEEL LIKE THERE MIGHT BE MORE.
HOW CAN I--
THERE IT IS AGAIN!
THAT VOICE!
YOU MUST'VE HEARD IT!
NO, KAL-EL.
MY MESSAGE IS FOR YOU AND YOU ALONE.
Huh?
WHO--?!
WAIT. I'VE SEEN YOU BEFORE.
YES.
BUT ALL YOU NEED TO KNOW--
AH!
SHRAKKT
--IS THAT YOU ARE DEALING WITH FORCES BEYOND YOU.
ALONE...
SKASSSHH

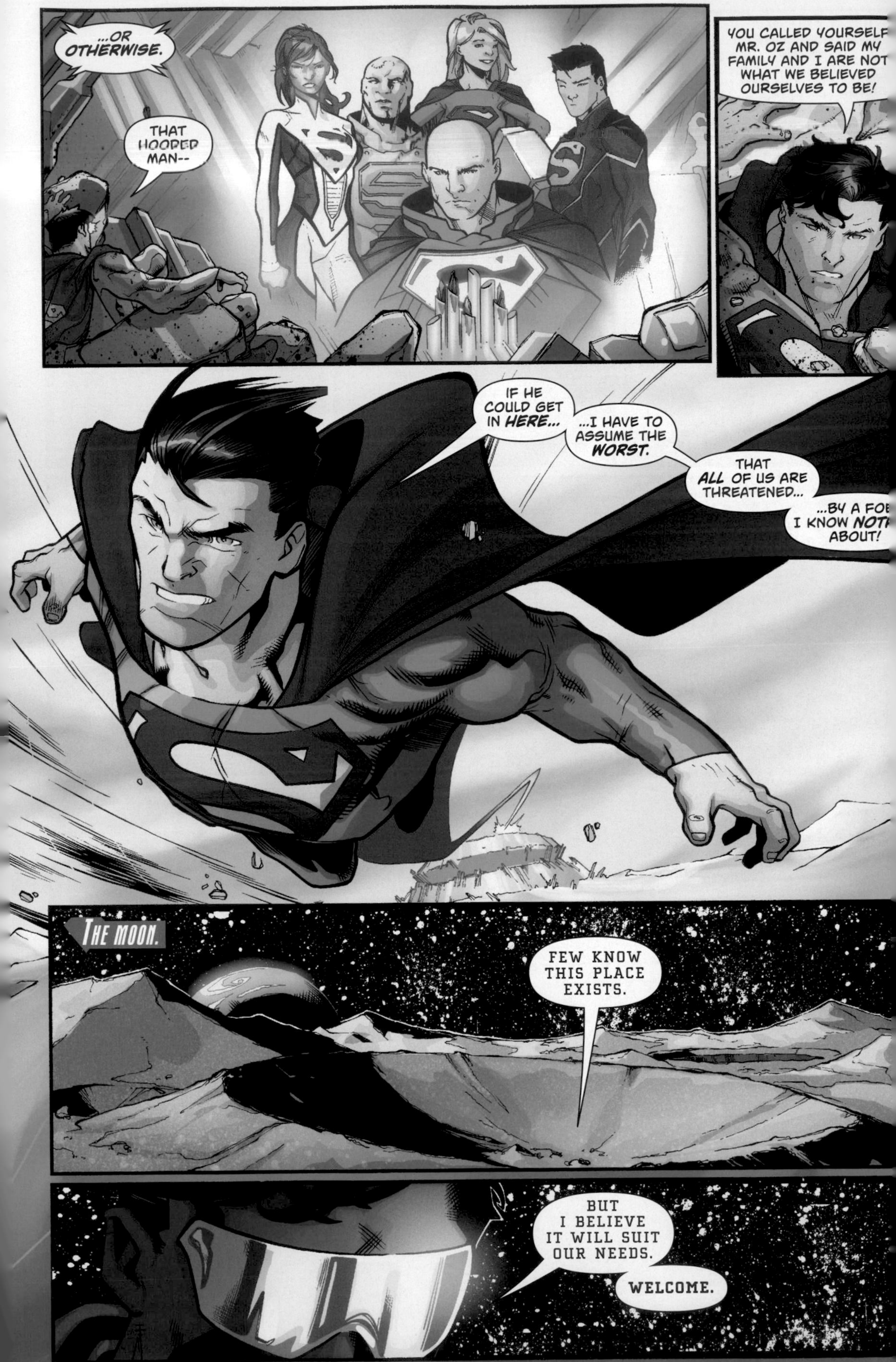

...OR OTHERWISE.
THAT HOODED MAN--
YOU CALLED YOURSELF MR. OZ AND SAID MY FAMILY AND I ARE NOT WHAT WE BELIEVED OURSELVES TO BE!
IF HE COULD GET IN HERE...
...I HAVE TO ASSUME THE WORST.
THAT ALL OF US ARE THREATENED...
...BY A FOE I KNOW NOTH ABOUT!
THE MOON.
FEW KNOW THIS PLACE EXISTS.
BUT I BELIEVE IT WILL SUIT OUR NEEDS.
WELCOME.

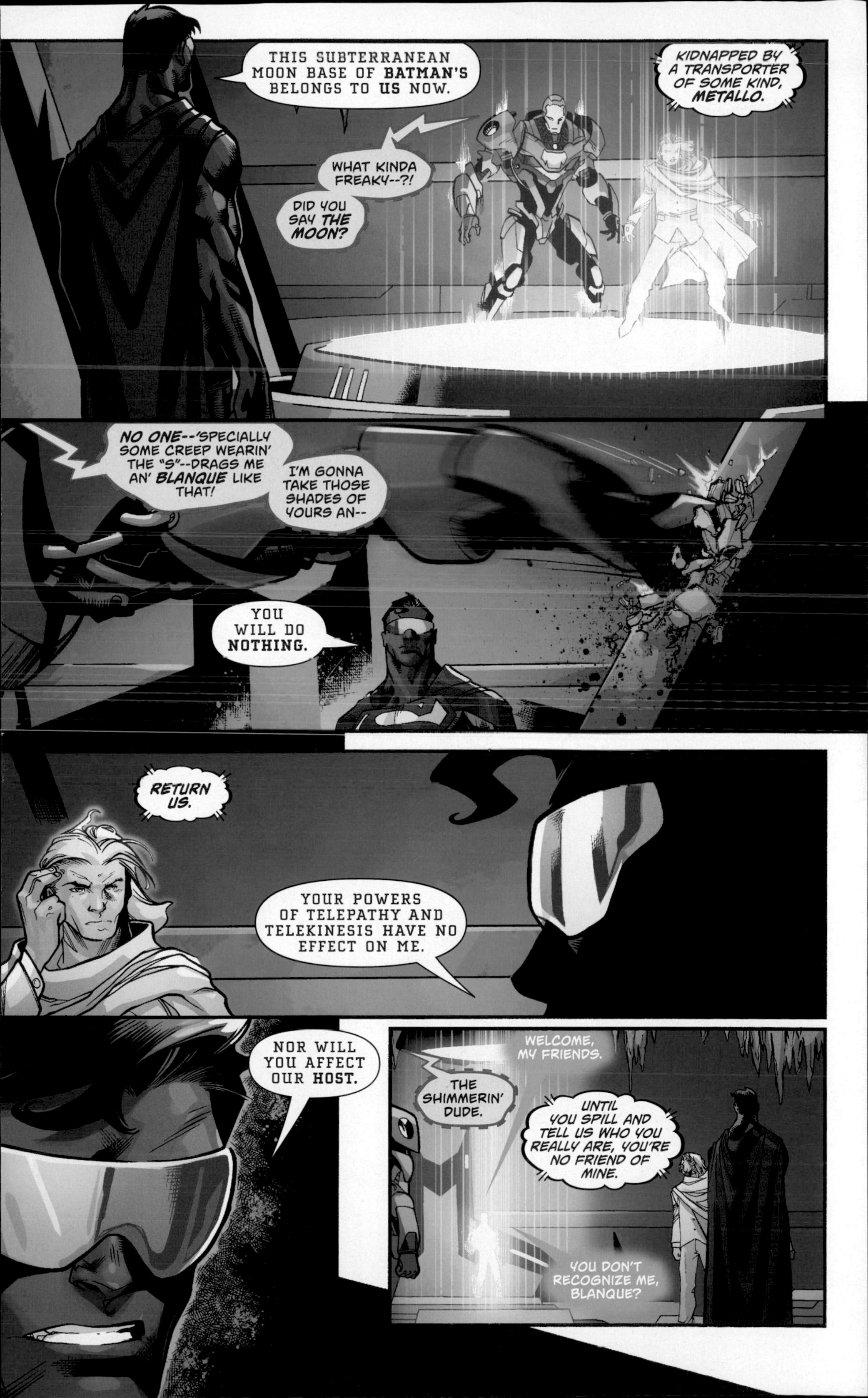
THIS SUBTERRANEAN MOON BASE OF BATMAN'S BELONGS TO US NOW.
KIDNAPPED BY A TRANSPORTER OF SOME KIND, METALLO.
WHAT KINDA FREAKY--?!
DID YOU SAY THE MOON?
NO ONE--'SPECIALLY SOME CREEP WEARIN' THE "S"--DRAGS ME AN' BLANQUE LIKE THAT!
I'M GONNA TAKE THOSE SHADES OF YOURS AN--
YOU WILL DO NOTHING.
RETURN US.
YOUR POWERS OF TELEPATHY AND TELEKINESIS HAVE NO EFFECT ON ME.
NOR WILL YOU AFFECT OUR HOST.
WELCOME, MY FRIENDS.
THE SHIMMERIN' DUDE.
UNTIL YOU SPILL AND TELL US WHO YOU REALLY ARE, YOU'RE NO FRIEND OF MINE.
YOU DON'T RECOGNIZE ME, BLANQUE?

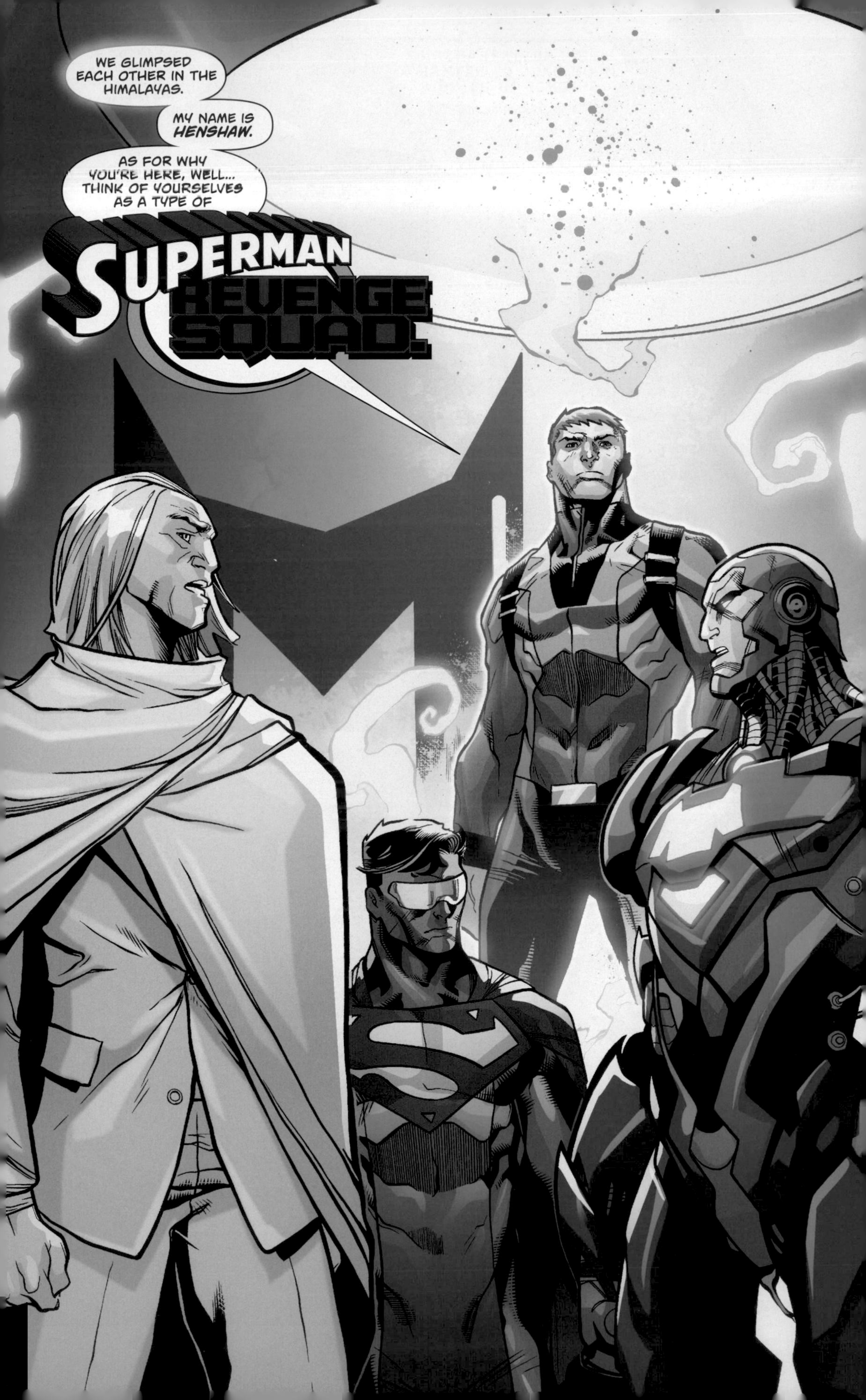
WE GLIMPSED EACH OTHER IN THE HIMALAYAS.
MY NAME IS HENSHAW.
AS FOR WHY YOU'RE HERE, WELL... THINK OF YOURSELVES AS A TYPE OF
SUPERMAN REVENGE SQUAD.

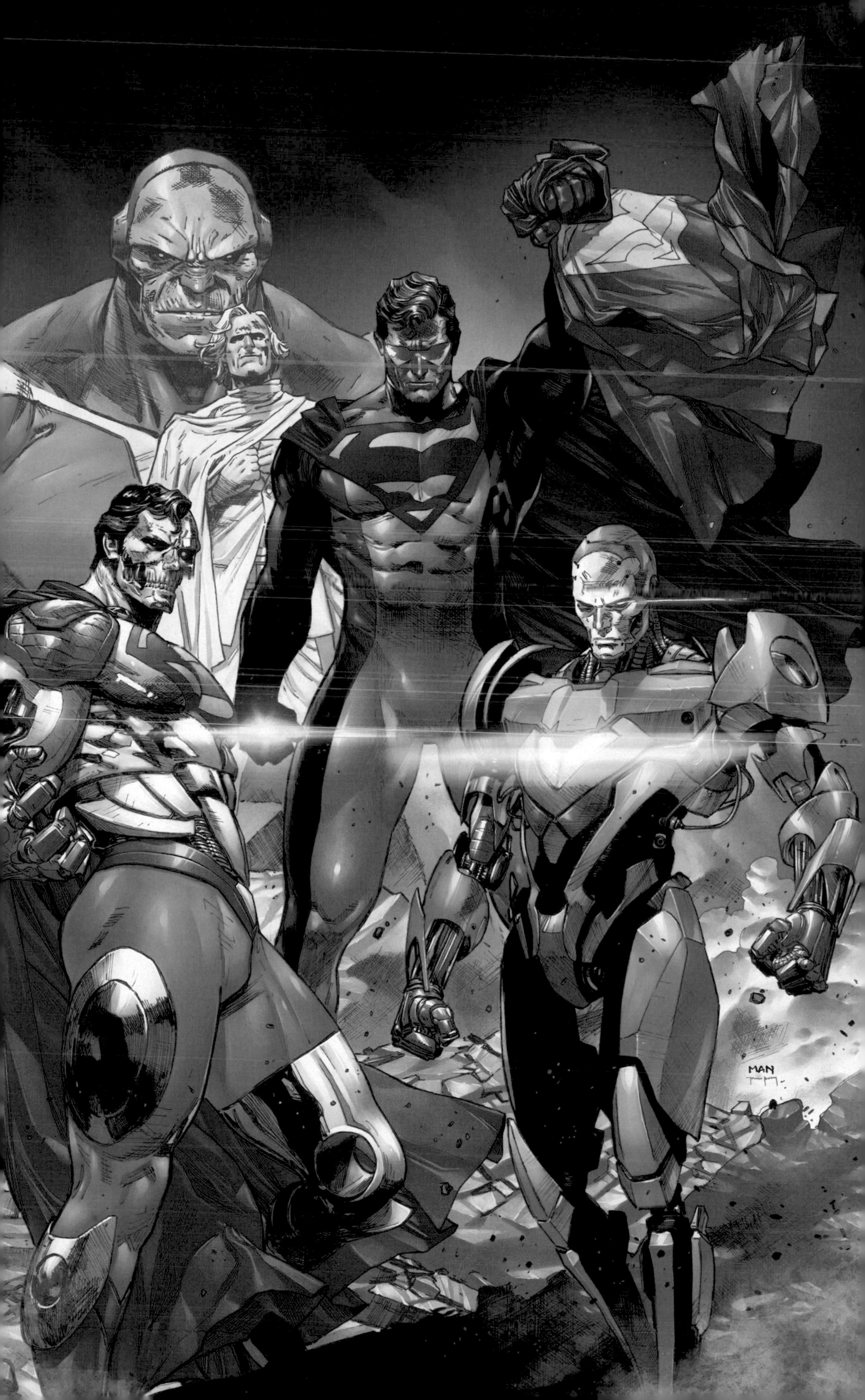
MAN

REVENGE PART 1

PATCH ZIRCHER artist * HI-FI colorist
CLAY MANN TOMEU MOREY cover artists

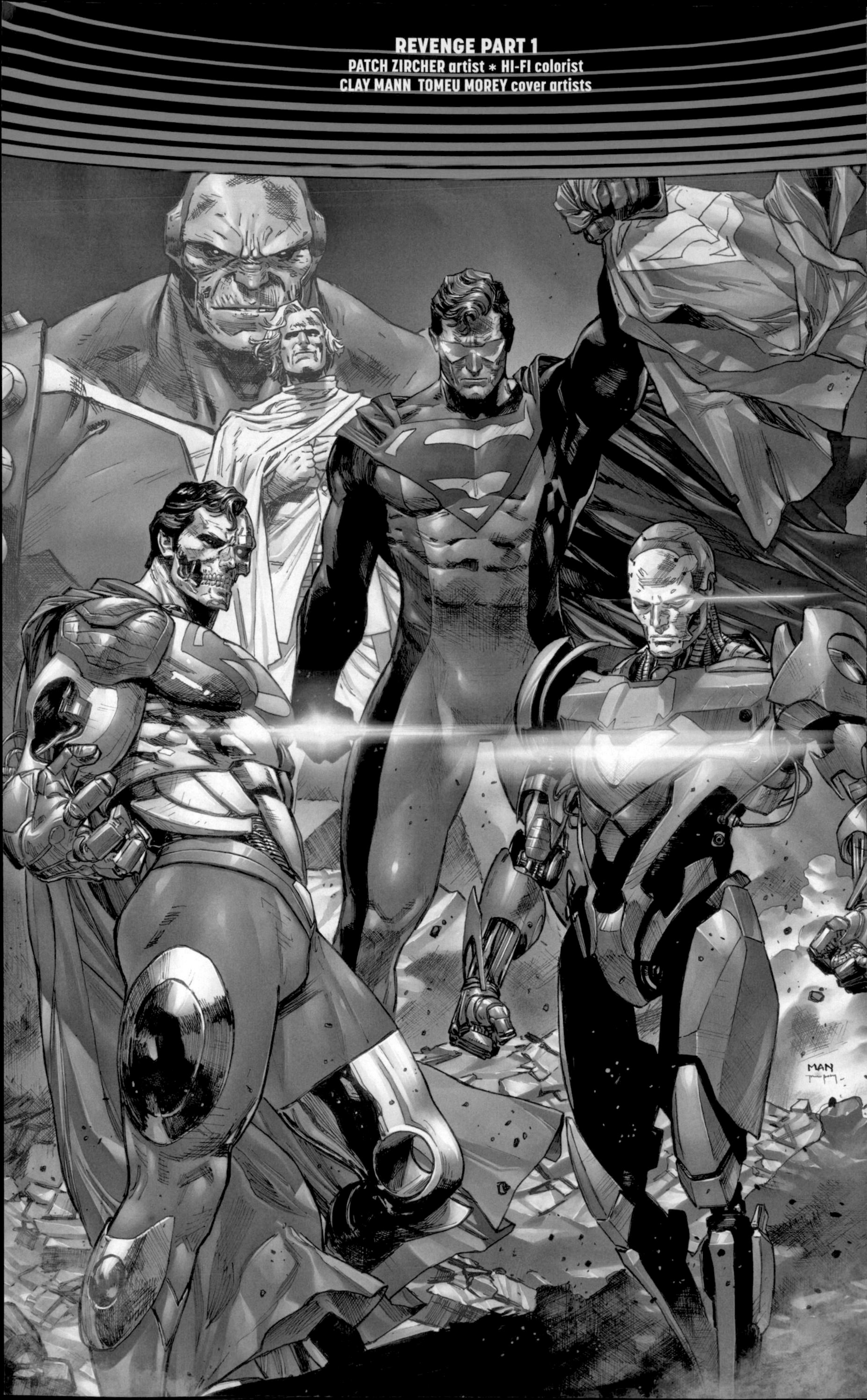

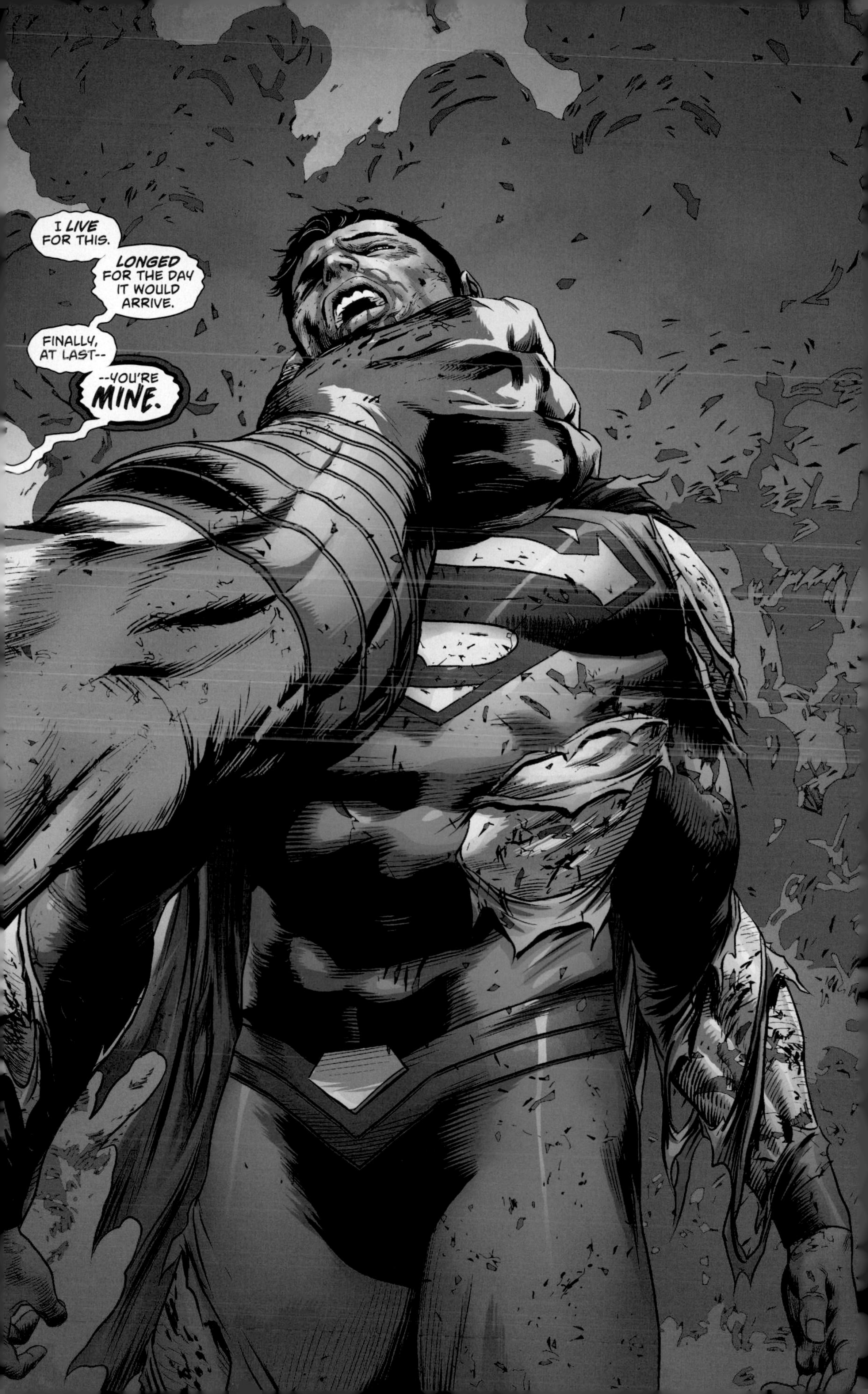
I *LIVE* FOR THIS.
LONGED FOR THE DAY IT WOULD ARRIVE.
FINALLY, AT LAST--
--YOU'RE **MINE.**

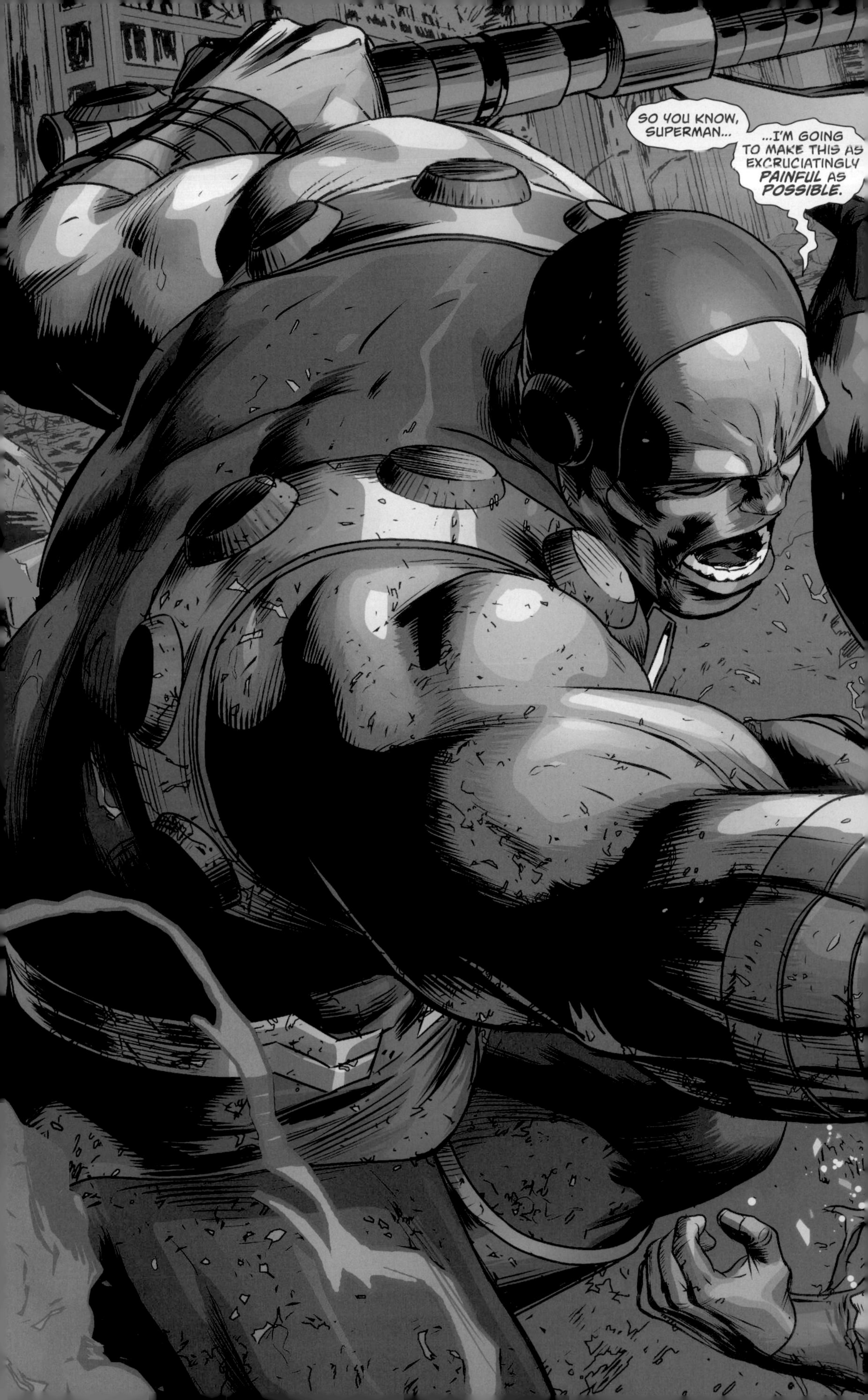
SO YOU KNOW, SUPERMAN...
...I'M GOING TO MAKE THIS AS EXCRUCIATINGLY *PAINFUL* AS *POSSIBLE.*

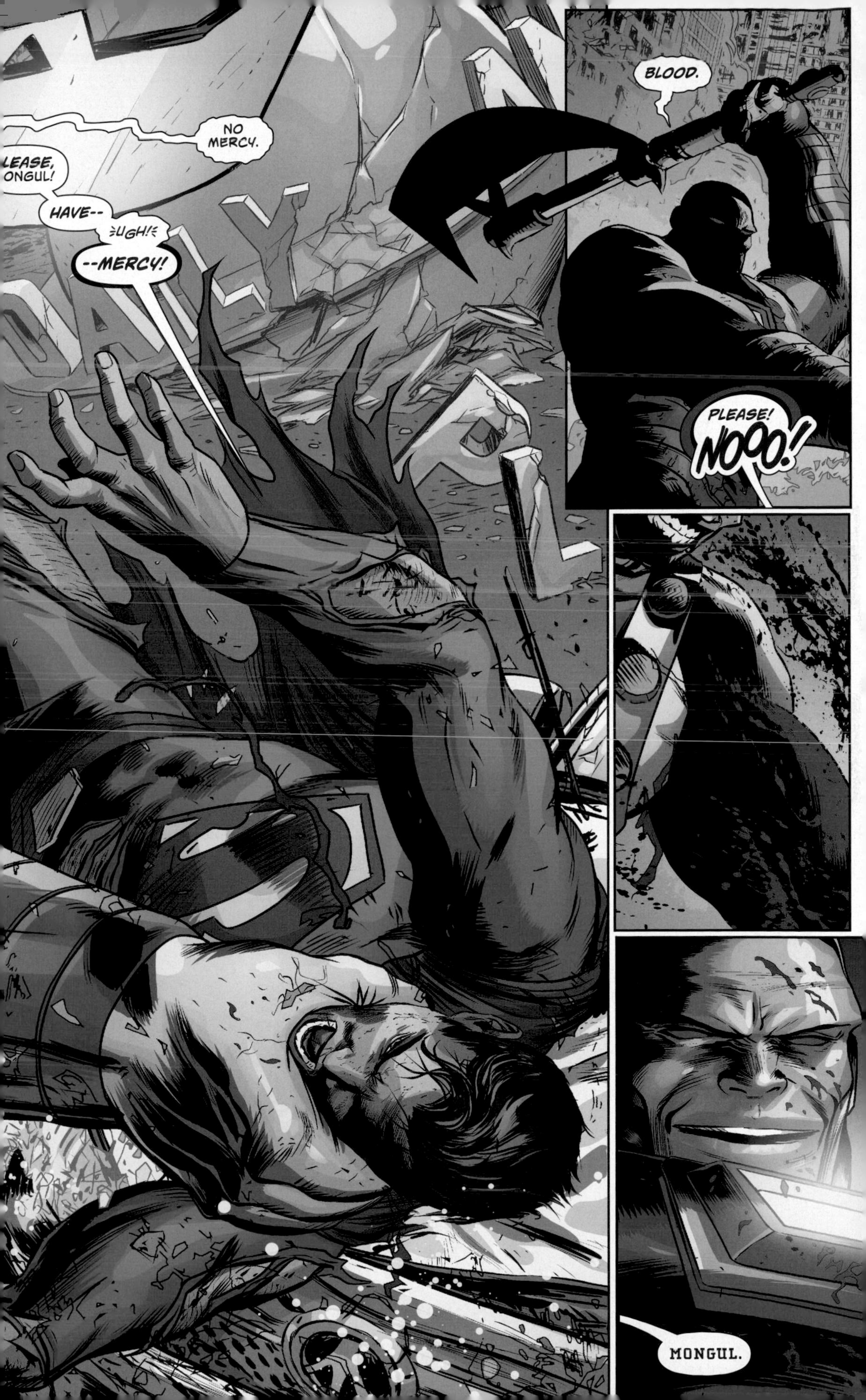
NO MERCY.
LEASE, ONGUL!
HAVE--
UGH!
--MERCY!
BLOOD.
PLEASE! NOOO!
MONGUL.

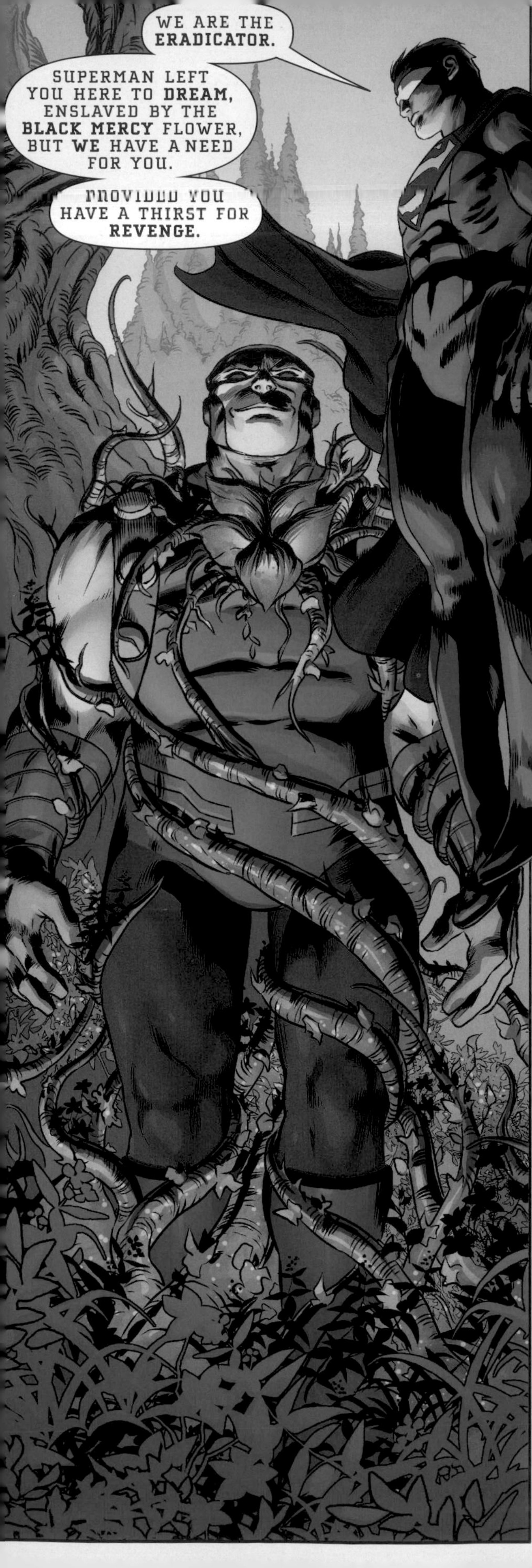
WE ARE THE ERADICATOR.
SUPERMAN LEFT YOU HERE TO DREAM, ENSLAVED BY THE BLACK MERCY FLOWER, BUT WE HAVE A NEED FOR YOU.
PROVIDED YOU HAVE A THIRST FOR REVENGE.

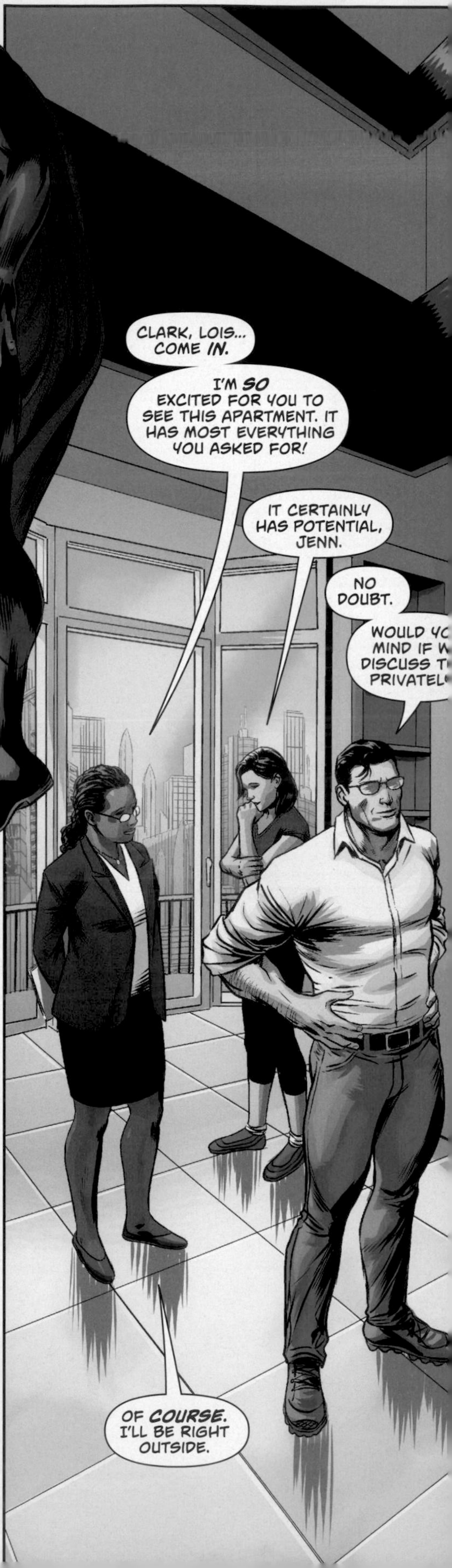
CLARK, LOIS... COME IN.
I'M SO EXCITED FOR YOU TO SEE THIS APARTMENT. IT HAS MOST EVERYTHING YOU ASKED FOR!
IT CERTAINLY HAS POTENTIAL, JENN.
NO DOUBT.
WOULD YO MIND IF W DISCUSS T PRIVATEL
OF COURSE. I'LL BE RIGHT OUTSIDE.

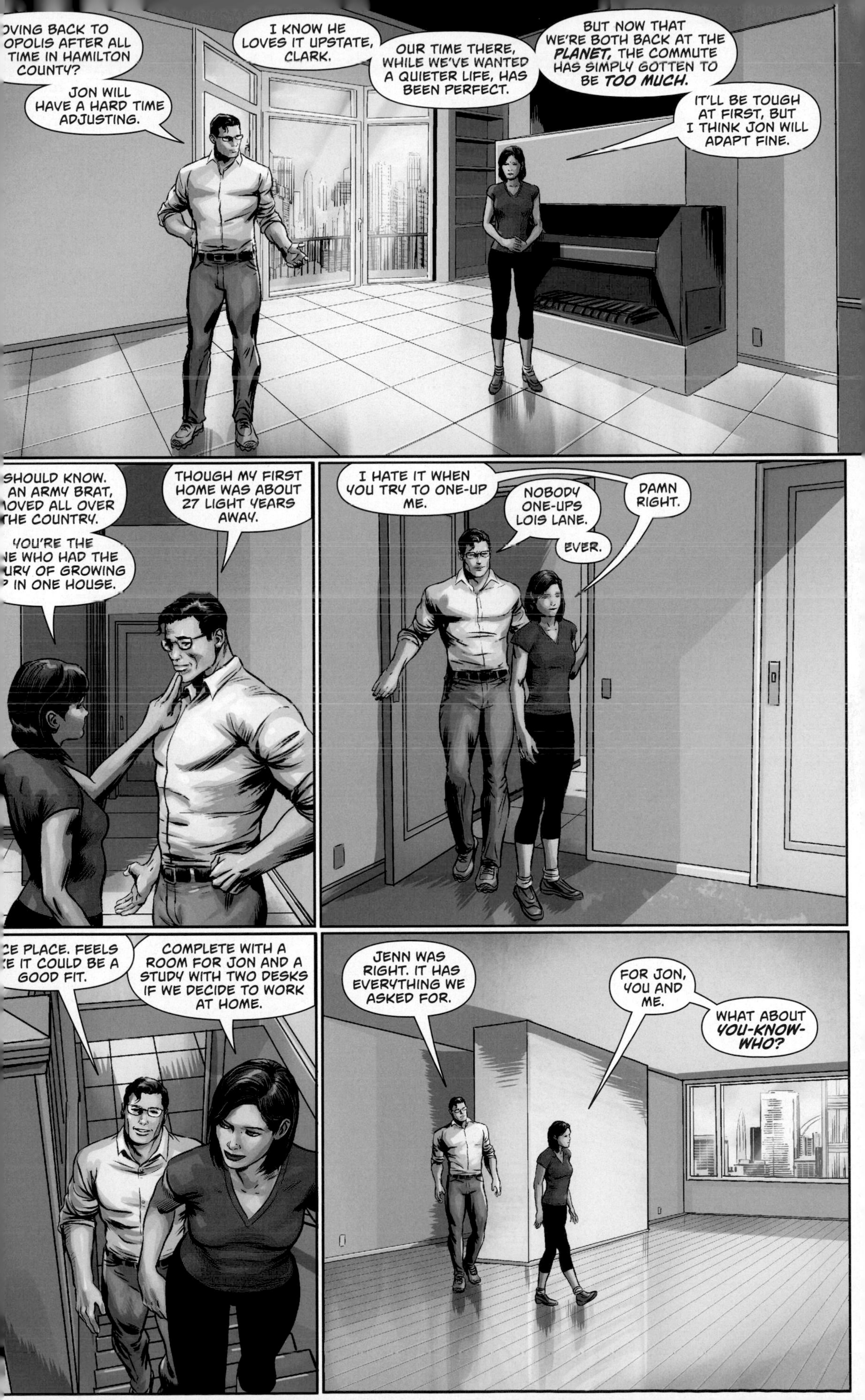

OVING BACK TO OPOLIS AFTER ALL TIME IN HAMILTON COUNTY?
JON WILL HAVE A HARD TIME ADJUSTING.
I KNOW HE LOVES IT UPSTATE, CLARK.
OUR TIME THERE, WHILE WE'VE WANTED A QUIETER LIFE, HAS BEEN PERFECT.
BUT NOW THAT WE'RE BOTH BACK AT THE PLANET, THE COMMUTE HAS SIMPLY GOTTEN TO BE TOO MUCH.
IT'LL BE TOUGH AT FIRST, BUT I THINK JON WILL ADAPT FINE.
SHOULD KNOW. AN ARMY BRAT, OVED ALL OVER THE COUNTRY.
YOU'RE THE E WHO HAD THE URY OF GROWING IN ONE HOUSE.
THOUGH MY FIRST HOME WAS ABOUT 27 LIGHT YEARS AWAY.
I HATE IT WHEN YOU TRY TO ONE-UP ME.
NOBODY ONE-UPS LOIS LANE.
EVER.
DAMN RIGHT.
CE PLACE. FEELS E IT COULD BE A GOOD FIT.
COMPLETE WITH A ROOM FOR JON AND A STUDY WITH TWO DESKS IF WE DECIDE TO WORK AT HOME.
JENN WAS RIGHT. IT HAS EVERYTHING WE ASKED FOR.
FOR JON, YOU AND ME.
WHAT ABOUT YOU-KNOW-WHO?

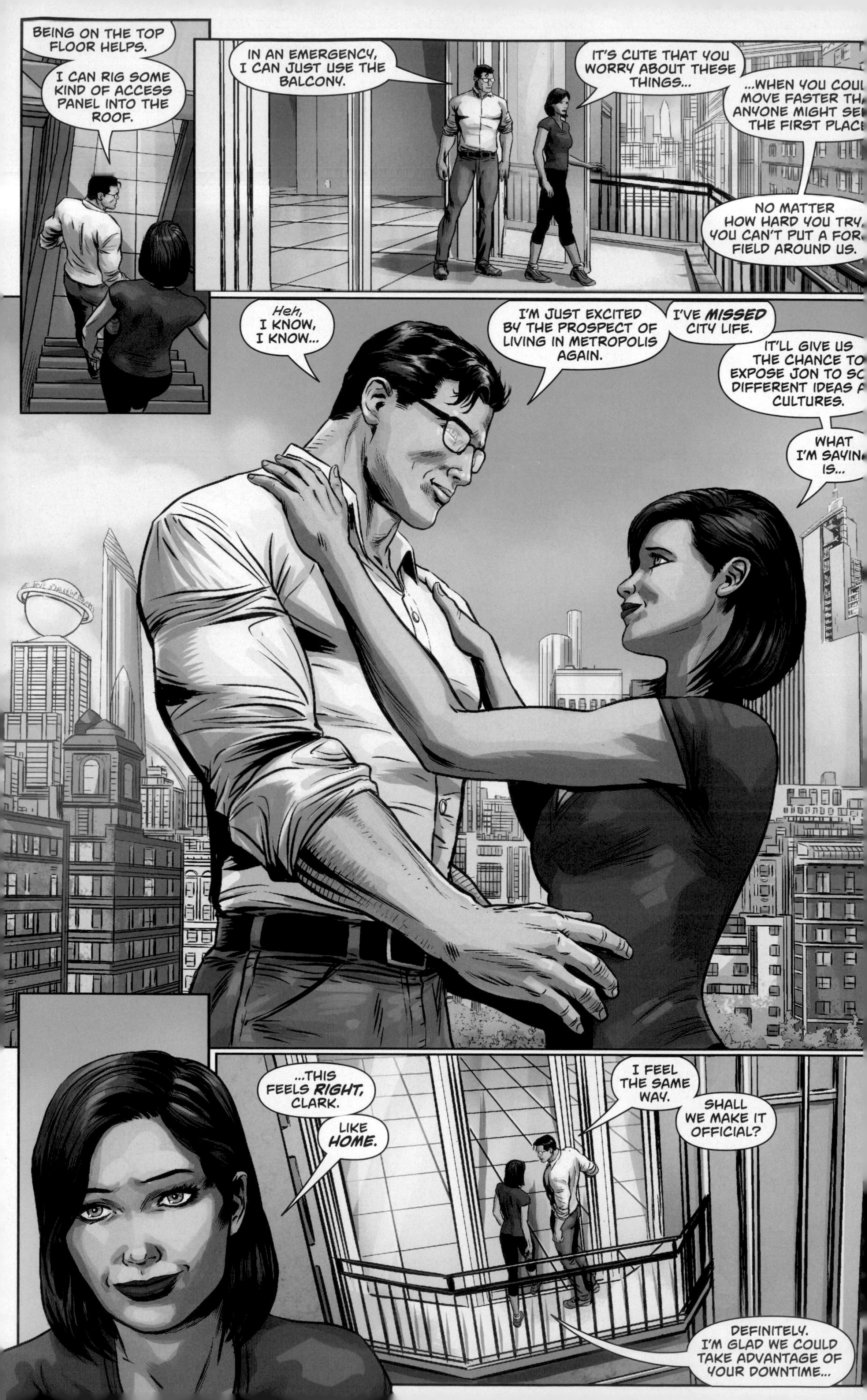
BEING ON THE TOP FLOOR HELPS.
I CAN RIG SOME KIND OF ACCESS PANEL INTO THE ROOF.
IN AN EMERGENCY, I CAN JUST USE THE BALCONY.
IT'S CUTE THAT YOU WORRY ABOUT THESE THINGS...
...WHEN YOU COUL MOVE FASTER TH ANYONE MIGHT SE THE FIRST PLAC
NO MATTER HOW HARD YOU TRY, YOU CAN'T PUT A FOR FIELD AROUND US.
Heh, I KNOW, I KNOW...
I'M JUST EXCITED BY THE PROSPECT OF LIVING IN METROPOLIS AGAIN.
I'VE ***MISSED*** CITY LIFE.
IT'LL GIVE US THE CHANCE TO EXPOSE JON TO SO DIFFERENT IDEAS A CULTURES.
WHAT I'M SAYIN IS...
...THIS FEELS ***RIGHT,*** CLARK.
LIKE ***HOME.***
I FEEL THE SAME WAY.
SHALL WE MAKE IT OFFICIAL?
DEFINITELY. I'M GLAD WE COULD TAKE ADVANTAGE OF YOUR DOWNTIME...

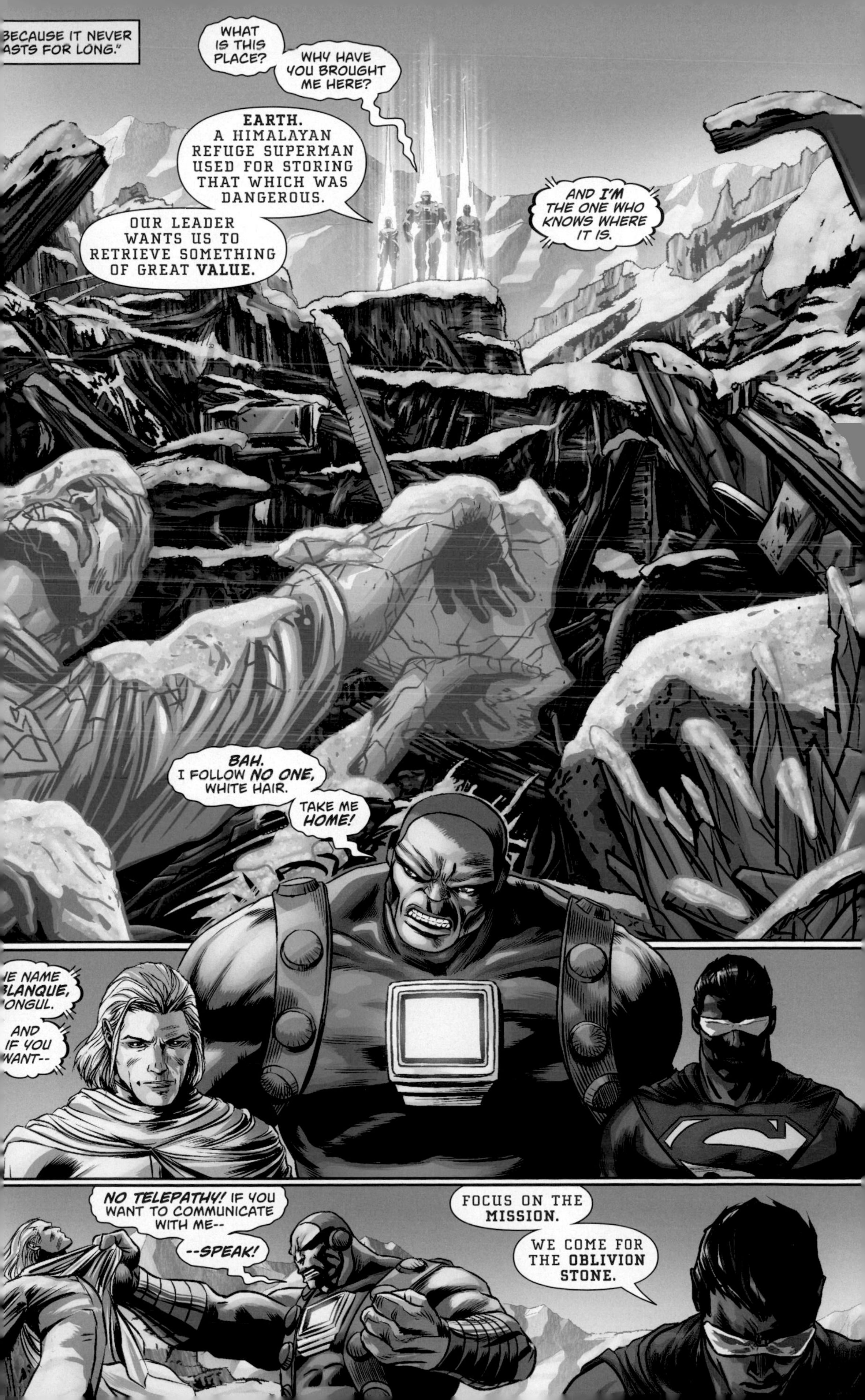

BECAUSE IT NEVER
ASTS FOR LONG."
WHAT IS THIS PLACE?
WHY HAVE YOU BROUGHT ME HERE?
EARTH. A HIMALAYAN REFUGE SUPERMAN USED FOR STORING THAT WHICH WAS DANGEROUS.
OUR LEADER WANTS US TO RETRIEVE SOMETHING OF GREAT VALUE.
AND I'M THE ONE WHO KNOWS WHERE IT IS.
BAH. I FOLLOW NO ONE, WHITE HAIR.
TAKE ME HOME!
E NAME
LANQUE,
ONGUL.
AND IF YOU WANT--
NO TELEPATHY! IF YOU WANT TO COMMUNICATE WITH ME--
--SPEAK!
FOCUS ON THE MISSION.
WE COME FOR THE OBLIVION STONE.

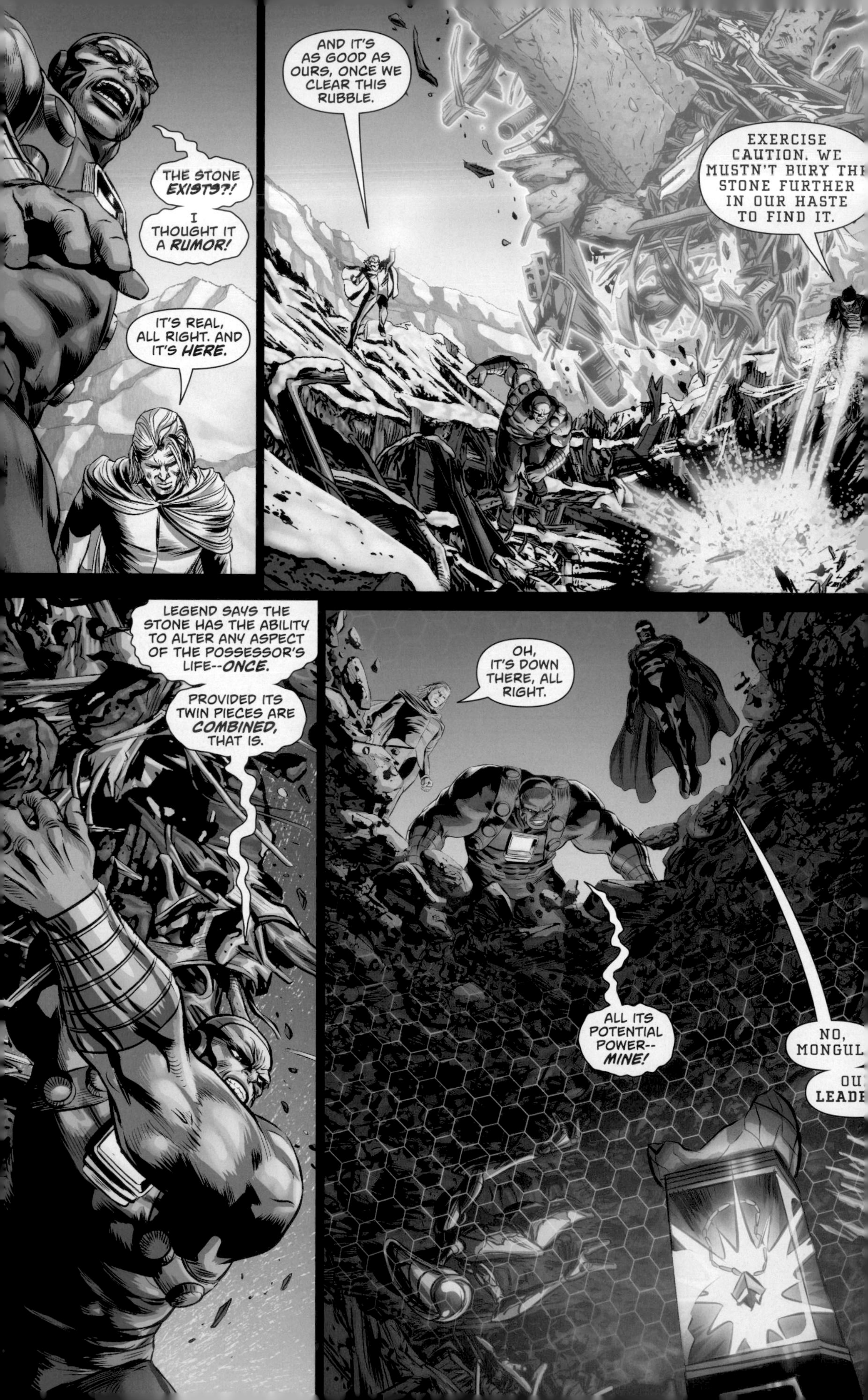
THE STONE EXISTS?!
I THOUGHT IT A RUMOR!
IT'S REAL, ALL RIGHT. AND IT'S HERE.
AND IT'S AS GOOD AS OURS, ONCE WE CLEAR THIS RUBBLE.
EXERCISE CAUTION. WE MUSTN'T BURY THE STONE FURTHER IN OUR HASTE TO FIND IT.
LEGEND SAYS THE STONE HAS THE ABILITY TO ALTER ANY ASPECT OF THE POSSESSOR'S LIFE--ONCE.
PROVIDED ITS TWIN PIECES ARE COMBINED, THAT IS.
OH, IT'S DOWN THERE, ALL RIGHT.
ALL ITS POTENTIAL POWER--MINE!
NO, MONGUL.

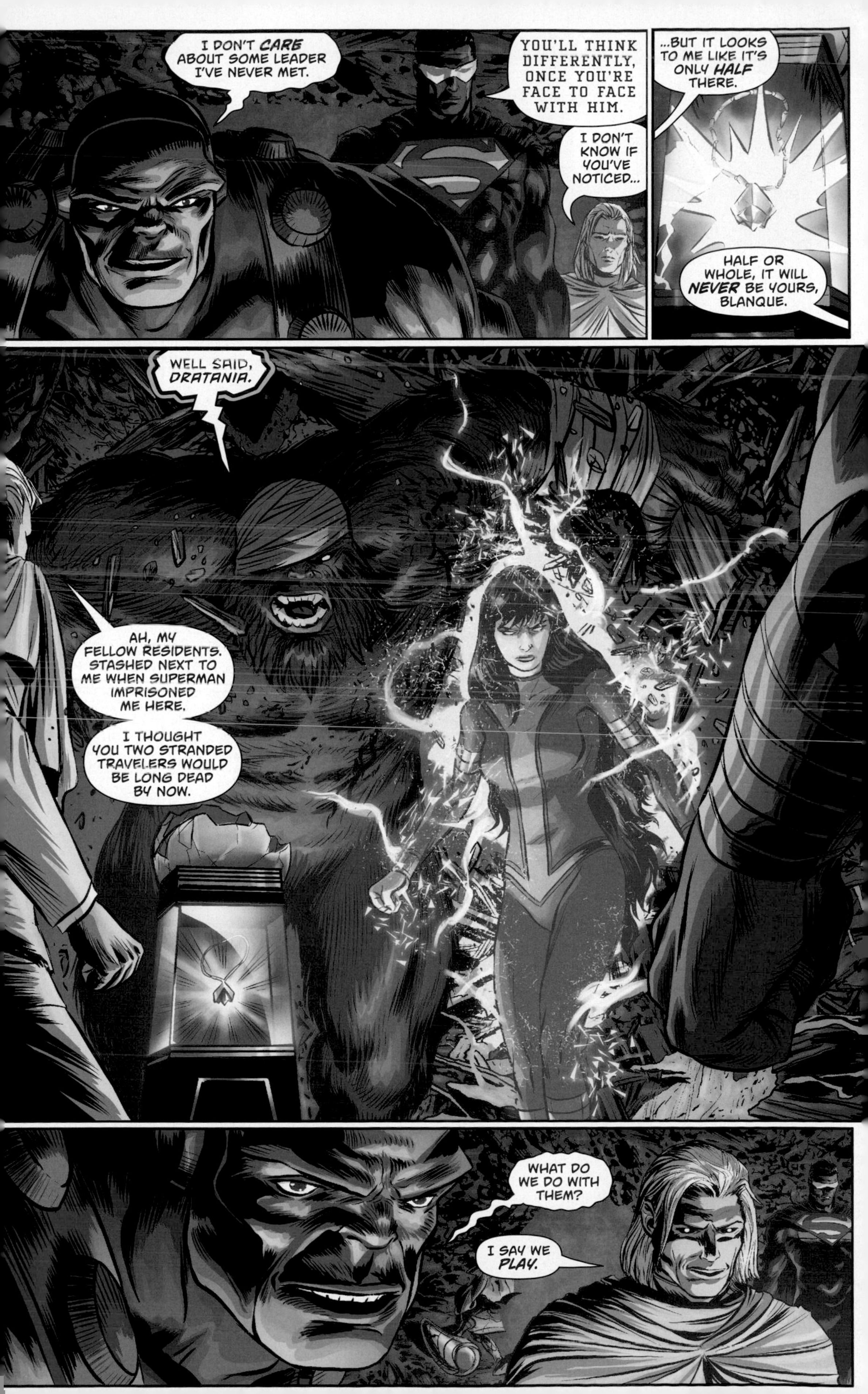
I DON'T CARE ABOUT SOME LEADER I'VE NEVER MET.
YOU'LL THINK DIFFERENTLY, ONCE YOU'RE FACE TO FACE WITH HIM.
I DON'T KNOW IF YOU'VE NOTICED...
...BUT IT LOOKS TO ME LIKE IT'S ONLY HALF THERE.
HALF OR WHOLE, IT WILL NEVER BE YOURS, BLANQUE.
WELL SAID, DRATANIA.
AH, MY FELLOW RESIDENTS. STASHED NEXT TO ME WHEN SUPERMAN IMPRISONED ME HERE.
I THOUGHT YOU TWO STRANDED TRAVELERS WOULD BE LONG DEAD BY NOW.
WHAT DO WE DO WITH THEM?
I SAY WE PLAY.

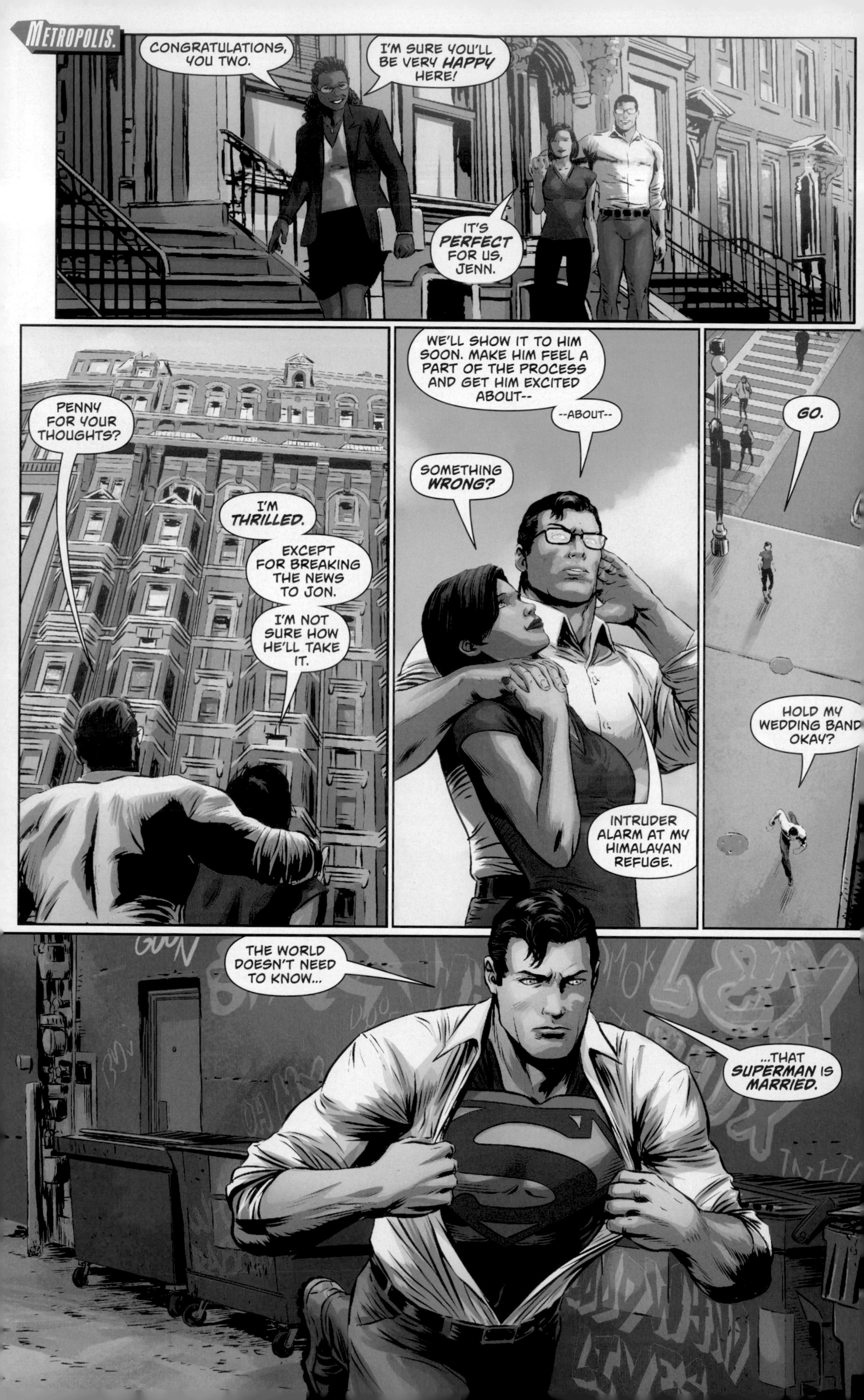
METROPOLIS.
CONGRATULATIONS, YOU TWO.
I'M SURE YOU'LL BE VERY HAPPY HERE!
IT'S PERFECT FOR US, JENN.
PENNY FOR YOUR THOUGHTS?
I'M THRILLED.
EXCEPT FOR BREAKING THE NEWS TO JON.
I'M NOT SURE HOW HE'LL TAKE IT.
WE'LL SHOW IT TO HIM SOON. MAKE HIM FEEL A PART OF THE PROCESS AND GET HIM EXCITED ABOUT--
--ABOUT--
SOMETHING WRONG?
INTRUDER ALARM AT MY HIMALAYAN REFUGE.
GO.
HOLD MY WEDDING BAND OKAY?
THE WORLD DOESN'T NEED TO KNOW...
...THAT SUPERMAN IS MARRIED.

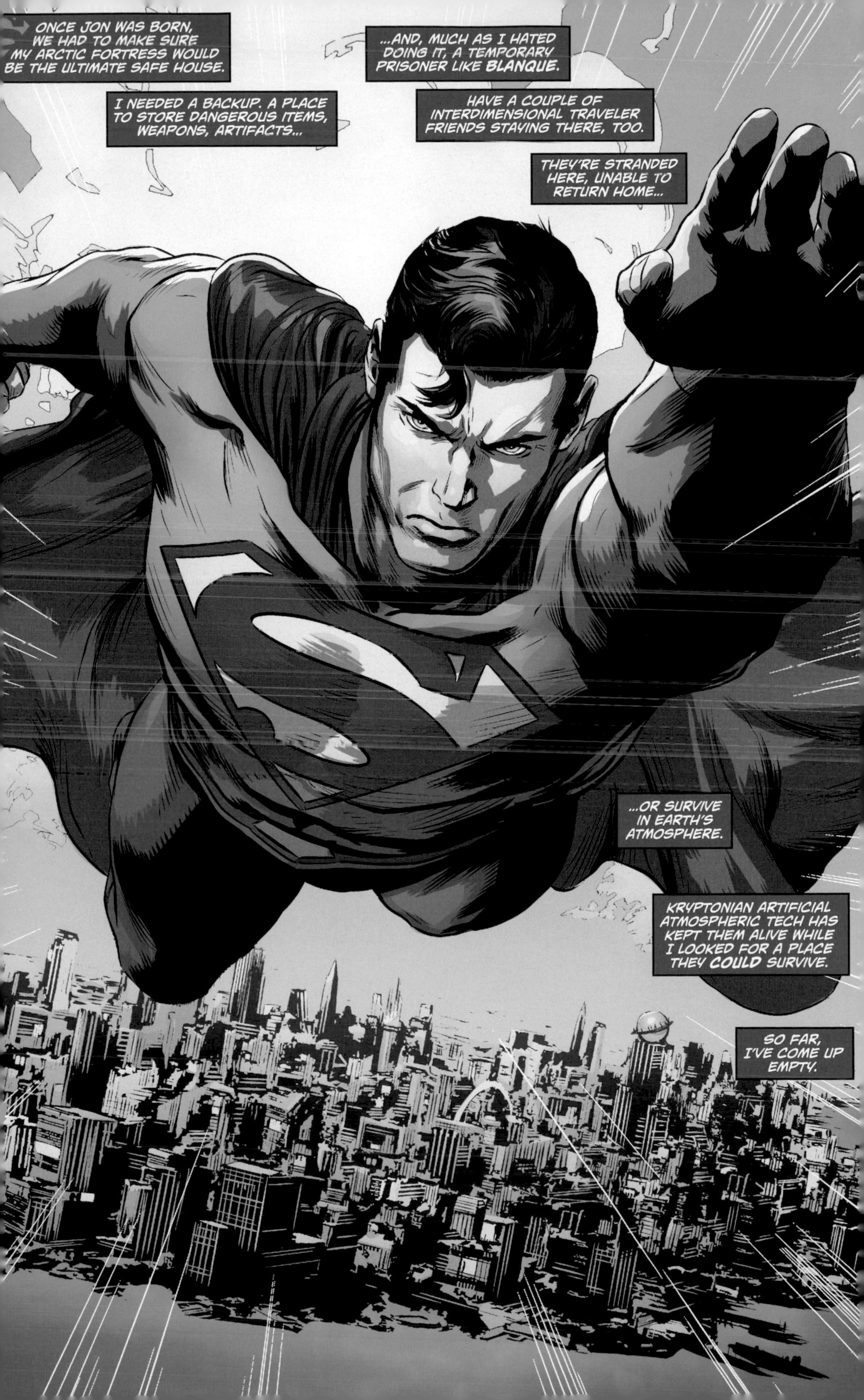
ONCE JON WAS BORN, WE HAD TO MAKE SURE MY ARCTIC FORTRESS WOULD BE THE ULTIMATE SAFE HOUSE.
I NEEDED A BACKUP. A PLACE TO STORE DANGEROUS ITEMS, WEAPONS, ARTIFACTS...
...AND, MUCH AS I HATED DOING IT, A TEMPORARY PRISONER LIKE BLANQUE.
HAVE A COUPLE OF INTERDIMENSIONAL TRAVELER FRIENDS STAYING THERE, TOO.
THEY'RE STRANDED HERE, UNABLE TO RETURN HOME...
...OR SURVIVE IN EARTH'S ATMOSPHERE.
KRYPTONIAN ARTIFICIAL ATMOSPHERIC TECH HAS KEPT THEM ALIVE WHILE I LOOKED FOR A PLACE THEY COULD SURVIVE.
SO FAR, I'VE COME UP EMPTY.

THE ALERT ABOUT A HELICOPTER SNOOPING AROUND THE AREA CAME IN A COUPLE OF DAYS AGO.

BUT KELEX II SENT THE ALL-CLEAR SIGNAL, AND THERE WERE OTHER...MITIGATING CIRCUMSTANCES I HAD TO ATTEND TO.

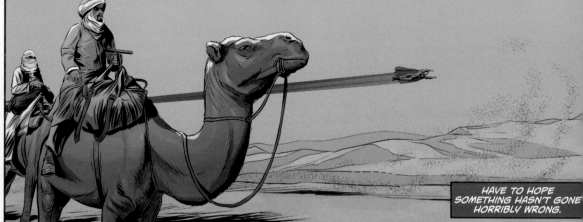

HAVE TO HOPE SOMETHING HASN'T GONE HORRIBLY WRONG.

THAT BLANQUE IS STILL IN HIS CELL AND--

DAMN.

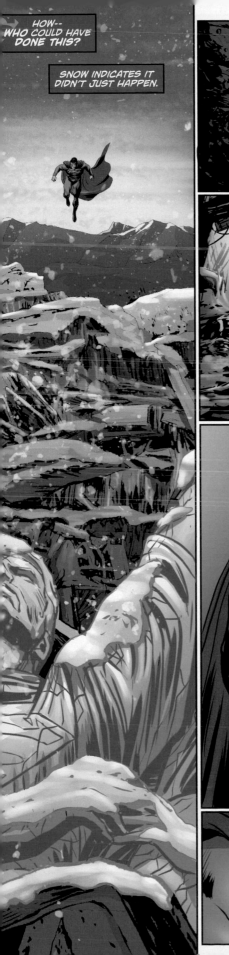

HOW-- WHO COULD HAVE DONE THIS?

SNOW INDICATES IT DIDN'T JUST HAPPEN.

IT MUST HAVE HAPPENED AROUND THE TIME OF THE FIRST ALERT.

BUT...WHY WOULD KELEX SIGNAL EVERYTHING WAS OKAY?

KAL-- KAL-- KAL-EL.

KELEX! WHAT HAPPENED HERE?

BLA-- BLA-- CHKT-- CHKT-- BLANQUE. FORCED--ALL-CLEAR MESSAGE.

TOOK THE ST-- CHKT-- ST-- CHKT-- CHKT--

OBLIVION STONE.

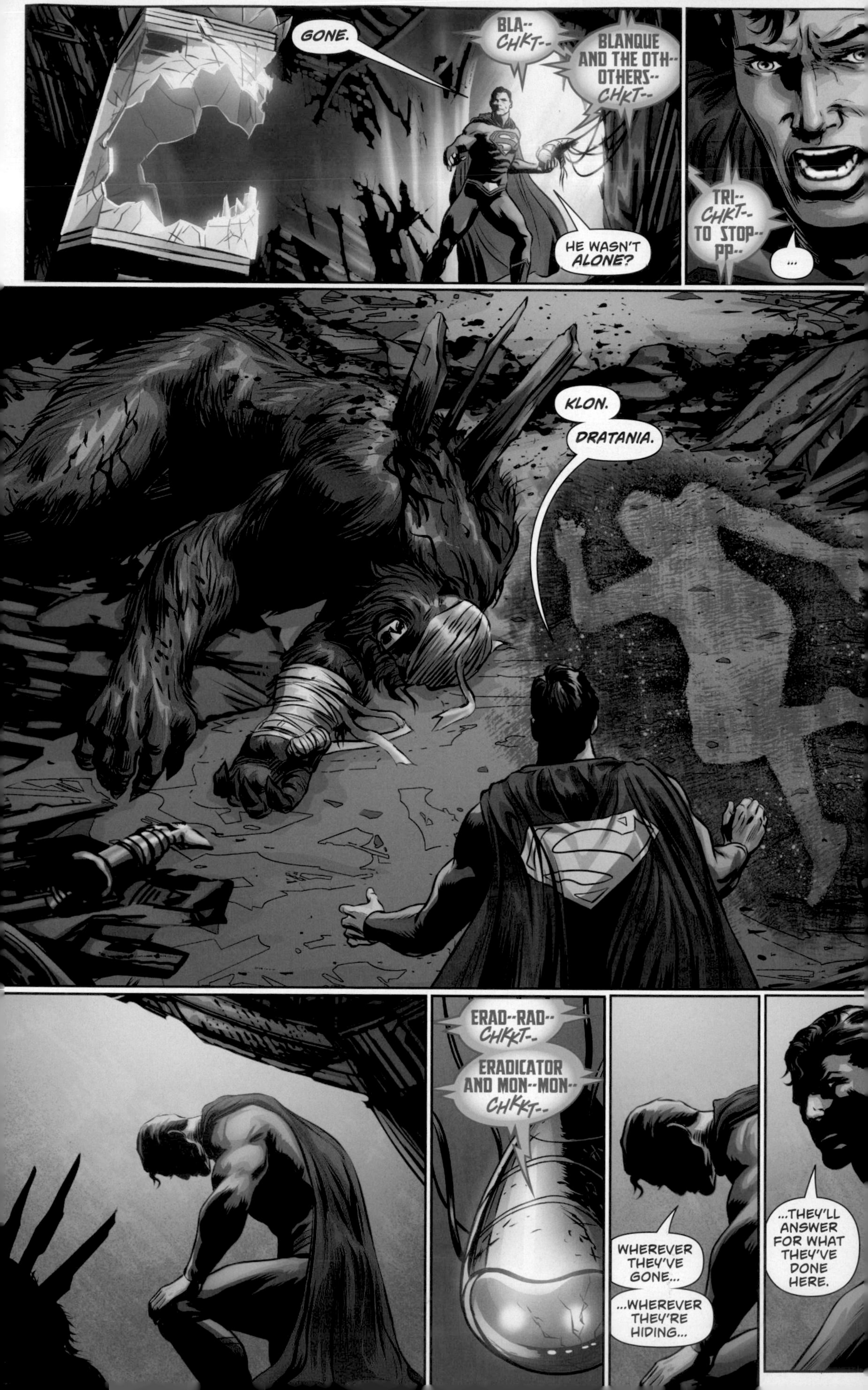
GONE.
BLA-- CHKT--
BLANQUE AND THE OTH-- OTHERS-- CHKT--
HE WASN'T ALONE?
TRI-- CHKT-- TO STOP-- PP--
...
KLON.
DRATANIA.
ERAD--RAD-- CHKKT--
ERADICATOR AND MON--MON-- CHKKT--
WHEREVER THEY'VE GONE...
...WHEREVER THEY'RE HIDING...
...THEY'LL ANSWER FOR WHAT THEY'VE DONE HERE.

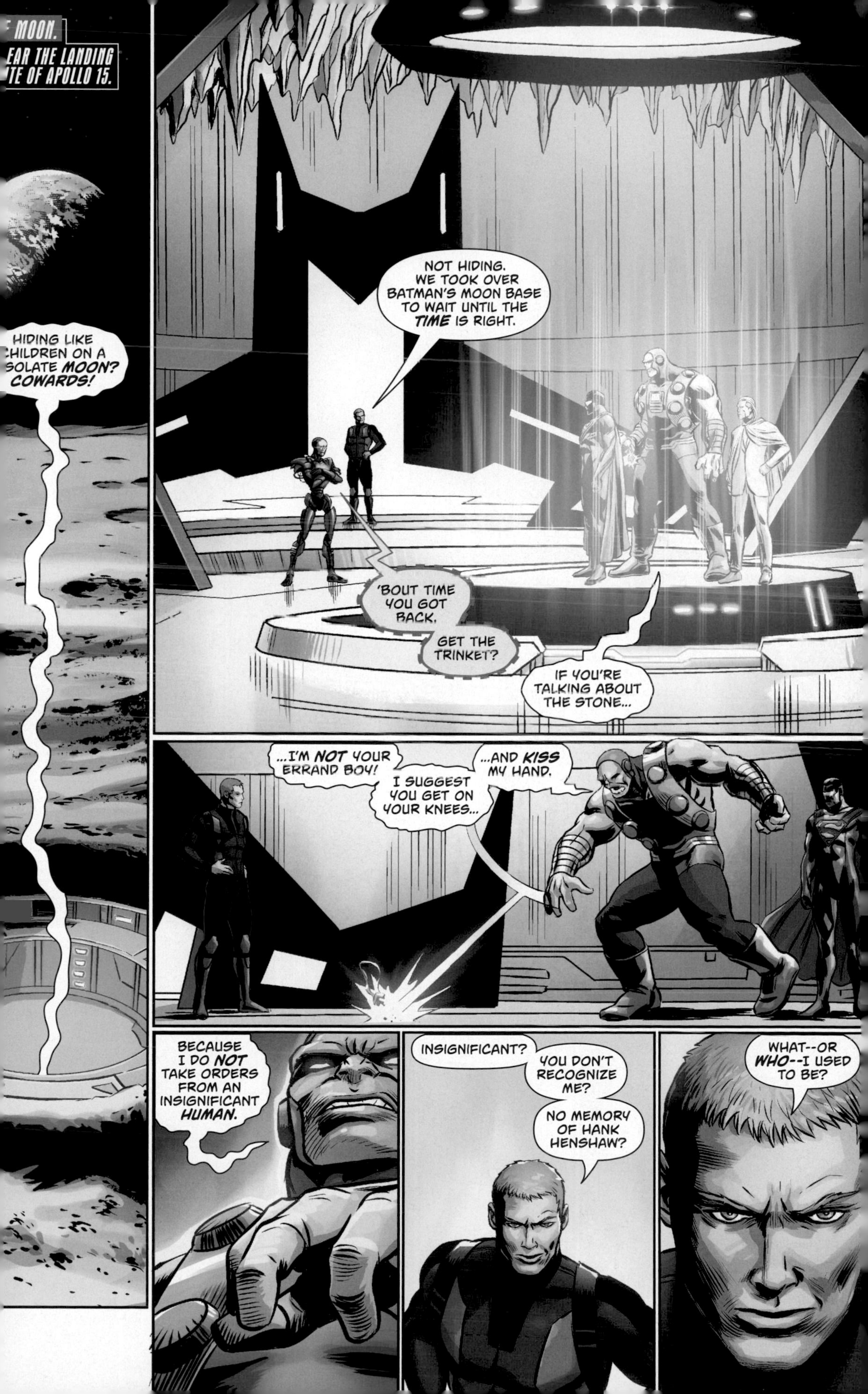
MOON.
EAR THE LANDING
TE OF APOLLO 15.
HIDING LIKE
CHILDREN ON A
SOLATE MOON?
COWARDS!
NOT HIDING. WE TOOK OVER BATMAN'S MOON BASE TO WAIT UNTIL THE TIME IS RIGHT.
'BOUT TIME YOU GOT BACK.
GET THE TRINKET?
IF YOU'RE TALKING ABOUT THE STONE...
...I'M NOT YOUR ERRAND BOY!
I SUGGEST YOU GET ON YOUR KNEES...
...AND KISS MY HAND.
BECAUSE I DO NOT TAKE ORDERS FROM AN INSIGNIFICANT HUMAN.
INSIGNIFICANT?
YOU DON'T RECOGNIZE ME?
NO MEMORY OF HANK HENSHAW?
WHAT--OR WHO--I USED TO BE?

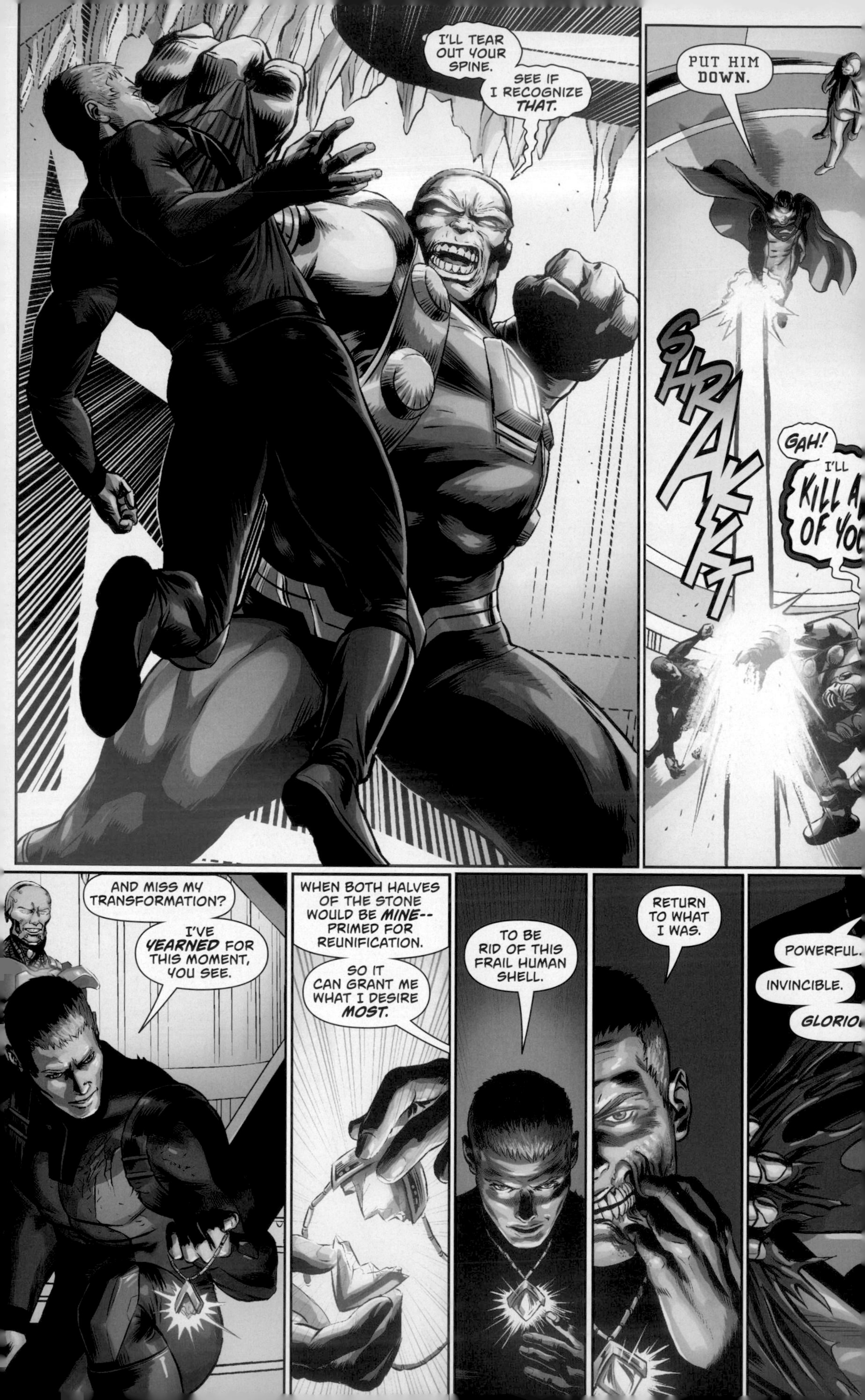

I'LL TEAR OUT YOUR SPINE.
SEE IF I RECOGNIZE *THAT.*
PUT HIM DOWN.
SHRAKKT
GAH!
I'LL KILL A
OF YO
AND MISS MY TRANSFORMATION?
I'VE *YEARNED* FOR THIS MOMENT, YOU SEE.
WHEN BOTH HALVES OF THE STONE WOULD BE *MINE*-- PRIMED FOR REUNIFICATION.
SO IT CAN GRANT ME WHAT I DESIRE *MOST.*
TO BE RID OF THIS FRAIL HUMAN SHELL.
RETURN TO WHAT I WAS.
POWERFUL.
INVINCIBLE.
GLORIO

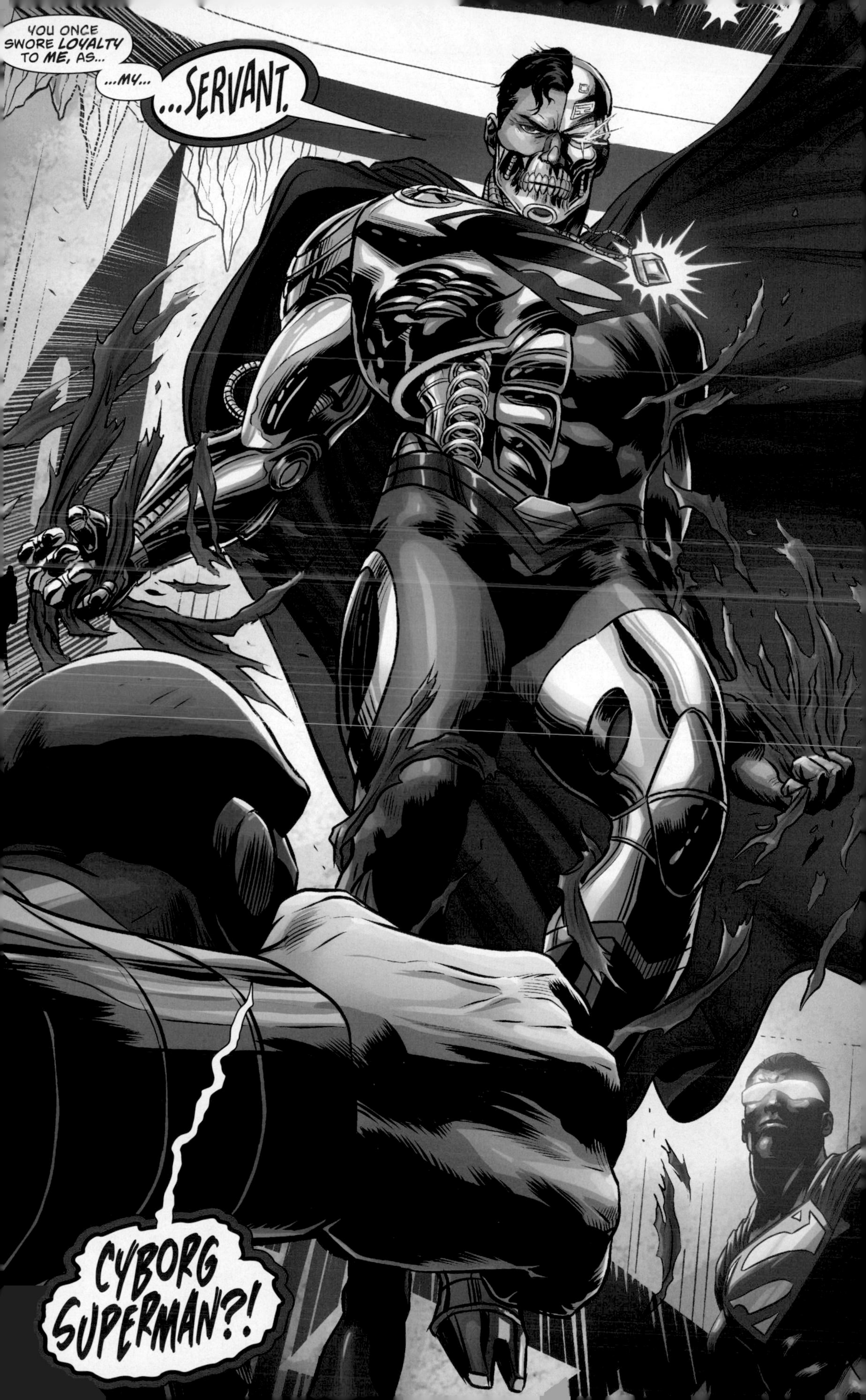
YOU ONCE SWORE LOYALTY TO ME, AS...
...MY...
...SERVANT.
CYBORG SUPERMAN?!

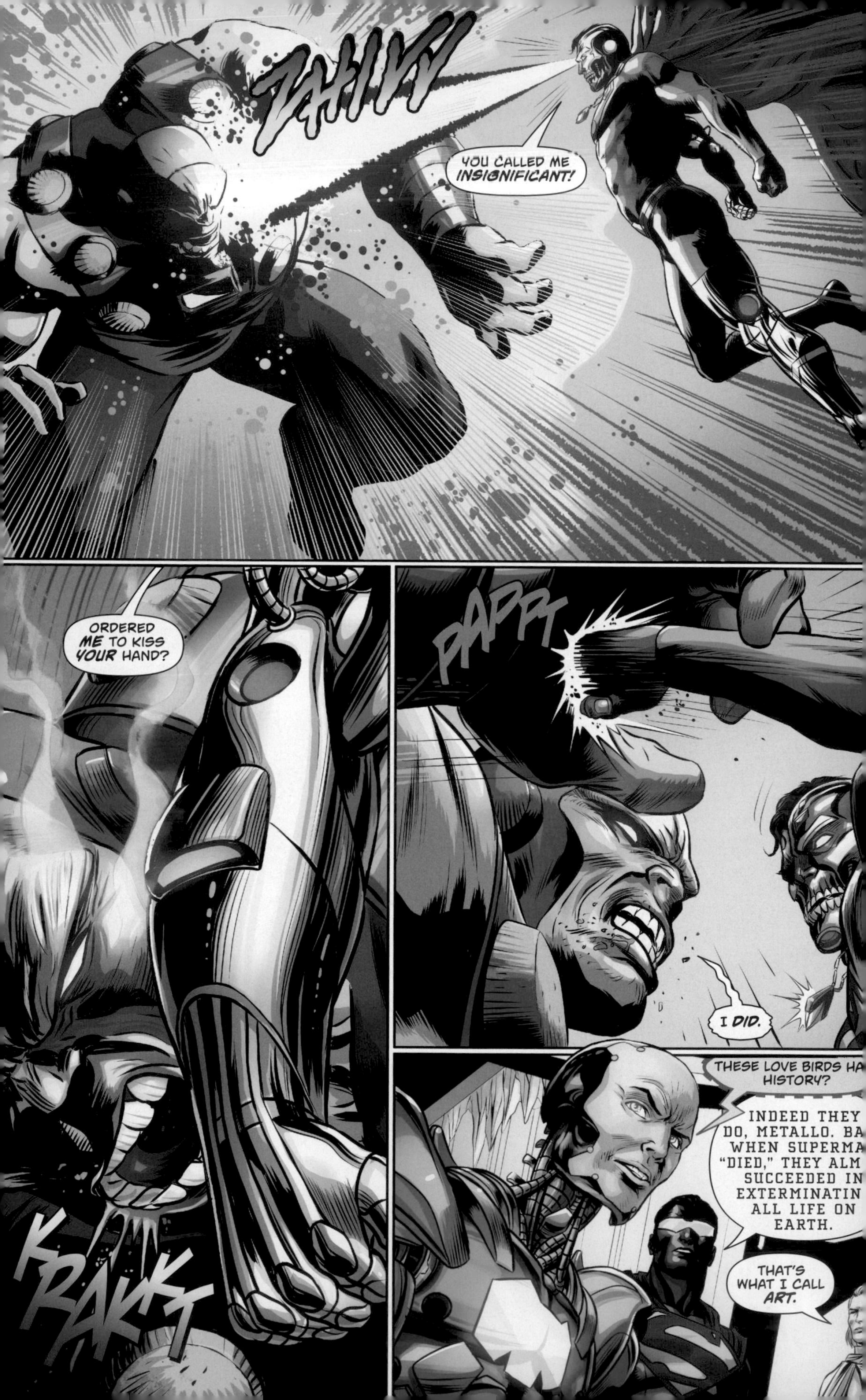
ZZHVVV
YOU CALLED ME INSIGNIFICANT!
ORDERED ME TO KISS YOUR HAND?
PAPPT
I DID.
KRAKKT
THESE LOVE BIRDS HA
HISTORY?
INDEED THEY DO, METALLO. BA WHEN SUPERMA "DIED," THEY ALM SUCCEEDED IN EXTERMINATIN ALL LIFE ON EARTH.
THAT'S WHAT I CALL ART.

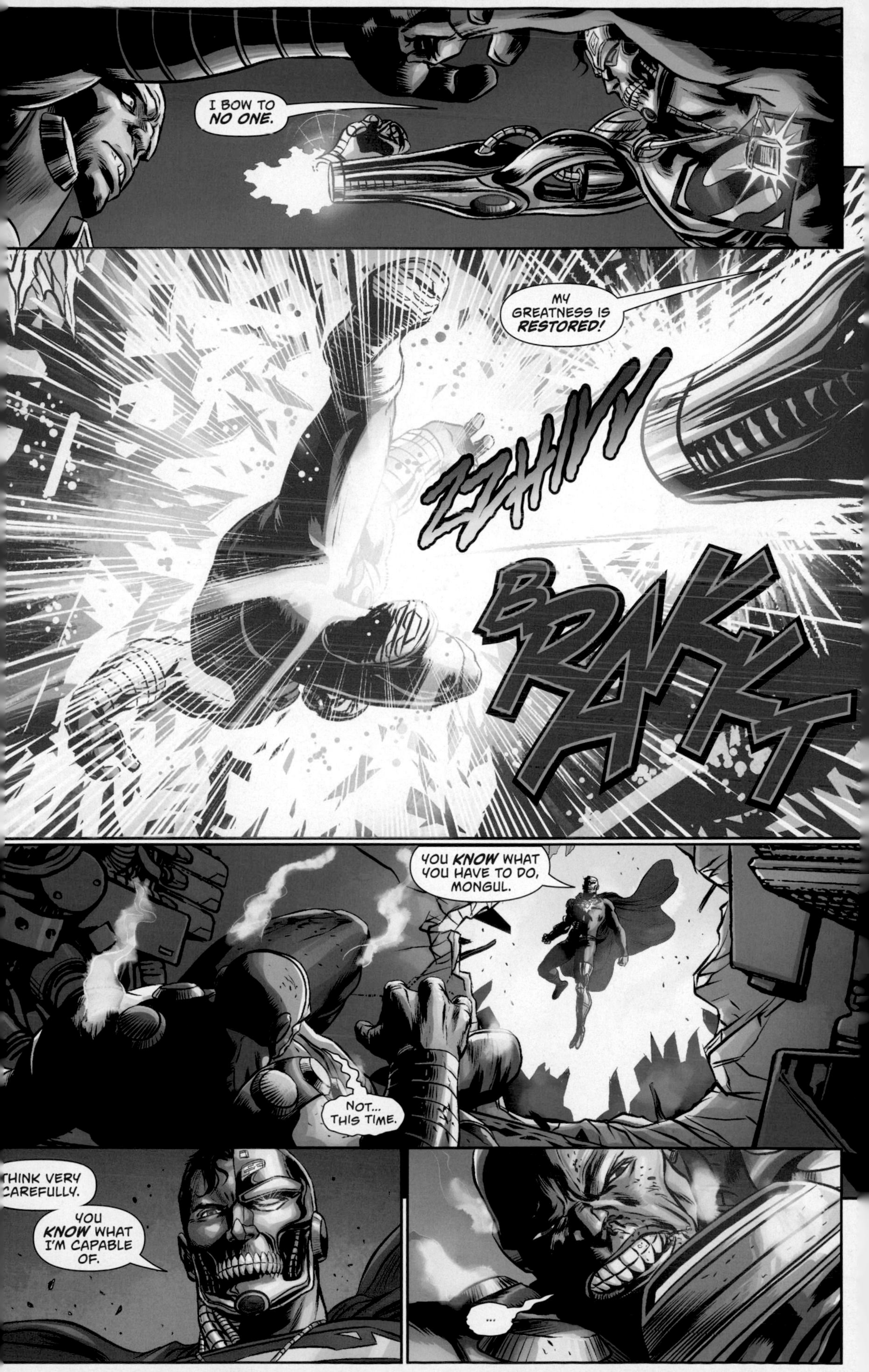
I BOW TO NO ONE.
MY GREATNESS IS RESTORED!
ZZHIVV
BRAKKT
YOU KNOW WHAT YOU HAVE TO DO, MONGUL.
NOT... THIS TIME.
THINK VERY CAREFULLY.
YOU KNOW WHAT I'M CAPABLE OF.
...

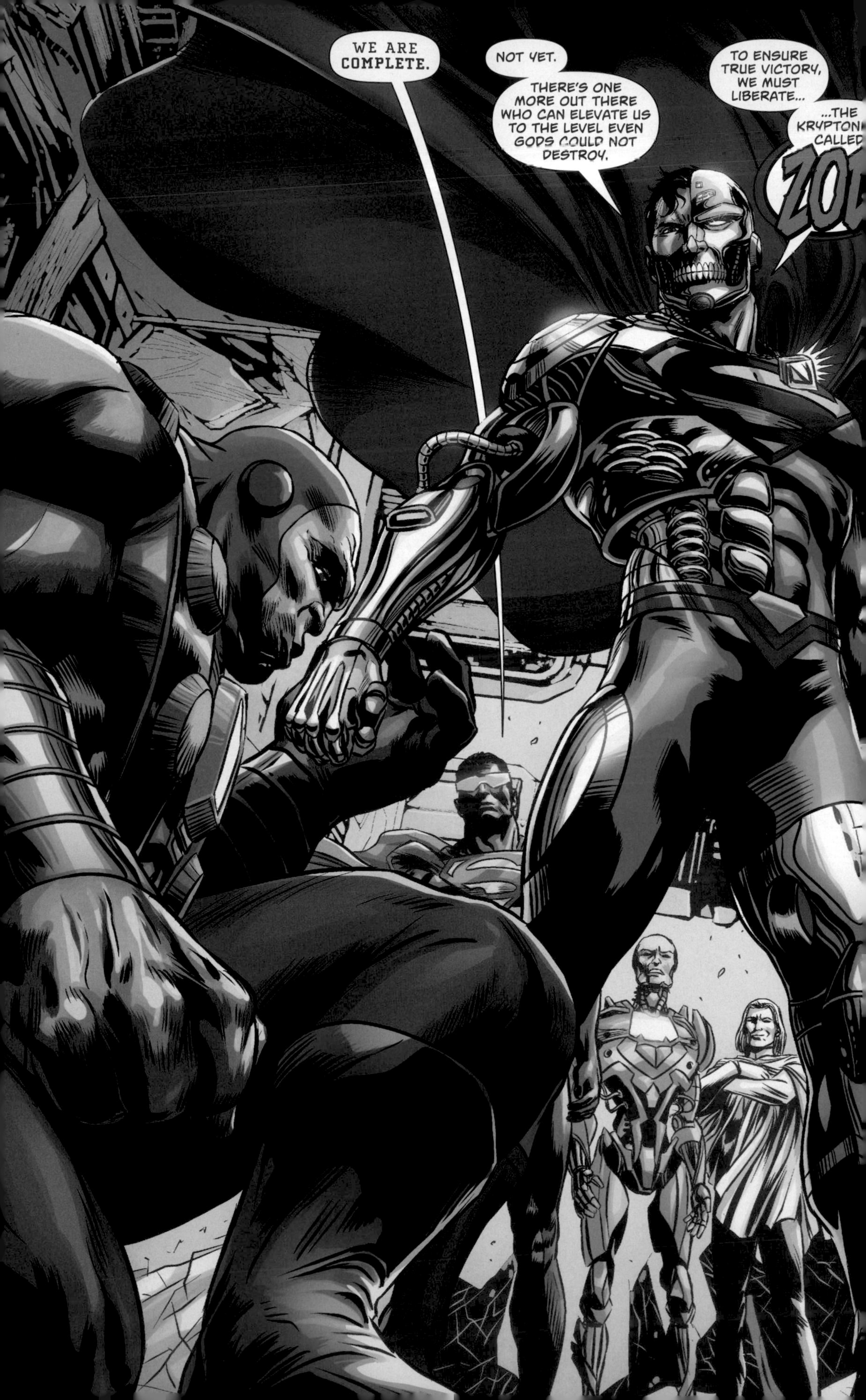

WE ARE COMPLETE.
NOT YET.
THERE'S ONE MORE OUT THERE WHO CAN ELEVATE US TO THE LEVEL EVEN GODS COULD NOT DESTROY.
TO ENSURE TRUE VICTORY, WE MUST LIBERATE...
...THE KRYPTON CALLED
ZO

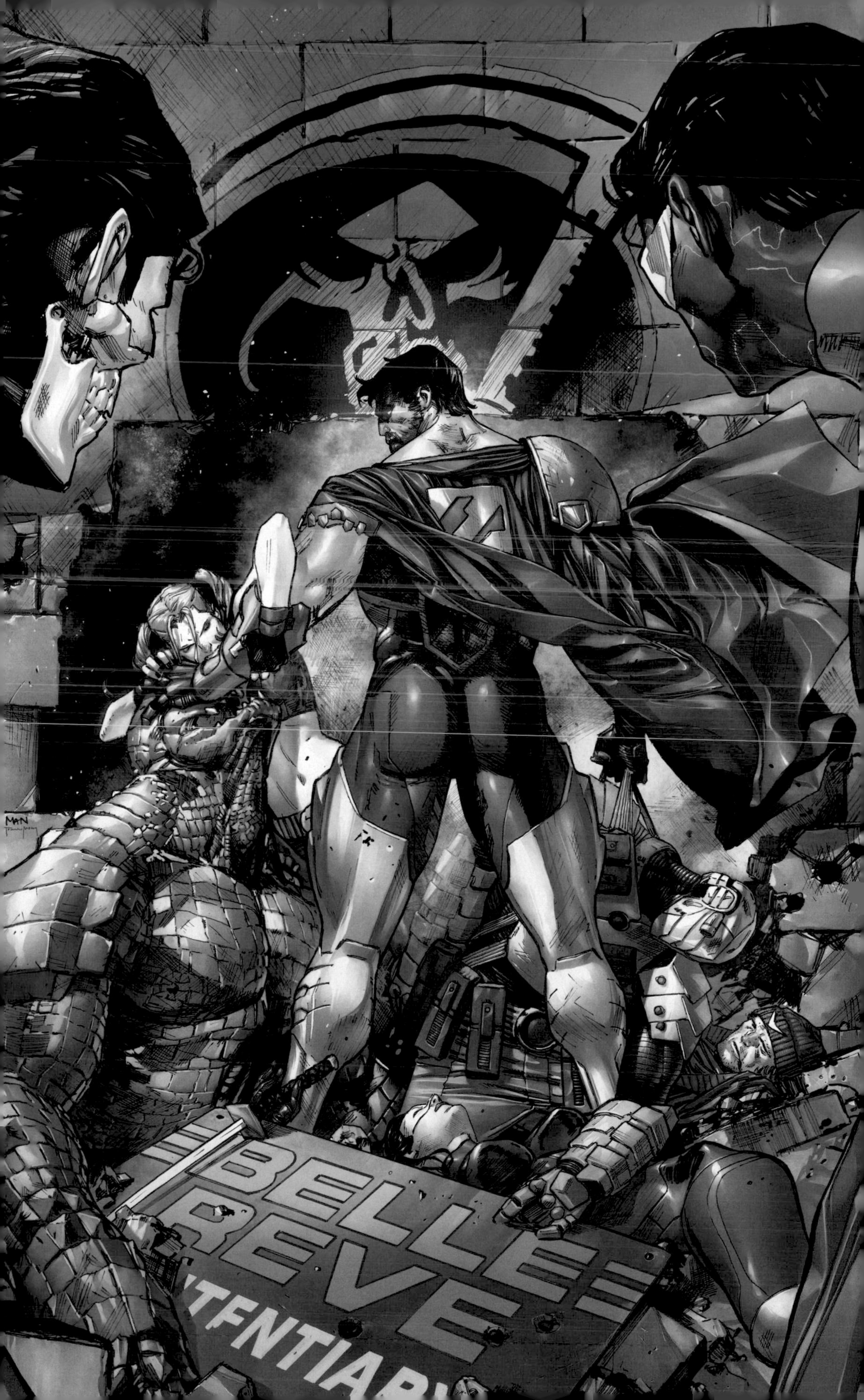
BELLE REVE

REVENGE PART 2

PATCH ZIRCHER artist * HI-FI colorist

CLAY MANN TOMEU MOREY cover artists

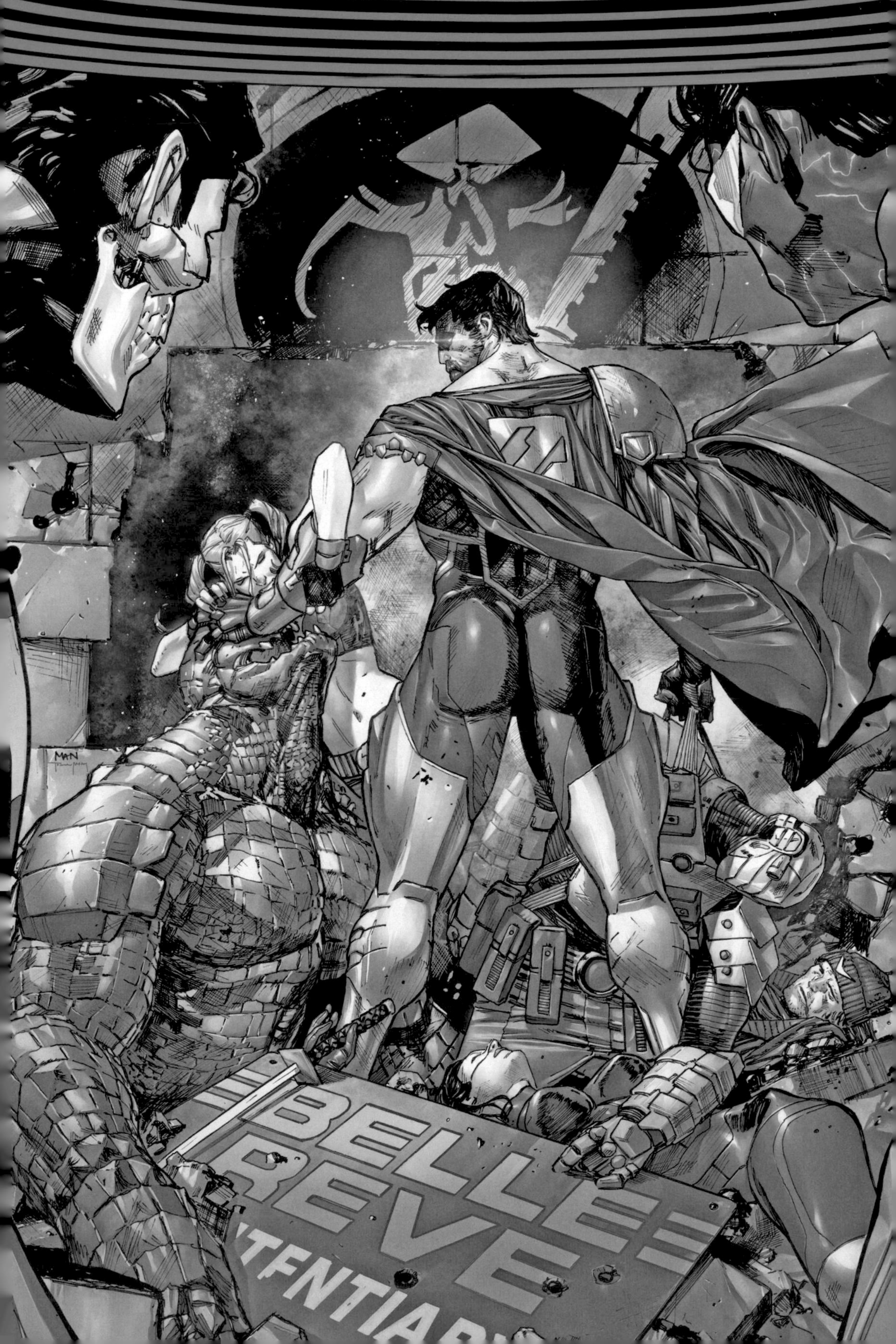
BELLE
REVE

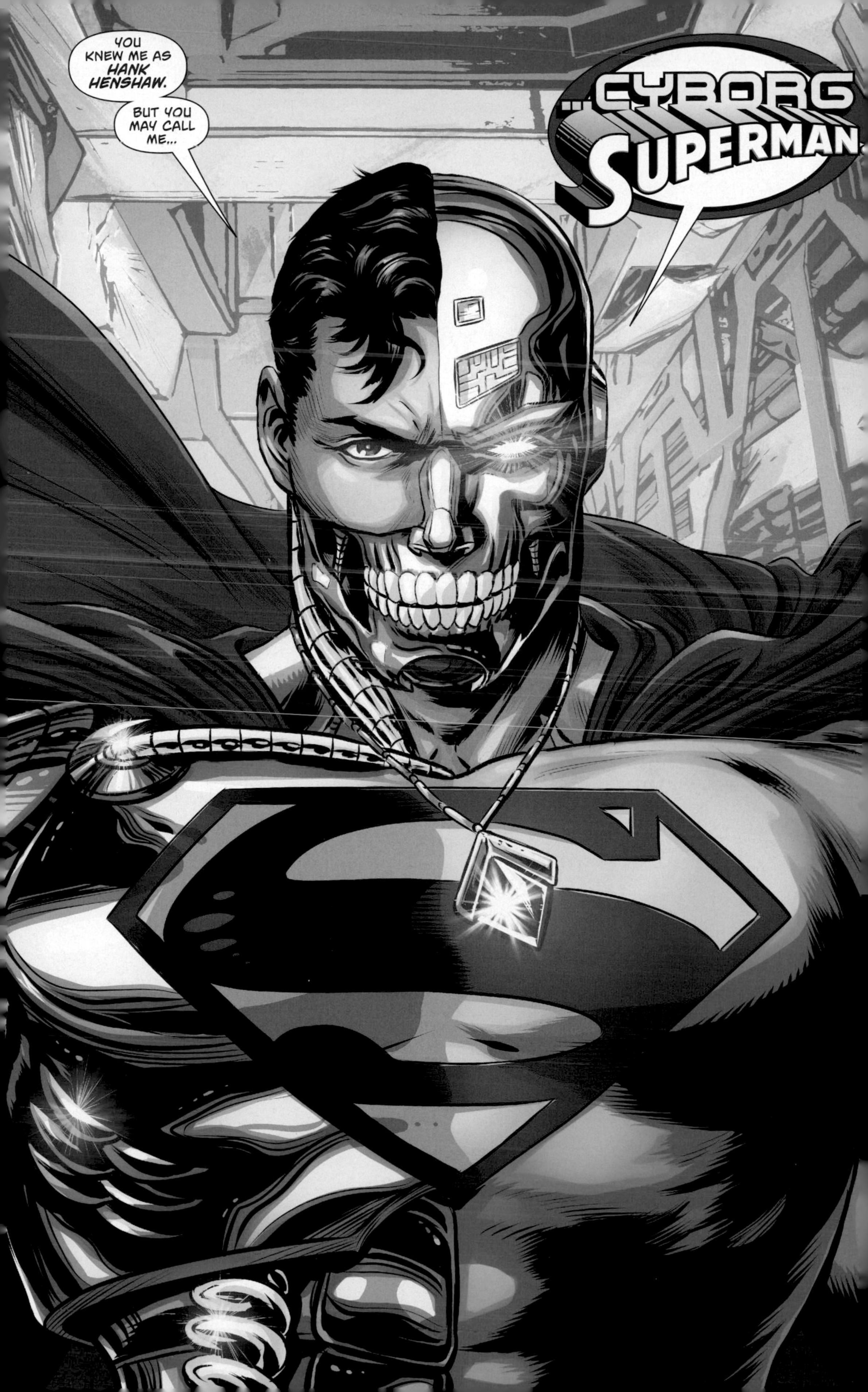

YOU KNEW ME AS HANK HENSHAW.
BUT YOU MAY CALL ME...
...CYBORG SUPERMAN.

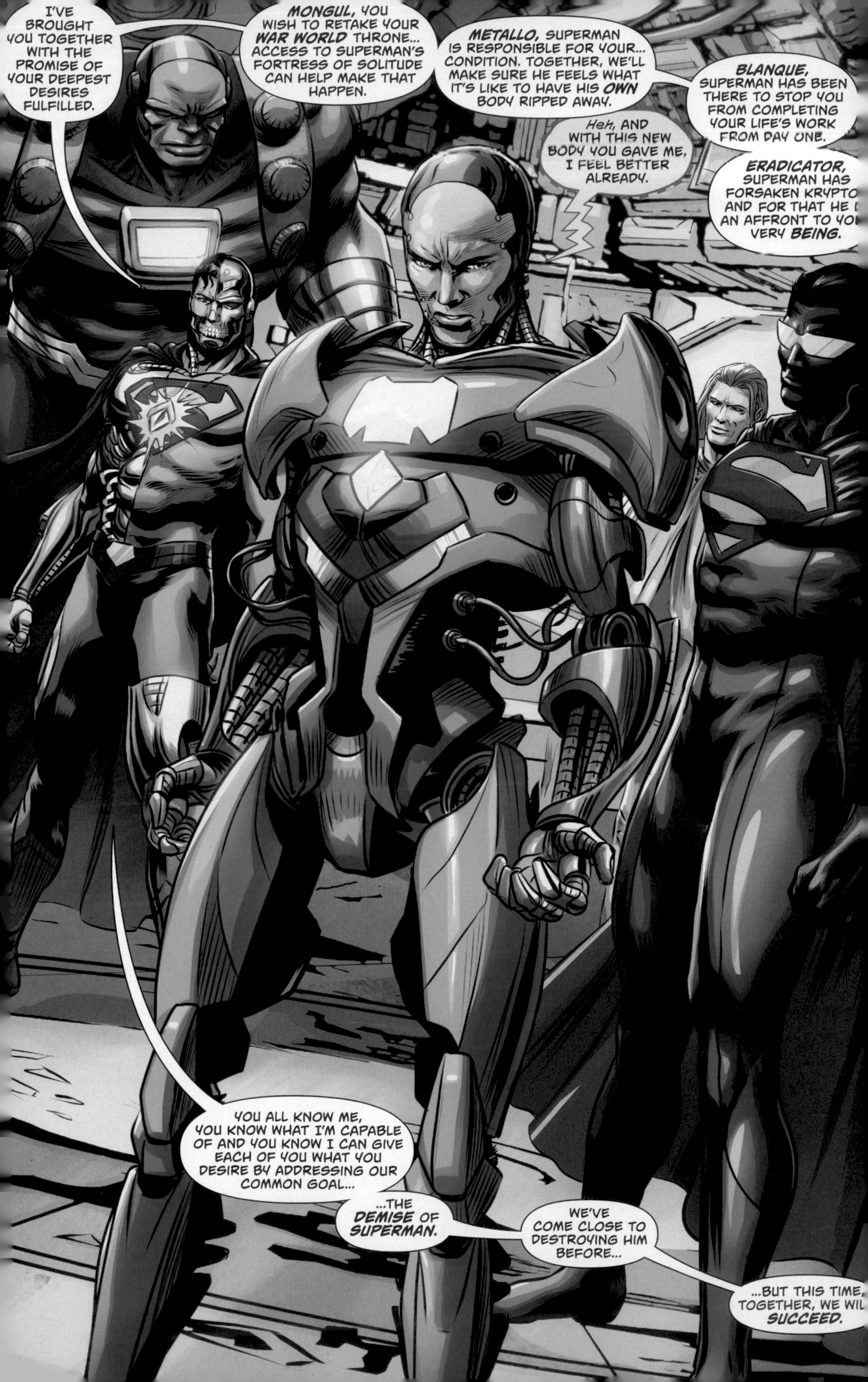
I'VE BROUGHT YOU TOGETHER WITH THE PROMISE OF YOUR DEEPEST DESIRES FULFILLED.
MONGUL, YOU WISH TO RETAKE YOUR *WAR WORLD* THRONE... ACCESS TO SUPERMAN'S FORTRESS OF SOLITUDE CAN HELP MAKE THAT HAPPEN.
METALLO, SUPERMAN IS RESPONSIBLE FOR YOUR... CONDITION. TOGETHER, WE'LL MAKE SURE HE FEELS WHAT IT'S LIKE TO HAVE HIS *OWN* BODY RIPPED AWAY.
Heh, AND WITH THIS NEW BODY YOU GAVE ME, I FEEL BETTER ALREADY.
BLANQUE, SUPERMAN HAS BEEN THERE TO STOP YOU FROM COMPLETING YOUR LIFE'S WORK FROM DAY ONE.
ERADICATOR, SUPERMAN HAS FORSAKEN KRYPTO AND FOR THAT HE AN AFFRONT TO YO VERY *BEING*.
YOU ALL KNOW ME, YOU KNOW WHAT I'M CAPABLE OF AND YOU KNOW I CAN GIVE EACH OF YOU WHAT YOU DESIRE BY ADDRESSING OUR COMMON GOAL...
...THE *DEMISE* OF *SUPERMAN*.
WE'VE COME CLOSE TO DESTROYING HIM BEFORE...
...BUT THIS TIME, TOGETHER, WE WIL *SUCCEED*.

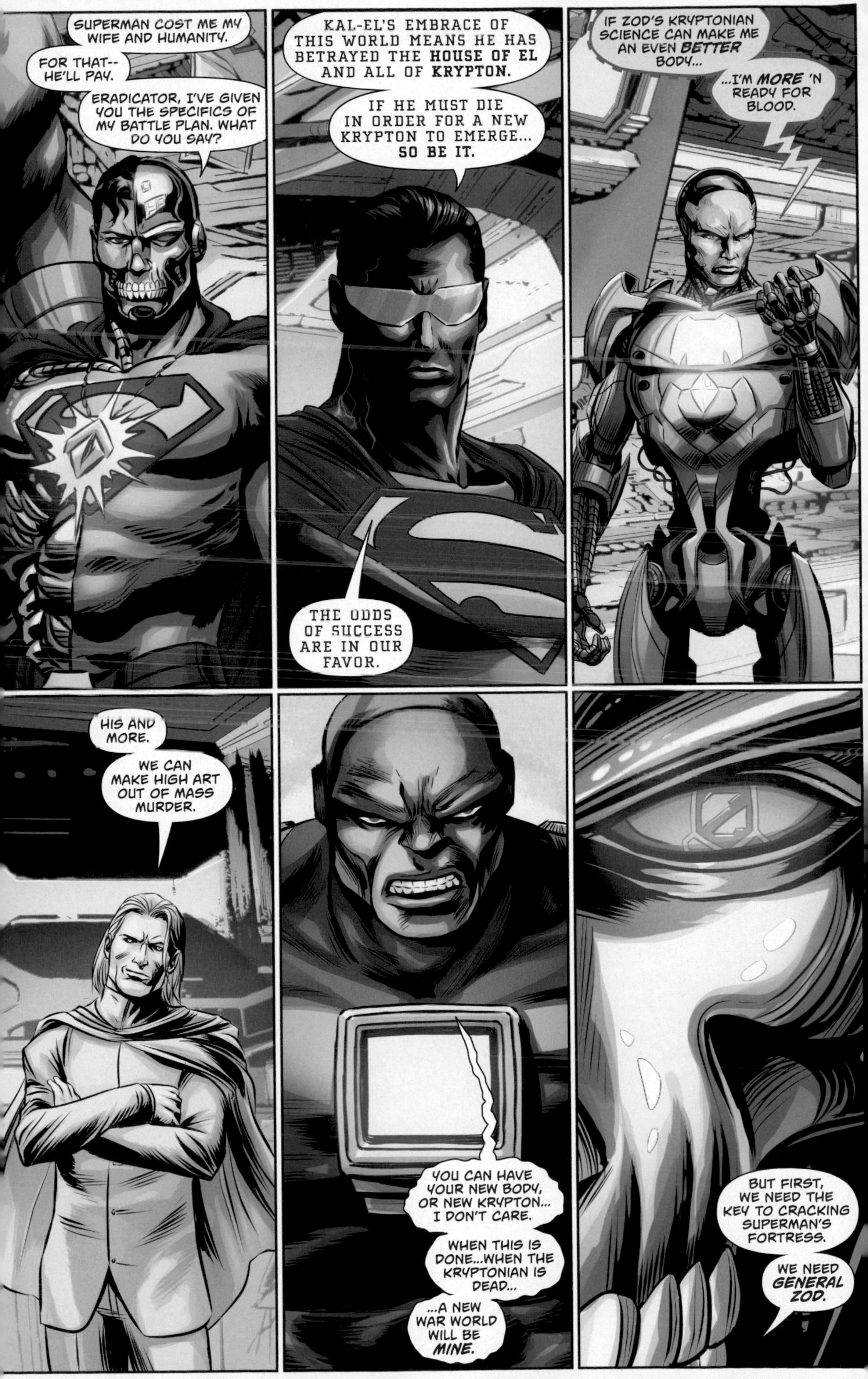
SUPERMAN COST ME MY WIFE AND HUMANITY.
FOR THAT-- HE'LL PAY.
ERADICATOR, I'VE GIVEN YOU THE SPECIFICS OF MY BATTLE PLAN. WHAT DO YOU SAY?
KAL-EL'S EMBRACE OF THIS WORLD MEANS HE HAS BETRAYED THE HOUSE OF EL AND ALL OF KRYPTON.
IF HE MUST DIE IN ORDER FOR A NEW KRYPTON TO EMERGE... SO BE IT.
THE ODDS OF SUCCESS ARE IN OUR FAVOR.
IF ZOD'S KRYPTONIAN SCIENCE CAN MAKE ME AN EVEN BETTER BODY...
...I'M MORE 'N READY FOR BLOOD.
HIS AND MORE.
WE CAN MAKE HIGH ART OUT OF MASS MURDER.
YOU CAN HAVE YOUR NEW BODY, OR NEW KRYPTON... I DON'T CARE.
WHEN THIS IS DONE...WHEN THE KRYPTONIAN IS DEAD...
...A NEW WAR WORLD WILL BE MINE.
BUT FIRST, WE NEED THE KEY TO CRACKING SUPERMAN'S FORTRESS.
WE NEED GENERAL ZOD.

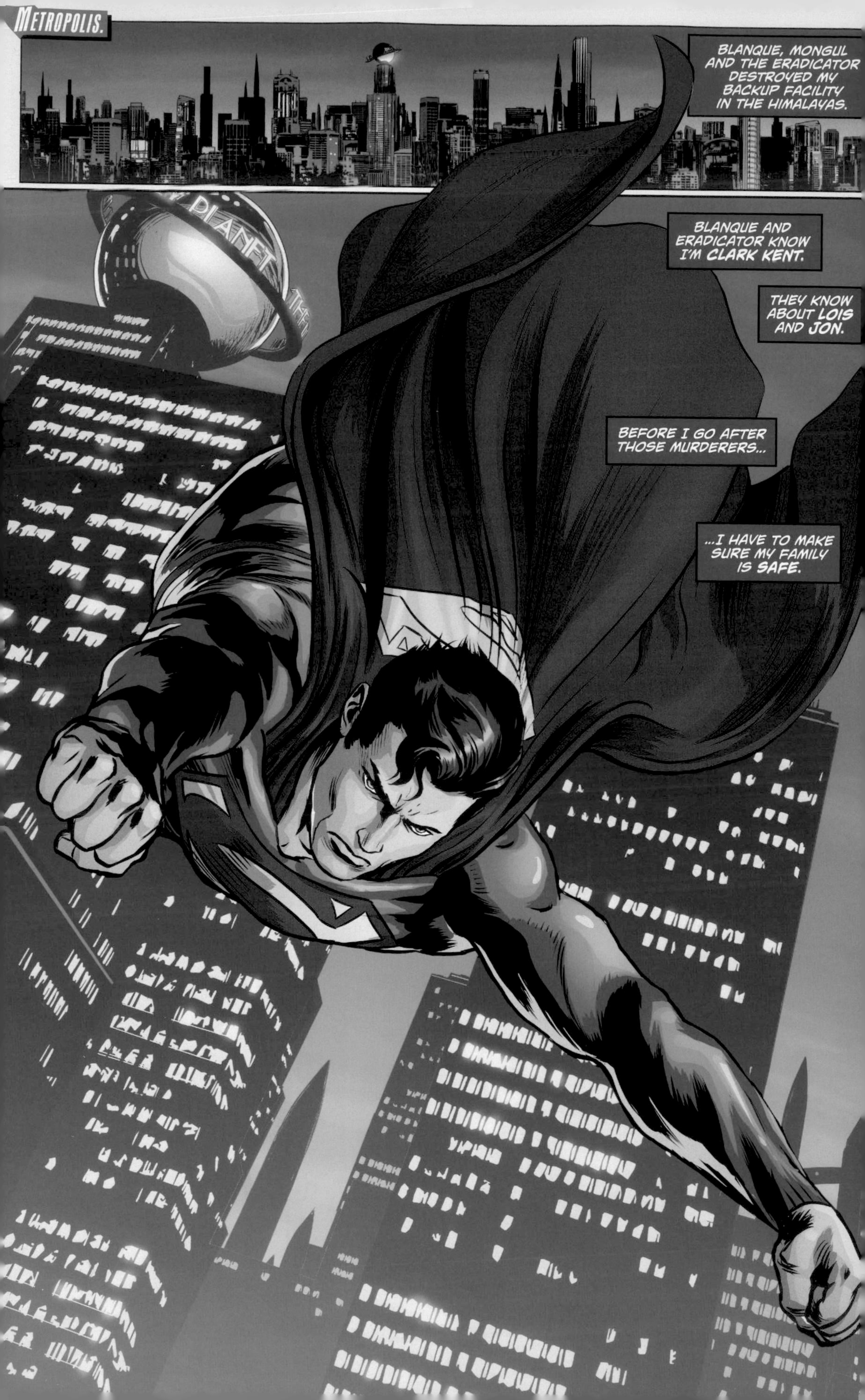
METROPOLIS.
BLANQUE, MONGUL AND THE ERADICATOR DESTROYED MY BACKUP FACILITY IN THE HIMALAYAS.
BLANQUE AND ERADICATOR KNOW I'M CLARK KENT.
THEY KNOW ABOUT LOIS AND JON.
BEFORE I GO AFTER THOSE MURDERERS...
...I HAVE TO MAKE SURE MY FAMILY IS SAFE.

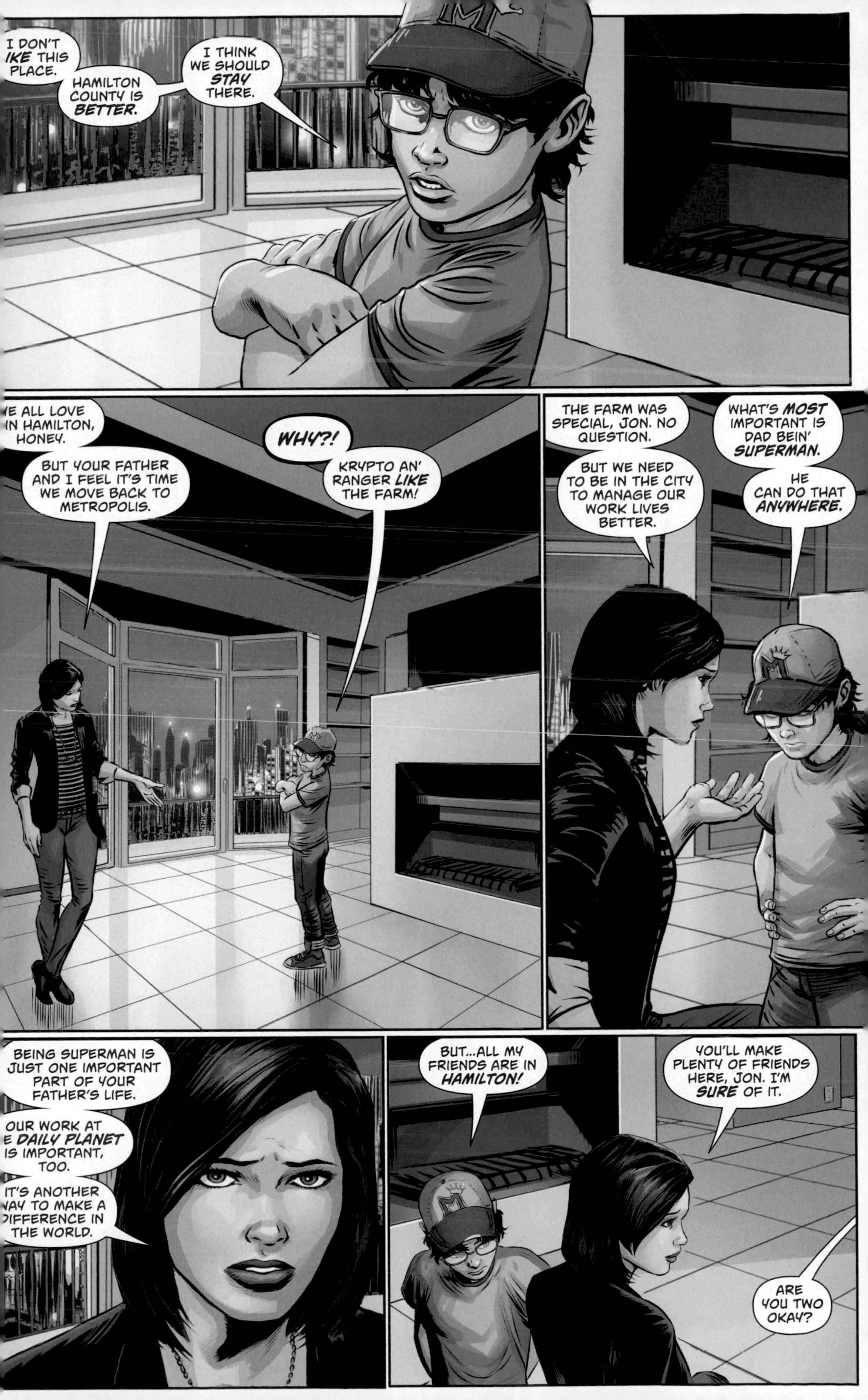
I DON'T
IKE THIS PLACE.
HAMILTON COUNTY IS BETTER.
I THINK WE SHOULD STAY THERE.
E ALL LOVE IN HAMILTON, HONEY.
BUT YOUR FATHER AND I FEEL IT'S TIME WE MOVE BACK TO METROPOLIS.
WHY?!
KRYPTO AN' RANGER LIKE THE FARM!
THE FARM WAS SPECIAL, JON. NO QUESTION.
BUT WE NEED TO BE IN THE CITY TO MANAGE OUR WORK LIVES BETTER.
WHAT'S MOST IMPORTANT IS DAD BEIN' SUPERMAN.
HE CAN DO THAT ANYWHERE.
BEING SUPERMAN IS JUST ONE IMPORTANT PART OF YOUR FATHER'S LIFE.
OUR WORK AT
E DAILY PLANET IS IMPORTANT, TOO.
IT'S ANOTHER
AY TO MAKE A
IFFERENCE IN THE WORLD.
BUT...ALL MY FRIENDS ARE IN HAMILTON!
YOU'LL MAKE PLENTY OF FRIENDS HERE, JON. I'M SURE OF IT.
ARE YOU TWO OKAY?

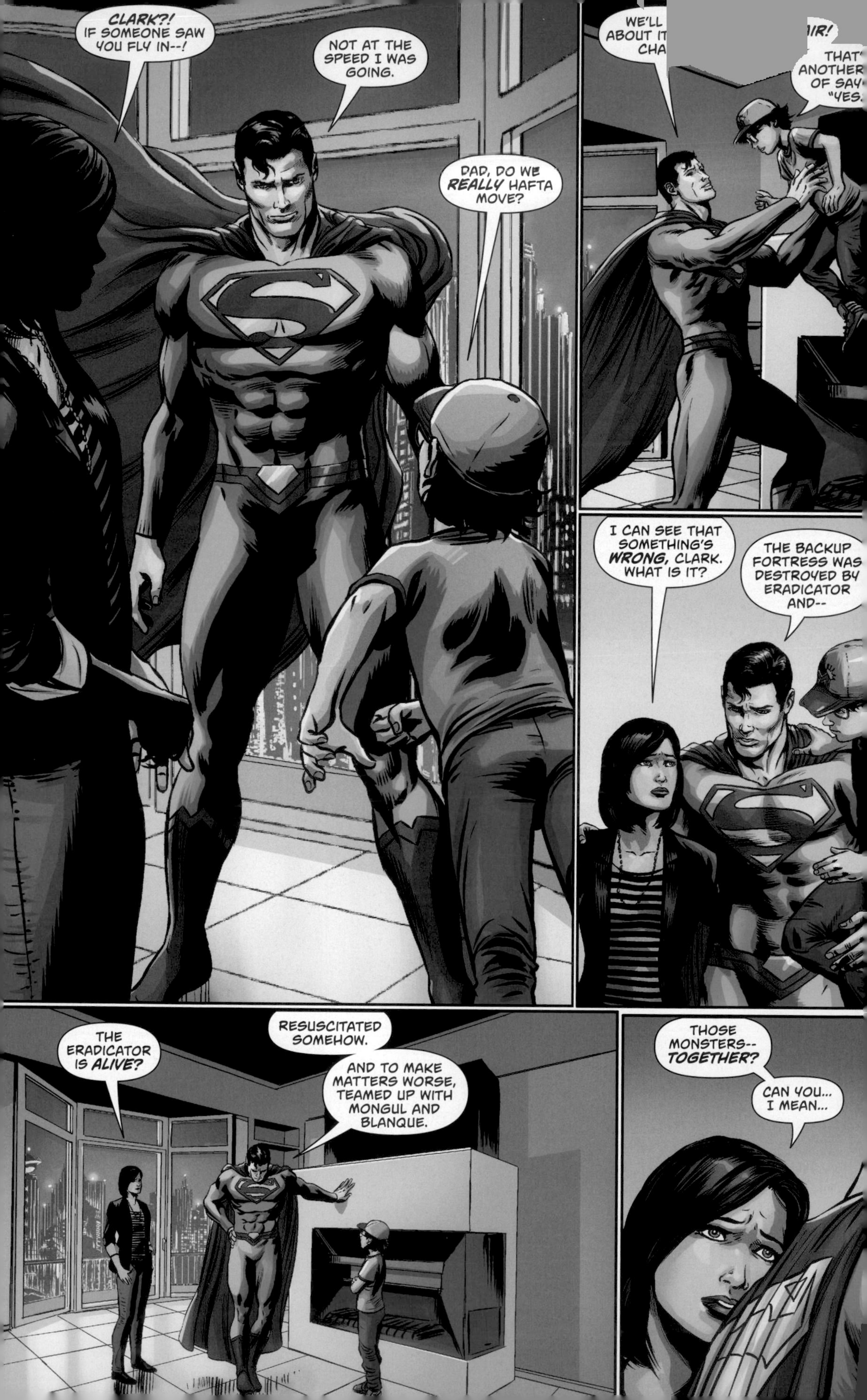
CLARK?! IF SOMEONE SAW YOU FLY IN--!
NOT AT THE SPEED I WAS GOING.
DAD, DO WE REALLY HAFTA MOVE?
I CAN SEE THAT SOMETHING'S WRONG, CLARK. WHAT IS IT?
THE BACKUP FORTRESS WAS DESTROYED BY ERADICATOR AND--
THE ERADICATOR IS ALIVE?
RESUSCITATED SOMEHOW.
AND TO MAKE MATTERS WORSE, TEAMED UP WITH MONGUL AND BLANQUE.
THOSE MONSTERS-- TOGETHER?
CAN YOU... I MEAN...

HANDLE THEM?

NO PROBLEM.

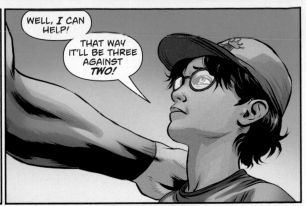

WELL, *I* CAN HELP! THAT WAY IT'LL BE THREE AGAINST *TWO*!

YOUR JOB IS TO WATCH OVER YOUR MOM.

HANG AROUND THE APARTMENT FOR A WHILE.

IT'S SO NEW, THEY WON'T KNOW TO LOOK HERE.

YOU WOULDN'T SAY THAT UNLESS...

EVERYTHING WILL BE FINE.

BUT I HAVE TO TAKE CARE OF THEM BEFORE THEY HURT ANYONE ELSE.

I'LL TRY TO HAVE THIS WRAPPED UP BY MORNING.

I CAN'T FOOL LOIS. NEVER COULD.

SHE KNOWS THIS IS SERIOUS.

BUT WE'LL HIDE THAT.

FOR JON...

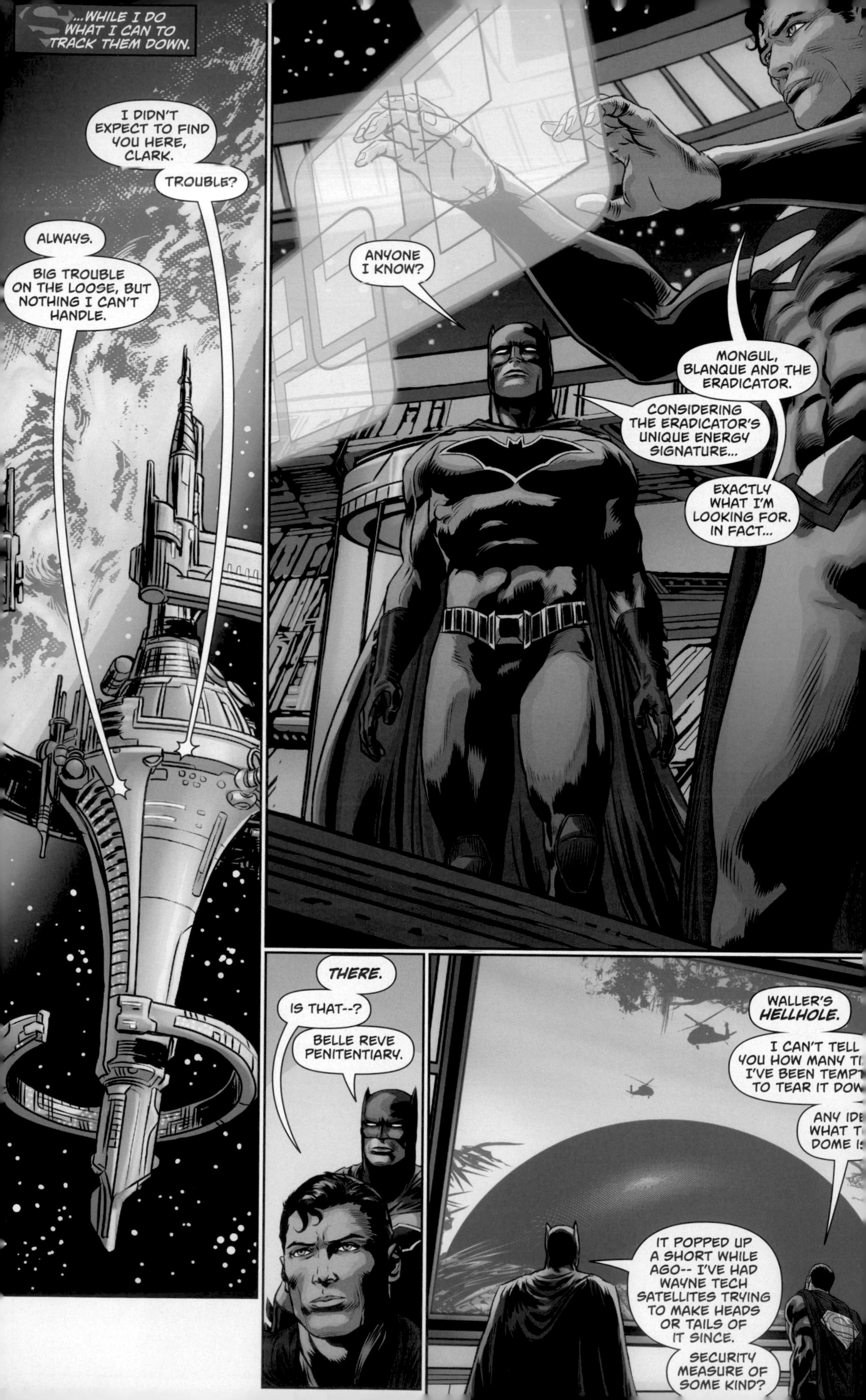
...WHILE I DO WHAT I CAN TO TRACK THEM DOWN.
I DIDN'T EXPECT TO FIND YOU HERE, CLARK.
TROUBLE?
ALWAYS.
BIG TROUBLE ON THE LOOSE, BUT NOTHING I CAN'T HANDLE.
ANYONE I KNOW?
MONGUL, BLANQUE AND THE ERADICATOR.
CONSIDERING THE ERADICATOR'S UNIQUE ENERGY SIGNATURE...
EXACTLY WHAT I'M LOOKING FOR. IN FACT...
THERE.
IS THAT--?
BELLE REVE PENITENTIARY.
WALLER'S HELLHOLE.
IT POPPED UP A SHORT WHILE AGO-- I'VE HAD WAYNE TECH SATELLITES TRYING TO MAKE HEADS OR TAILS OF IT SINCE.
SECURITY MEASURE OF SOME KIND?

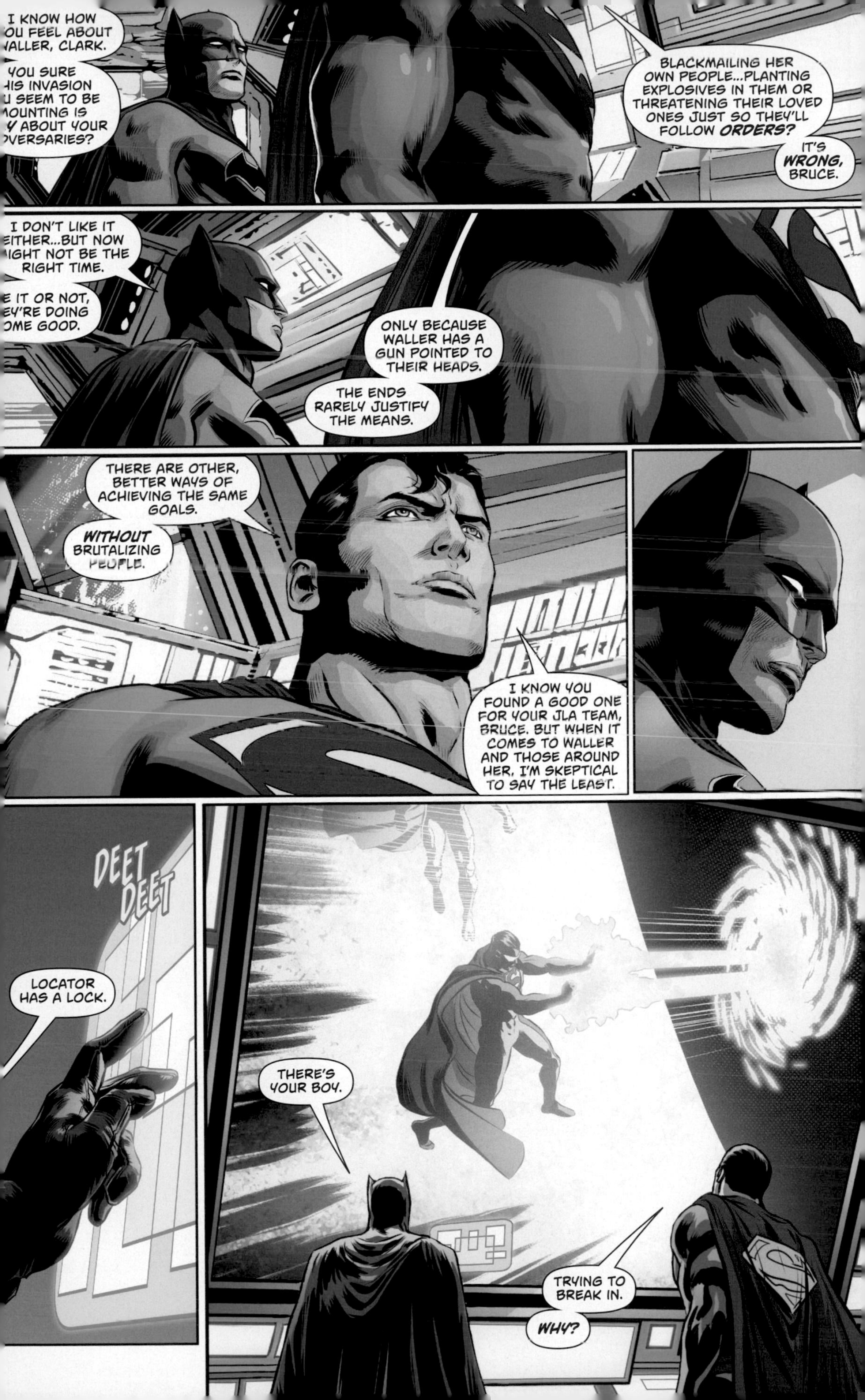
I KNOW HOW
OU FEEL ABOUT
ALLER, CLARK.
YOU SURE
HIS INVASION
U SEEM TO BE
MOUNTING IS
Y ABOUT YOUR
VERSARIES?
BLACKMAILING HER OWN PEOPLE...PLANTING EXPLOSIVES IN THEM OR THREATENING THEIR LOVED ONES JUST SO THEY'LL FOLLOW ORDERS?
IT'S WRONG, BRUCE.
I DON'T LIKE IT
EITHER...BUT NOW
IGHT NOT BE THE
RIGHT TIME.
E IT OR NOT,
EY'RE DOING
OME GOOD.
ONLY BECAUSE WALLER HAS A GUN POINTED TO THEIR HEADS.
THE ENDS RARELY JUSTIFY THE MEANS.
THERE ARE OTHER, BETTER WAYS OF ACHIEVING THE SAME GOALS.
WITHOUT BRUTALIZING PEOPLE.
I KNOW YOU FOUND A GOOD ONE FOR YOUR JLA TEAM, BRUCE. BUT WHEN IT COMES TO WALLER AND THOSE AROUND HER, I'M SKEPTICAL TO SAY THE LEAST.
DEET DEET
LOCATOR HAS A LOCK.
THERE'S YOUR BOY.
TRYING TO BREAK IN.
WHY?

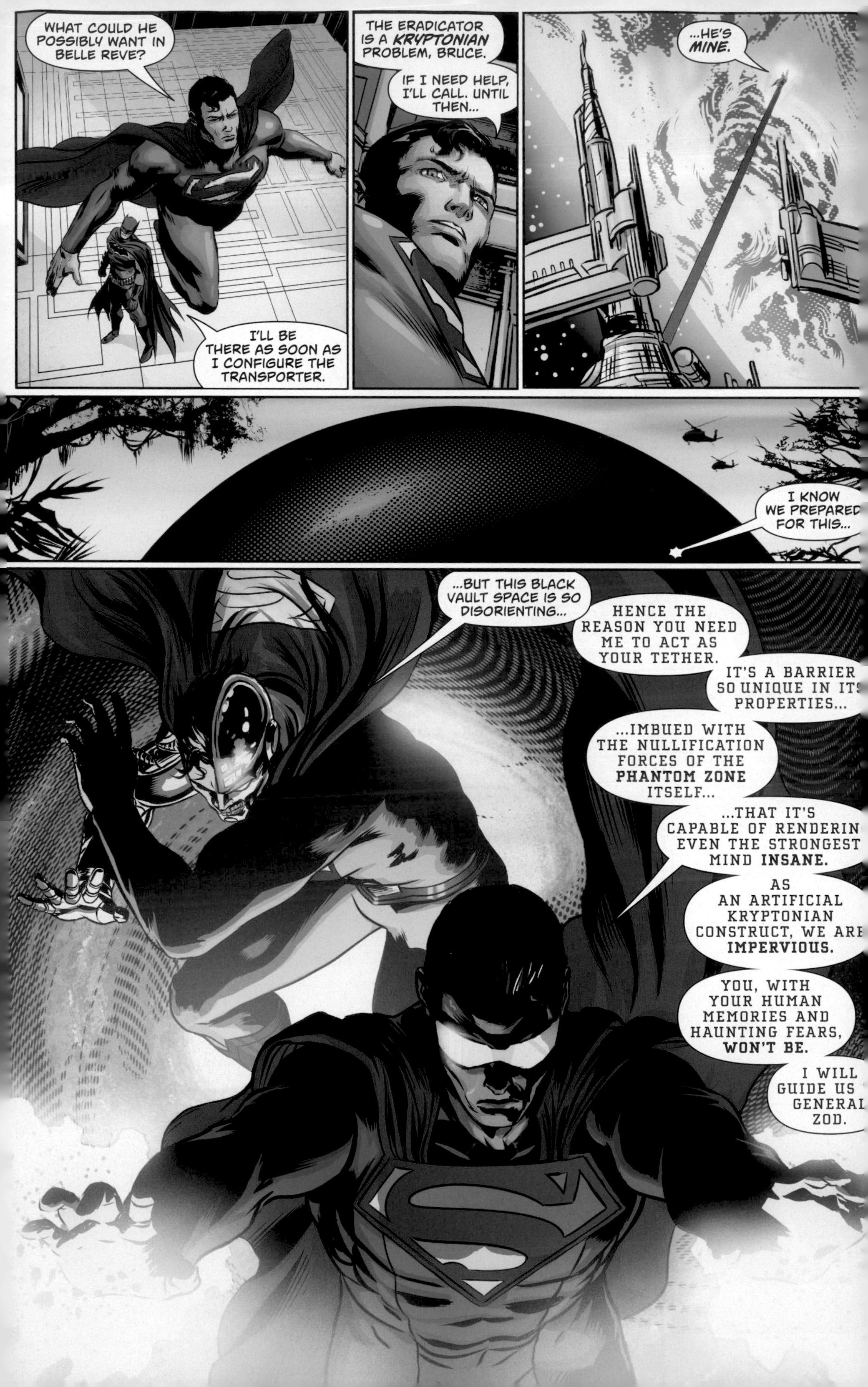
WHAT COULD HE POSSIBLY WANT IN BELLE REVE?
I'LL BE THERE AS SOON AS I CONFIGURE THE TRANSPORTER.
THE ERADICATOR IS A KRYPTONIAN PROBLEM, BRUCE.
IF I NEED HELP, I'LL CALL. UNTIL THEN...
...HE'S MINE.
I KNOW WE PREPARED FOR THIS...
...BUT THIS BLACK VAULT SPACE IS SO DISORIENTING...
HENCE THE REASON YOU NEED ME TO ACT AS YOUR TETHER.
IT'S A BARRIER SO UNIQUE IN ITS PROPERTIES...
...IMBUED WITH THE NULLIFICATION FORCES OF THE PHANTOM ZONE ITSELF...
...THAT IT'S CAPABLE OF RENDERIN EVEN THE STRONGEST MIND INSANE.
AS AN ARTIFICIAL KRYPTONIAN CONSTRUCT, WE ARE IMPERVIOUS.
YOU, WITH YOUR HUMAN MEMORIES AND HAUNTING FEARS, WON'T BE.
I WILL GUIDE US GENERAL ZOD.

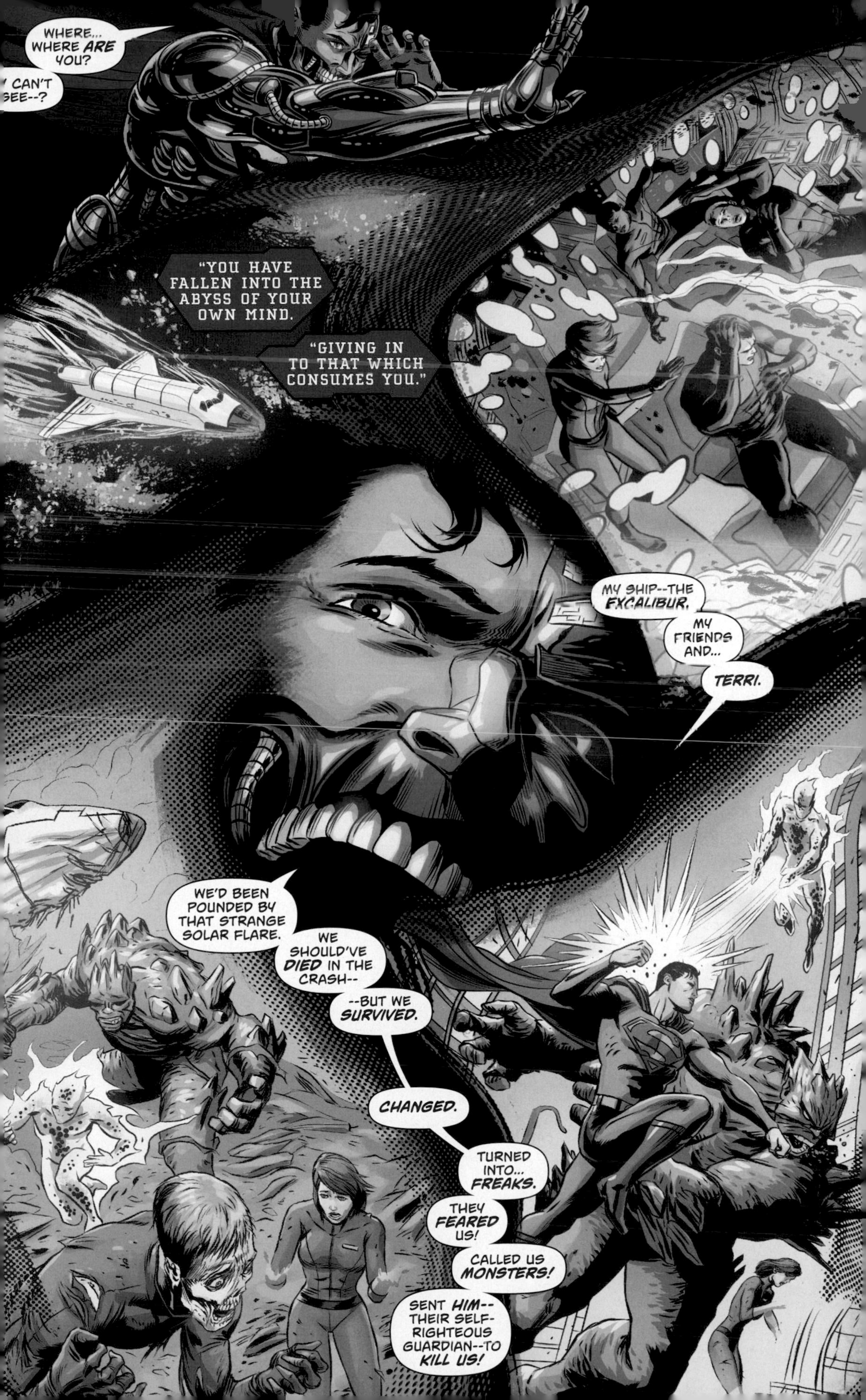
WHERE... WHERE ARE YOU?
I CAN'T SEE--?
"YOU HAVE FALLEN INTO THE ABYSS OF YOUR OWN MIND.
"GIVING IN TO THAT WHICH CONSUMES YOU."
MY SHIP--THE EXCALIBUR.
MY FRIENDS AND...
TERRI.
WE'D BEEN POUNDED BY THAT STRANGE SOLAR FLARE.
WE SHOULD'VE DIED IN THE CRASH--
--BUT WE SURVIVED.
CHANGED.
TURNED INTO... FREAKS.
THEY FEARED US!
CALLED US MONSTERS!
SENT HIM--THEIR SELF-RIGHTEOUS GUARDIAN--TO KILL US!

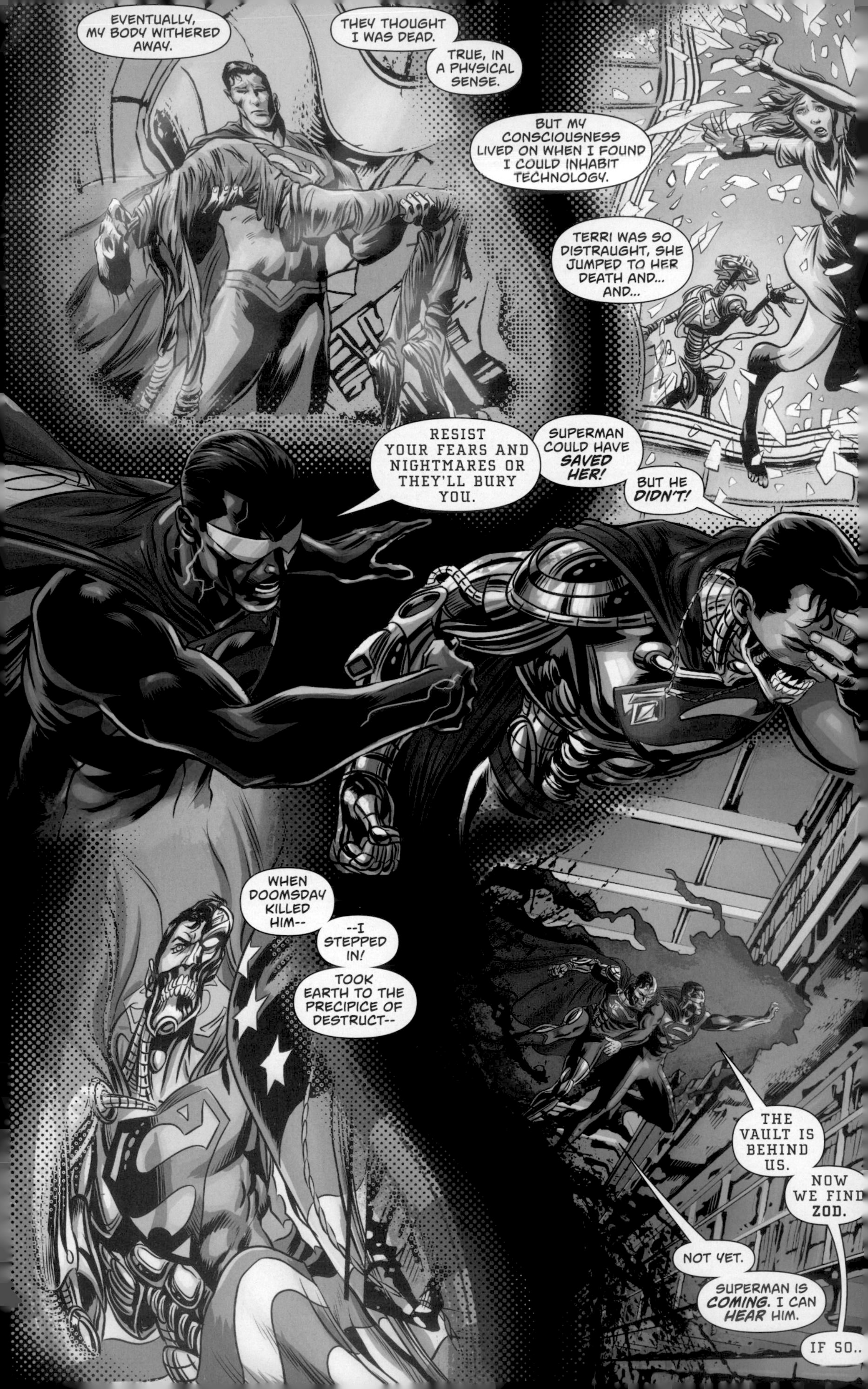
EVENTUALLY, MY BODY WITHERED AWAY.
THEY THOUGHT I WAS DEAD.
TRUE, IN A PHYSICAL SENSE.
BUT MY CONSCIOUSNESS LIVED ON WHEN I FOUND I COULD INHABIT TECHNOLOGY.
TERRI WAS SO DISTRAUGHT, SHE JUMPED TO HER DEATH AND... AND...
RESIST YOUR FEARS AND NIGHTMARES OR THEY'LL BURY YOU.
SUPERMAN COULD HAVE SAVED HER!
BUT HE DIDN'T!
WHEN DOOMSDAY KILLED HIM--
--I STEPPED IN!
TOOK EARTH TO THE PRECIPICE OF DESTRUCT--
THE VAULT IS BEHIND US.
NOW WE FIND ZOD.
NOT YET.
SUPERMAN IS COMING. I CAN HEAR HIM.
IF SO..

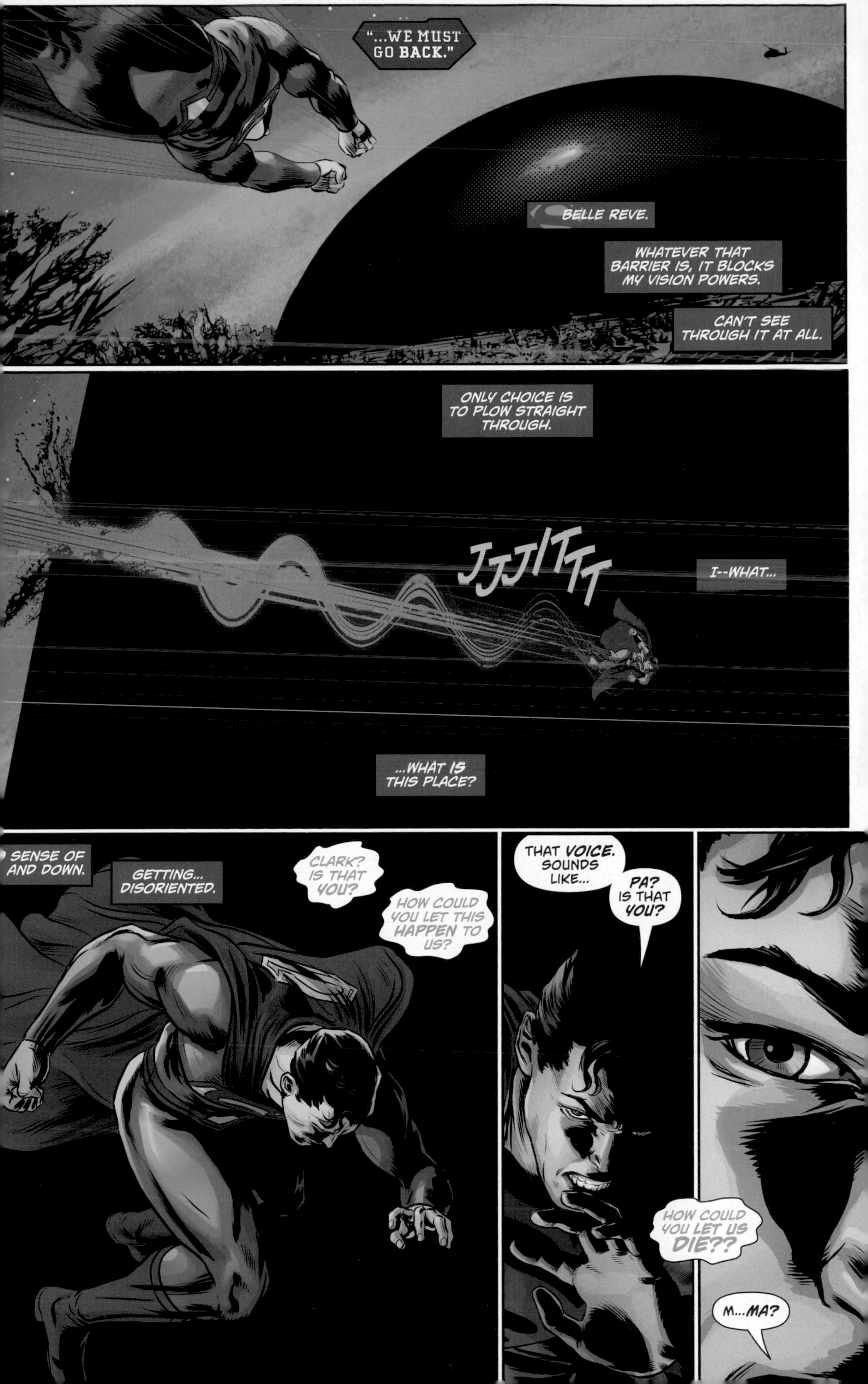
"...WE MUST GO BACK."
BELLE REVE.
WHATEVER THAT BARRIER IS, IT BLOCKS MY VISION POWERS.
CAN'T SEE THROUGH IT AT ALL.
ONLY CHOICE IS TO PLOW STRAIGHT THROUGH.
JJJ/TTT
I--WHAT...
...WHAT IS THIS PLACE?
SENSE OF AND DOWN.
GETTING... DISORIENTED.
CLARK? IS THAT YOU?
HOW COULD YOU LET THIS HAPPEN TO US?
THAT VOICE. SOUNDS LIKE...
PA? IS THAT YOU?
HOW COULD YOU LET US DIE??
M...MA?

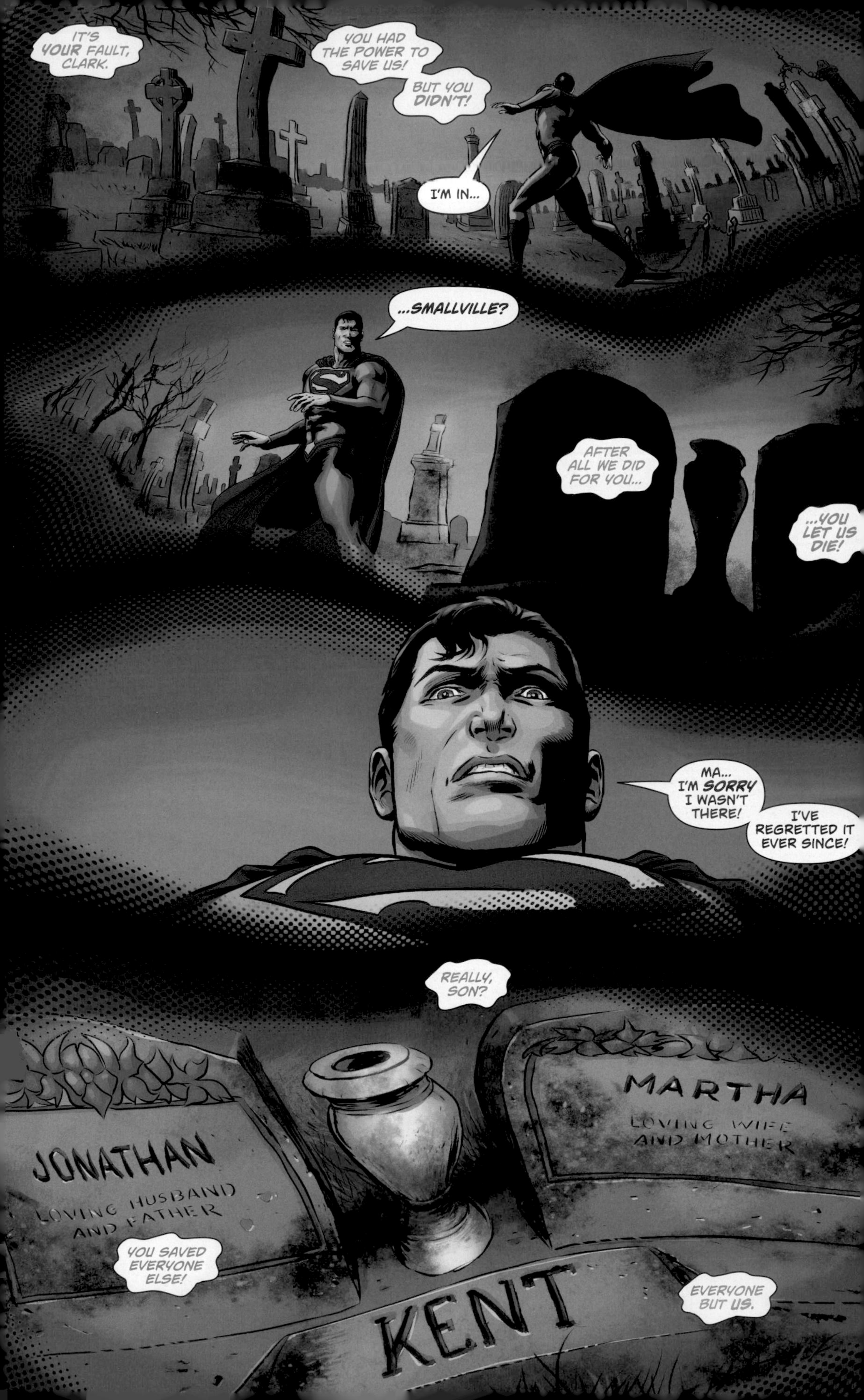
IT'S YOUR FAULT, CLARK.
YOU HAD THE POWER TO SAVE US!
BUT YOU DIDN'T!
I'M IN...
...SMALLVILLE?
AFTER ALL WE DID FOR YOU...
...YOU LET US DIE!
MA... I'M SORRY I WASN'T THERE!
I'VE REGRETTED IT EVER SINCE!
REALLY, SON?
MARTHA
LOVING WIFE AND MOTHER
JONATHAN
LOVING HUSBAND AND FATHER
YOU SAVED EVERYONE ELSE!
EVERYONE BUT US.
KENT

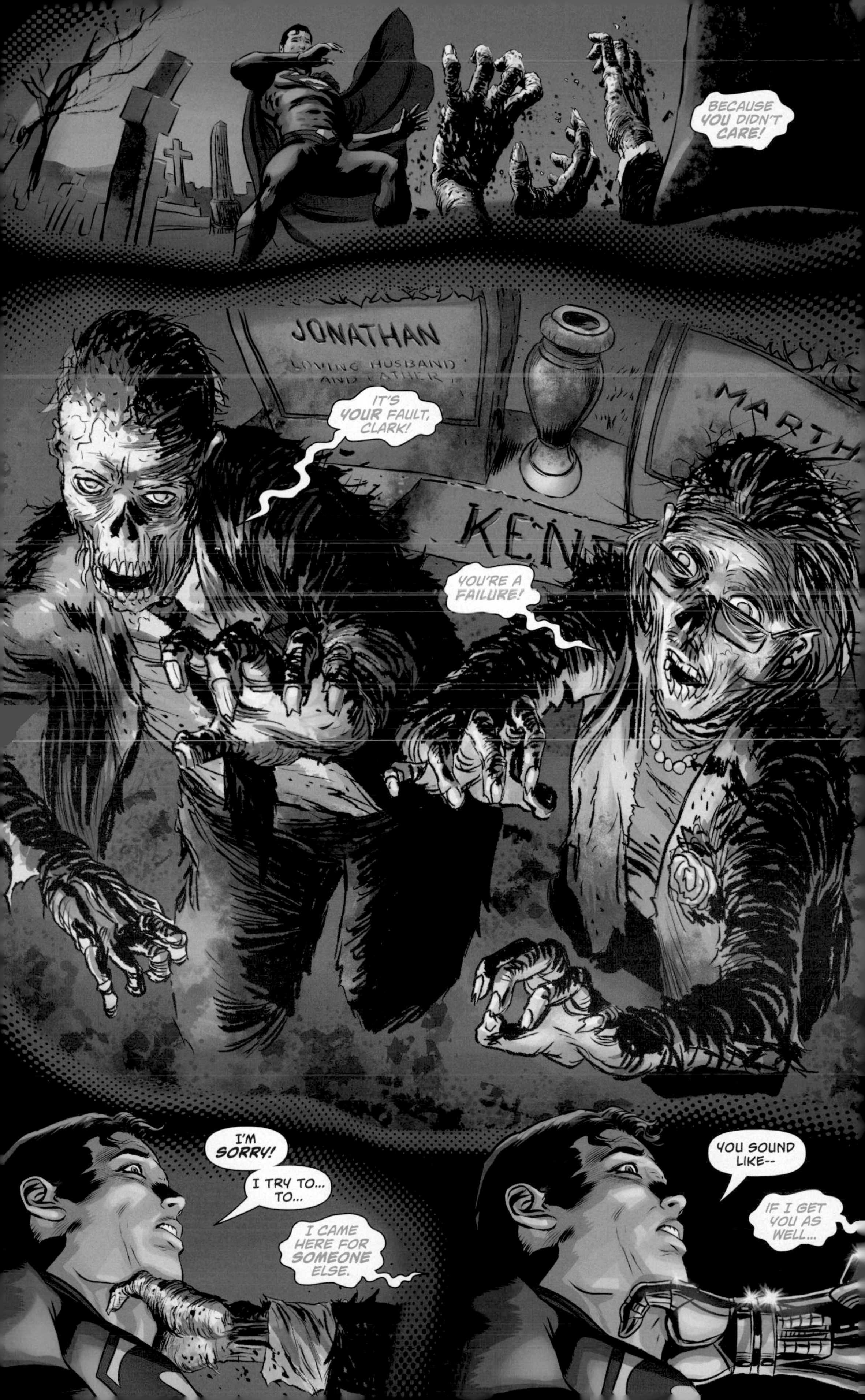
BECAUSE YOU DIDN'T CARE!
JONATHAN
LOVING HUSBAND AND FATHER
MARTH
KENT
IT'S YOUR FAULT, CLARK!
YOU'RE A FAILURE!
I'M SORRY!
I TRY TO... TO...
I CAME HERE FOR SOMEONE ELSE.
YOU SOUND LIKE--
IF I GET YOU AS WELL...

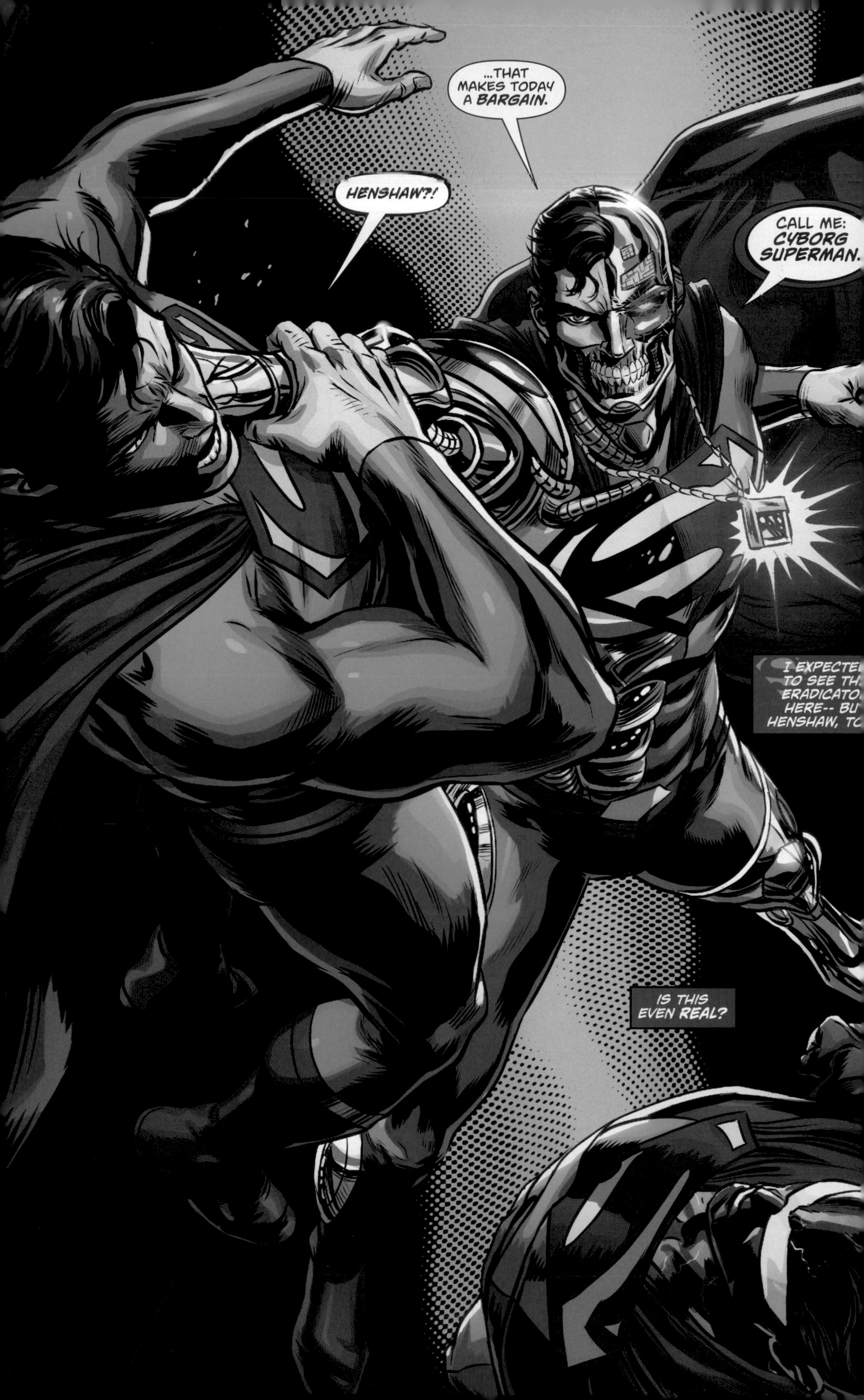
...THAT MAKES TODAY A BARGAIN.
HENSHAW?!
CALL ME: CYBORG SUPERMAN.
I EXPECTE TO SEE TH ERADICATO HERE-- BU HENSHAW, TO
IS THIS EVEN REAL?

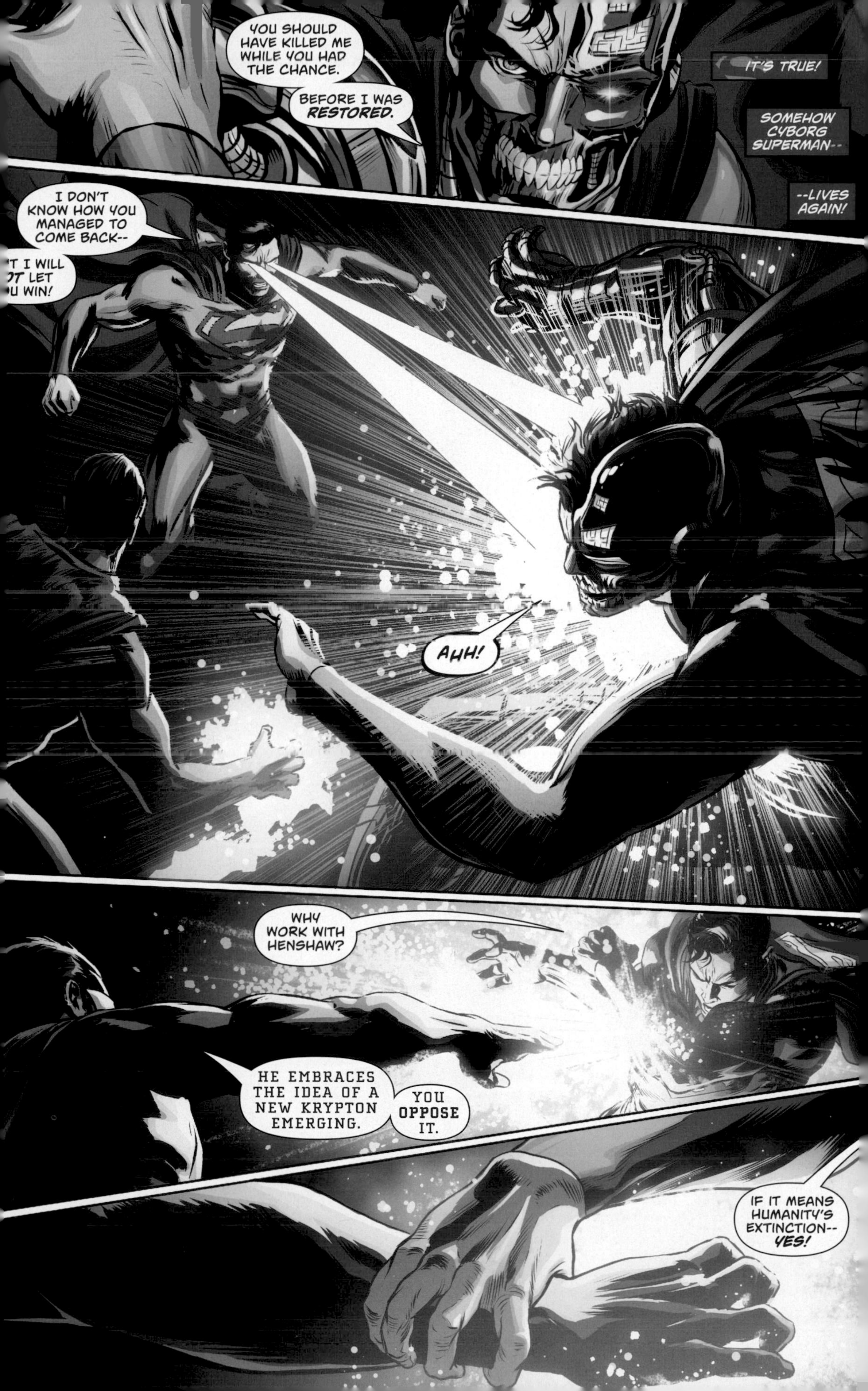
YOU SHOULD HAVE KILLED ME WHILE YOU HAD THE CHANCE.
BEFORE I WAS RESTORED.
IT'S TRUE!
SOMEHOW CYBORG SUPERMAN--
--LIVES AGAIN!
I DON'T KNOW HOW YOU MANAGED TO COME BACK--
AHH!
WHY WORK WITH HENSHAW?
HE EMBRACES THE IDEA OF A NEW KRYPTON EMERGING.
YOU OPPOSE IT.
IF IT MEANS HUMANITY'S EXTINCTION-- YES!

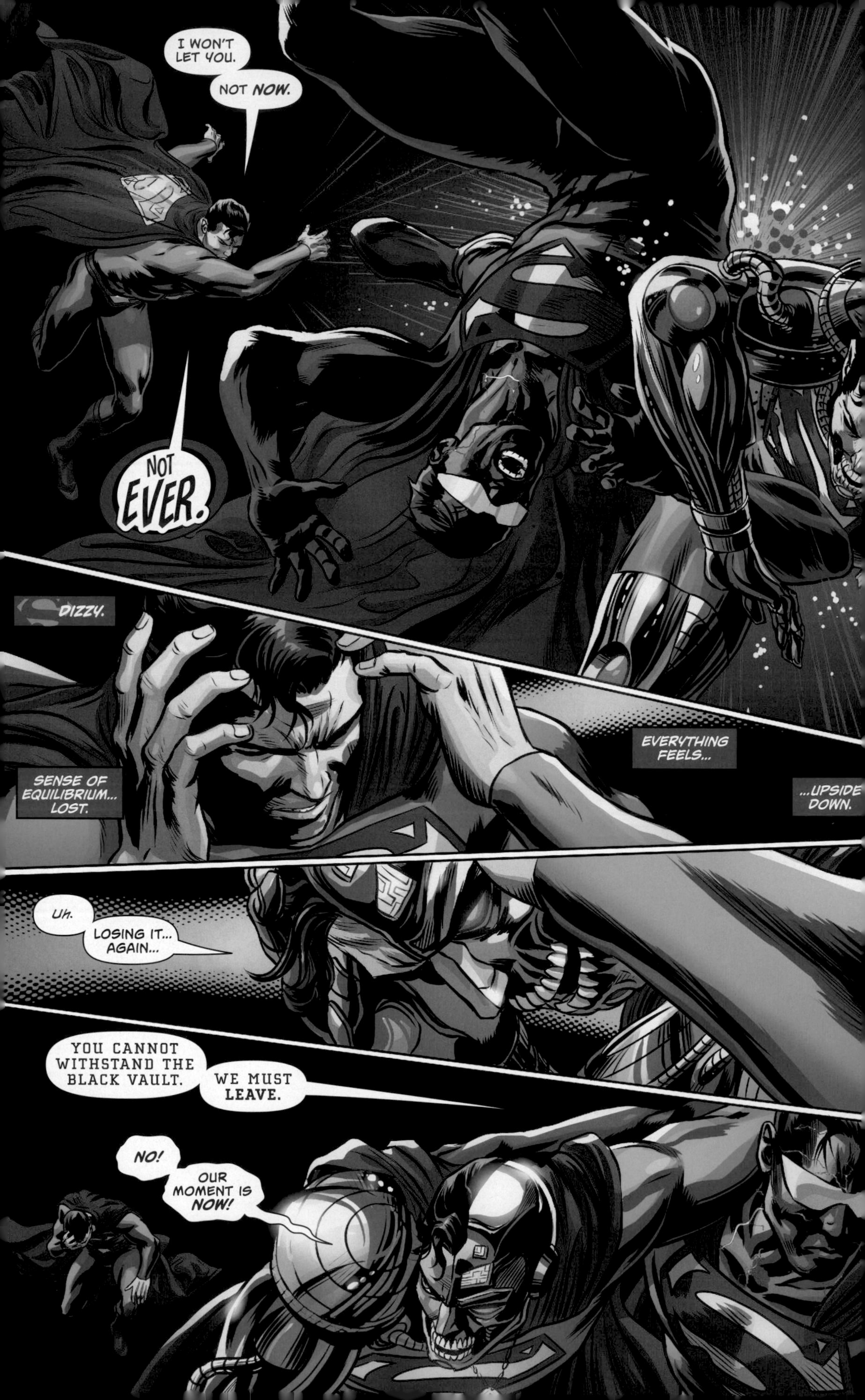
I WON'T LET YOU.
NOT NOW.
NOT EVER.
DIZZY.
SENSE OF EQUILIBRIUM... LOST.
EVERYTHING FEELS...
...UPSIDE DOWN.
Uh.
LOSING IT... AGAIN...
YOU CANNOT WITHSTAND THE BLACK VAULT.
WE MUST LEAVE.
NO!
OUR MOMENT IS NOW!

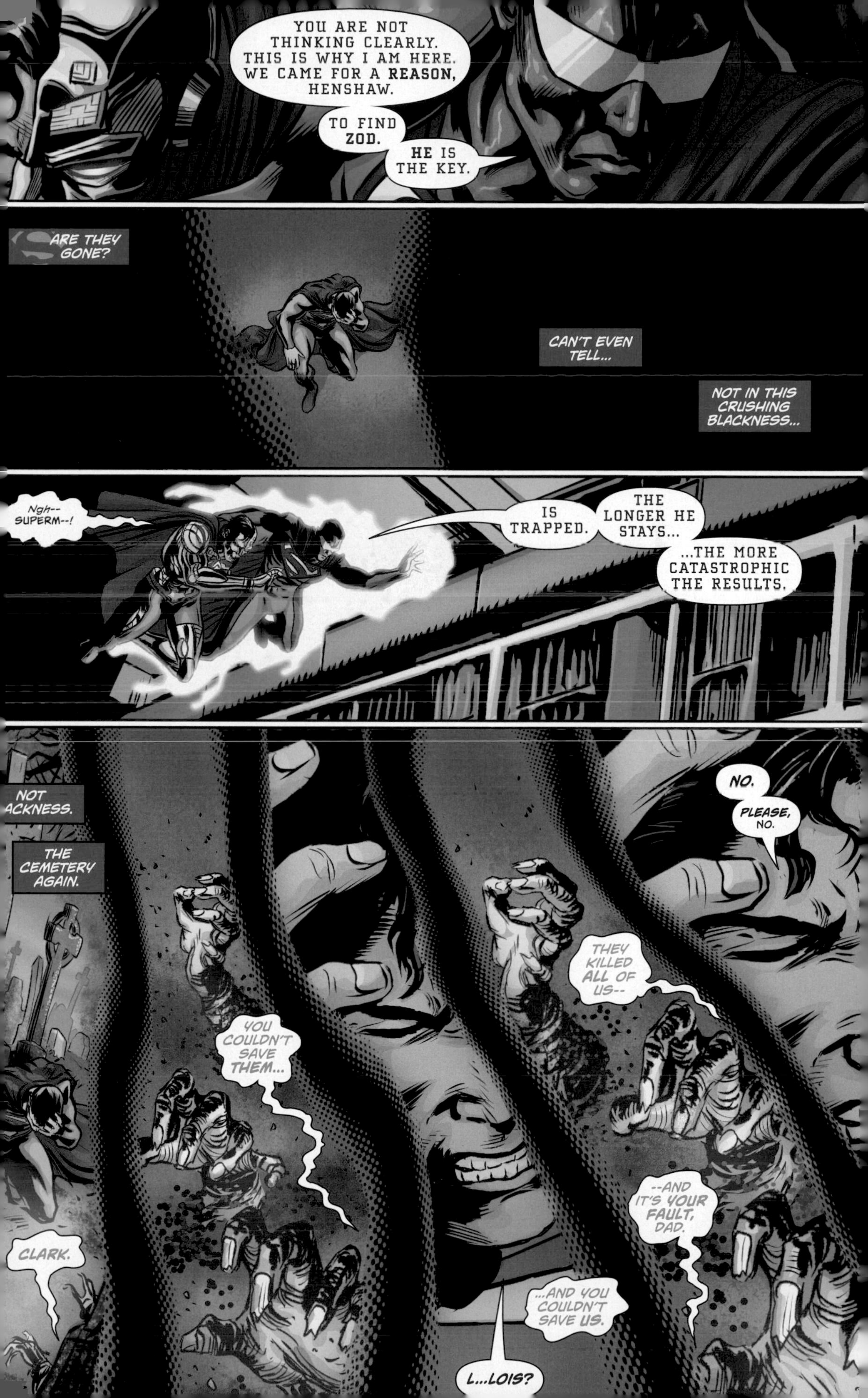
YOU ARE NOT THINKING CLEARLY. THIS IS WHY I AM HERE. WE CAME FOR A REASON, HENSHAW.
TO FIND ZOD.
HE IS THE KEY.
ARE THEY GONE?
CAN'T EVEN TELL...
NOT IN THIS CRUSHING BLACKNESS...
Ngh-- SUPERM--!
IS TRAPPED.
THE LONGER HE STAYS...
...THE MORE CATASTROPHIC THE RESULTS.
NOT ACKNESS.
THE CEMETERY AGAIN.
NO.
PLEASE, NO.
THEY KILLED ALL OF US--
YOU COULDN'T SAVE THEM...
--AND IT'S YOUR FAULT, DAD.
CLARK.
...AND YOU COULDN'T SAVE US.
L...LOIS?

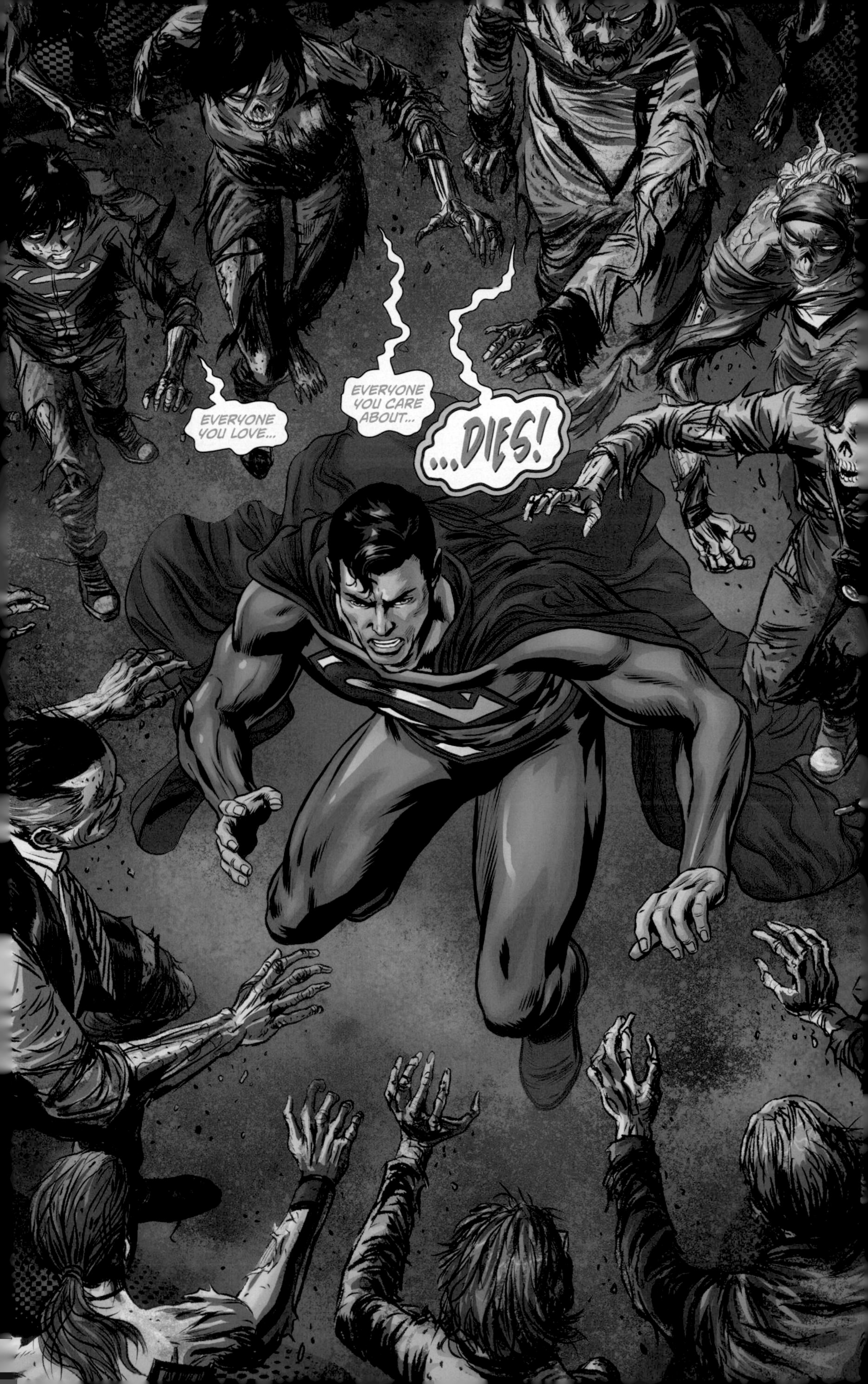
EVERYONE YOU LOVE...
EVERYONE YOU CARE ABOUT...
...DIES!

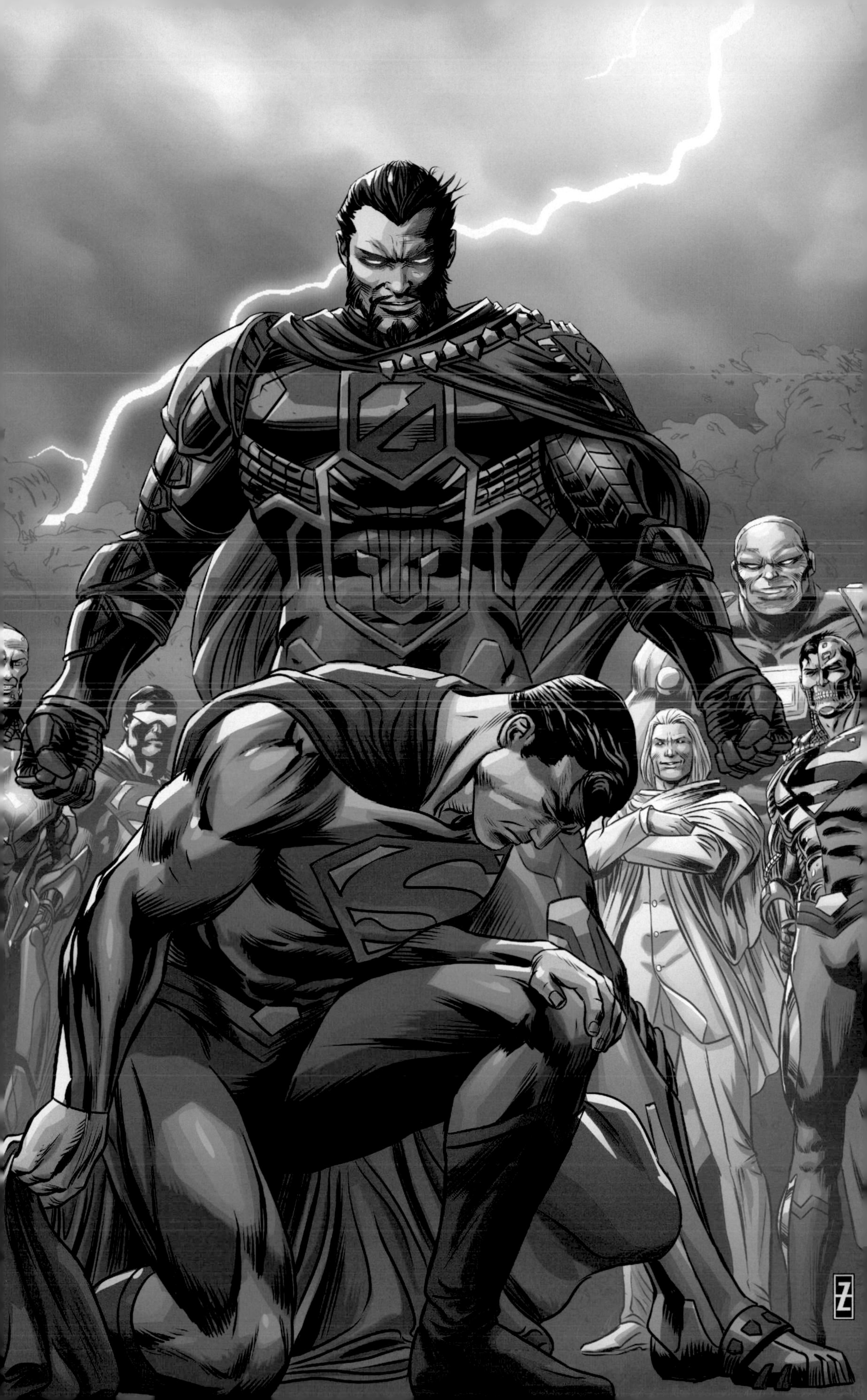

REVENGE PART 3

JACK HERBERT artist * HI-FI colorist

PATRICK ZIRCHER HI-FI cover artists

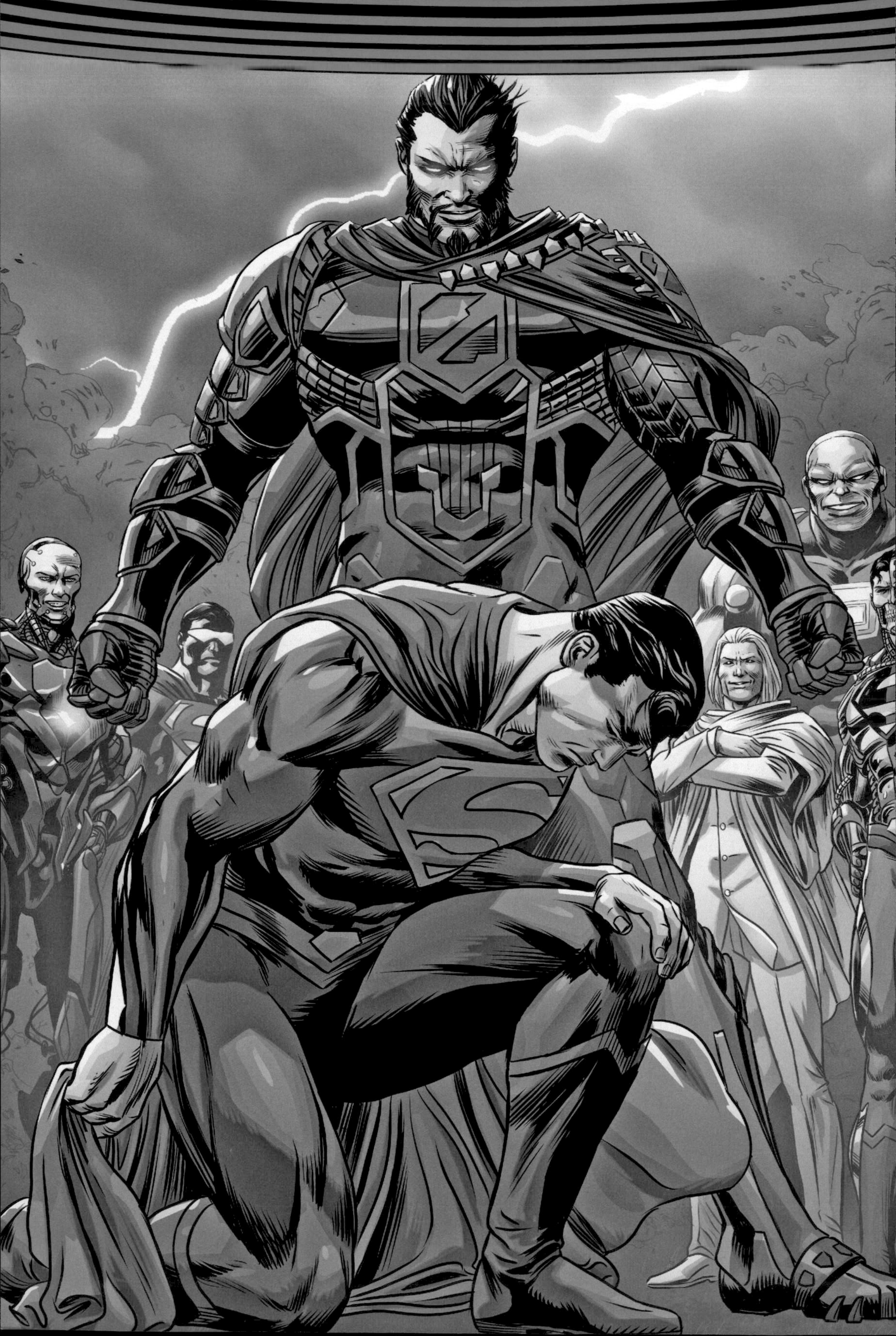

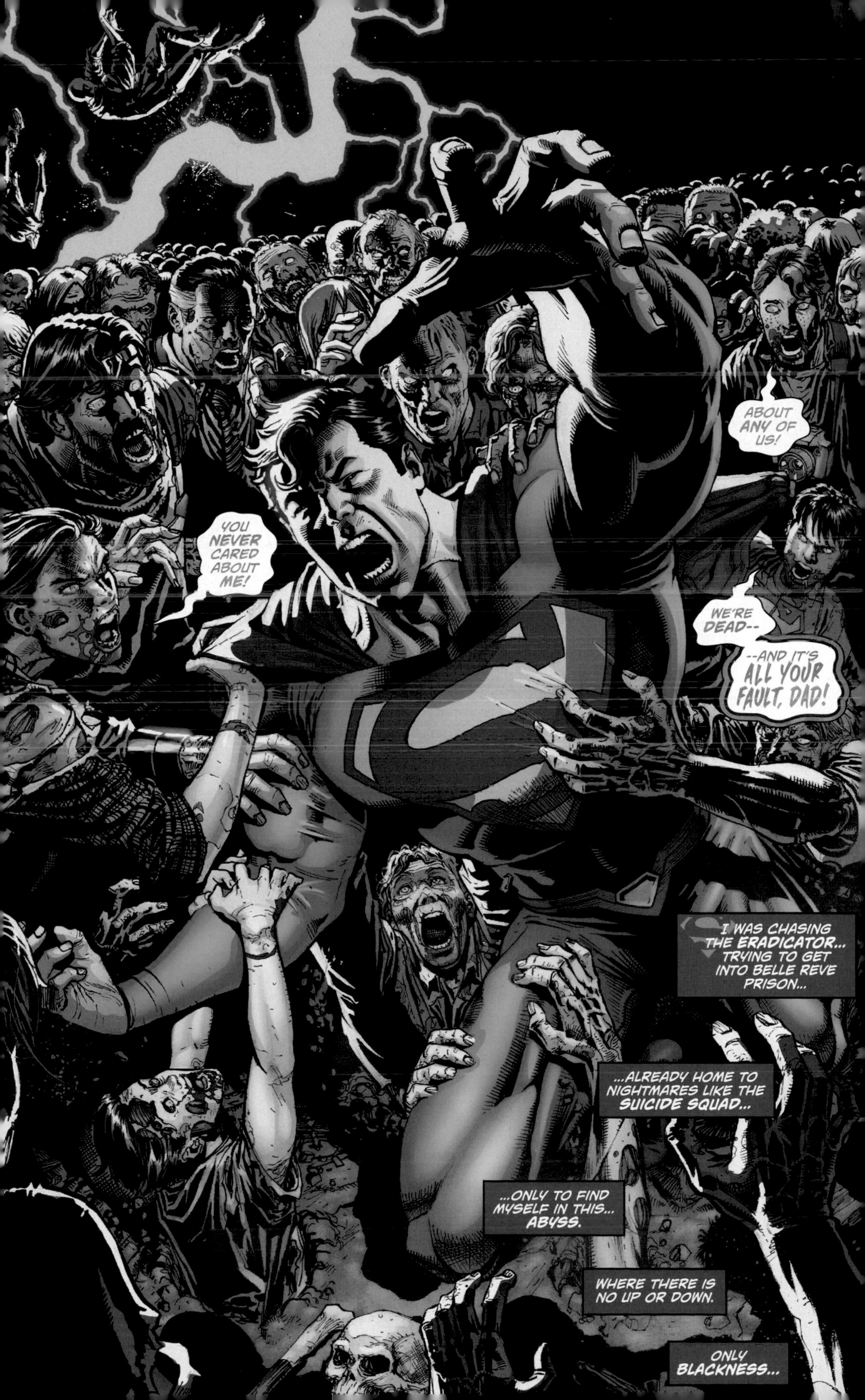
YOU NEVER CARED ABOUT ME!
ABOUT ANY OF US!
WE'RE DEAD--
--AND IT'S ALL YOUR FAULT, DAD!
I WAS CHASING THE ERADICATOR... TRYING TO GET INTO BELLE REVE PRISON...
...ALREADY HOME TO NIGHTMARES LIKE THE SUICIDE SQUAD...
...ONLY TO FIND MYSELF IN THIS... ABYSS.
WHERE THERE IS NO UP OR DOWN.
ONLY BLACKNESS...

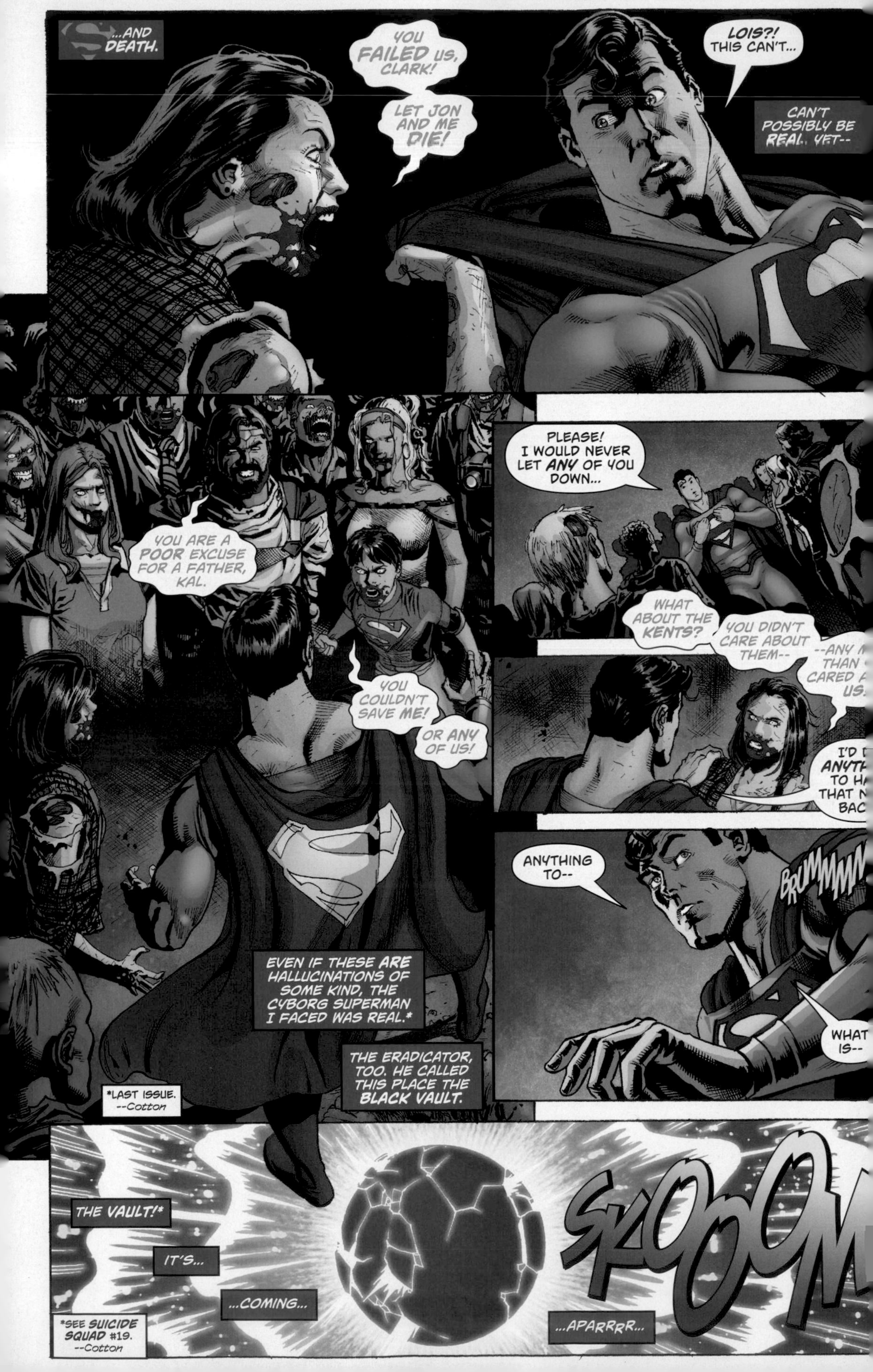
...AND DEATH.
YOU FAILED US, CLARK!
LET JON AND ME DIE!
LOIS?! THIS CAN'T...
CAN'T POSSIBLY BE REAL. YET--
YOU ARE A POOR EXCUSE FOR A FATHER, KAL.
YOU COULDN'T SAVE ME!
OR ANY OF US!
EVEN IF THESE ARE HALLUCINATIONS OF SOME KIND, THE CYBORG SUPERMAN I FACED WAS REAL.*
THE ERADICATOR, TOO. HE CALLED THIS PLACE THE BLACK VAULT.
*LAST ISSUE. --Cotton
PLEASE! I WOULD NEVER LET ANY OF YOU DOWN...
WHAT ABOUT THE KENTS?
YOU DIDN'T CARE ABOUT THEM--
ANYTHING TO--
WHAT IS--
THE VAULT!*
IT'S...
...COMING...
...APARRRR...
*SEE SUICIDE SQUAD #19. --Cotton

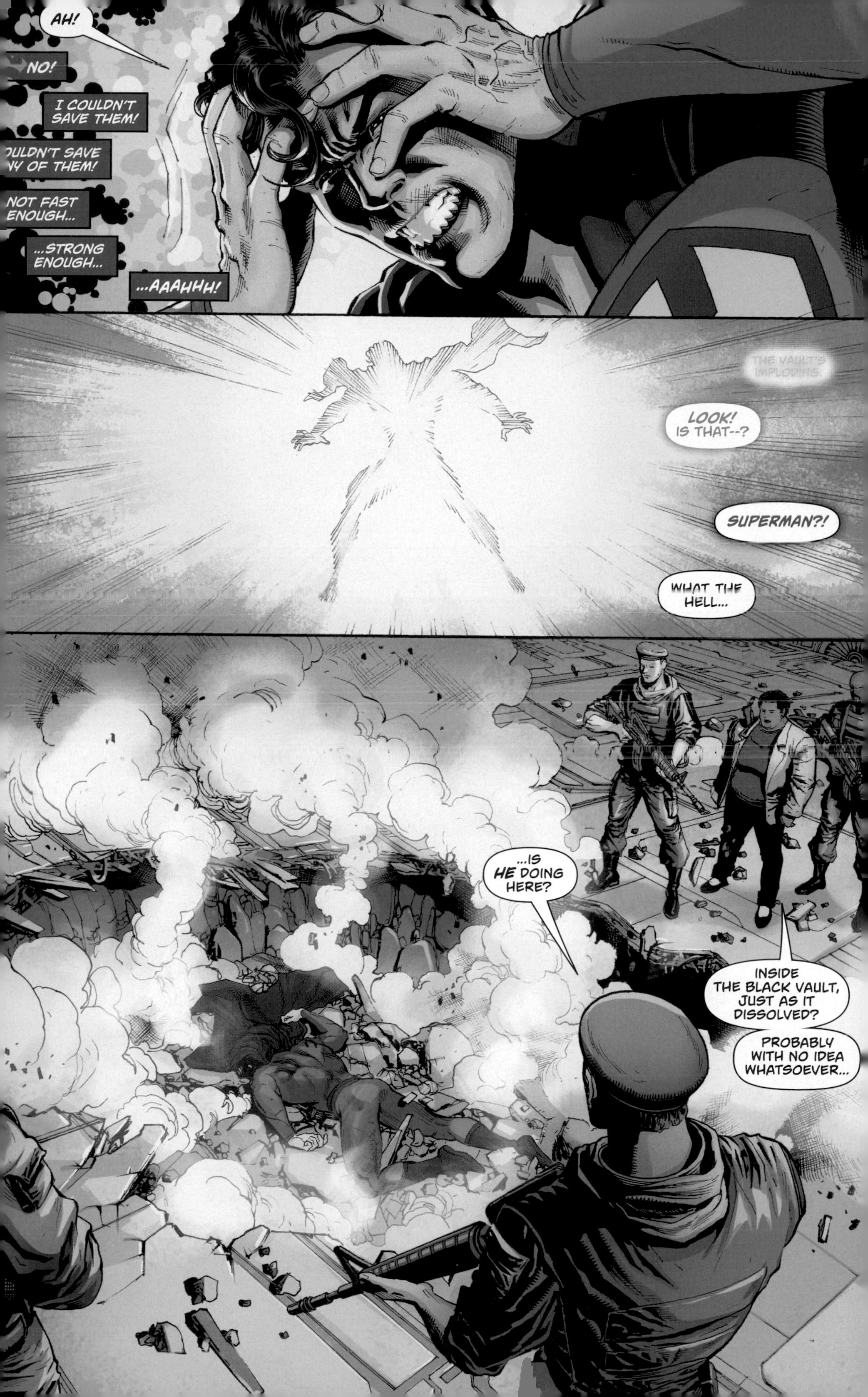
AH!
NO!
I COULDN'T SAVE THEM!
OULDN'T SAVE NY OF THEM!
NOT FAST ENOUGH...
...STRONG ENOUGH...
...AAAHHH!
THE VAULT'S IMPLODING.
LOOK! IS THAT--?
SUPERMAN?!
WHAT THE HELL...
...IS HE DOING HERE?
INSIDE THE BLACK VAULT, JUST AS IT DISSOLVED?
PROBABLY WITH NO IDEA WHATSOEVER...

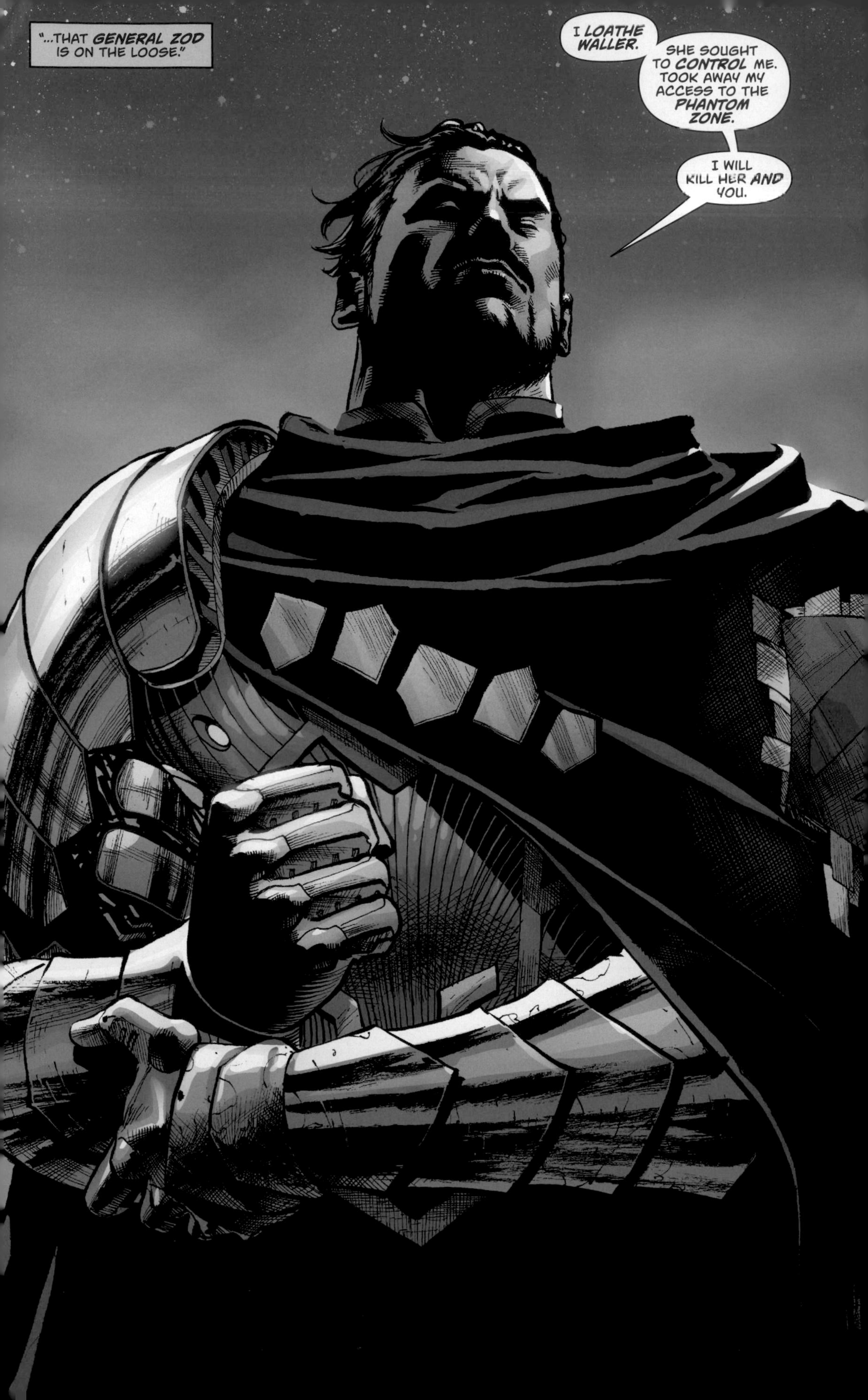
"...THAT GENERAL ZOD IS ON THE LOOSE."
I LOATHE WALLER.
SHE SOUGHT TO CONTROL ME. TOOK AWAY MY ACCESS TO THE PHANTOM ZONE.
I WILL KILL HER AND YOU.

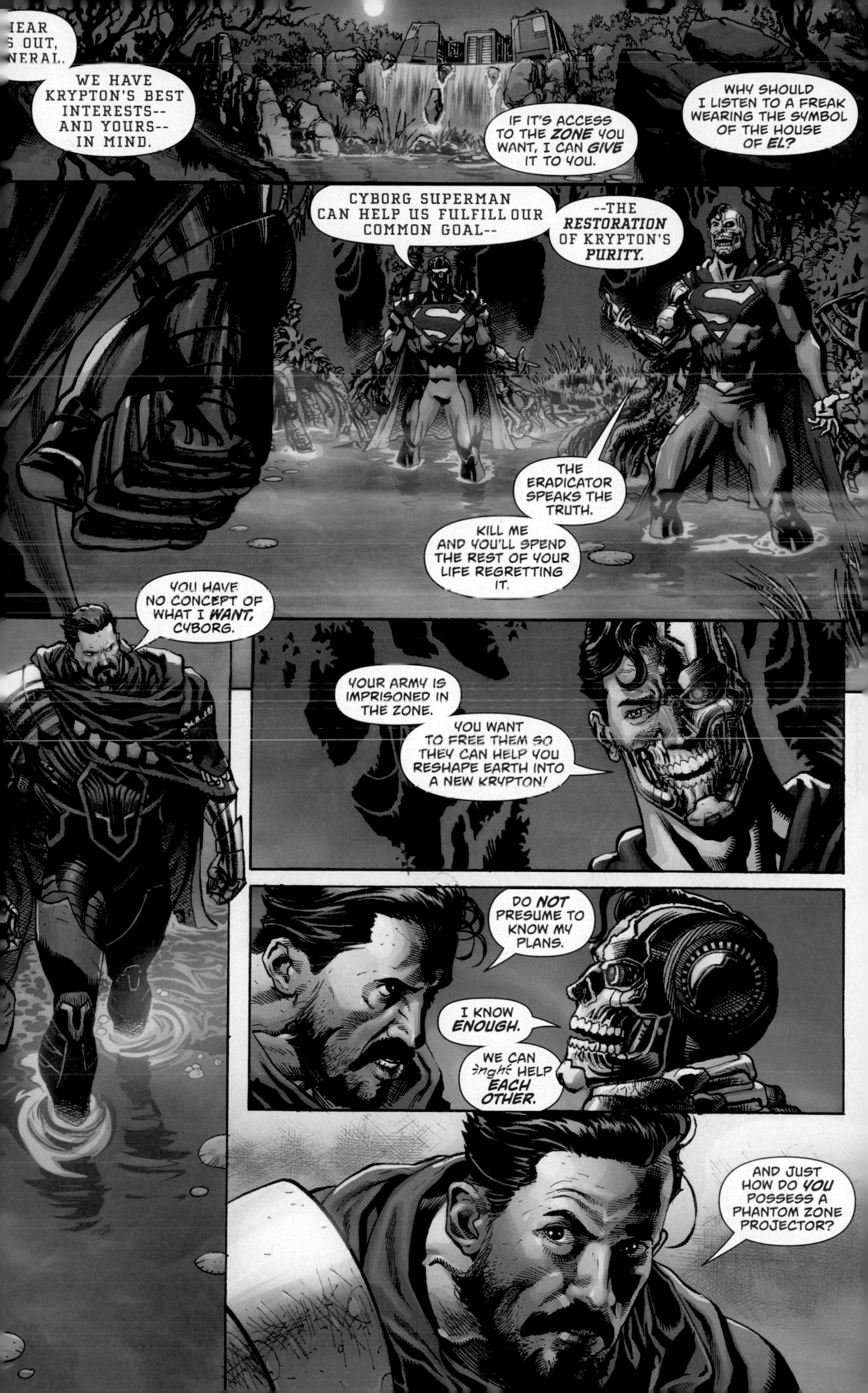

HEAR
S OUT,
NERAL.
WE HAVE KRYPTON'S BEST INTERESTS-- AND YOURS-- IN MIND.
IF IT'S ACCESS TO THE ZONE YOU WANT, I CAN GIVE IT TO YOU.
WHY SHOULD I LISTEN TO A FREAK WEARING THE SYMBOL OF THE HOUSE OF EL?
CYBORG SUPERMAN CAN HELP US FULFILL OUR COMMON GOAL--
--THE RESTORATION OF KRYPTON'S PURITY.
THE ERADICATOR SPEAKS THE TRUTH.
KILL ME AND YOU'LL SPEND THE REST OF YOUR LIFE REGRETTING IT.
YOU HAVE NO CONCEPT OF WHAT I WANT, CYBORG.
YOUR ARMY IS IMPRISONED IN THE ZONE.
YOU WANT TO FREE THEM SO THEY CAN HELP YOU RESHAPE EARTH INTO A NEW KRYPTON!
DO NOT PRESUME TO KNOW MY PLANS.
I KNOW ENOUGH.
WE CAN *ngh* HELP EACH OTHER.
AND JUST HOW DO YOU POSSESS A PHANTOM ZONE PROJECTOR?

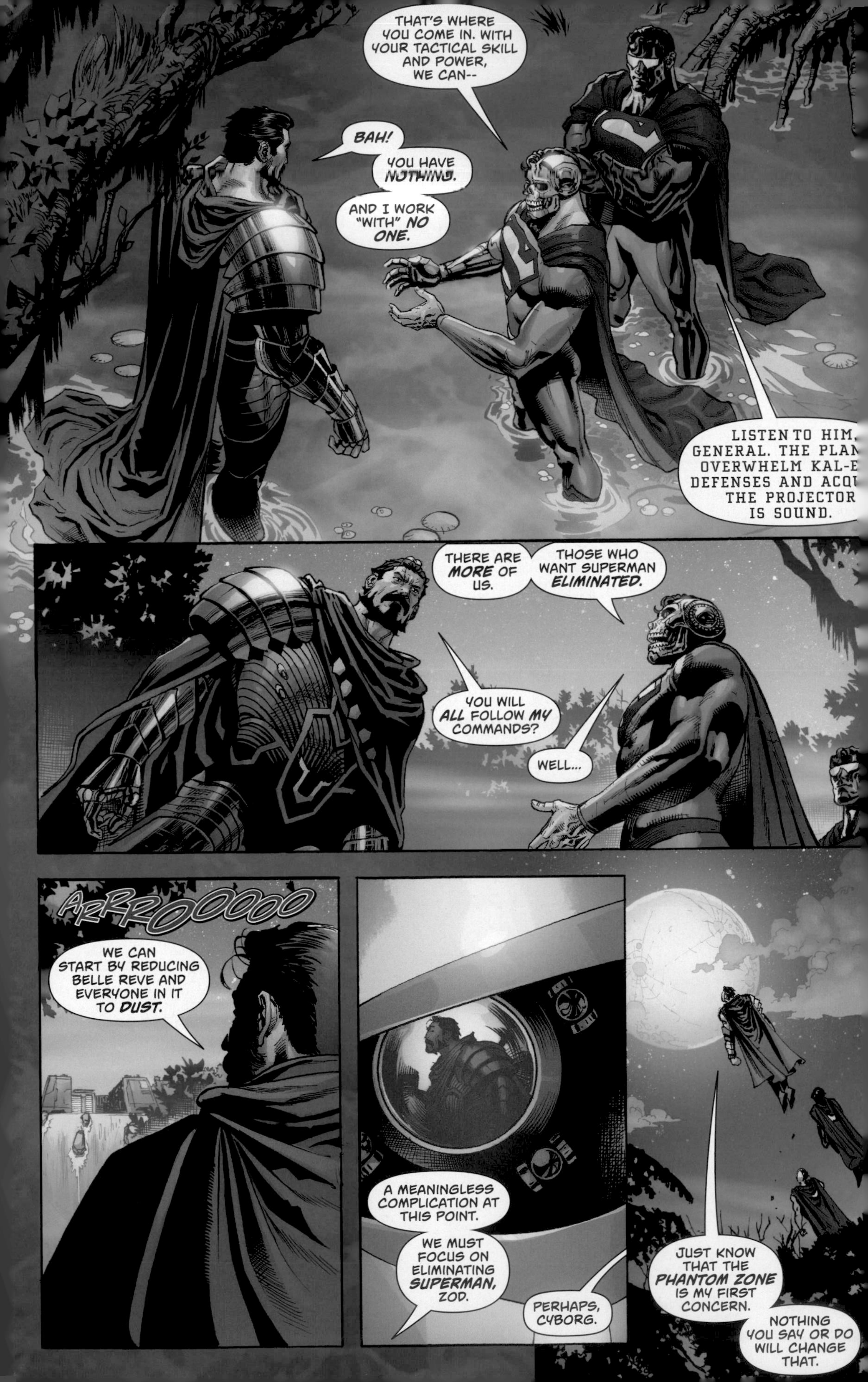

THAT'S WHERE YOU COME IN. WITH YOUR TACTICAL SKILL AND POWER, WE CAN--
BAH!
YOU HAVE NOTHING.
AND I WORK "WITH" NO ONE.
LISTEN TO HIM, GENERAL. THE PLAN OVERWHELM KAL-E DEFENSES AND ACQU THE PROJECTOR IS SOUND.
THERE ARE MORE OF US.
THOSE WHO WANT SUPERMAN ELIMINATED.
YOU WILL ALL FOLLOW MY COMMANDS?
WELL...
ARRROOOOOO
WE CAN START BY REDUCING BELLE REVE AND EVERYONE IN IT TO DUST.
A MEANINGLESS COMPLICATION AT THIS POINT.
WE MUST FOCUS ON ELIMINATING SUPERMAN, ZOD.
PERHAPS, CYBORG.
JUST KNOW THAT THE PHANTOM ZONE IS MY FIRST CONCERN.
NOTHING YOU SAY OR DO WILL CHANGE THAT.

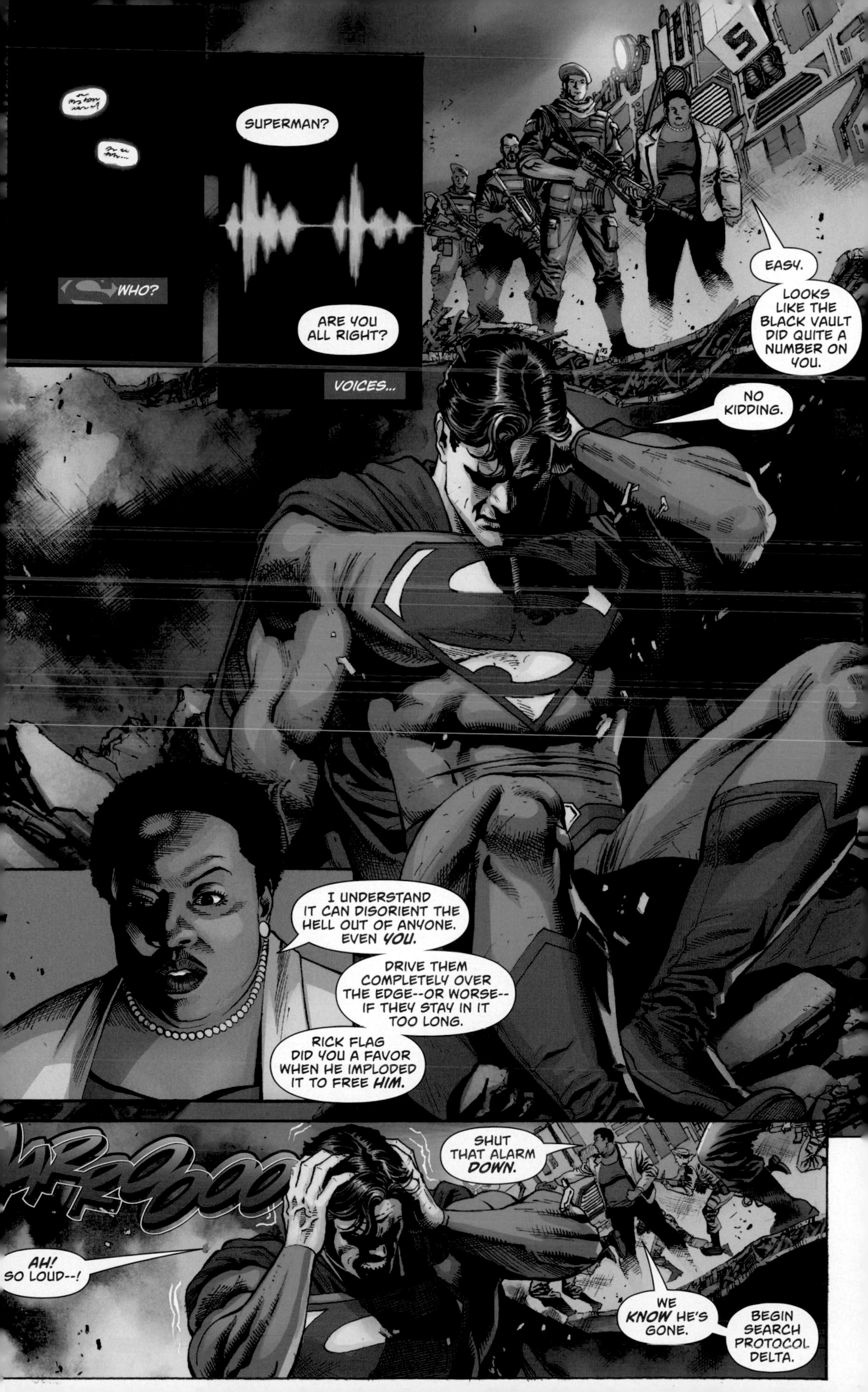
WHO?
SUPERMAN?
ARE YOU ALL RIGHT?
VOICES...
EASY.
LOOKS LIKE THE BLACK VAULT DID QUITE A NUMBER ON YOU.
NO KIDDING.
I UNDERSTAND IT CAN DISORIENT THE HELL OUT OF ANYONE. EVEN *YOU.*
DRIVE THEM COMPLETELY OVER THE EDGE--OR WORSE--IF THEY STAY IN IT TOO LONG.
RICK FLAG DID YOU A FAVOR WHEN HE IMPLODED IT TO FREE *HIM.*
AH! SO LOUD--!
SHUT THAT ALARM *DOWN.*
WE *KNOW* HE'S GONE.
BEGIN SEARCH PROTOCOL DELTA.

PLEASE— CAN YOU—?

DRIVES ME NUTS, TOO, BUT IT'S OFF NOW.

NO SIGN OF Z... DIRECTOR WA... WHEREVER H... WENT, HE'S L... GONE.

MY GOD. I CAN'T—

DID YOU SAY— **ZOD?!**

HE WAS **HERE?**

YES. UNDER MY CONTROL.

WHY?

TO ACT AS THE ULTIMATE WEAPON, OF COURSE.

EVEN AGAINST **YOU,** IF NECESSARY.

HAVE TO GO. **BEFORE** WALLER REALIZES WHAT'S HAPPENED.

YOUR TACTICS ARE **DEPLORABLE.**

DON'T GET SO HIGH AND MIGHTY WITH ME, SUPERMAN.

MY JOB IS TO KEEP PEOPLE SAFE, AND ZOD HELPED ME DO THAT.

YOU MIGHT HAVE TO MAKE CHOICE YOURS... SOMEDAY.

KILL— OR LET SOMEONE YOU LOVE **DIE.**

WHAT WILL YOU DO?

CAN'T ARGUE NOW.

HAVE TO FIND ZOD...

SOME...

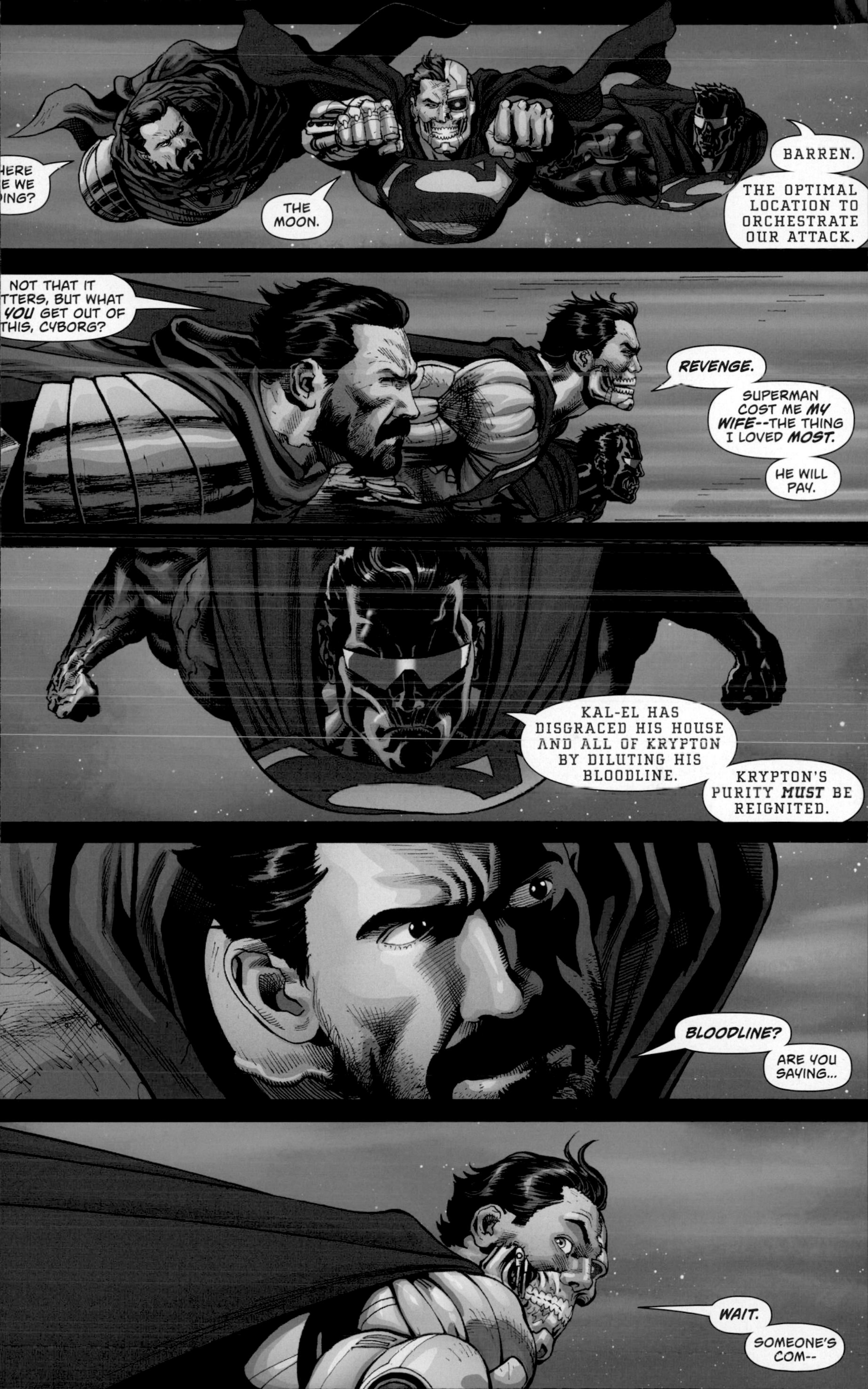
HERE
E WE
ING?
THE MOON.
BARREN.
THE OPTIMAL LOCATION TO ORCHESTRATE OUR ATTACK.
NOT THAT IT
TTERS, BUT WHAT
YOU GET OUT OF
THIS, CYBORG?
REVENGE.
SUPERMAN COST ME MY WIFE--THE THING I LOVED MOST.
HE WILL PAY.
KAL-EL HAS DISGRACED HIS HOUSE AND ALL OF KRYPTON BY DILUTING HIS BLOODLINE.
KRYPTON'S PURITY MUST BE REIGNITED.
BLOODLINE?
ARE YOU SAYING...
WAIT.
SOMEONE'S COM--

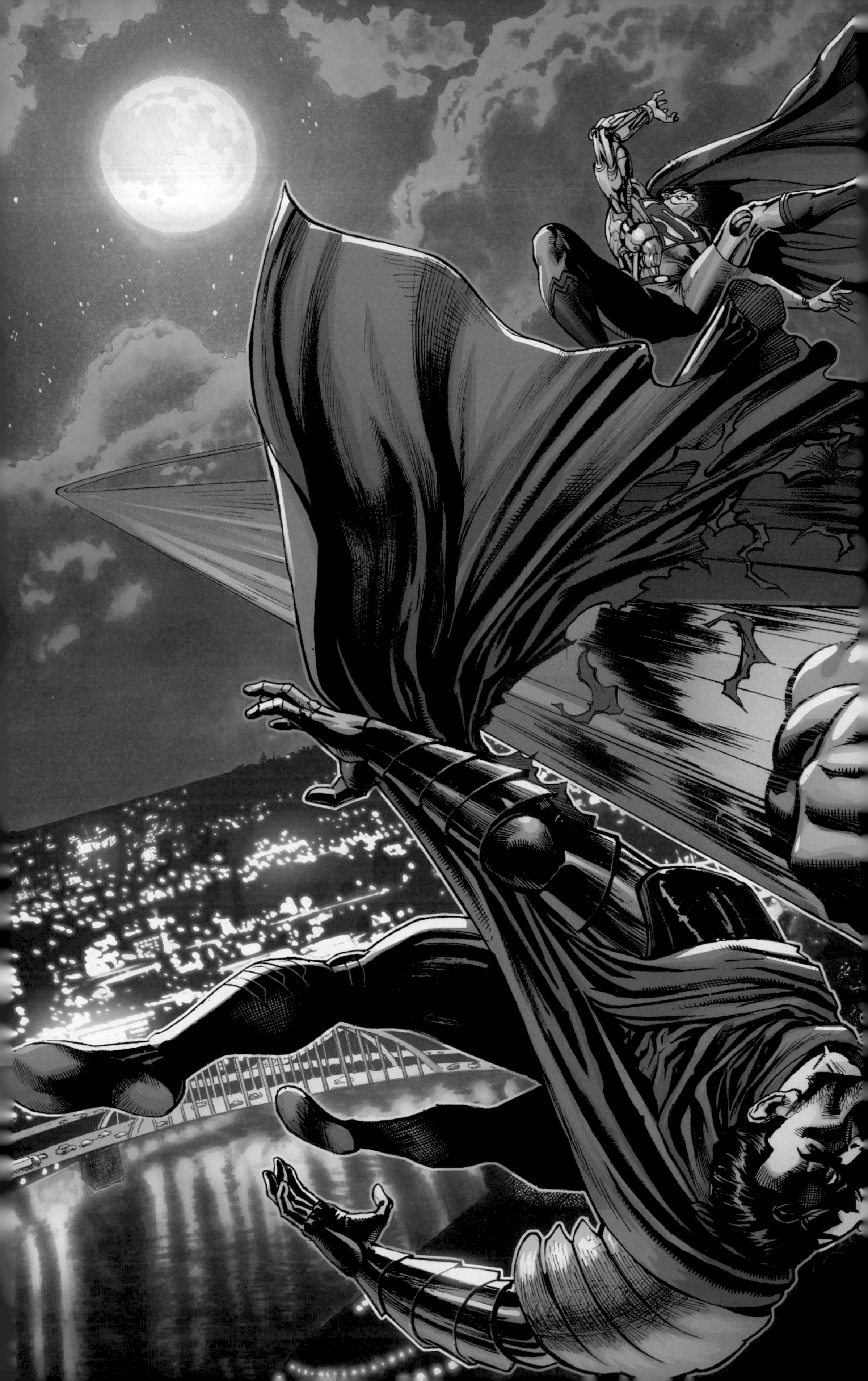

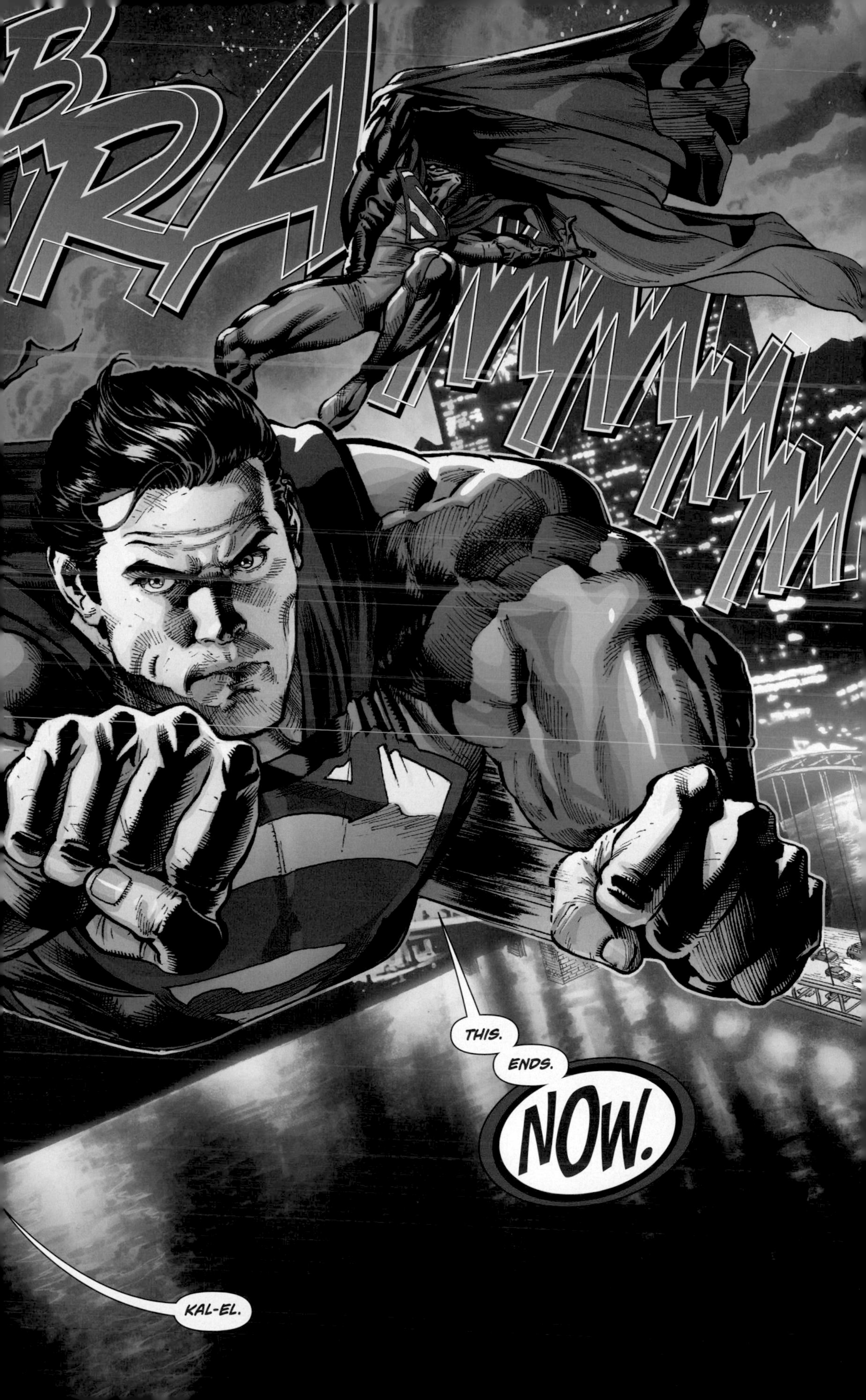
BRAMMMM
THIS.
ENDS.
NOW.
KAL-EL.

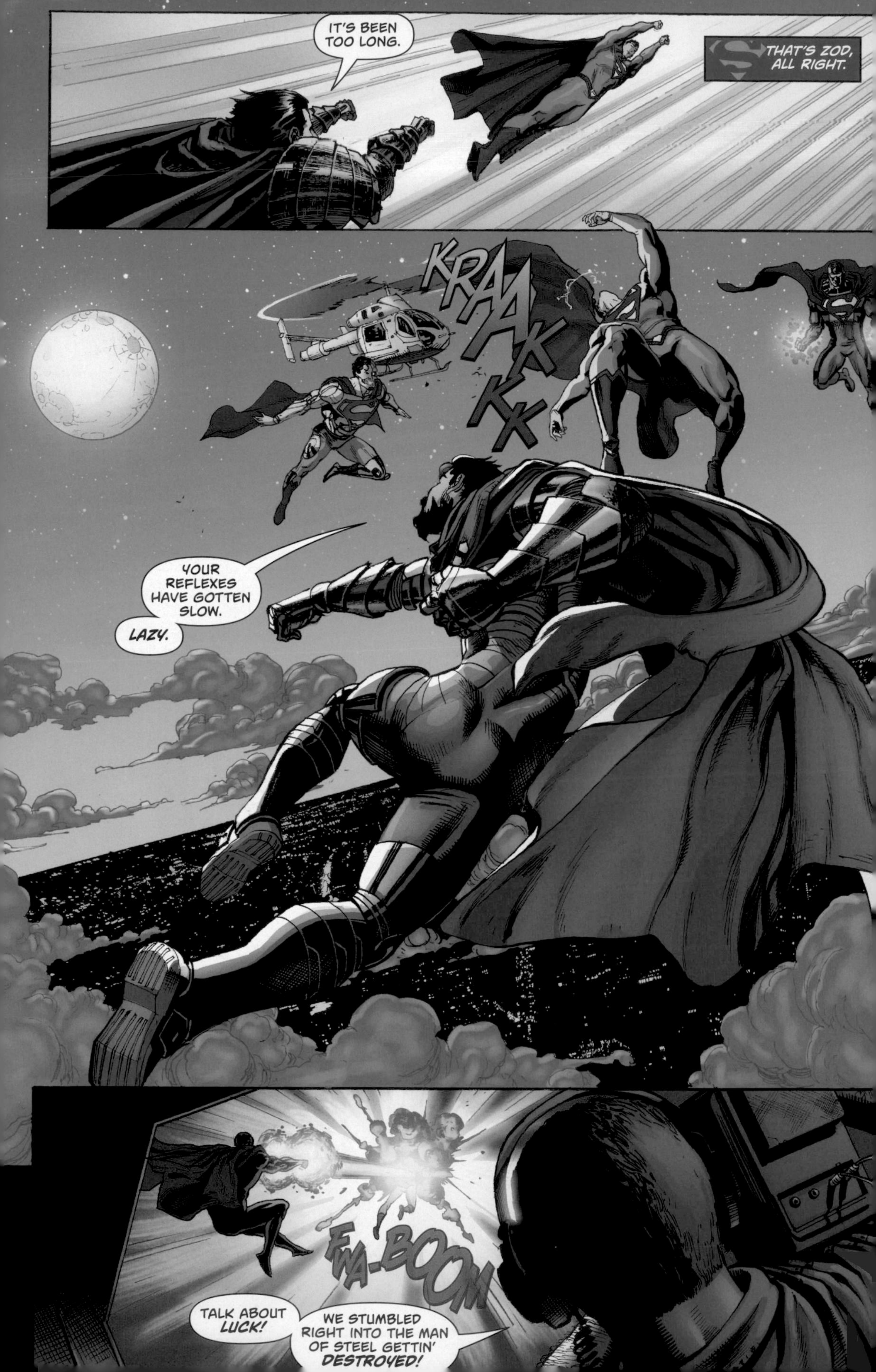

IT'S BEEN TOO LONG.
THAT'S ZOD, ALL RIGHT.
KRAAAKKK
YOUR REFLEXES HAVE GOTTEN SLOW.
LAZY.
FWA-BOOM
TALK ABOUT LUCK!
WE STUMBLED RIGHT INTO THE MAN OF STEEL GETTIN' DESTROYED!

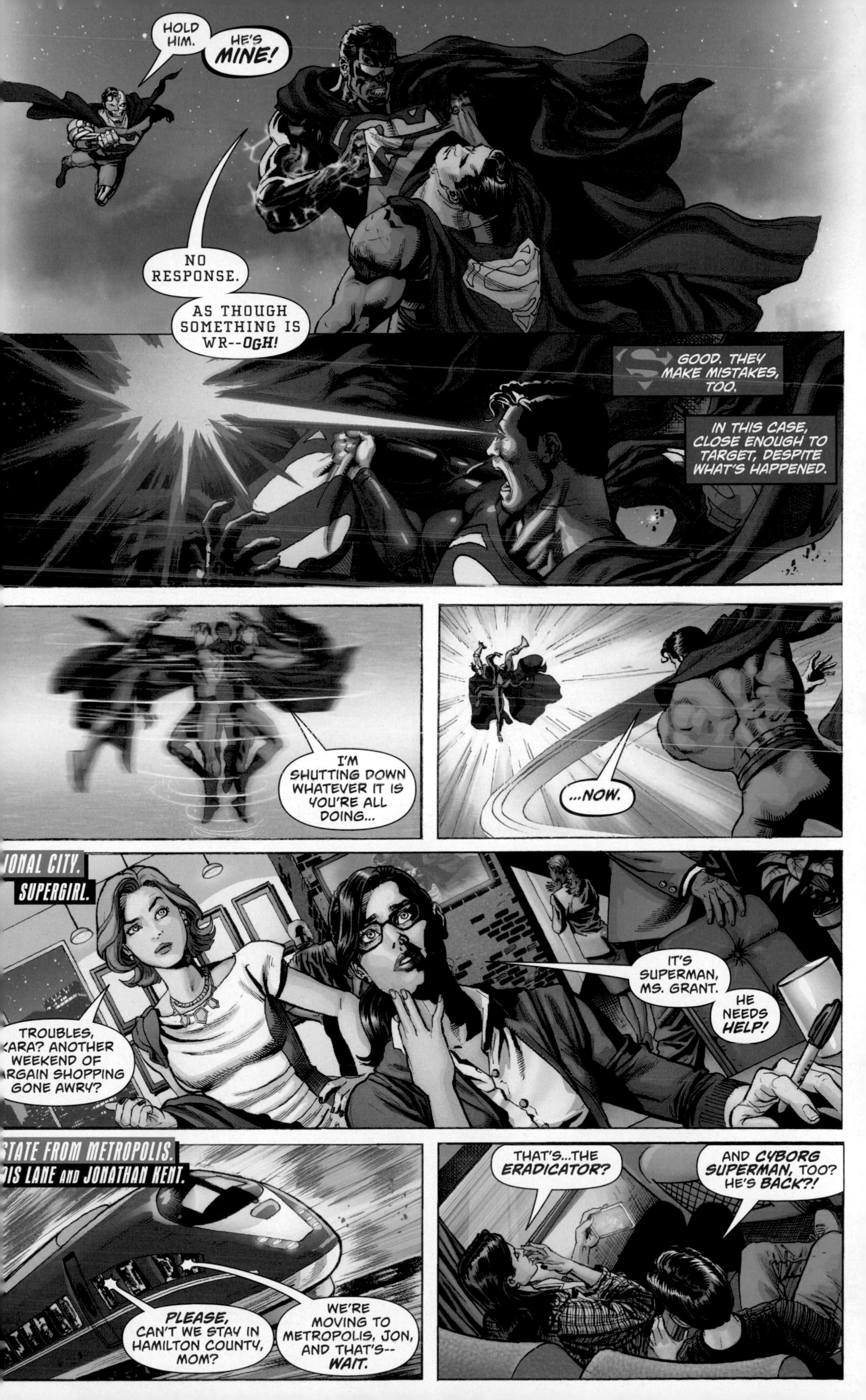
HOLD HIM.
HE'S MINE!
NO RESPONSE.
AS THOUGH SOMETHING IS WR--OGH!
GOOD. THEY MAKE MISTAKES, TOO.
IN THIS CASE, CLOSE ENOUGH TO TARGET, DESPITE WHAT'S HAPPENED.
I'M SHUTTING DOWN WHATEVER IT IS YOU'RE ALL DOING...
...NOW.
IONAL CITY.
SUPERGIRL.
TROUBLES, KARA? ANOTHER WEEKEND OF ARGAIN SHOPPING GONE AWRY?
IT'S SUPERMAN, MS. GRANT.
HE NEEDS HELP!
STATE FROM METROPOLIS.
OIS LANE AND JONATHAN KENT.
PLEASE, CAN'T WE STAY IN HAMILTON COUNTY, MOM?
WE'RE MOVING TO METROPOLIS, JON, AND THAT'S-- WAIT.
THAT'S...THE ERADICATOR?
AND CYBORG SUPERMAN, TOO? HE'S BACK?!

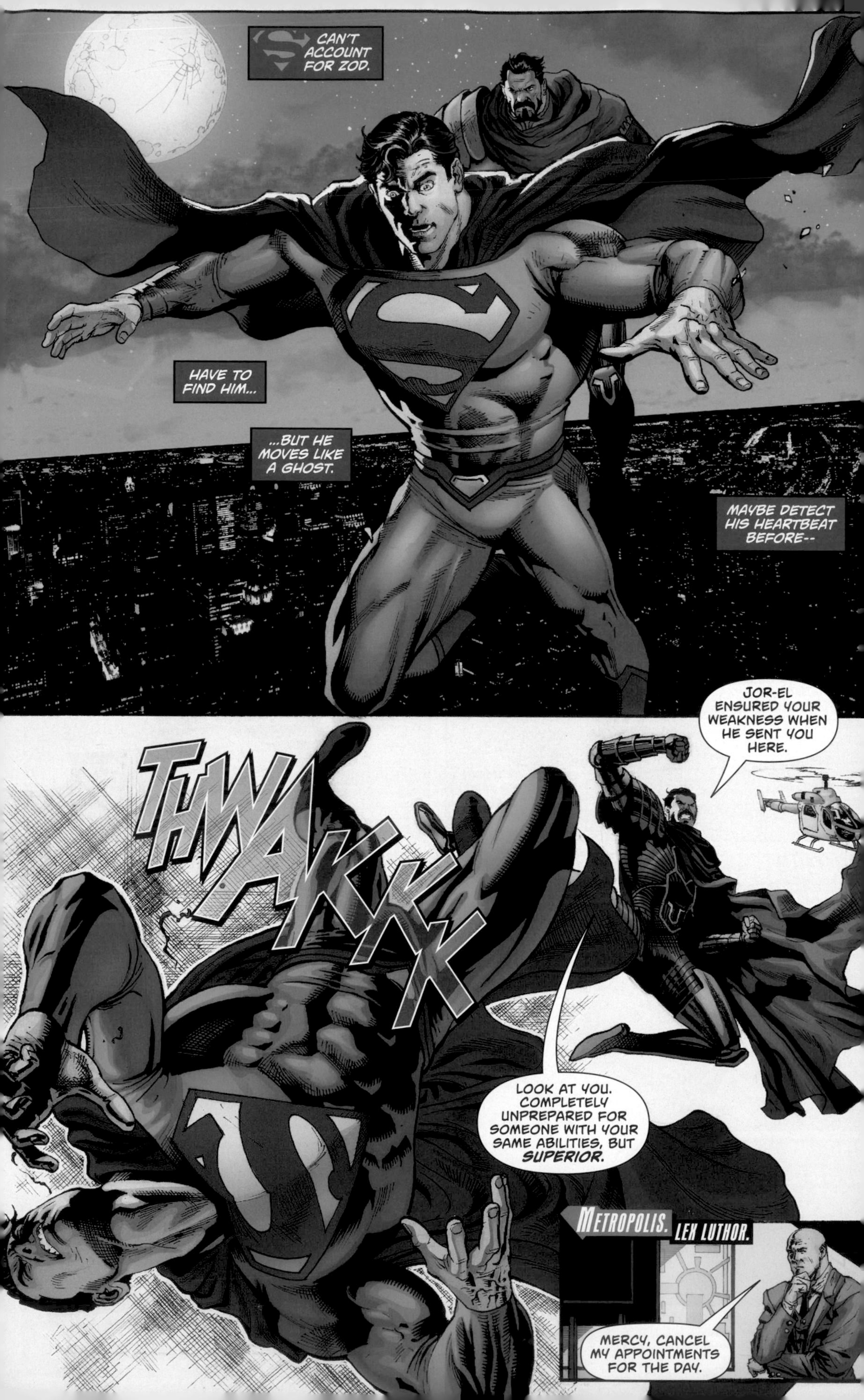
CAN'T ACCOUNT FOR ZOD.
HAVE TO FIND HIM...
...BUT HE MOVES LIKE A GHOST.
MAYBE DETECT HIS HEARTBEAT BEFORE--
THWAKKK
JOR-EL ENSURED YOUR WEAKNESS WHEN HE SENT YOU HERE.
LOOK AT YOU. COMPLETELY UNPREPARED FOR SOMEONE WITH YOUR SAME ABILITIES, BUT SUPERIOR.
METROPOLIS. LEX LUTHOR.
MERCY, CANCEL MY APPOINTMENTS FOR THE DAY.

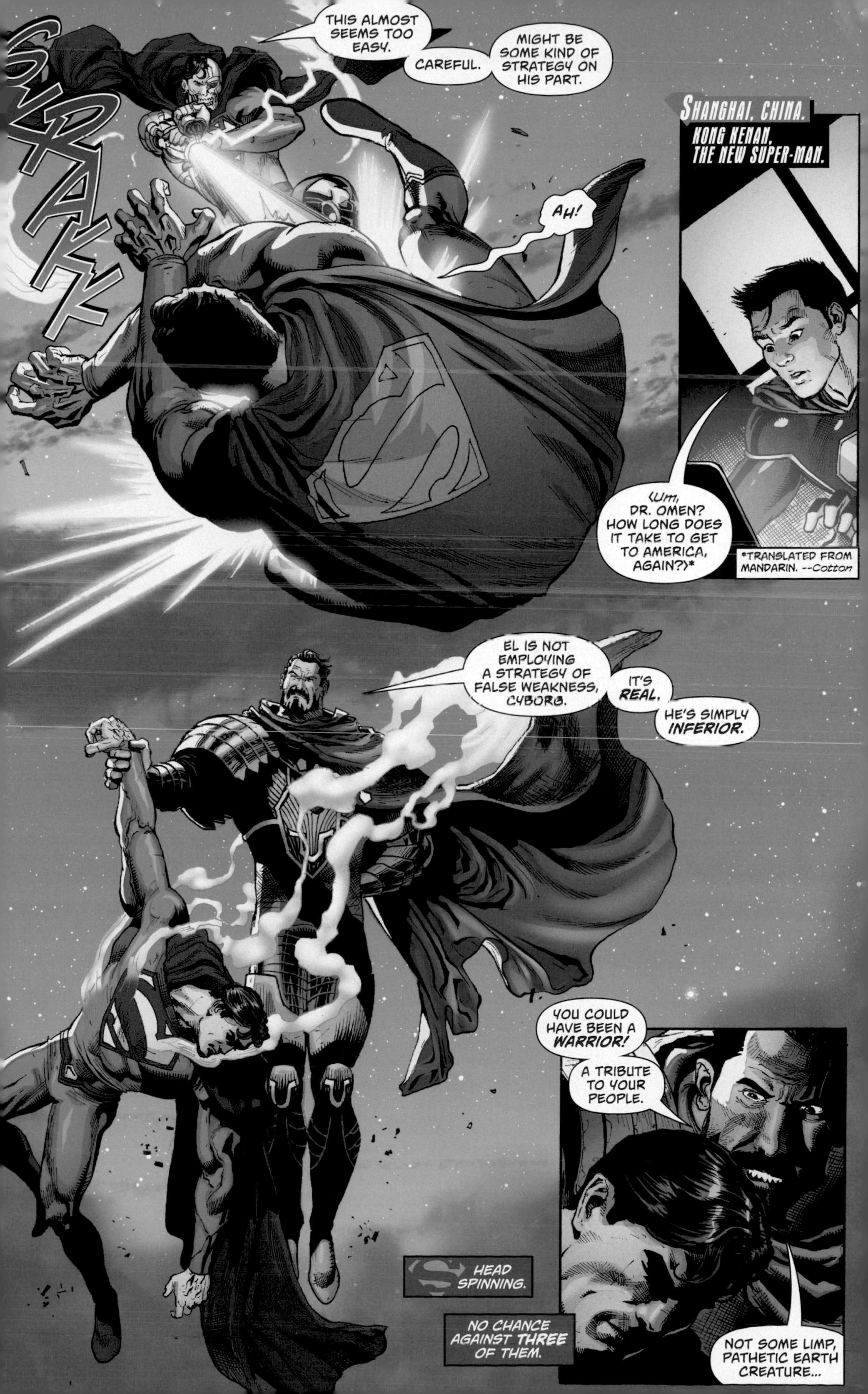
SKRAKK
THIS ALMOST SEEMS TOO EASY.
CAREFUL.
MIGHT BE SOME KIND OF STRATEGY ON HIS PART.
AH!
SHANGHAI, CHINA.
KONG KENAN, THE NEW SUPER-MAN.
⟨UM, DR. OMEN? HOW LONG DOES IT TAKE TO GET TO AMERICA, AGAIN?⟩*
*TRANSLATED FROM MANDARIN. --Cotton
EL IS NOT EMPLOYING A STRATEGY OF FALSE WEAKNESS, CYBORG.
IT'S REAL.
HE'S SIMPLY INFERIOR.
YOU COULD HAVE BEEN A WARRIOR!
A TRIBUTE TO YOUR PEOPLE.
NOT SOME LIMP, PATHETIC EARTH CREATURE...
HEAD SPINNING.
NO CHANCE AGAINST THREE OF THEM.

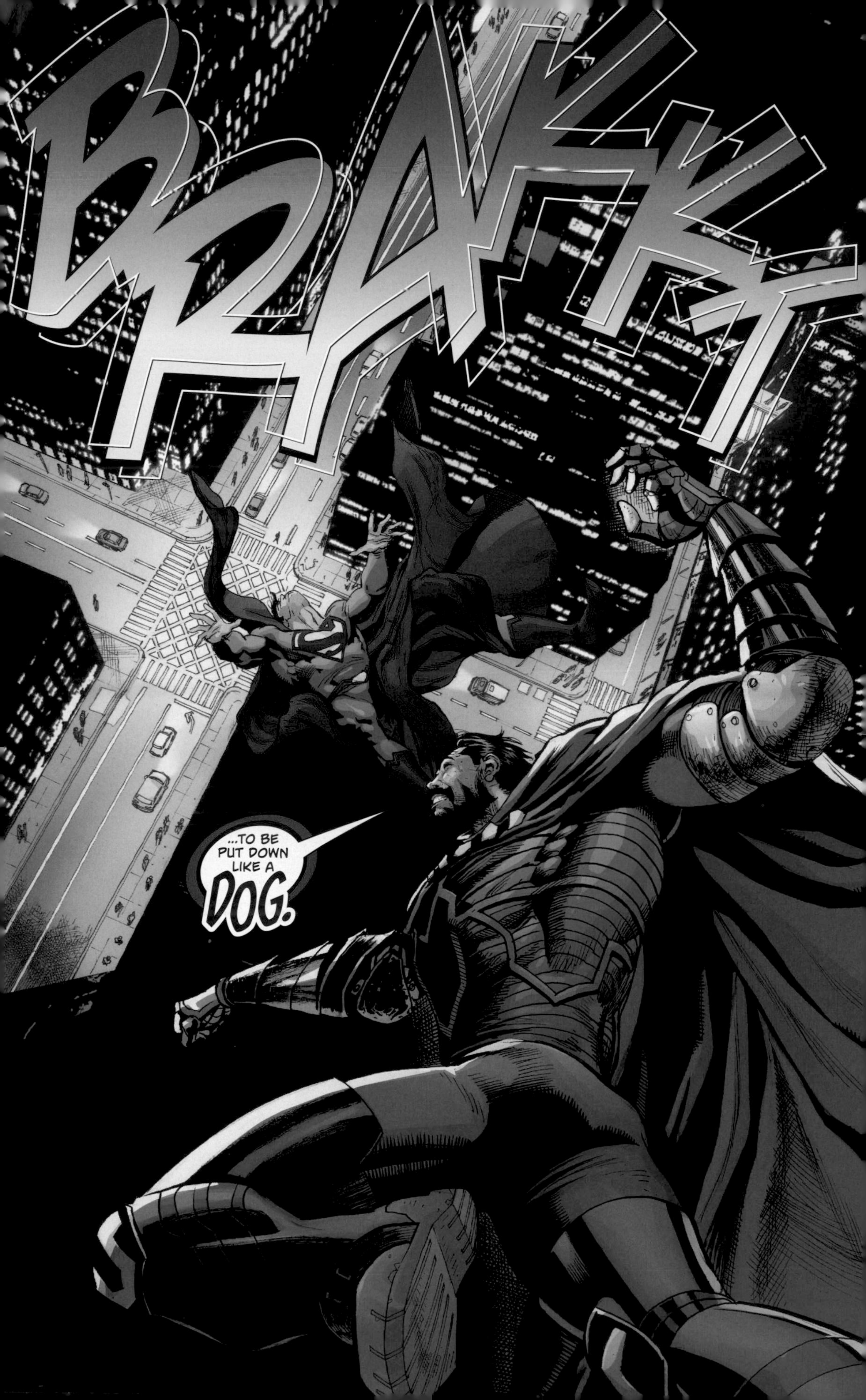
BRAKT
...TO BE PUT DOWN LIKE A DOG.

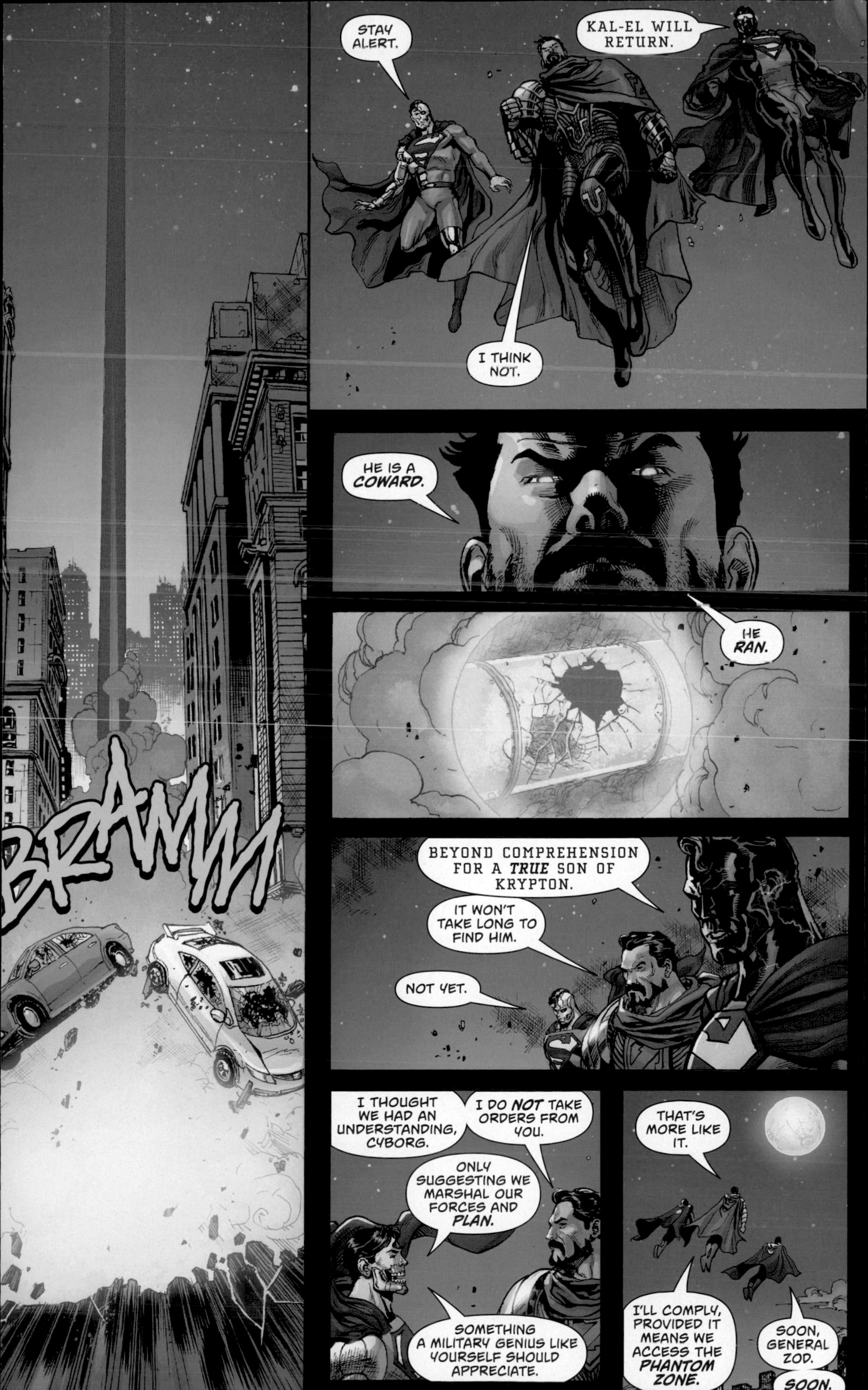
BRAMM
STAY ALERT.
KAL-EL WILL RETURN.
I THINK NOT.
HE IS A COWARD.
HE RAN.
BEYOND COMPREHENSION FOR A TRUE SON OF KRYPTON.
IT WON'T TAKE LONG TO FIND HIM.
NOT YET.
I THOUGHT WE HAD AN UNDERSTANDING, CYBORG.
I DO NOT TAKE ORDERS FROM YOU.
ONLY SUGGESTING WE MARSHAL OUR FORCES AND PLAN.
SOMETHING A MILITARY GENIUS LIKE YOURSELF SHOULD APPRECIATE.
THAT'S MORE LIKE IT.
I'LL COMPLY, PROVIDED IT MEANS WE ACCESS THE PHANTOM ZONE.
SOON, GENERAL ZOD.
SOON.

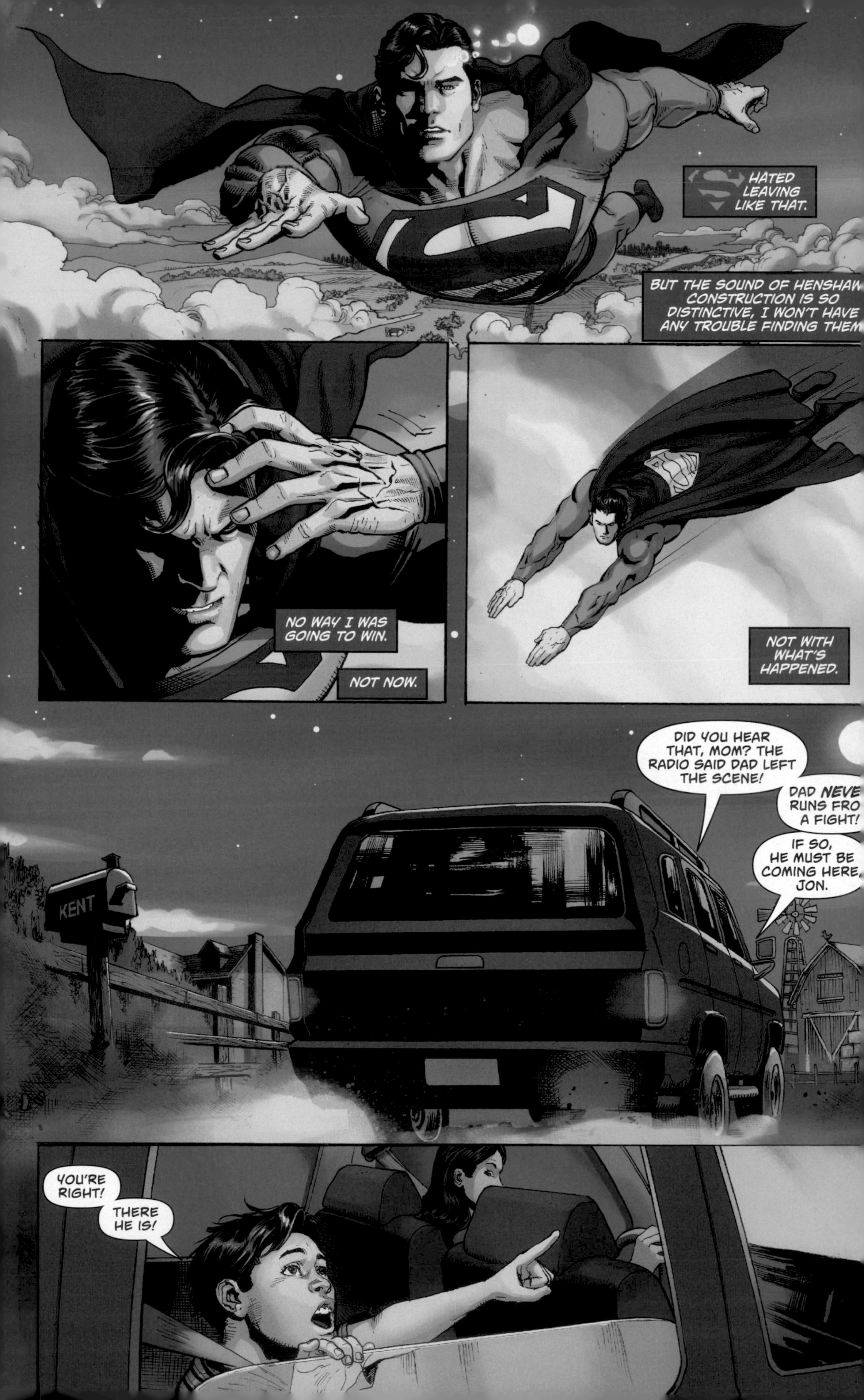

HATED LEAVING LIKE THAT.
BUT THE SOUND OF HENSHAW CONSTRUCTION IS SO DISTINCTIVE, I WON'T HAVE ANY TROUBLE FINDING THEM
NO WAY I WAS GOING TO WIN.
NOT NOW.
NOT WITH WHAT'S HAPPENED.
DID YOU HEAR THAT, MOM? THE RADIO SAID DAD LEFT THE SCENE!
DAD NEVE RUNS FRO A FIGHT!
IF SO, HE MUST BE COMING HERE, JON.
KENT
YOU'RE RIGHT!
THERE HE IS!

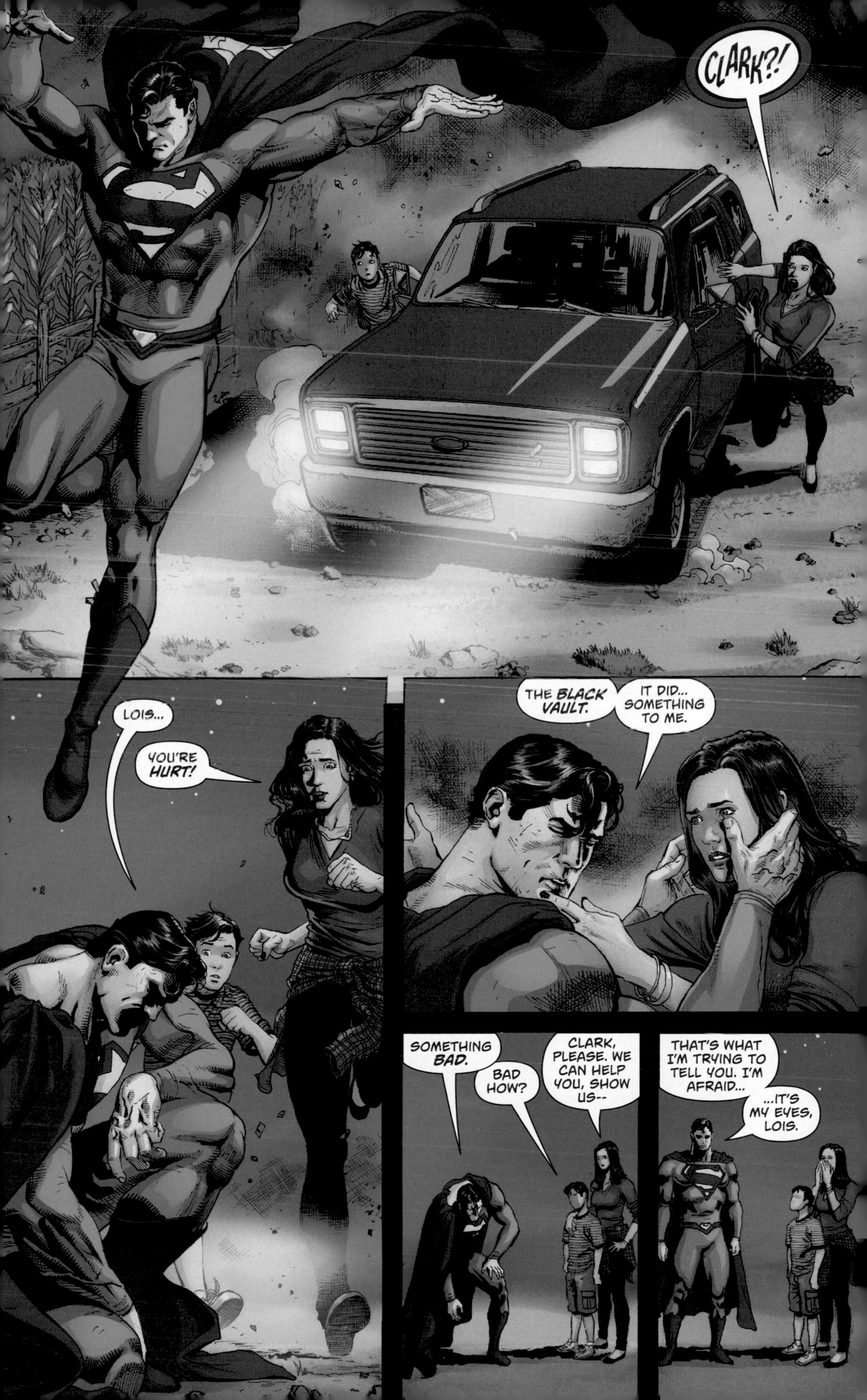
CLARK?!
LOIS...
YOU'RE HURT!
THE BLACK VAULT.
IT DID... SOMETHING TO ME.
SOMETHING BAD.
BAD HOW?
CLARK, PLEASE. WE CAN HELP YOU, SHOW US--
THAT'S WHAT I'M TRYING TO TELL YOU. I'M AFRAID...
...IT'S MY EYES, LOIS.

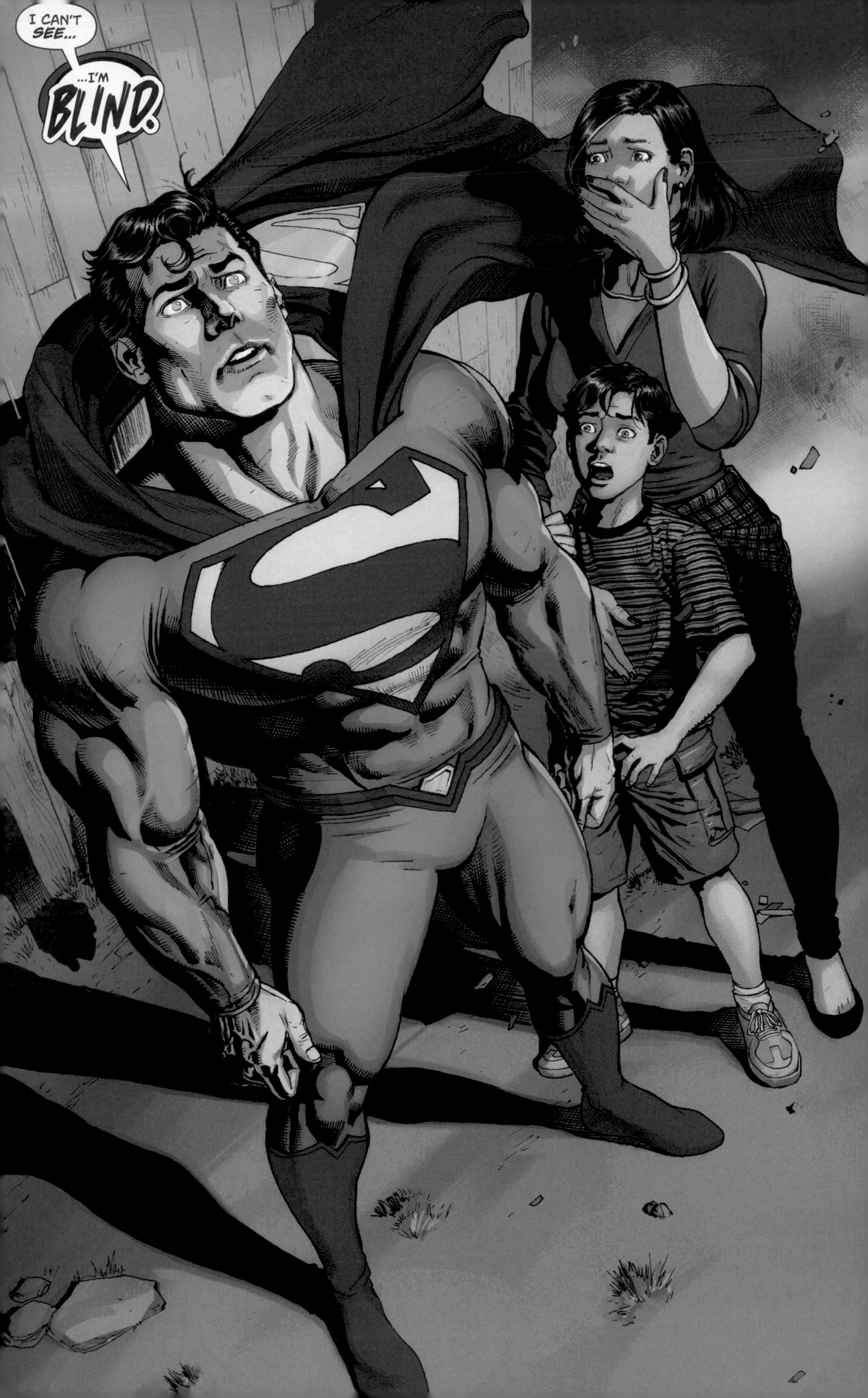
I CAN'T SEE...
...I'M BLIND.

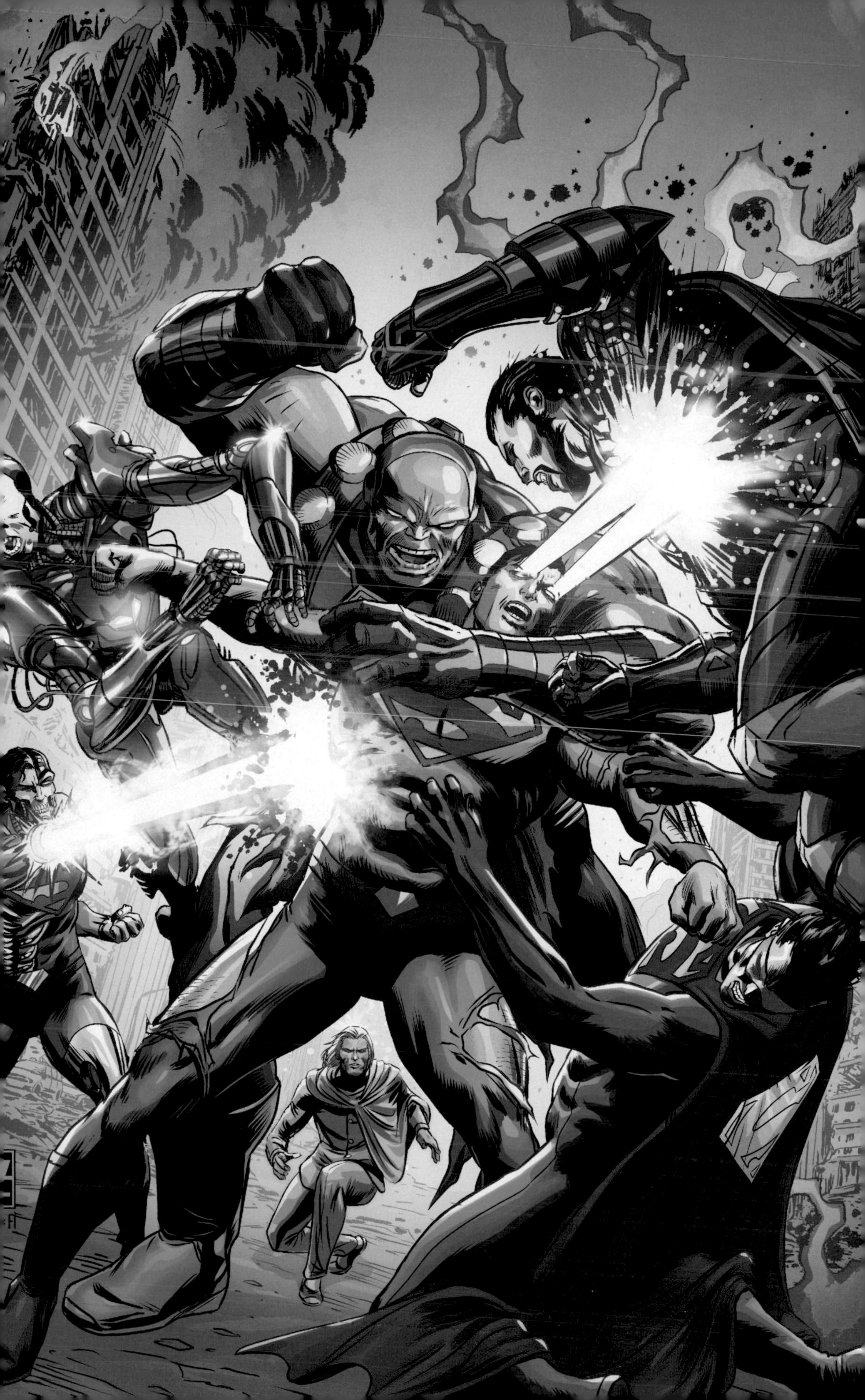

REVENGE PART 4

JACK HERBERT JOSE LUIS artists * JACK HERBERT RAY McCARTHY inkers
PATRICK ZIRCHER HI-FI cover artists

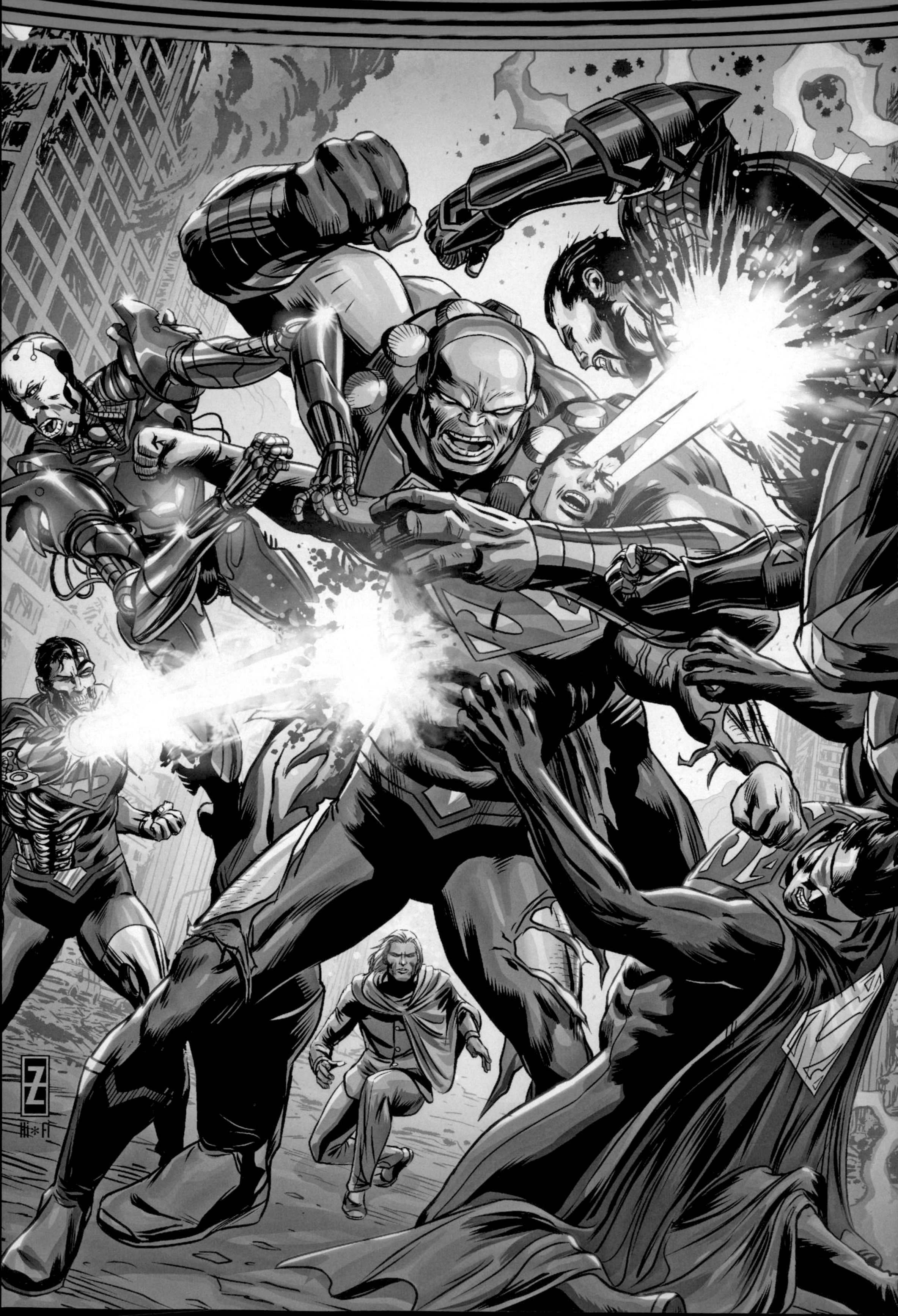

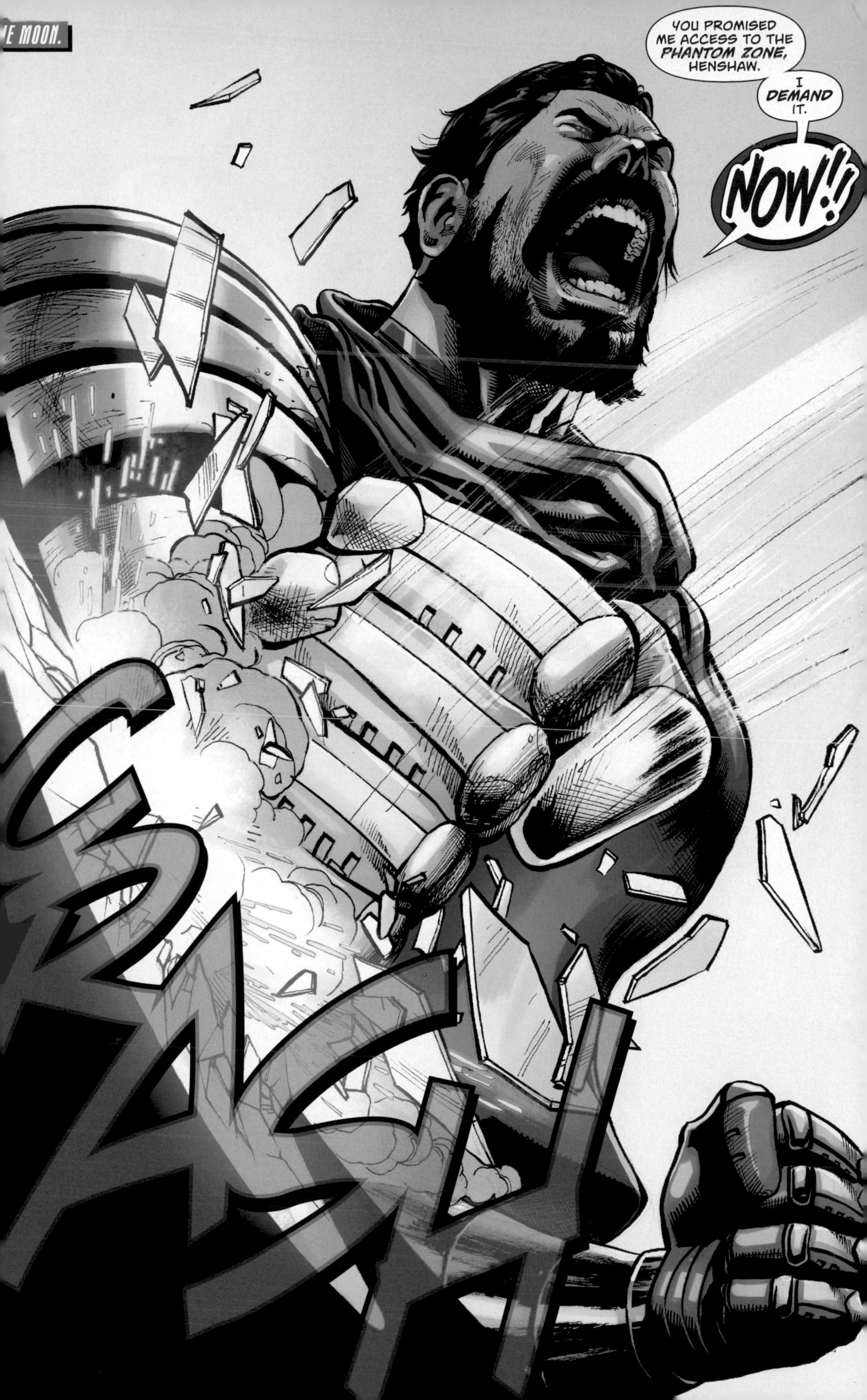
E MOON.
YOU PROMISED ME ACCESS TO THE PHANTOM ZONE, HENSHAW.
I DEMAND IT.
NOW!!

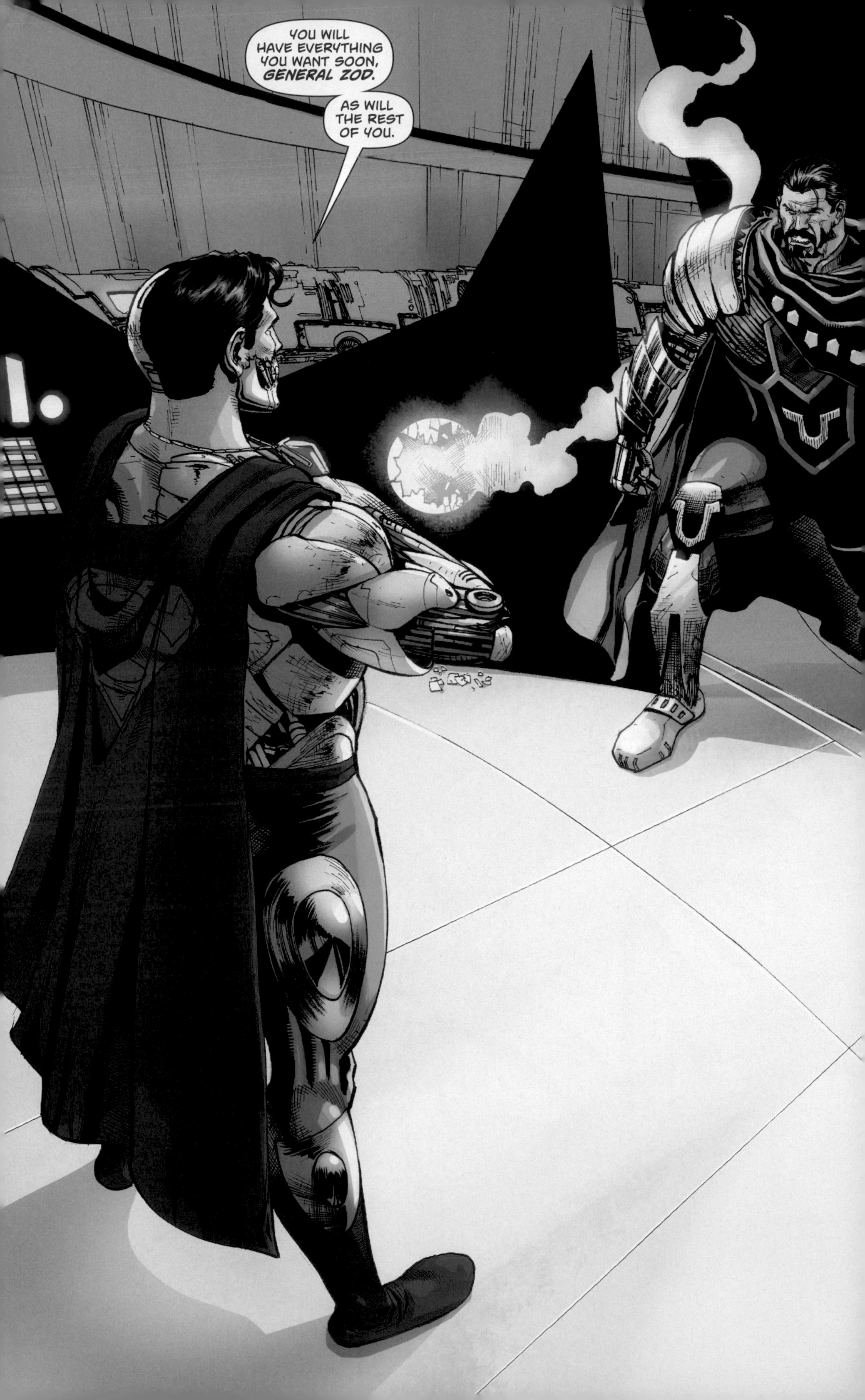
YOU WILL HAVE EVERYTHING YOU WANT SOON, GENERAL ZOD.
AS WILL THE REST OF YOU.

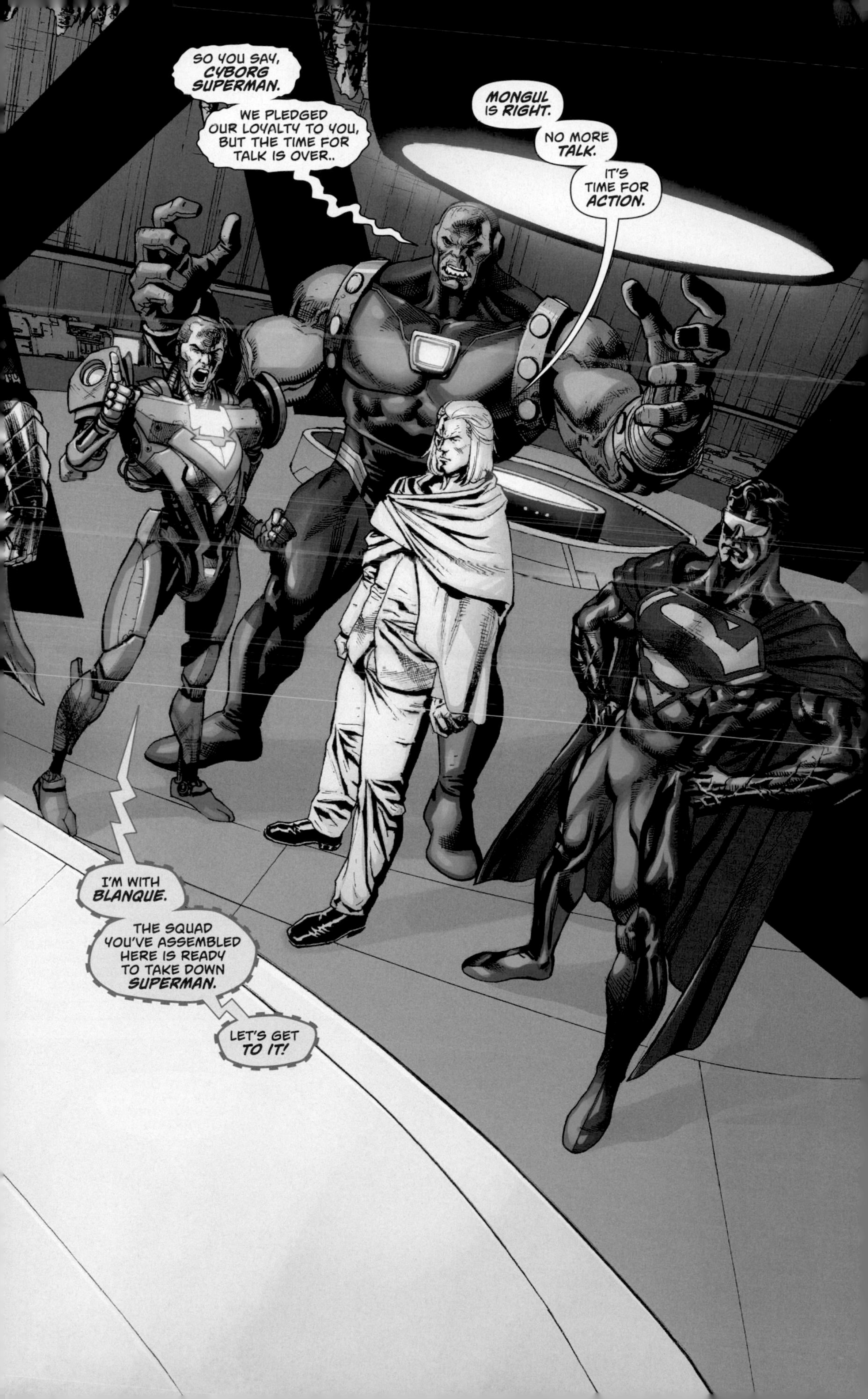
SO YOU SAY, CYBORG SUPERMAN.
WE PLEDGED OUR LOYALTY TO YOU, BUT THE TIME FOR TALK IS OVER..
MONGUL IS RIGHT.
NO MORE TALK.
IT'S TIME FOR ACTION.
I'M WITH BLANQUE.
THE SQUAD YOU'VE ASSEMBLED HERE IS READY TO TAKE DOWN SUPERMAN.
LET'S GET TO IT!

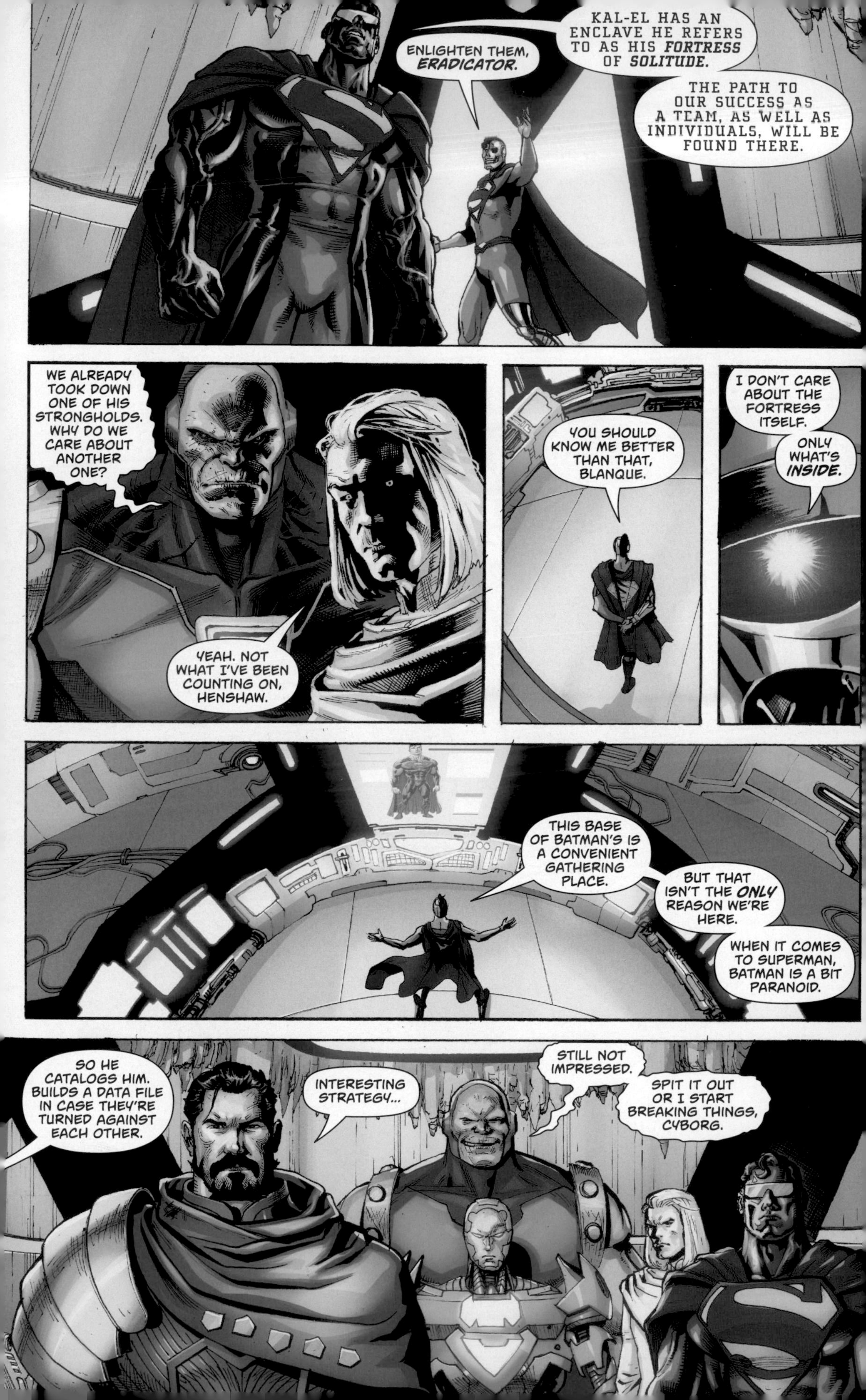
ENLIGHTEN THEM, ERADICATOR.
KAL-EL HAS AN ENCLAVE HE REFERS TO AS HIS FORTRESS OF SOLITUDE.
THE PATH TO OUR SUCCESS AS A TEAM, AS WELL AS INDIVIDUALS, WILL BE FOUND THERE.
WE ALREADY TOOK DOWN ONE OF HIS STRONGHOLDS. WHY DO WE CARE ABOUT ANOTHER ONE?
YEAH. NOT WHAT I'VE BEEN COUNTING ON, HENSHAW.
YOU SHOULD KNOW ME BETTER THAN THAT, BLANQUE.
I DON'T CARE ABOUT THE FORTRESS ITSELF.
ONLY WHAT'S INSIDE.
THIS BASE OF BATMAN'S IS A CONVENIENT GATHERING PLACE.
BUT THAT ISN'T THE ONLY REASON WE'RE HERE.
WHEN IT COMES TO SUPERMAN, BATMAN IS A BIT PARANOID.
SO HE CATALOGS HIM. BUILDS A DATA FILE IN CASE THEY'RE TURNED AGAINST EACH OTHER.
INTERESTING STRATEGY...
STILL NOT IMPRESSED.
SPIT IT OUT OR I START BREAKING THINGS, CYBORG.

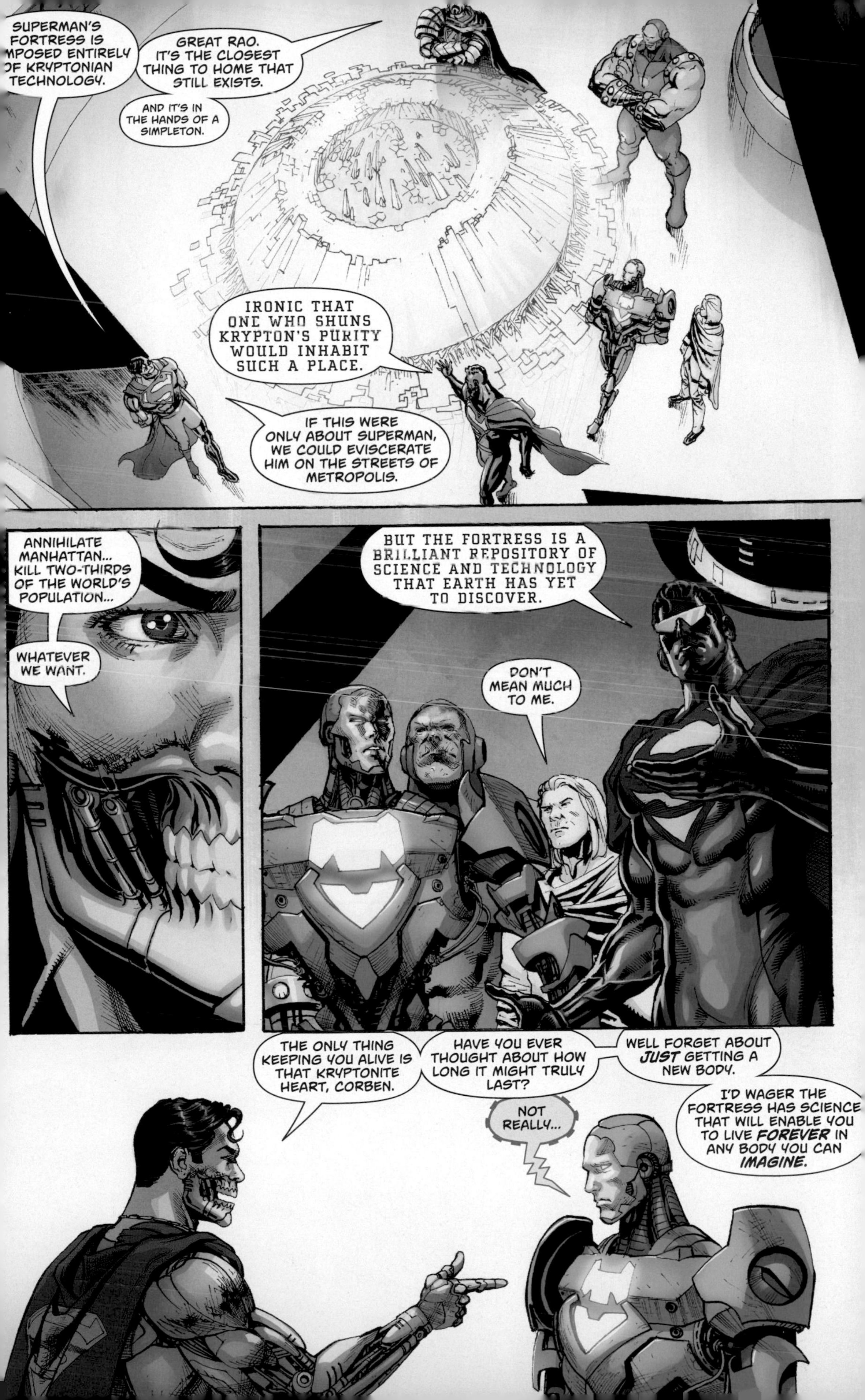
SUPERMAN'S FORTRESS IS COMPOSED ENTIRELY OF KRYPTONIAN TECHNOLOGY.
GREAT RAO. IT'S THE CLOSEST THING TO HOME THAT STILL EXISTS.
AND IT'S IN THE HANDS OF A SIMPLETON.
IRONIC THAT ONE WHO SHUNS KRYPTON'S PURITY WOULD INHABIT SUCH A PLACE.
IF THIS WERE ONLY ABOUT SUPERMAN, WE COULD EVISCERATE HIM ON THE STREETS OF METROPOLIS.
ANNIHILATE MANHATTAN... KILL TWO-THIRDS OF THE WORLD'S POPULATION...
WHATEVER WE WANT.
BUT THE FORTRESS IS A BRILLIANT REPOSITORY OF SCIENCE AND TECHNOLOGY THAT EARTH HAS YET TO DISCOVER.
DON'T MEAN MUCH TO ME.
THE ONLY THING KEEPING YOU ALIVE IS THAT KRYPTONITE HEART, CORBEN.
HAVE YOU EVER THOUGHT ABOUT HOW LONG IT MIGHT TRULY LAST?
NOT REALLY...
WELL FORGET ABOUT JUST GETTING A NEW BODY.
I'D WAGER THE FORTRESS HAS SCIENCE THAT WILL ENABLE YOU TO LIVE FOREVER IN ANY BODY YOU CAN IMAGINE.

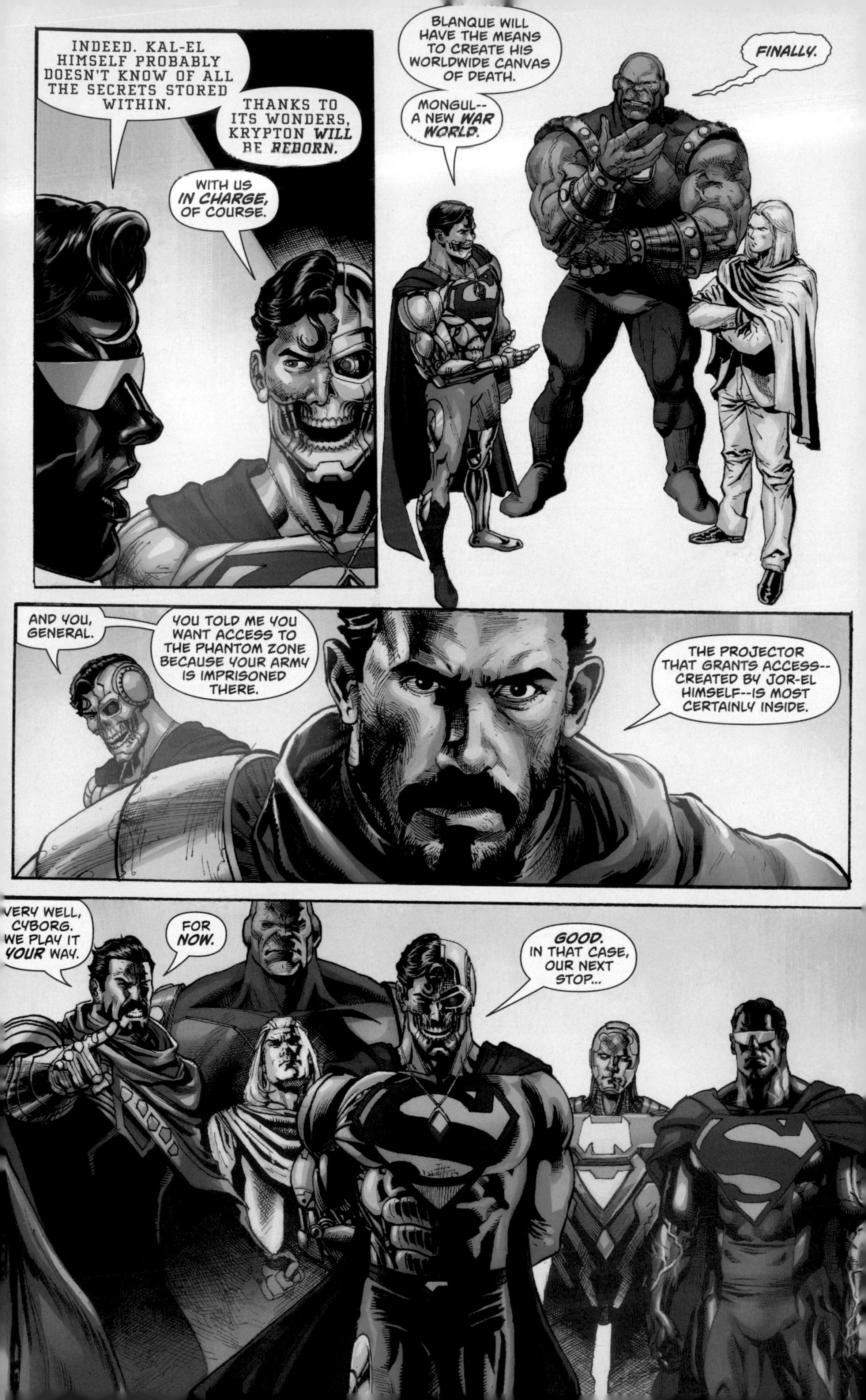
INDEED. KAL-EL HIMSELF PROBABLY DOESN'T KNOW OF ALL THE SECRETS STORED WITHIN.
THANKS TO ITS WONDERS, KRYPTON WILL BE REBORN.
WITH US IN CHARGE, OF COURSE.
BLANQUE WILL HAVE THE MEANS TO CREATE HIS WORLDWIDE CANVAS OF DEATH.
MONGUL-- A NEW WAR WORLD.
FINALLY.
AND YOU, GENERAL.
YOU TOLD ME YOU WANT ACCESS TO THE PHANTOM ZONE BECAUSE YOUR ARMY IS IMPRISONED THERE.
THE PROJECTOR THAT GRANTS ACCESS-- CREATED BY JOR-EL HIMSELF--IS MOST CERTAINLY INSIDE.
VERY WELL, CYBORG. WE PLAY IT YOUR WAY.
FOR NOW.
GOOD. IN THAT CASE, OUR NEXT STOP...

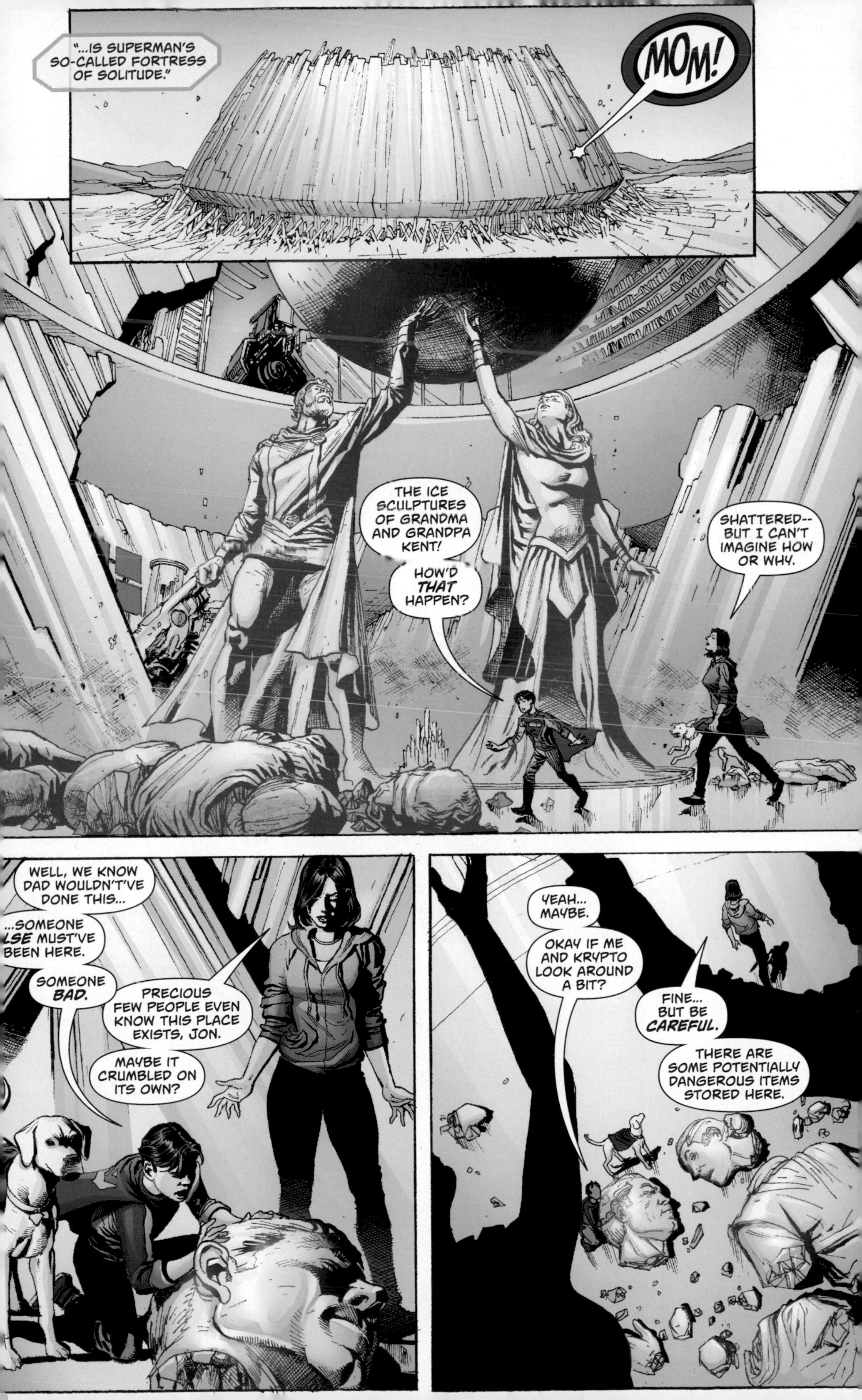
"...IS SUPERMAN'S SO-CALLED FORTRESS OF SOLITUDE."
MOM!
THE ICE SCULPTURES OF GRANDMA AND GRANDPA KENT!
HOW'D THAT HAPPEN?
SHATTERED-- BUT I CAN'T IMAGINE HOW OR WHY.
WELL, WE KNOW DAD WOULDN'T'VE DONE THIS...
...SOMEONE LSE MUST'VE BEEN HERE.
SOMEONE BAD.
PRECIOUS FEW PEOPLE EVEN KNOW THIS PLACE EXISTS, JON.
MAYBE IT CRUMBLED ON ITS OWN?
YEAH... MAYBE.
OKAY IF ME AND KRYPTO LOOK AROUND A BIT?
FINE... BUT BE CAREFUL.
THERE ARE SOME POTENTIALLY DANGEROUS ITEMS STORED HERE.

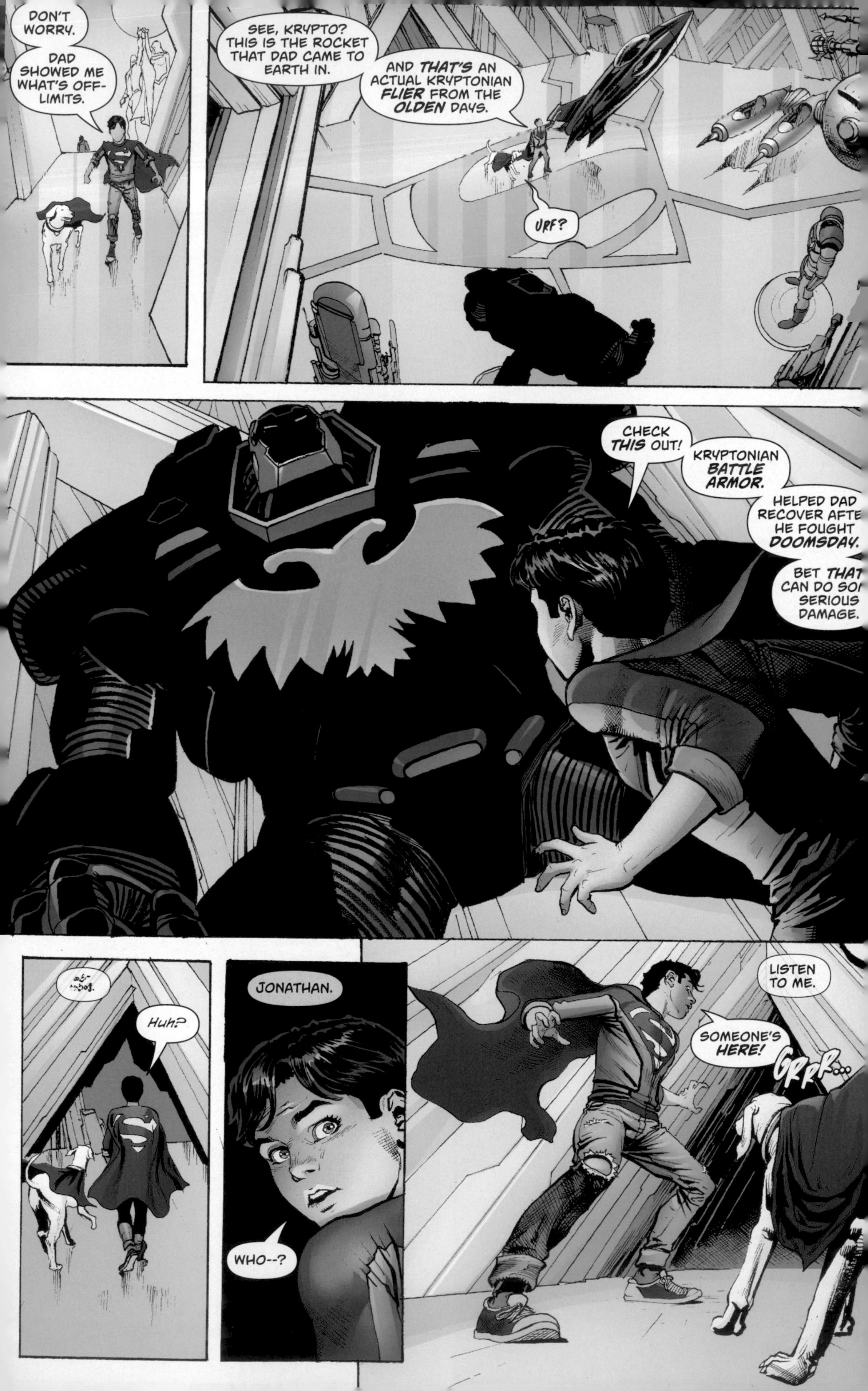

DON'T WORRY.
DAD SHOWED ME WHAT'S OFF-LIMITS.
SEE, KRYPTO? THIS IS THE ROCKET THAT DAD CAME TO EARTH IN.
AND THAT'S AN ACTUAL KRYPTONIAN FLIER FROM THE OLDEN DAYS.
URF?
CHECK THIS OUT!
KRYPTONIAN BATTLE ARMOR.
HELPED DAD RECOVER AFTE HE FOUGHT DOOMSDAY.
BET THAT CAN DO SO SERIOUS DAMAGE.
Huh?
JONATHAN.
WHO--?
LISTEN TO ME.
SOMEONE'S HERE!
GRRR...

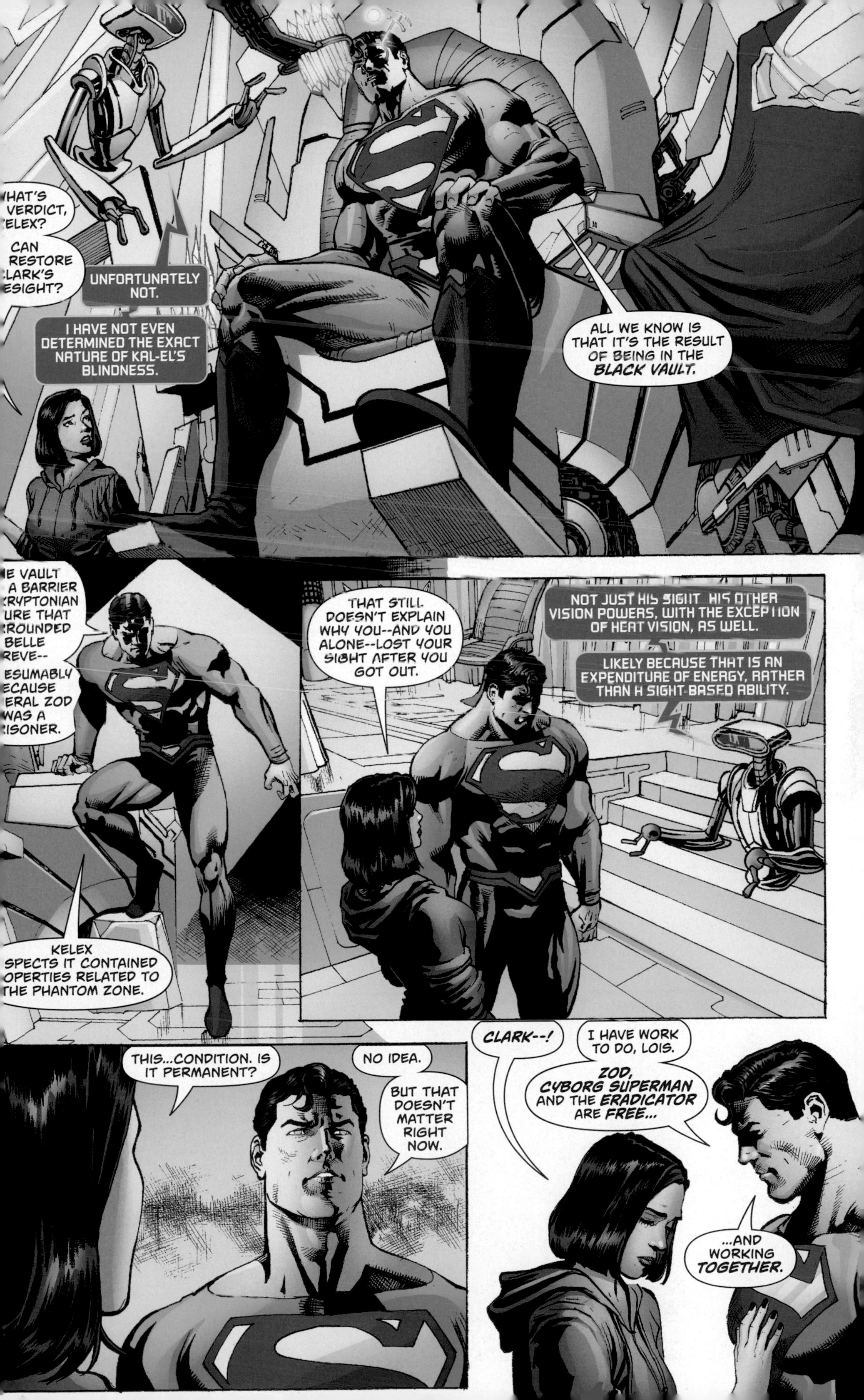
HAT'S VERDICT, ELEX?
CAN RESTORE LARK'S ESIGHT?
UNFORTUNATELY NOT.
I HAVE NOT EVEN DETERMINED THE EXACT NATURE OF KAL-EL'S BLINDNESS.
ALL WE KNOW IS THAT IT'S THE RESULT OF BEING IN THE BLACK VAULT.
E VAULT A BARRIER KRYPTONIAN URE THAT RROUNDED BELLE REVE--
ESUMABLY ECAUSE ERAL ZOD WAS A RISONER.
KELEX SPECTS IT CONTAINED OPERTIES RELATED TO THE PHANTOM ZONE.
THAT STILL DOESN'T EXPLAIN WHY YOU--AND YOU ALONE--LOST YOUR SIGHT AFTER YOU GOT OUT.
NOT JUST HIS SIGHT HIS OTHER VISION POWERS, WITH THE EXCEPTION OF HEAT VISION, AS WELL.
LIKELY BECAUSE THAT IS AN EXPENDITURE OF ENERGY, RATHER THAN A SIGHT-BASED ABILITY.
THIS...CONDITION. IS IT PERMANENT?
NO IDEA.
BUT THAT DOESN'T MATTER RIGHT NOW.
CLARK--!
I HAVE WORK TO DO, LOIS.
ZOD, CYBORG SUPERMAN AND THE ERADICATOR ARE FREE...
...AND WORKING TOGETHER.

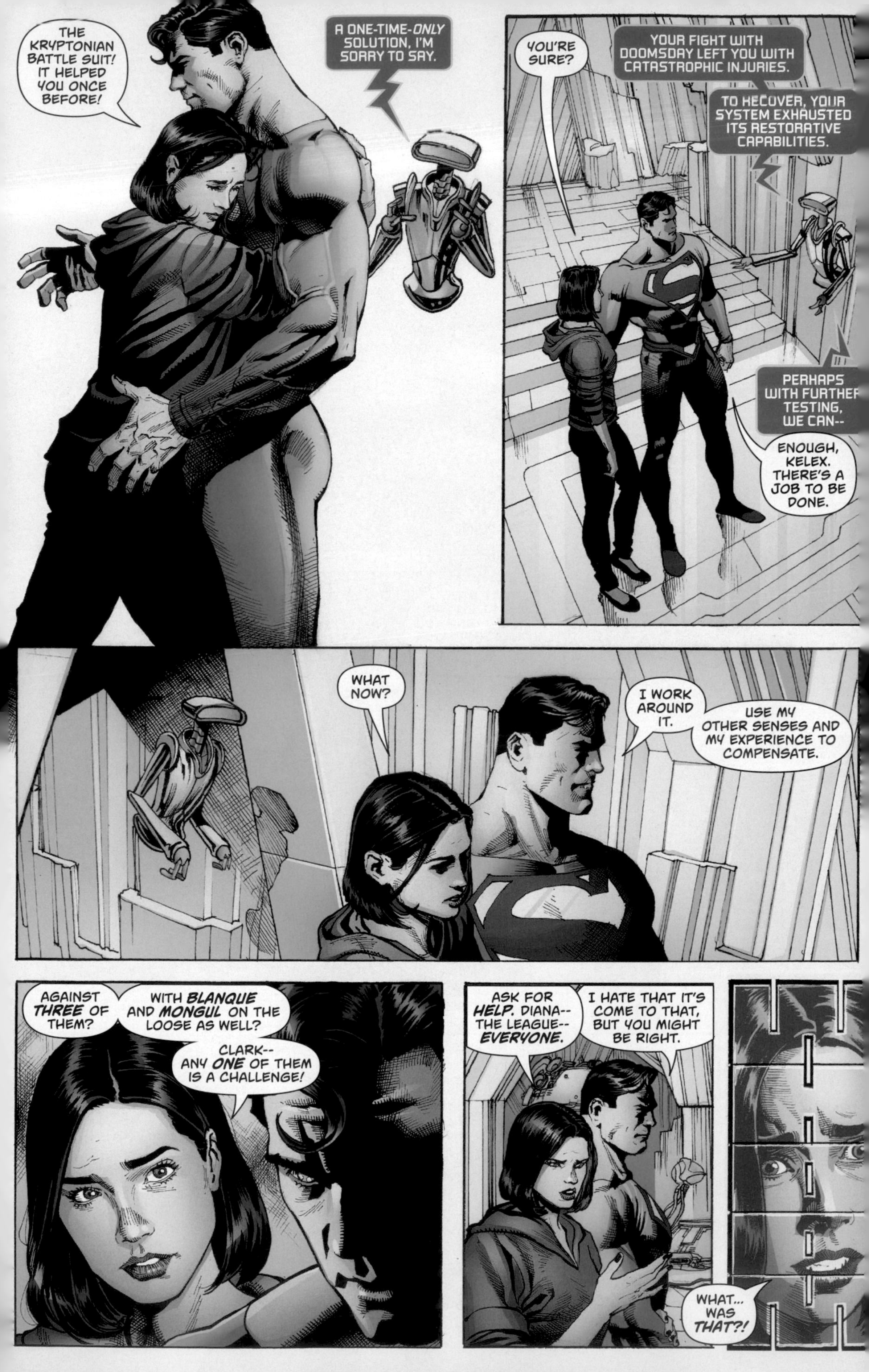
THE KRYPTONIAN BATTLE SUIT! IT HELPED YOU ONCE BEFORE!
A ONE-TIME-ONLY SOLUTION, I'M SORRY TO SAY.
YOU'RE SURE?
YOUR FIGHT WITH DOOMSDAY LEFT YOU WITH CATASTROPHIC INJURIES.
TO RECOVER, YOUR SYSTEM EXHAUSTED ITS RESTORATIVE CAPABILITIES.
PERHAPS WITH FURTHER TESTING, WE CAN--
ENOUGH, KELEX. THERE'S A JOB TO BE DONE.
WHAT NOW?
I WORK AROUND IT.
USE MY OTHER SENSES AND MY EXPERIENCE TO COMPENSATE.
AGAINST THREE OF THEM?
WITH BLANQUE AND MONGUL ON THE LOOSE AS WELL?
CLARK-- ANY ONE OF THEM IS A CHALLENGE!
ASK FOR HELP. DIANA-- THE LEAGUE-- EVERYONE.
I HATE THAT IT'S COME TO THAT, BUT YOU MIGHT BE RIGHT.
WHAT... WAS THAT?!

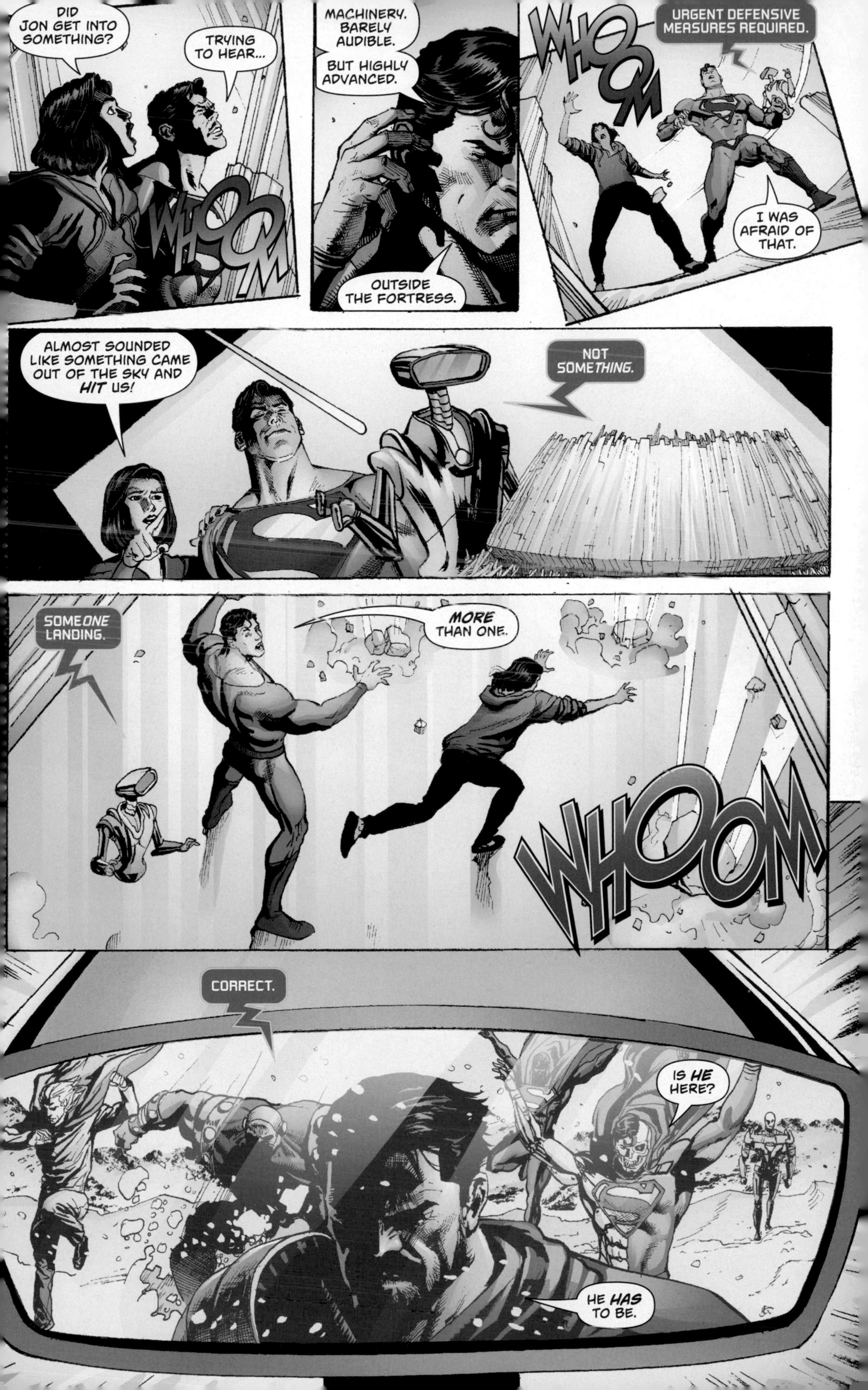
DID JON GET INTO SOMETHING?
TRYING TO HEAR...
WHOOM
MACHINERY. BARELY AUDIBLE.
BUT HIGHLY ADVANCED.
OUTSIDE THE FORTRESS.
WHOOM
URGENT DEFENSIVE MEASURES REQUIRED.
I WAS AFRAID OF THAT.
ALMOST SOUNDED LIKE SOMETHING CAME OUT OF THE SKY AND HIT US!
NOT SOMETHING.
SOMEONE LANDING.
MORE THAN ONE.
WHOOM
CORRECT.
IS HE HERE?
HE HAS TO BE.

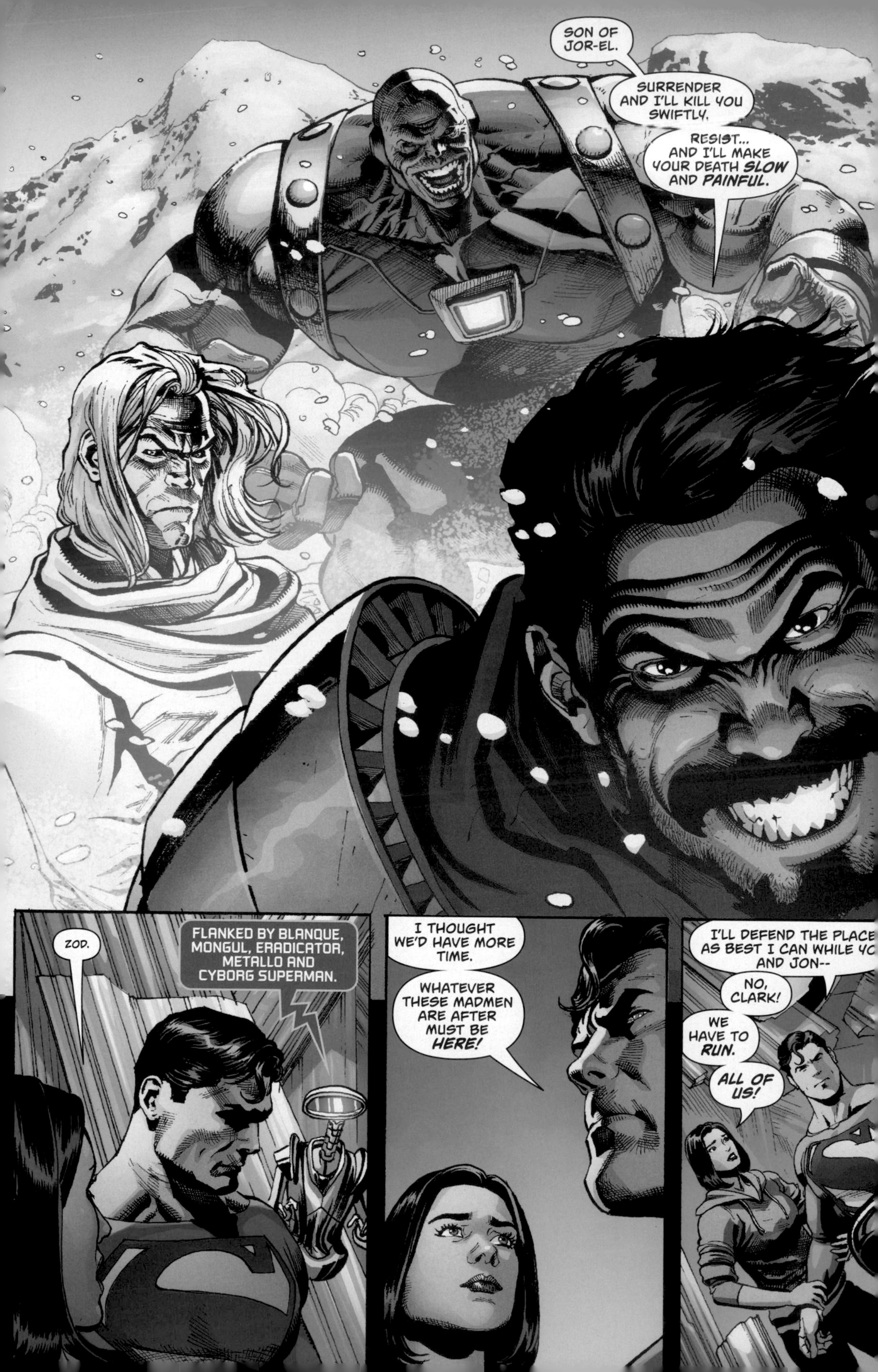
SON OF JOR-EL.
SURRENDER AND I'LL KILL YOU SWIFTLY.
RESIST... AND I'LL MAKE YOUR DEATH SLOW AND PAINFUL.
ZOD.
FLANKED BY BLANQUE, MONGUL, ERADICATOR, METALLO AND CYBORG SUPERMAN.
I THOUGHT WE'D HAVE MORE TIME.
WHATEVER THESE MADMEN ARE AFTER MUST BE HERE!
I'LL DEFEND THE PLACE AS BEST I CAN WHILE YO AND JON--
NO, CLARK!
WE HAVE TO RUN.
ALL OF US!

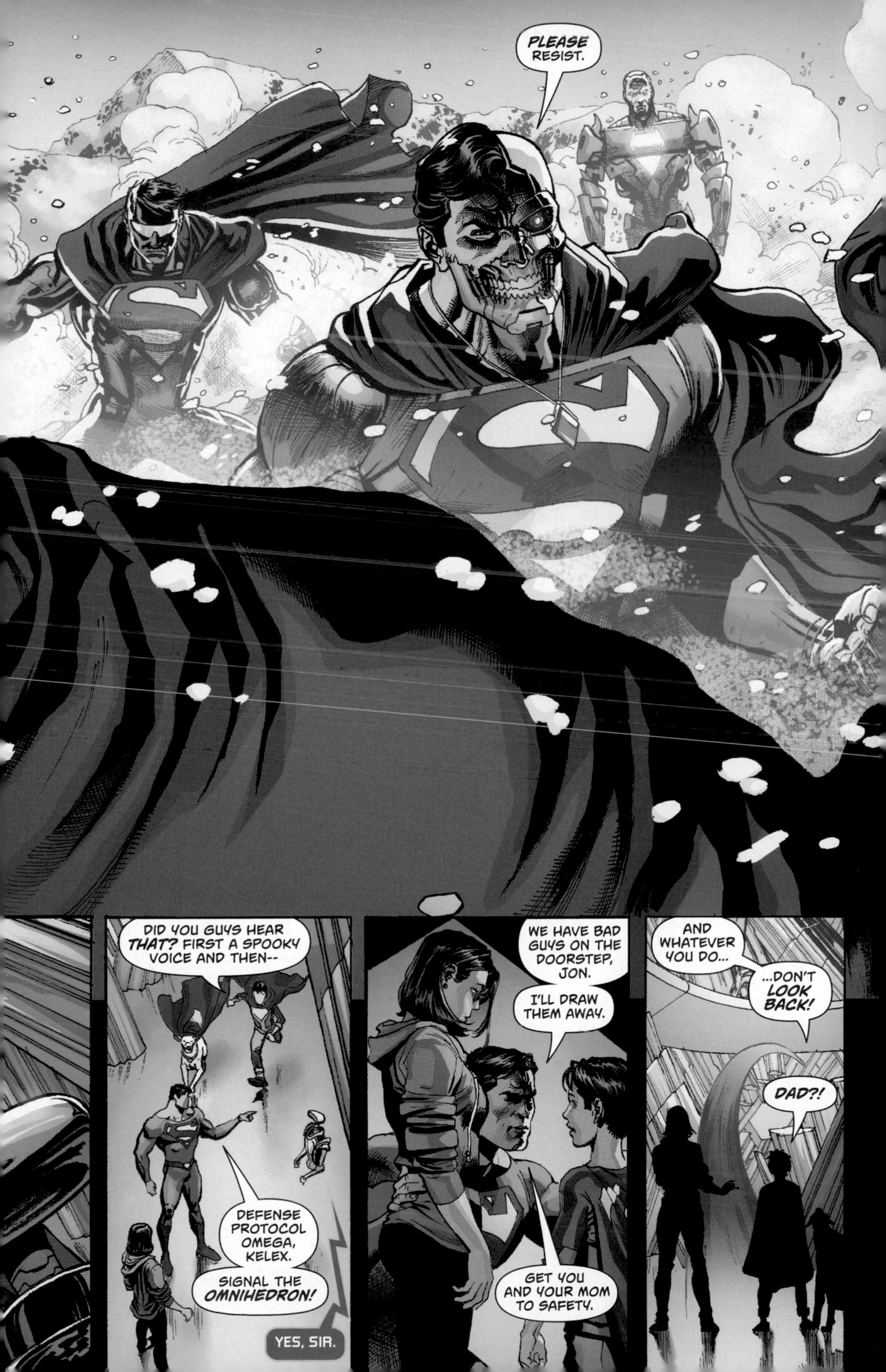
PLEASE RESIST.
DID YOU GUYS HEAR THAT? FIRST A SPOOKY VOICE AND THEN--
DEFENSE PROTOCOL OMEGA, KELEX.
SIGNAL THE OMNIHEDRON!
YES, SIR.
WE HAVE BAD GUYS ON THE DOORSTEP, JON.
I'LL DRAW THEM AWAY.
GET YOU AND YOUR MOM TO SAFETY.
AND WHATEVER YOU DO...
...DON'T LOOK BACK!
DAD?!

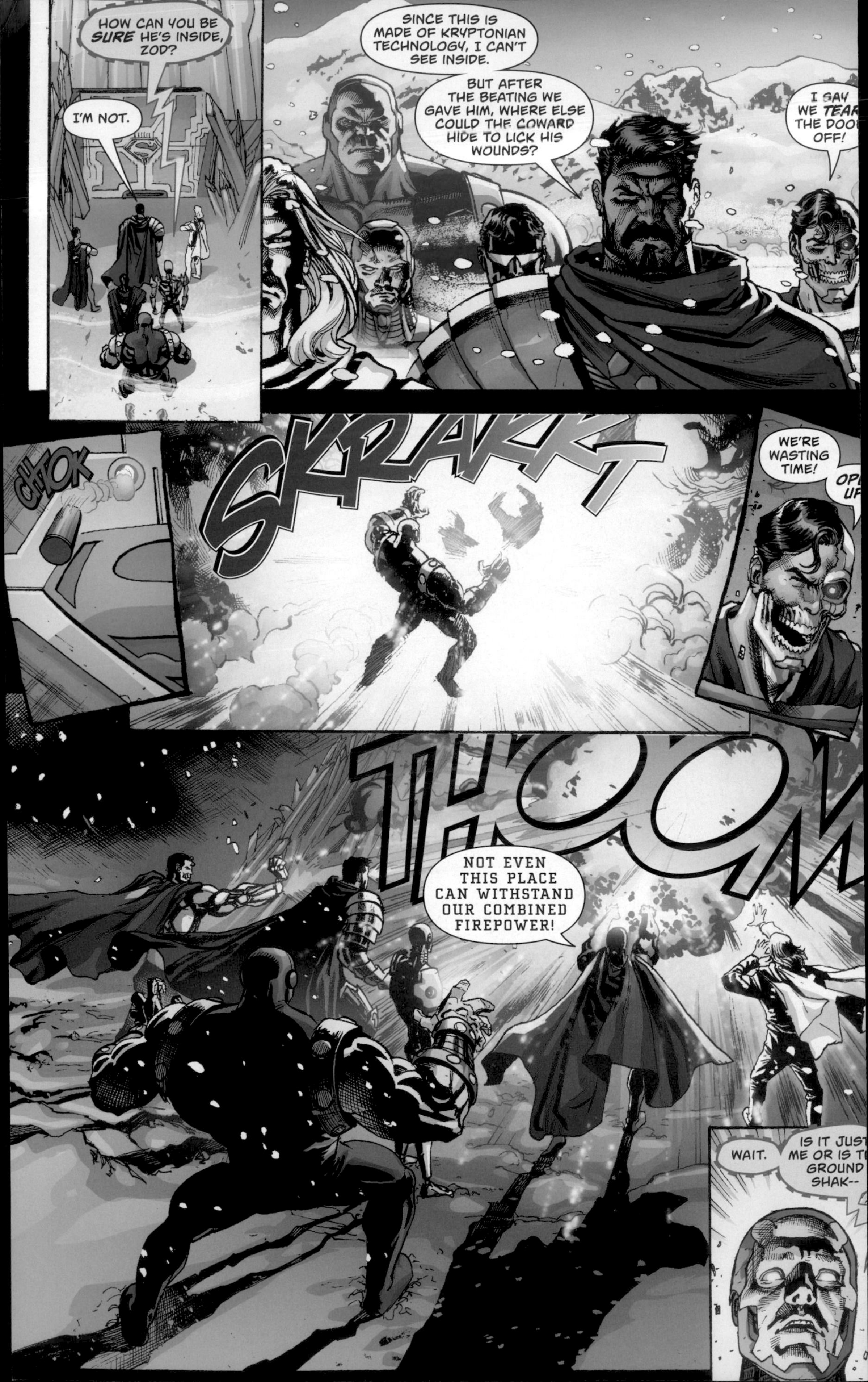
HOW CAN YOU BE SURE HE'S INSIDE, ZOD?
I'M NOT.
SINCE THIS IS MADE OF KRYPTONIAN TECHNOLOGY, I CAN'T SEE INSIDE.
BUT AFTER THE BEATING WE GAVE HIM, WHERE ELSE COULD THE COWARD HIDE TO LICK HIS WOUNDS?
I SAY WE TEAR THE DOO OFF!
CHTOK
SKRAKKT
WE'RE WASTING TIME!
OP UP
THOOM
NOT EVEN THIS PLACE CAN WITHSTAND OUR COMBINED FIREPOWER!
WAIT.
IS IT JUST ME OR IS T GROUND SHAK--

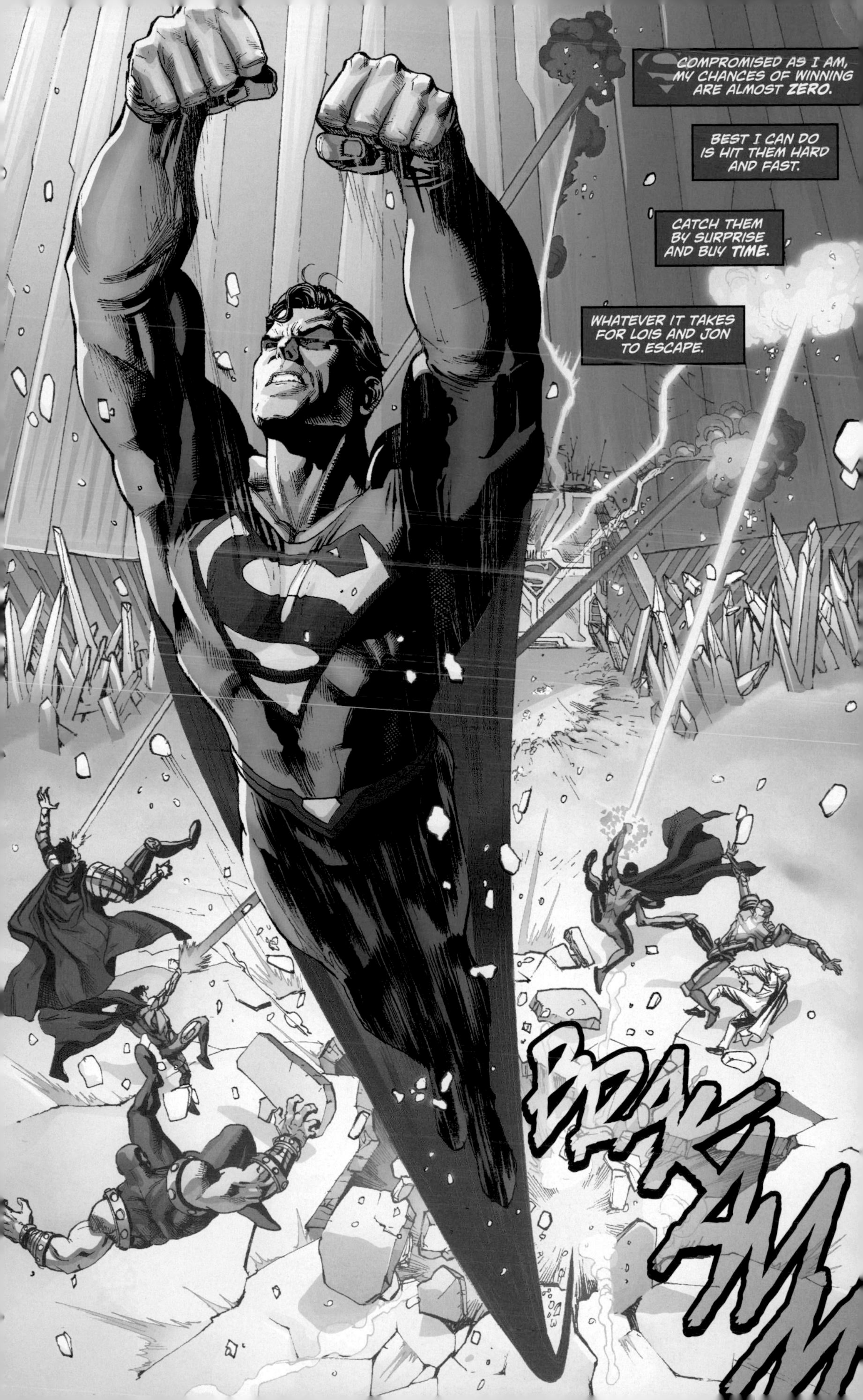

COMPROMISED AS I AM, MY CHANCES OF WINNING ARE ALMOST ZERO.
BEST I CAN DO IS HIT THEM HARD AND FAST.
CATCH THEM BY SURPRISE AND BUY TIME.
WHATEVER IT TAKES FOR LOIS AND JON TO ESCAPE.

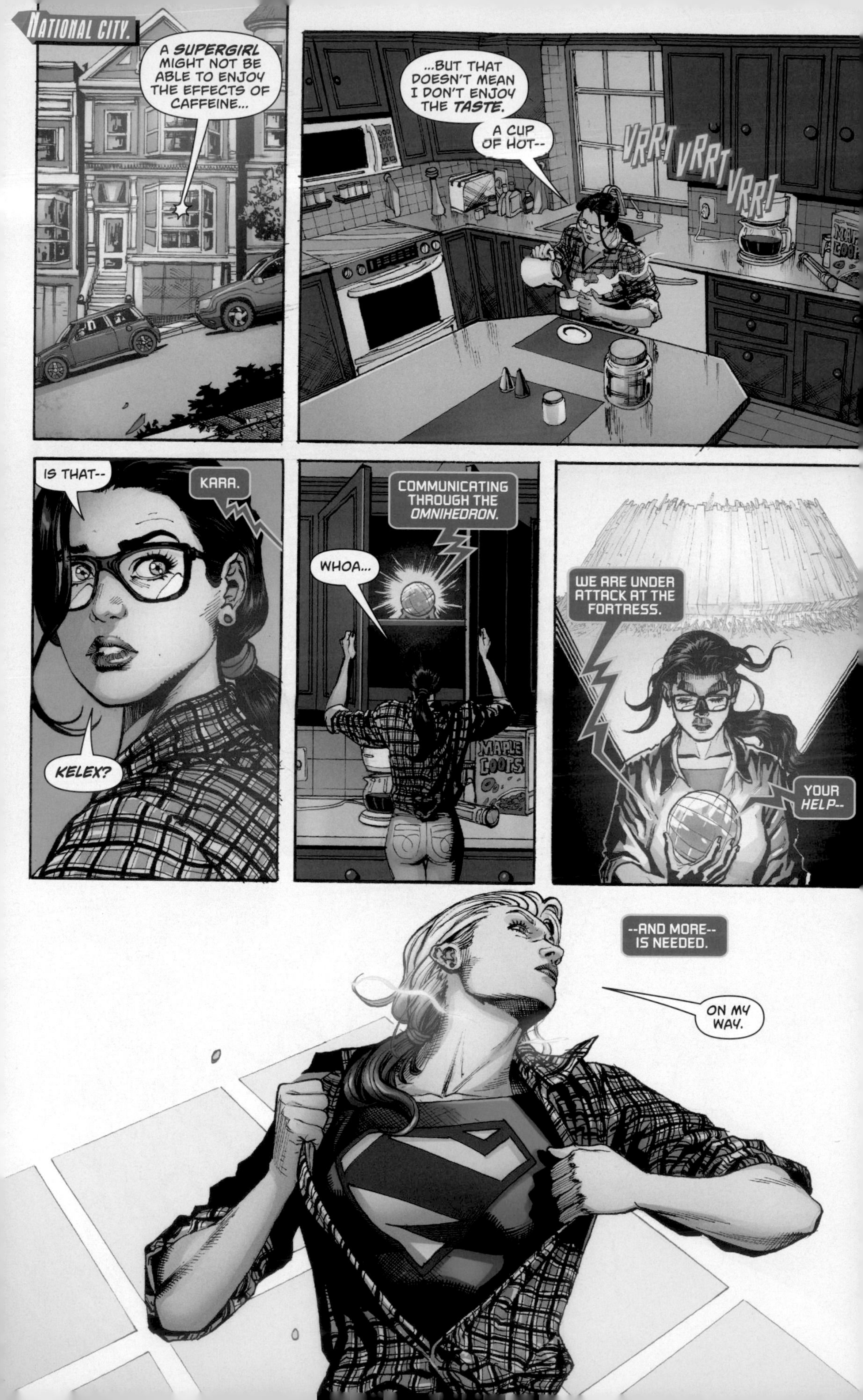
NATIONAL CITY.
A SUPERGIRL MIGHT NOT BE ABLE TO ENJOY THE EFFECTS OF CAFFEINE...
...BUT THAT DOESN'T MEAN I DON'T ENJOY THE TASTE.
A CUP OF HOT--
VRRT VRRT VRRT
IS THAT--
KARA.
KELEX?
COMMUNICATING THROUGH THE OMNIHEDRON.
WHOA...
MAPLE COOPS
WE ARE UNDER ATTACK AT THE FORTRESS.
YOUR HELP--
--AND MORE--IS NEEDED.
ON MY WAY.

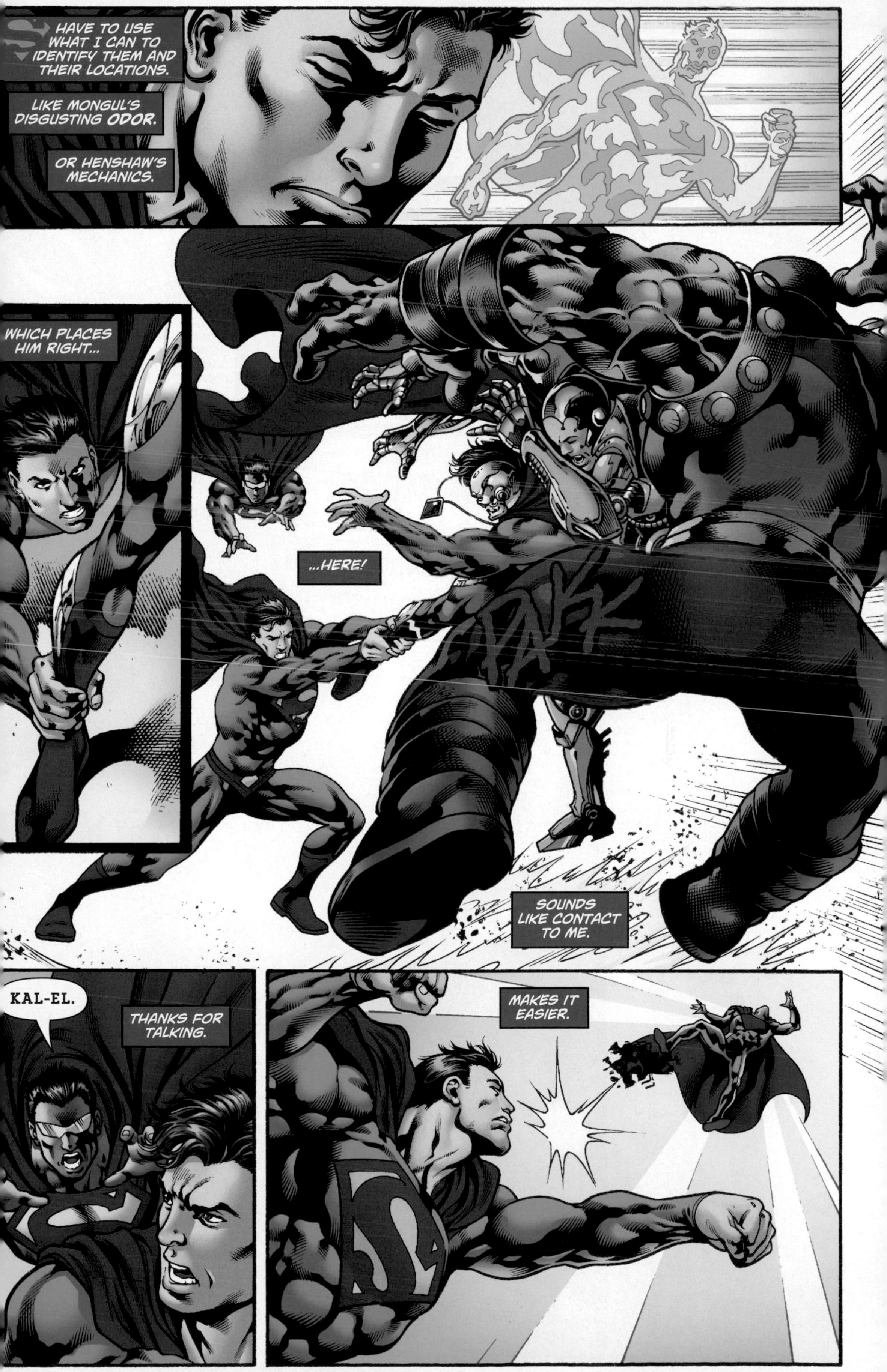

HAVE TO USE WHAT I CAN TO IDENTIFY THEM AND THEIR LOCATIONS.
LIKE MONGUL'S DISGUSTING ODOR.
OR HENSHAW'S MECHANICS.
WHICH PLACES HIM RIGHT...
...HERE!
SOUNDS LIKE CONTACT TO ME.
KAL-EL.
THANKS FOR TALKING.
MAKES IT EASIER.

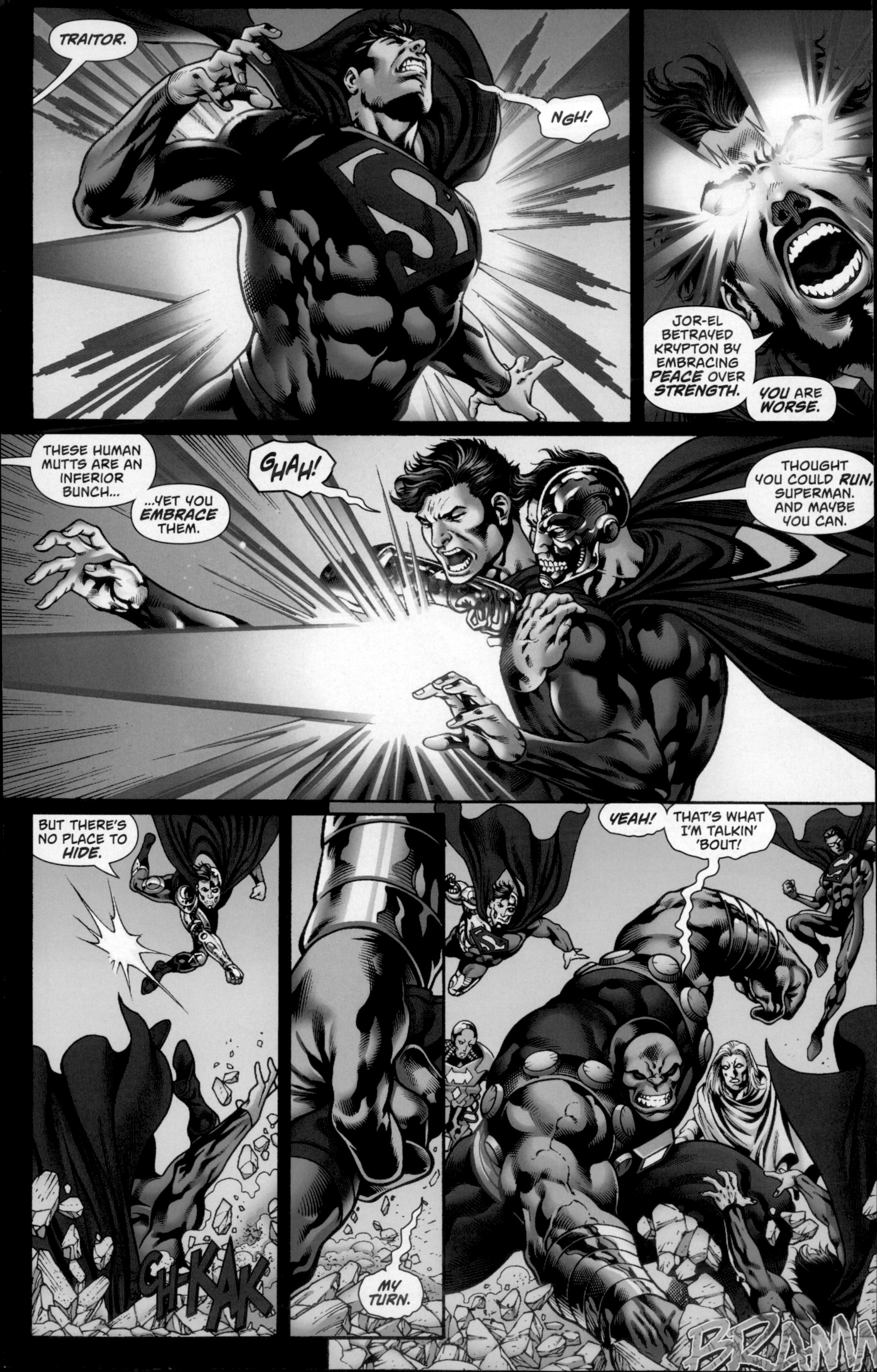
TRAITOR.
NGH!
JOR-EL BETRAYED KRYPTON BY EMBRACING PEACE OVER STRENGTH.
YOU ARE WORSE.
THESE HUMAN MUTTS ARE AN INFERIOR BUNCH...
...YET YOU EMBRACE THEM.
GHAH!
THOUGHT YOU COULD RUN, SUPERMAN. AND MAYBE YOU CAN.
BUT THERE'S NO PLACE TO HIDE.
CH-KAK
MY TURN.
YEAH!
THAT'S WHAT I'M TALKIN' 'BOUT!

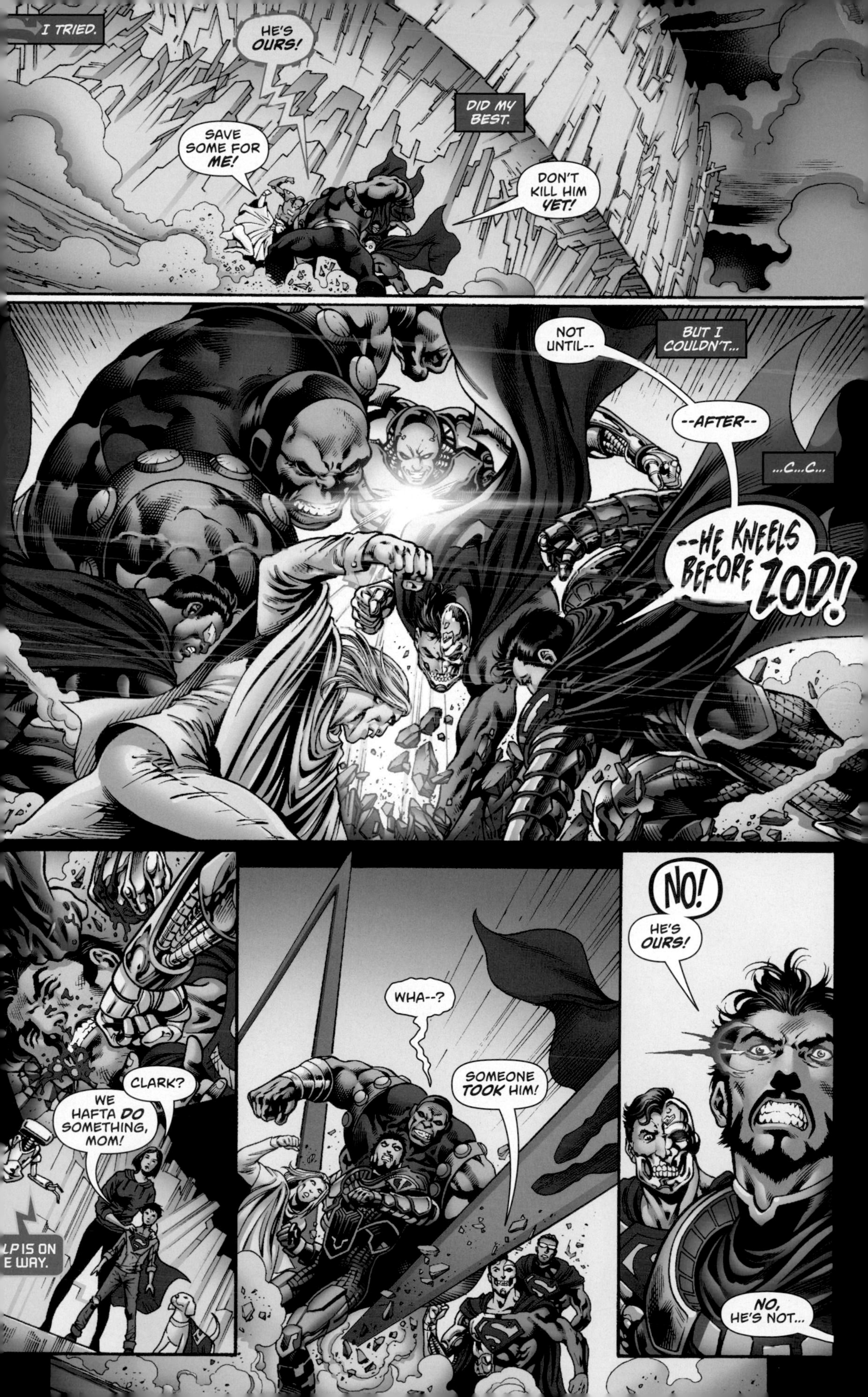
I TRIED.
HE'S OURS!
DID MY BEST.
SAVE SOME FOR ME!
DON'T KILL HIM YET!
NOT UNTIL--
BUT I COULDN'T...
--AFTER--
...C...C...
--HE KNEELS BEFORE ZOD!
CLARK?
WE HAFTA DO SOMETHING, MOM!
LP IS ON
E WAY.
WHA--?
SOMEONE TOOK HIM!
NO!
HE'S OURS!
NO, HE'S NOT...

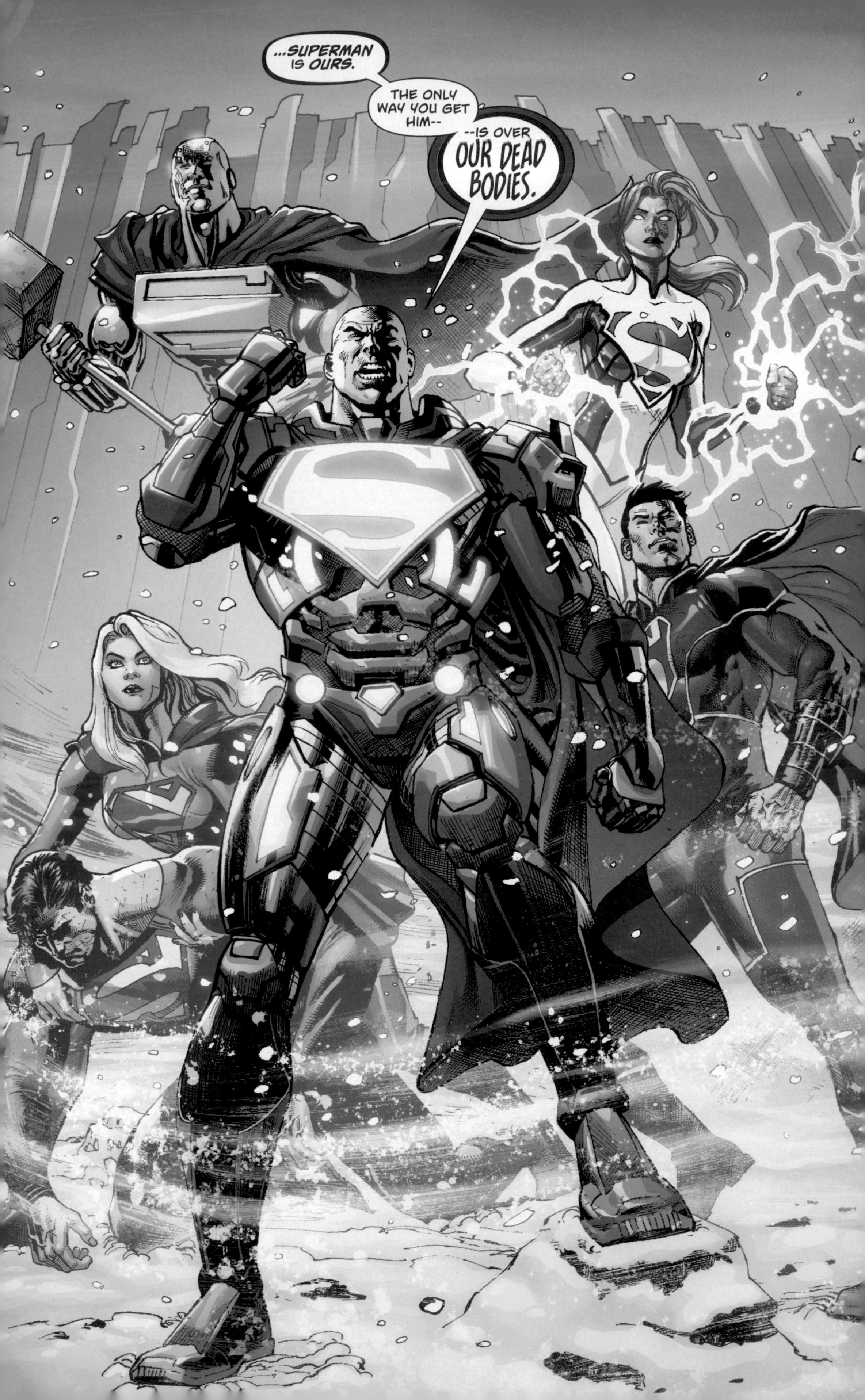
...SUPERMAN IS OURS.
THE ONLY WAY YOU GET HIM--
--IS OVER OUR DEAD BODIES.

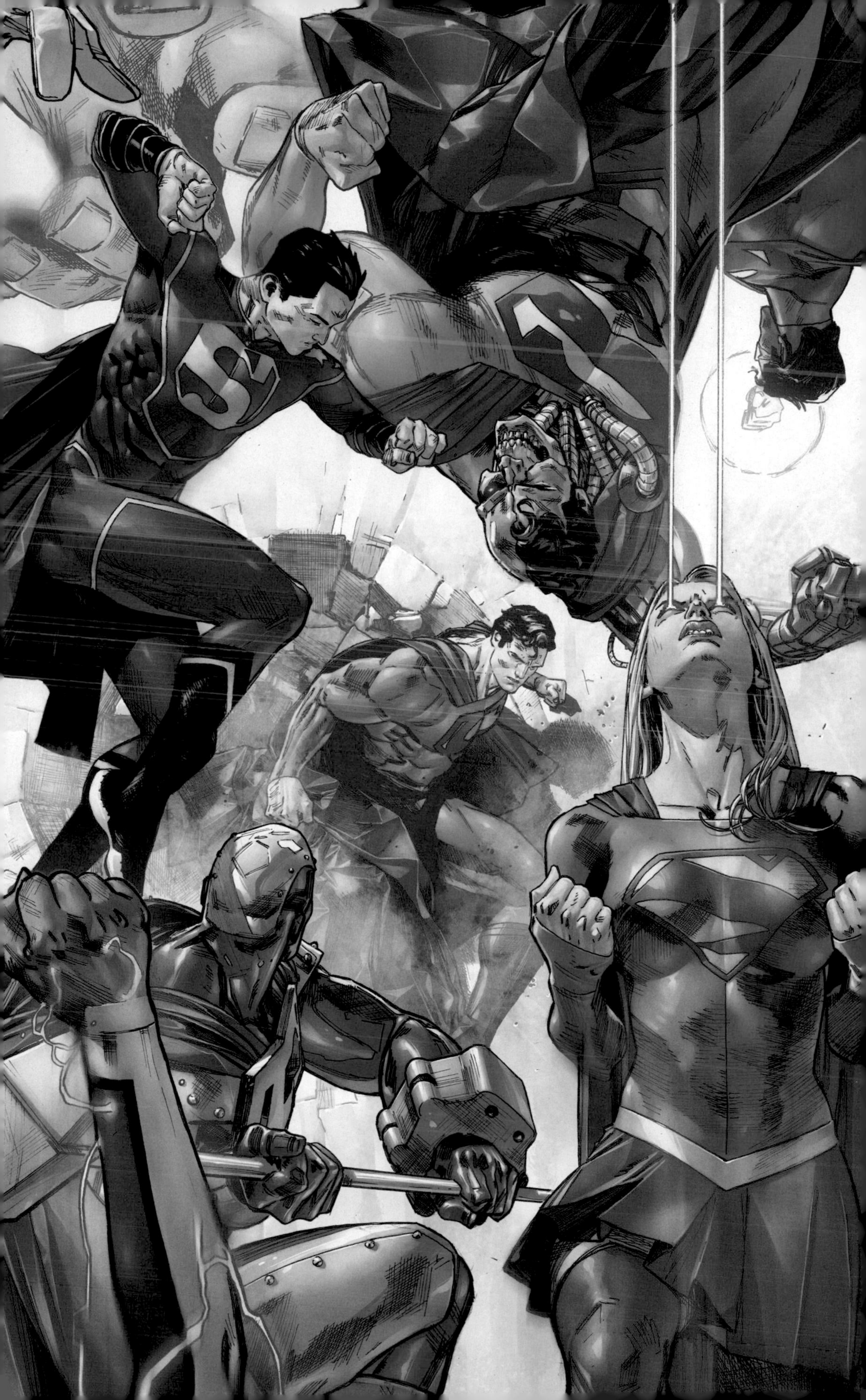

REVENGE PART 5

VIKTOR BOGDANOVIC penciller * VIKTOR BOGDANOVIC JONATHAN GLAPION inkers * MIKE SPICER colorist
CLAY MANN TOMEU MOREY cover artists

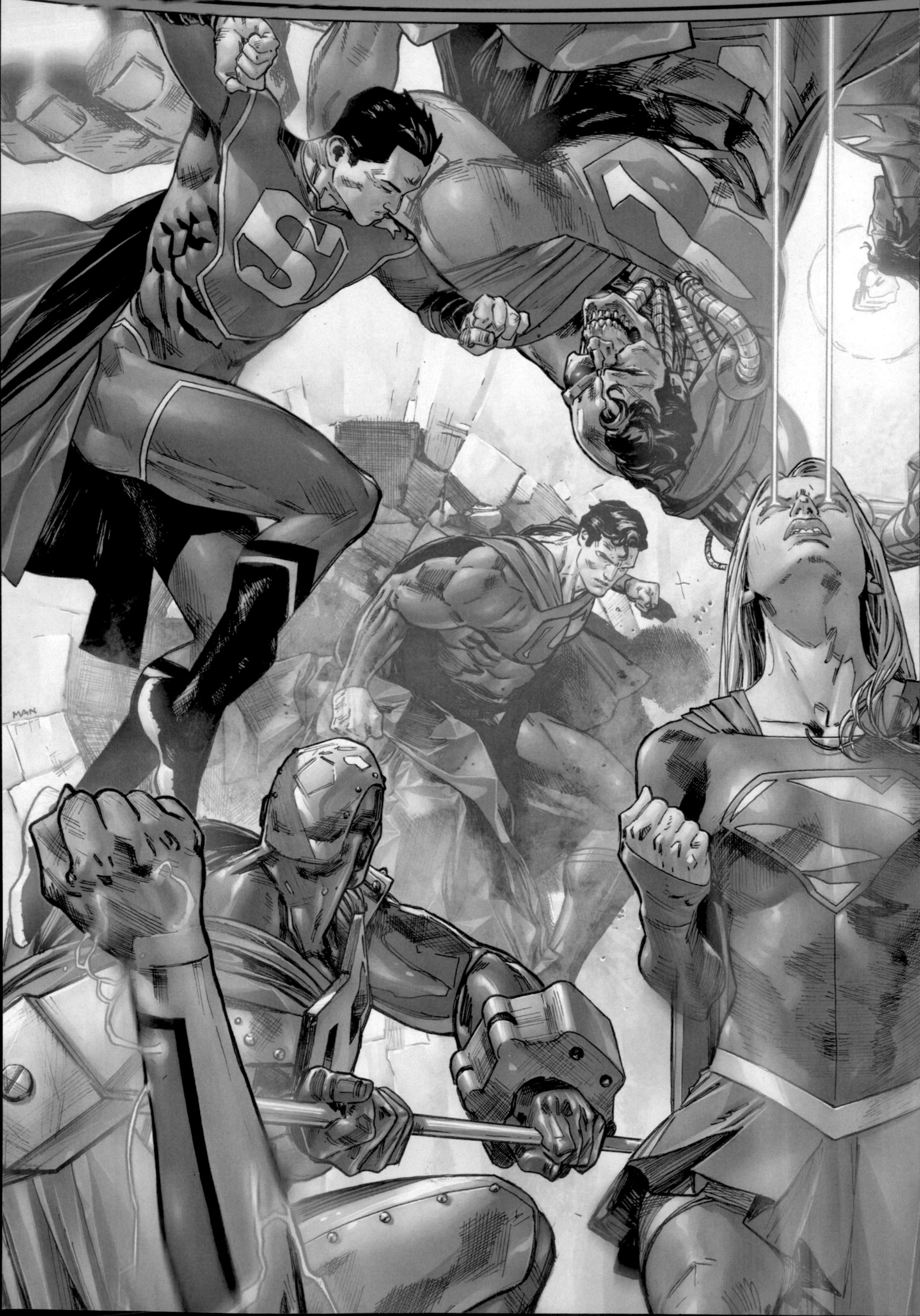

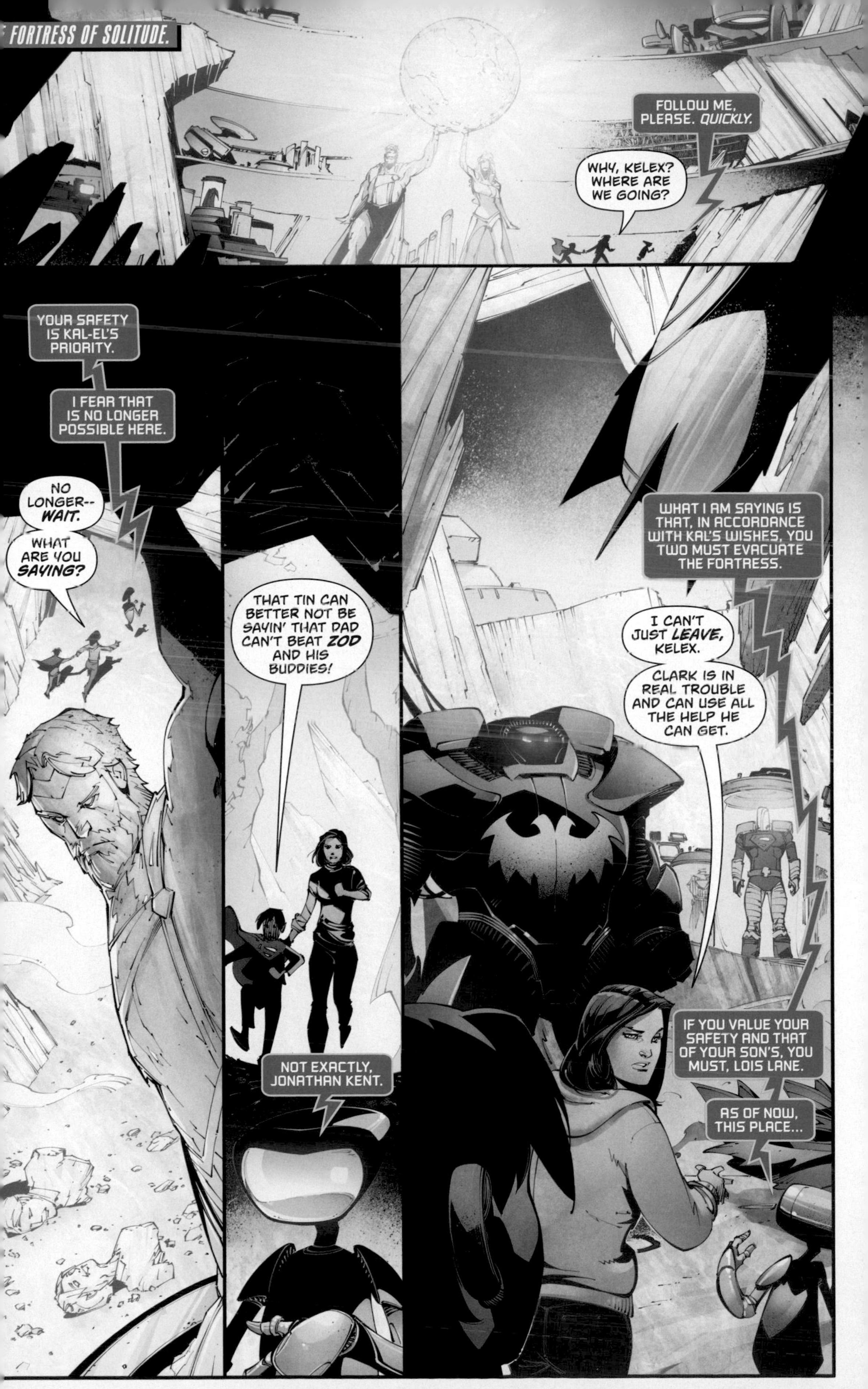

FORTRESS OF SOLITUDE.
FOLLOW ME, PLEASE. QUICKLY.
WHY, KELEX? WHERE ARE WE GOING?
YOUR SAFETY IS KAL-EL'S PRIORITY.
I FEAR THAT IS NO LONGER POSSIBLE HERE.
NO LONGER-- WAIT.
WHAT ARE YOU SAYING?
THAT TIN CAN BETTER NOT BE SAYIN' THAT DAD CAN'T BEAT ZOD AND HIS BUDDIES!
NOT EXACTLY, JONATHAN KENT.
WHAT I AM SAYING IS THAT, IN ACCORDANCE WITH KAL'S WISHES, YOU TWO MUST EVACUATE THE FORTRESS.
I CAN'T JUST LEAVE, KELEX.
CLARK IS IN REAL TROUBLE AND CAN USE ALL THE HELP HE CAN GET.
IF YOU VALUE YOUR SAFETY AND THAT OF YOUR SON'S, YOU MUST, LOIS LANE.
AS OF NOW, THIS PLACE...

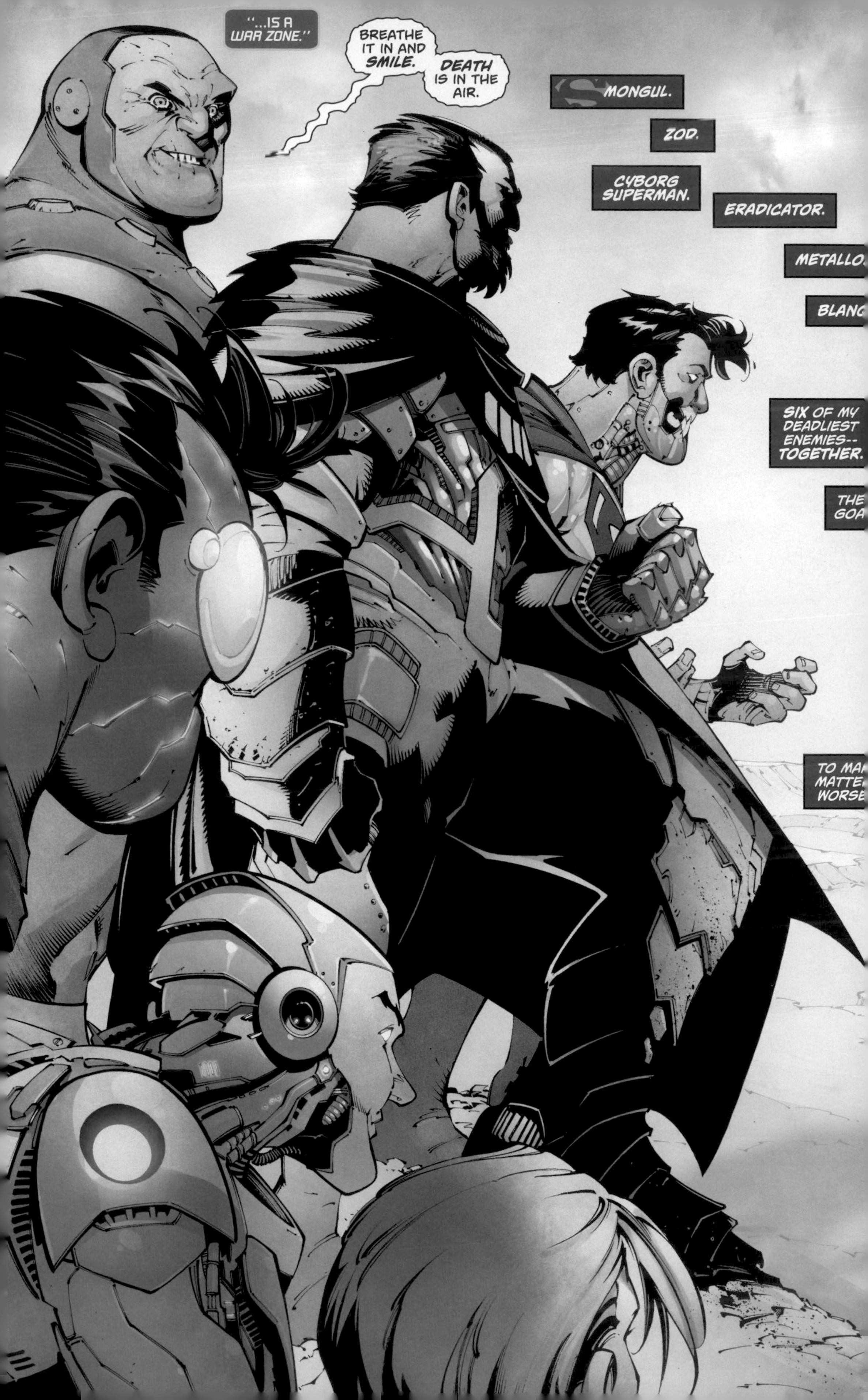
"...IS A WAR ZONE."
BREATHE IT IN AND SMILE.
DEATH IS IN THE AIR.
MONGUL.
ZOD.
CYBORG SUPERMAN.
ERADICATOR.
METALLO.
SIX OF MY DEADLIEST ENEMIES-- TOGETHER.

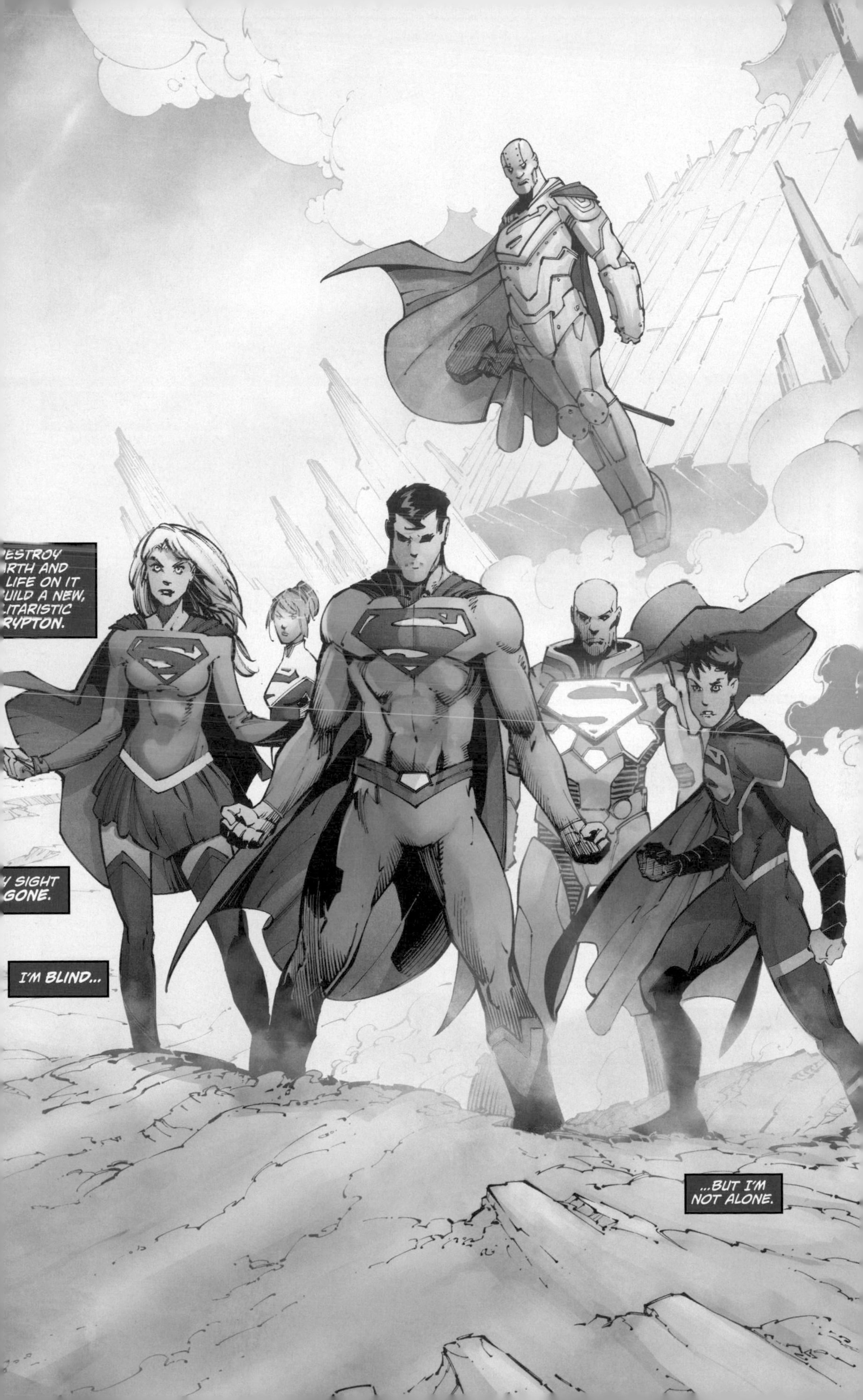
ESTROY RTH AND LIFE ON IT UILD A NEW, LITARISTIC RYPTON.
Y SIGHT GONE.
I'M BLIND...
...BUT I'M NOT ALONE.

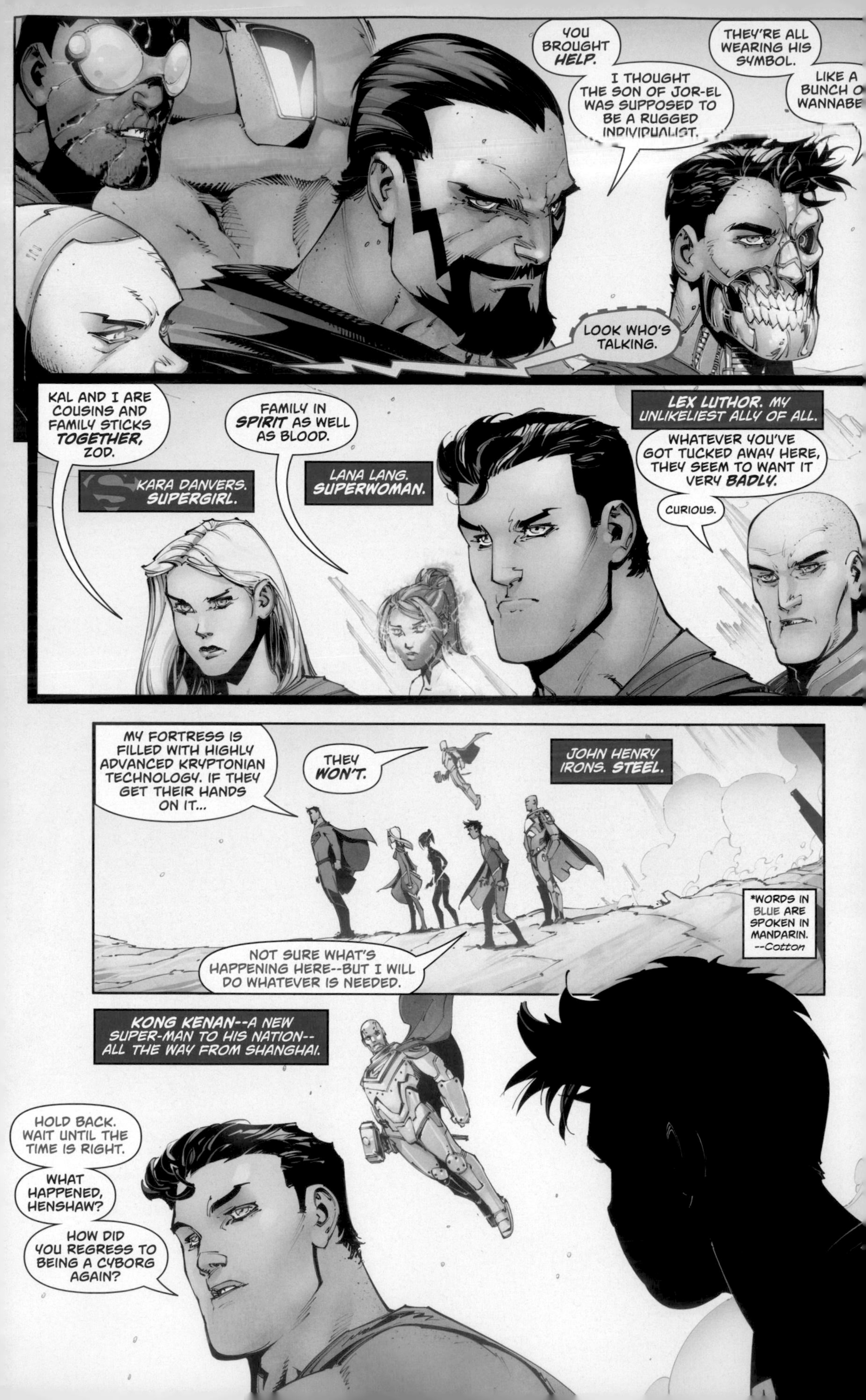
YOU BROUGHT HELP.
I THOUGHT THE SON OF JOR-EL WAS SUPPOSED TO BE A RUGGED INDIVIDUALIST.
THEY'RE ALL WEARING HIS SYMBOL.
LIKE A BUNCH O WANNABE
LOOK WHO'S TALKING.
KAL AND I ARE COUSINS AND FAMILY STICKS TOGETHER, ZOD.
KARA DANVERS. SUPERGIRL.
FAMILY IN SPIRIT AS WELL AS BLOOD.
LANA LANG. SUPERWOMAN.
LEX LUTHOR. MY UNLIKELIEST ALLY OF ALL.
WHATEVER YOU'VE GOT TUCKED AWAY HERE, THEY SEEM TO WANT IT VERY BADLY.
CURIOUS.
MY FORTRESS IS FILLED WITH HIGHLY ADVANCED KRYPTONIAN TECHNOLOGY. IF THEY GET THEIR HANDS ON IT...
THEY WON'T.
JOHN HENRY IRONS. STEEL.
NOT SURE WHAT'S HAPPENING HERE--BUT I WILL DO WHATEVER IS NEEDED.
*WORDS IN BLUE ARE SPOKEN IN MANDARIN. --Cotton
KONG KENAN--A NEW SUPER-MAN TO HIS NATION--ALL THE WAY FROM SHANGHAI.
HOLD BACK. WAIT UNTIL THE TIME IS RIGHT.
WHAT HAPPENED, HENSHAW?
HOW DID YOU REGRESS TO BEING A CYBORG AGAIN?

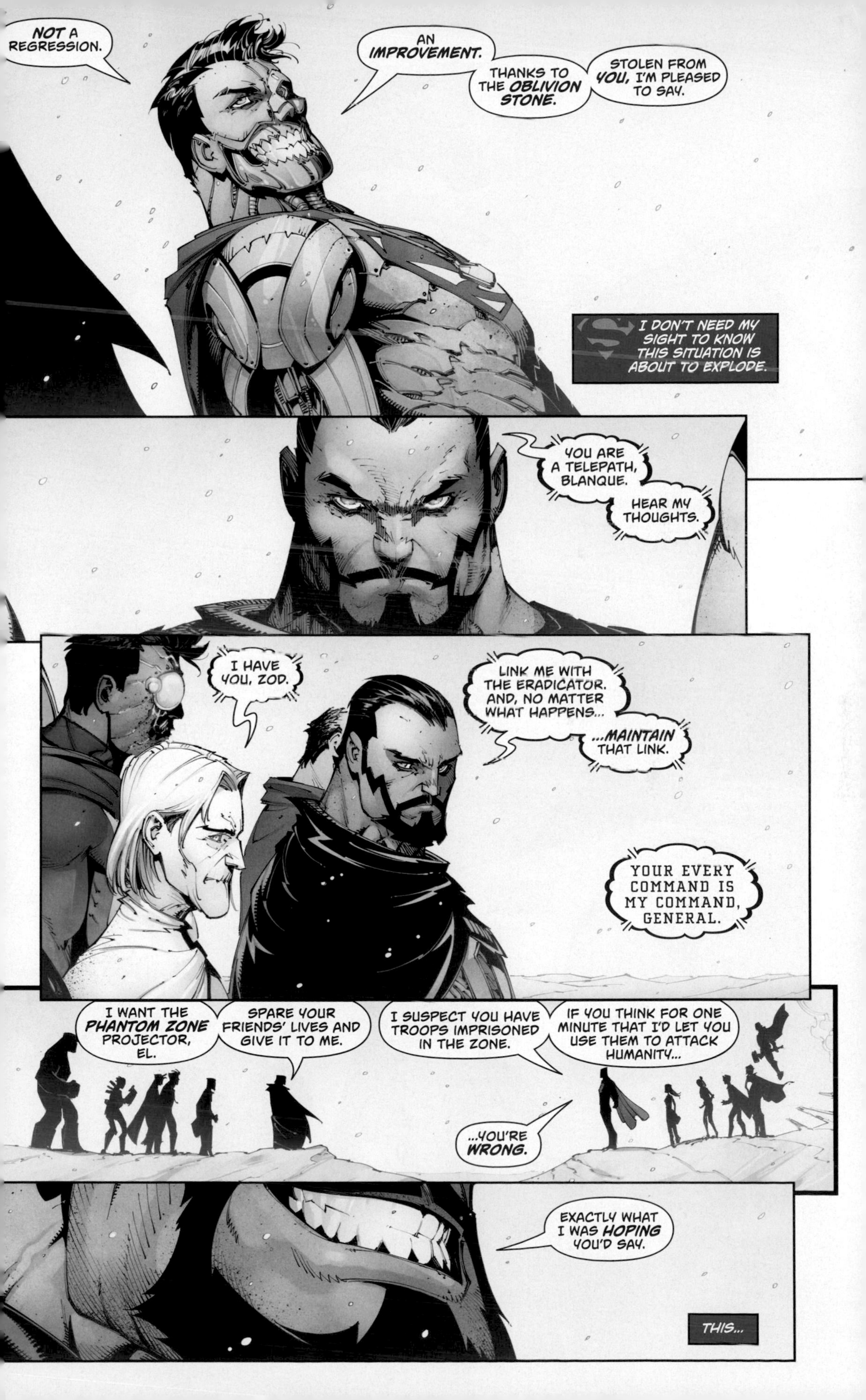
NOT A REGRESSION.
AN IMPROVEMENT.
THANKS TO THE OBLIVION STONE.
STOLEN FROM YOU, I'M PLEASED TO SAY.
I DON'T NEED MY SIGHT TO KNOW THIS SITUATION IS ABOUT TO EXPLODE.
YOU ARE A TELEPATH, BLANQUE.
HEAR MY THOUGHTS.
I HAVE YOU, ZOD.
LINK ME WITH THE ERADICATOR. AND, NO MATTER WHAT HAPPENS...
...MAINTAIN THAT LINK.
YOUR EVERY COMMAND IS MY COMMAND, GENERAL.
I WANT THE PHANTOM ZONE PROJECTOR, EL.
SPARE YOUR FRIENDS' LIVES AND GIVE IT TO ME.
I SUSPECT YOU HAVE TROOPS IMPRISONED IN THE ZONE.
IF YOU THINK FOR ONE MINUTE THAT I'D LET YOU USE THEM TO ATTACK HUMANITY...
...YOU'RE WRONG.
EXACTLY WHAT I WAS HOPING YOU'D SAY.
THIS...

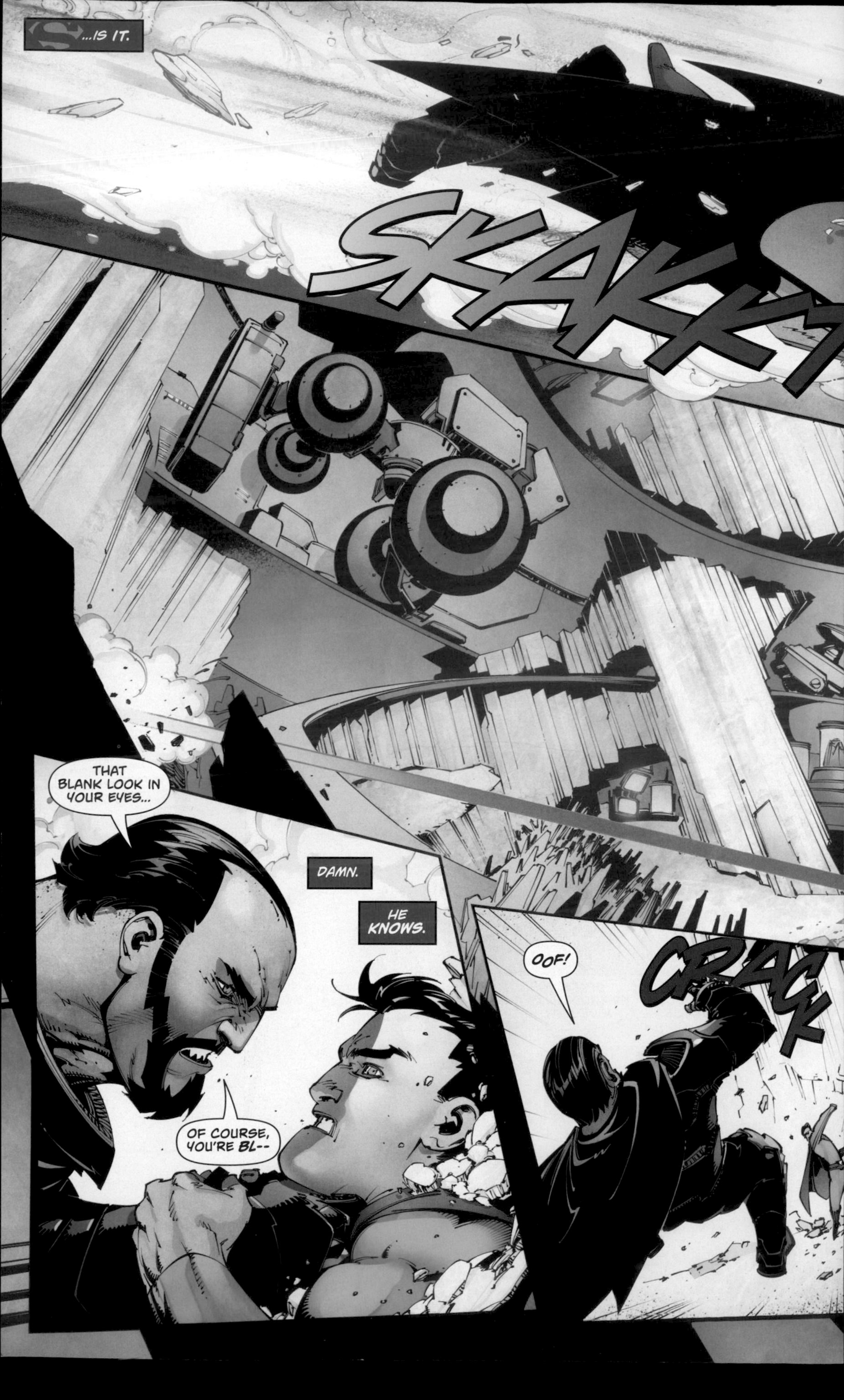
...IS IT.
SKAKT
THAT BLANK LOOK IN YOUR EYES...
DAMN.
HE KNOWS.
OF COURSE, YOU'RE BL--
OOF!
CRACK

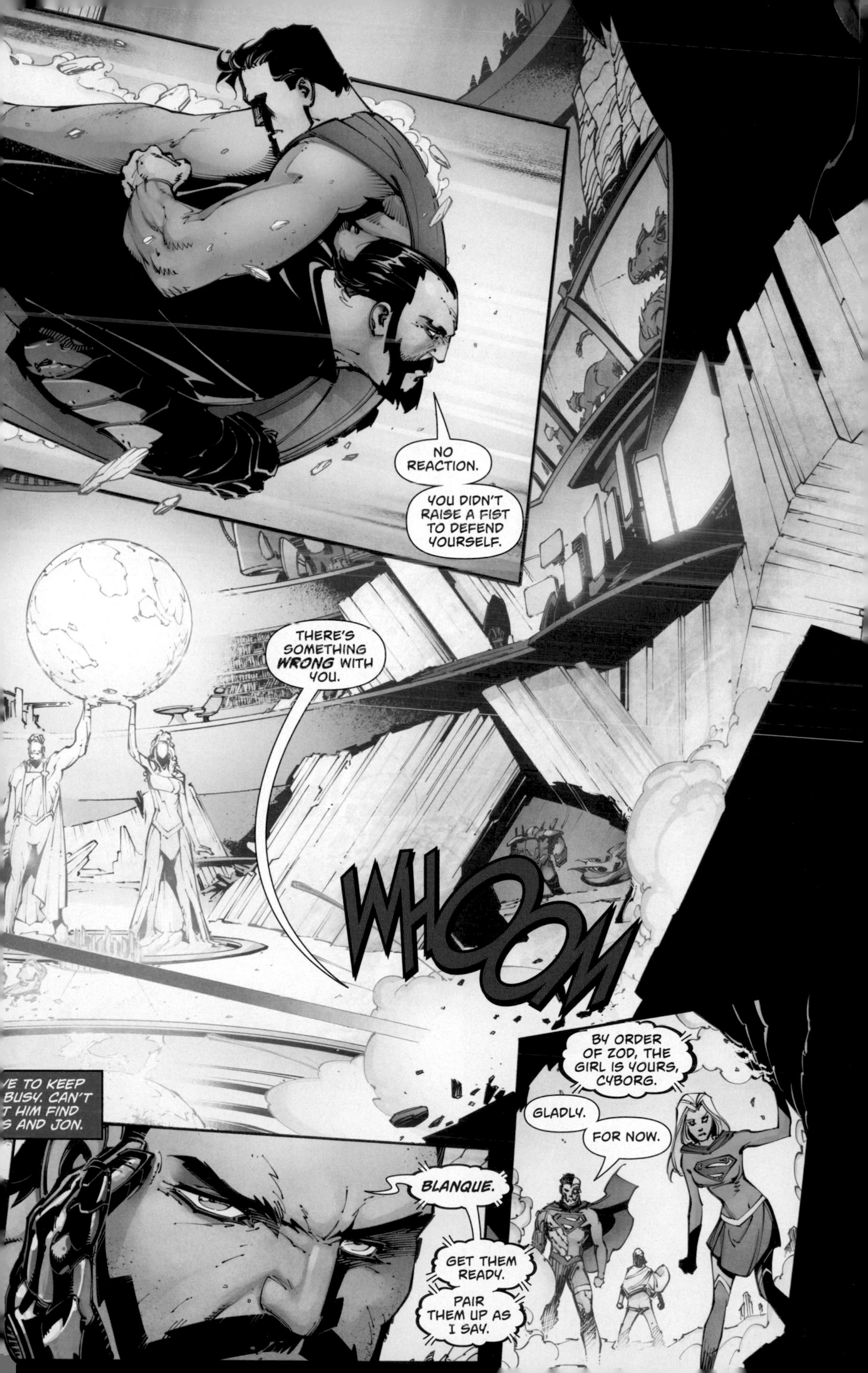
NO REACTION.
YOU DIDN'T RAISE A FIST TO DEFEND YOURSELF.
THERE'S SOMETHING WRONG WITH YOU.
WHOOM
VE TO KEEP BUSY. CAN'T T HIM FIND S AND JON.
BLANQUE.
GET THEM READY.
PAIR THEM UP AS I SAY.
BY ORDER OF ZOD, THE GIRL IS YOURS, CYBORG.
GLADLY.
FOR NOW.

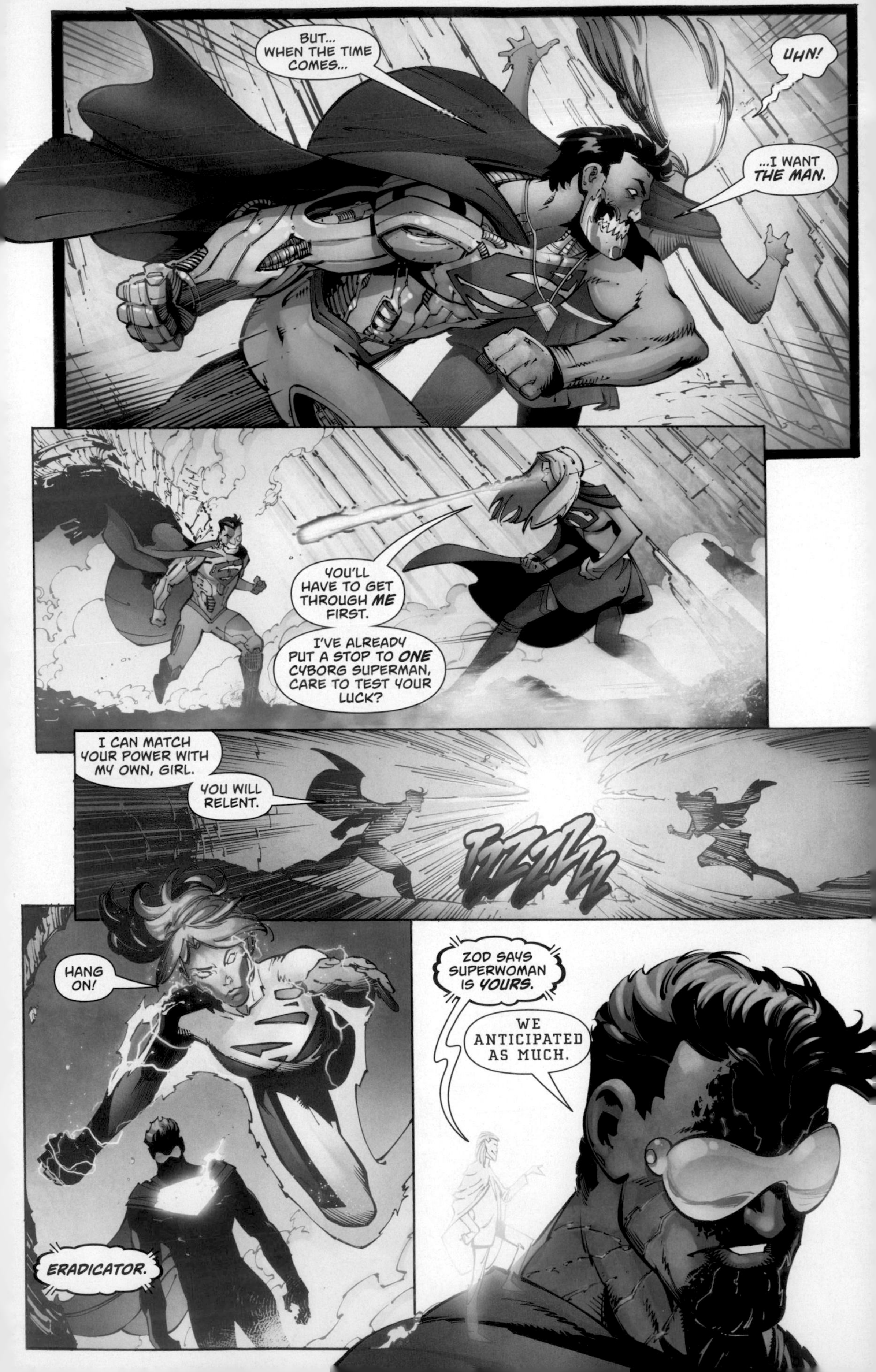
BUT... WHEN THE TIME COMES...
UHN!
...I WANT THE MAN.
YOU'LL HAVE TO GET THROUGH ME FIRST.
I'VE ALREADY PUT A STOP TO ONE CYBORG SUPERMAN, CARE TO TEST YOUR LUCK?
I CAN MATCH YOUR POWER WITH MY OWN, GIRL.
YOU WILL RELENT.
TZZZZZZ
HANG ON!
ERADICATOR.
ZOD SAYS SUPERWOMAN IS YOURS.
WE ANTICIPATED AS MUCH.

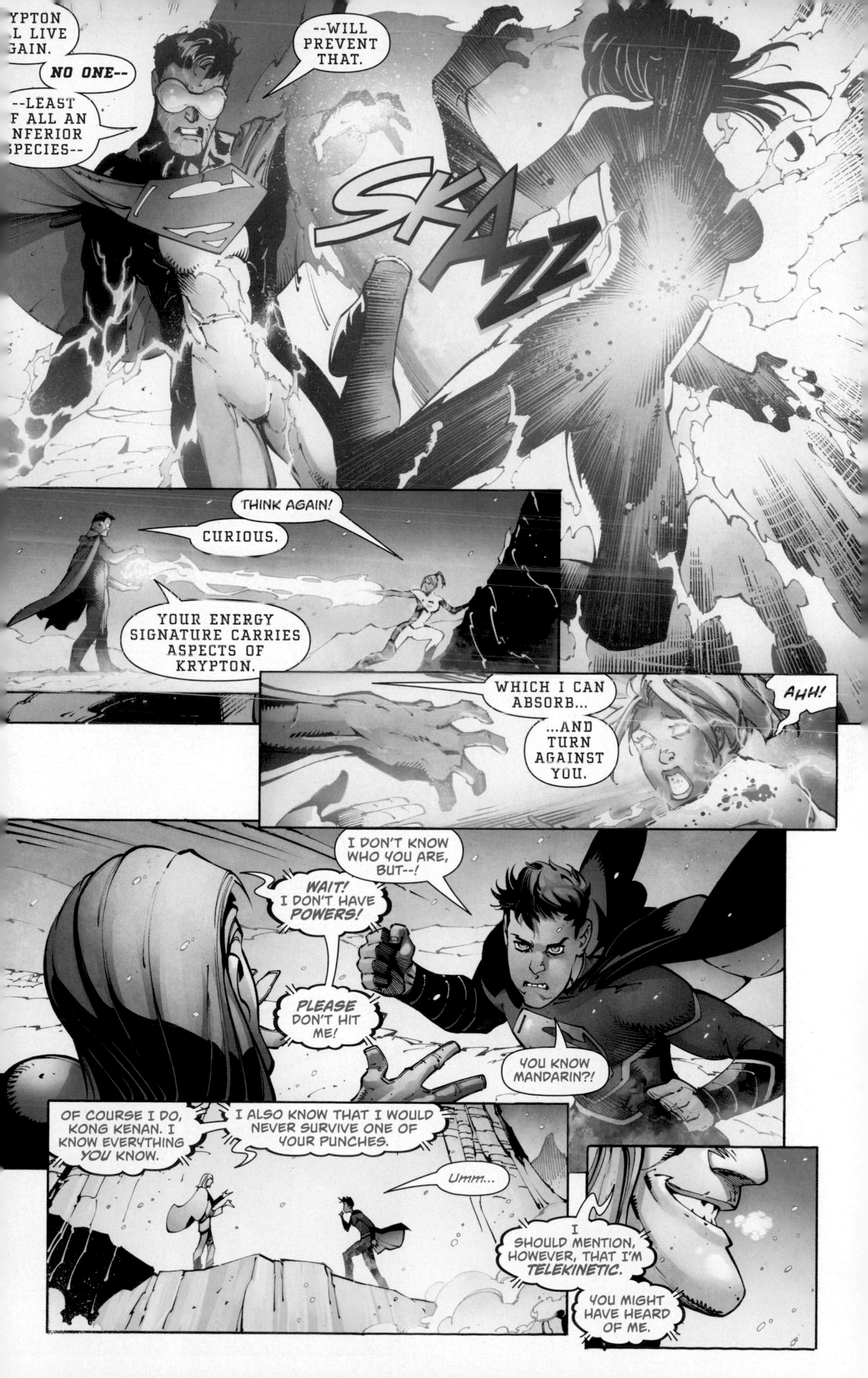
YPTON L LIVE GAIN.
NO ONE--
--WILL PREVENT THAT.
--LEAST F ALL AN NFERIOR SPECIES--
SKAZZ
THINK AGAIN!
CURIOUS.
YOUR ENERGY SIGNATURE CARRIES ASPECTS OF KRYPTON.
WHICH I CAN ABSORB...
...AND TURN AGAINST YOU.
AHH!
I DON'T KNOW WHO YOU ARE, BUT--!
WAIT! I DON'T HAVE POWERS!
PLEASE DON'T HIT ME!
YOU KNOW MANDARIN?!
OF COURSE I DO, KONG KENAN. I KNOW EVERYTHING YOU KNOW.
I ALSO KNOW THAT I WOULD NEVER SURVIVE ONE OF YOUR PUNCHES.
Umm...
I SHOULD MENTION, HOWEVER, THAT I'M TELEKINETIC.
YOU MIGHT HAVE HEARD OF ME.

THE NAME'S BLANQUE.

I *KILL* PEOPLE.

CCCRRKK

Huh?

BOODE

AND I'M ALWAYS GLAD TO ADD MORE TO THE LIST.

IT'S SOUNDING PRETTY BAD OUT THERE, MOM.

DAD *NEEDS* ME!

NO, JON.

KELEX WAS RIGHT. GETTING *YOU* TO SAFETY IS THE PRIORITY HERE.

THE SOONER THE BETTER.

BUT--!

GENERAL ZOD IS A STONE-COLD *KILLER,* JON.

I DON'T EVEN WANT HIM KNOWING YOU *EXIST!*

INTO THE FLIER. *QUICKLY.*

THAT OPEN COCKPIT THING? LOOKS LIKE A SNOWBALL COULD BRING IT DOWN!

UNFORTUNAT IT'S OUR ON OPTION.

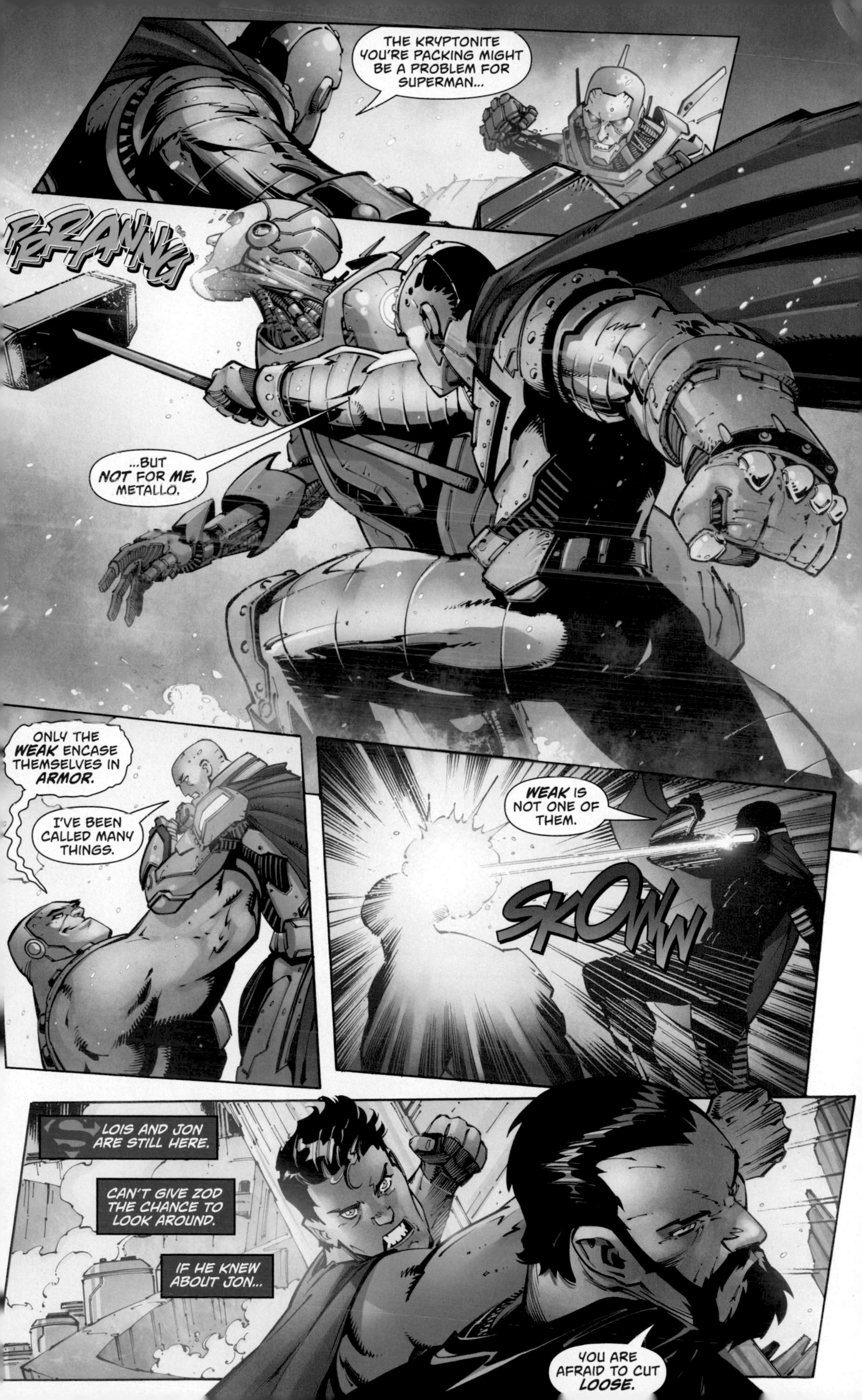
THE KRYPTONITE YOU'RE PACKING MIGHT BE A PROBLEM FOR SUPERMAN...
PRRANNG
...BUT NOT FOR ME, METALLO.
ONLY THE WEAK ENCASE THEMSELVES IN ARMOR.
I'VE BEEN CALLED MANY THINGS.
WEAK IS NOT ONE OF THEM.
SKOWW
LOIS AND JON ARE STILL HERE.
CAN'T GIVE ZOD THE CHANCE TO LOOK AROUND.
IF HE KNEW ABOUT JON...
YOU ARE AFRAID TO CUT LOOSE.

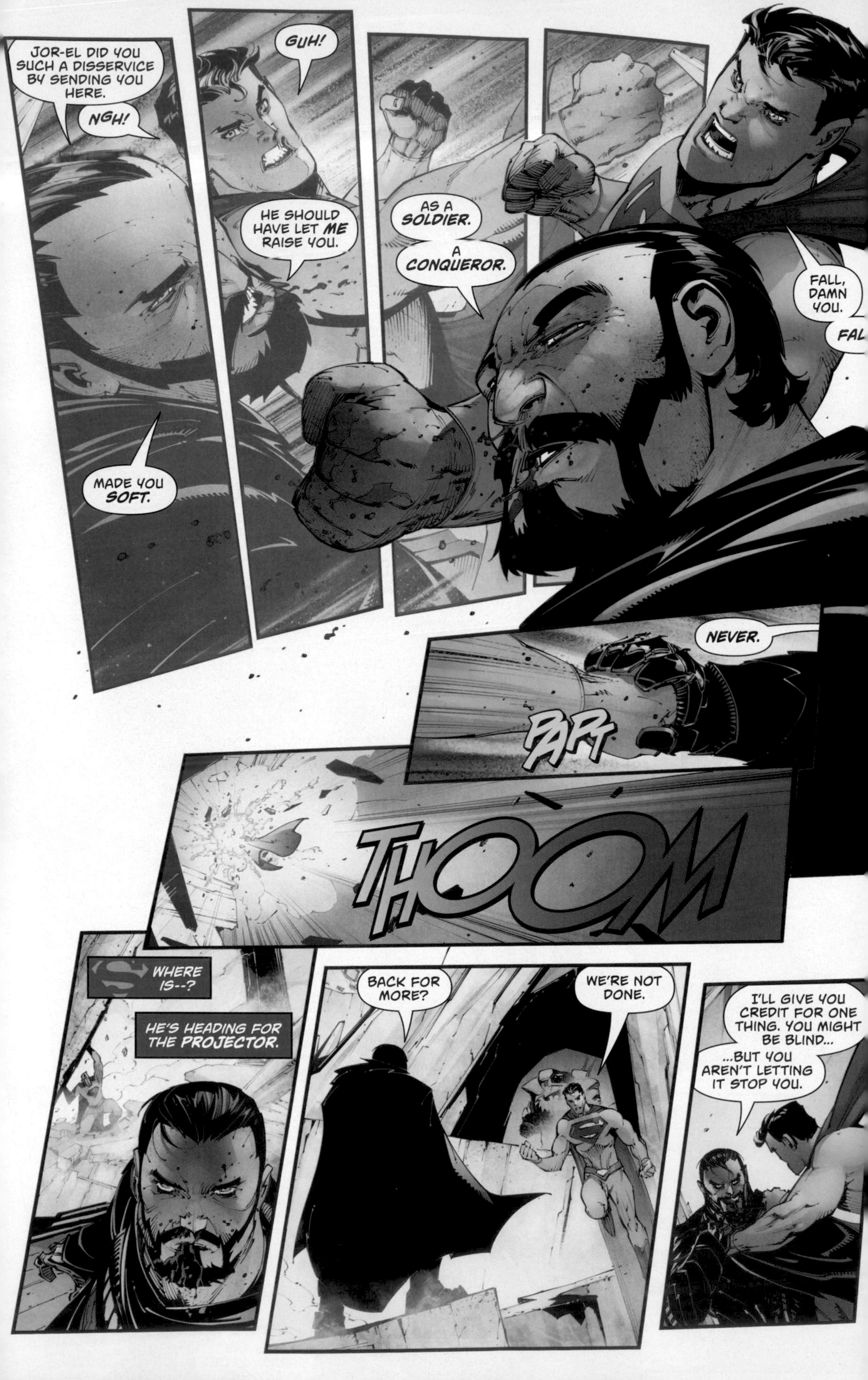
JOR-EL DID YOU SUCH A DISSERVICE BY SENDING YOU HERE.
NGH!
MADE YOU SOFT.
GUH!
HE SHOULD HAVE LET ME RAISE YOU.
AS A SOLDIER.
A CONQUEROR.
FALL, DAMN YOU.
FAL
NEVER.
PAP
THOOM
WHERE IS--?
HE'S HEADING FOR THE PROJECTOR.
BACK FOR MORE?
WE'RE NOT DONE.
I'LL GIVE YOU CREDIT FOR ONE THING. YOU MIGHT BE BLIND...
...BUT YOU AREN'T LETTING IT STOP YOU.

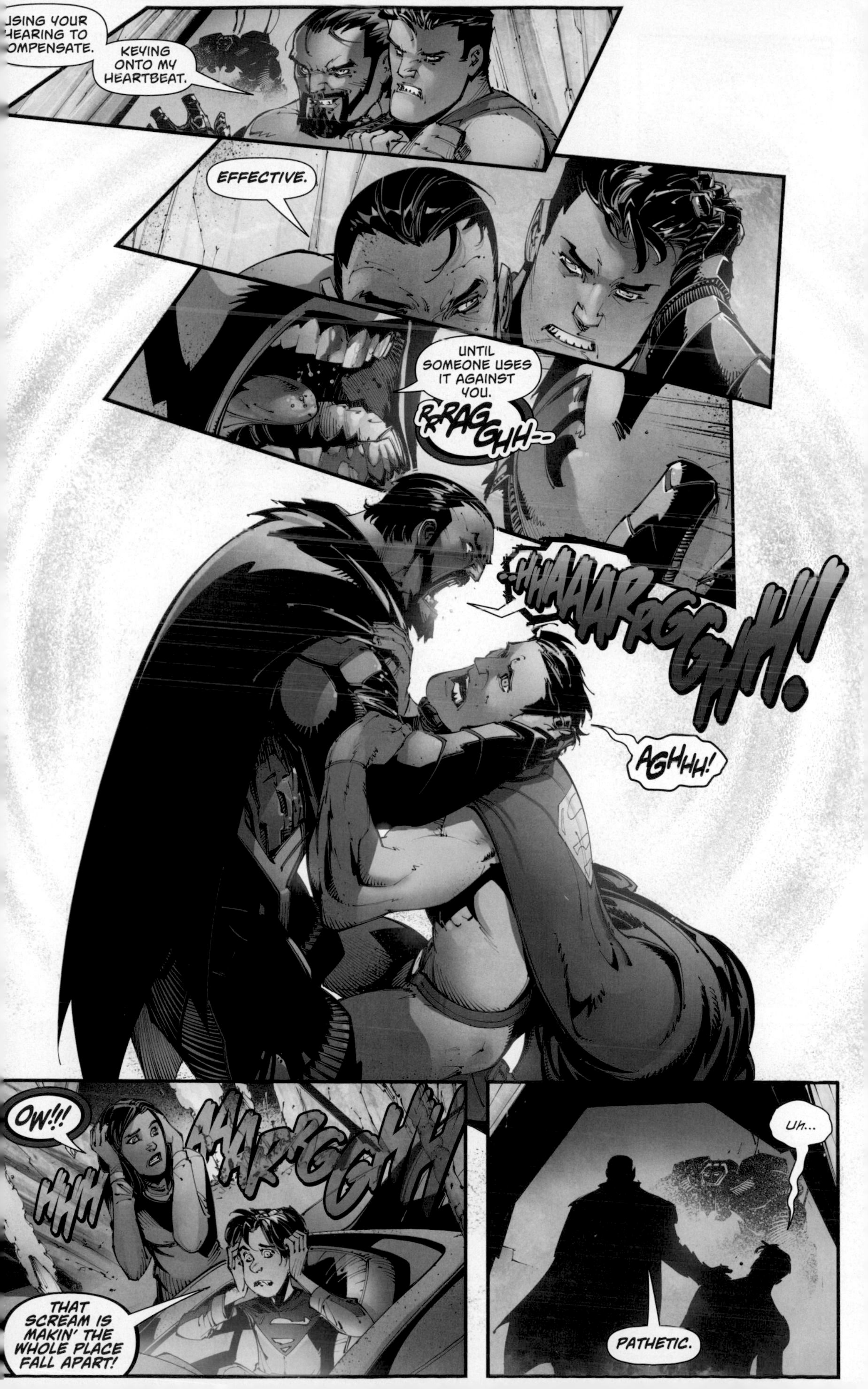
USING YOUR HEARING TO COMPENSATE.
KEYING ONTO MY HEARTBEAT.
EFFECTIVE.
UNTIL SOMEONE USES IT AGAINST YOU.
RRRAGGHH--
-HHAAAARRGGHH!!
AGHHH!
OW!!!
AAARGGHH
HHH
THAT SCREAM IS MAKIN' THE WHOLE PLACE FALL APART!
Uh...
PATHETIC.

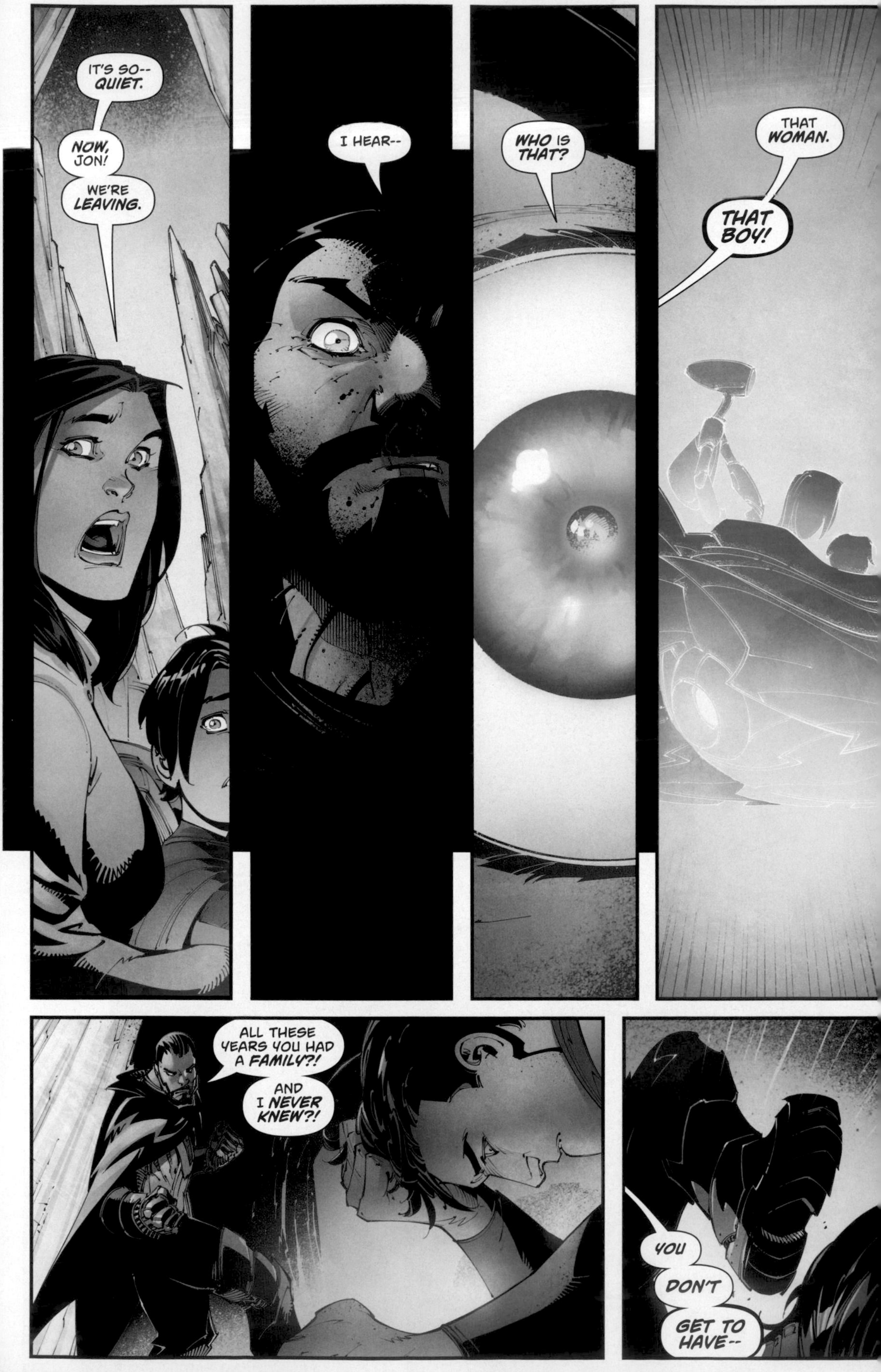
IT'S SO--
QUIET.
NOW, JON!
WE'RE LEAVING.
I HEAR--
WHO IS THAT?
THAT WOMAN.
THAT BOY!
ALL THESE YEARS YOU HAD A FAMILY?!
AND I NEVER KNEW?!
YOU
DON'T
GET TO HAVE--

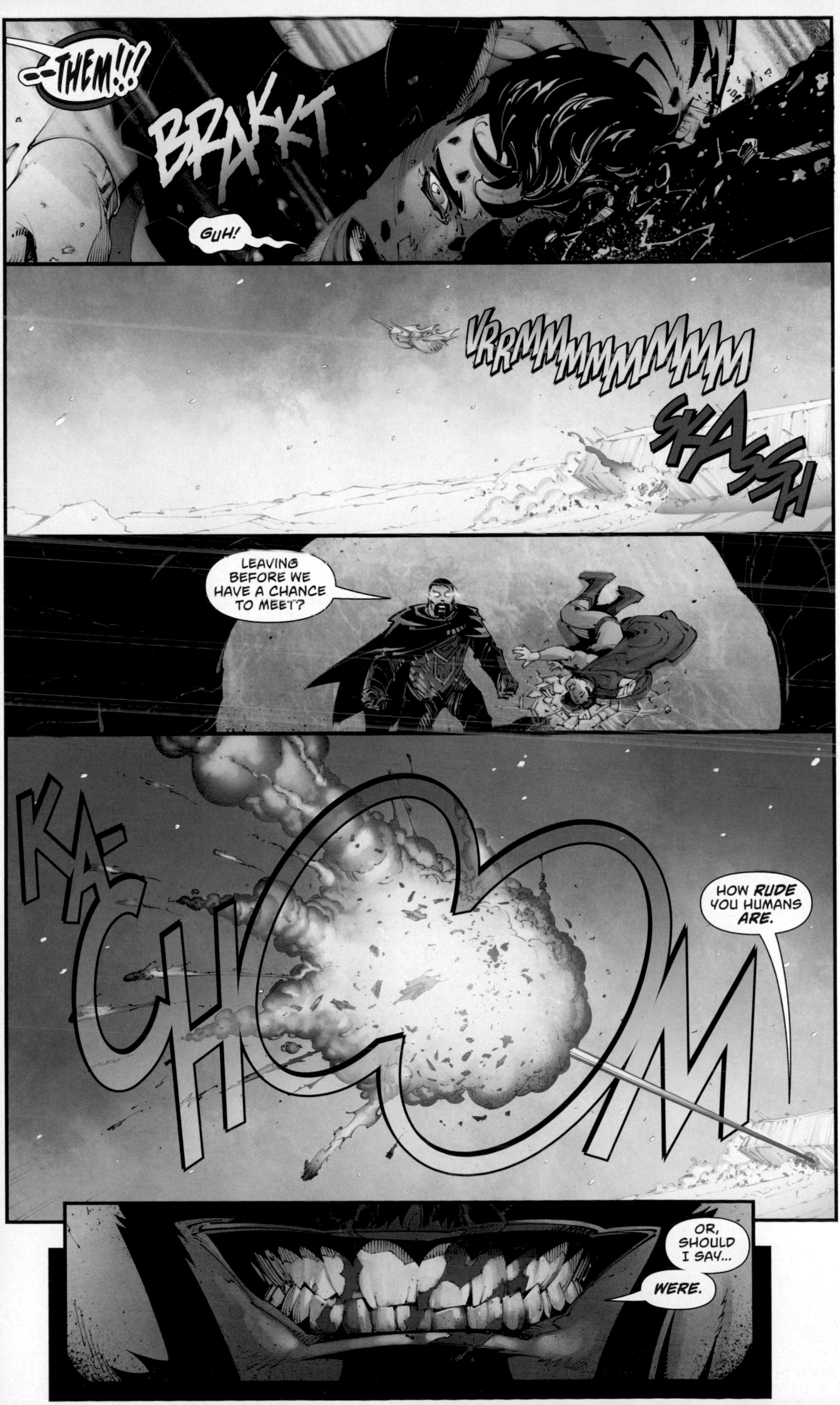

-THEM!!!
BRAKT
GUH!
VRRMMMMMMMMMM
SKASSH
LEAVING BEFORE WE HAVE A CHANCE TO MEET?
KA-CHOOM
HOW RUDE YOU HUMANS ARE.
OR, SHOULD I SAY...
WERE.

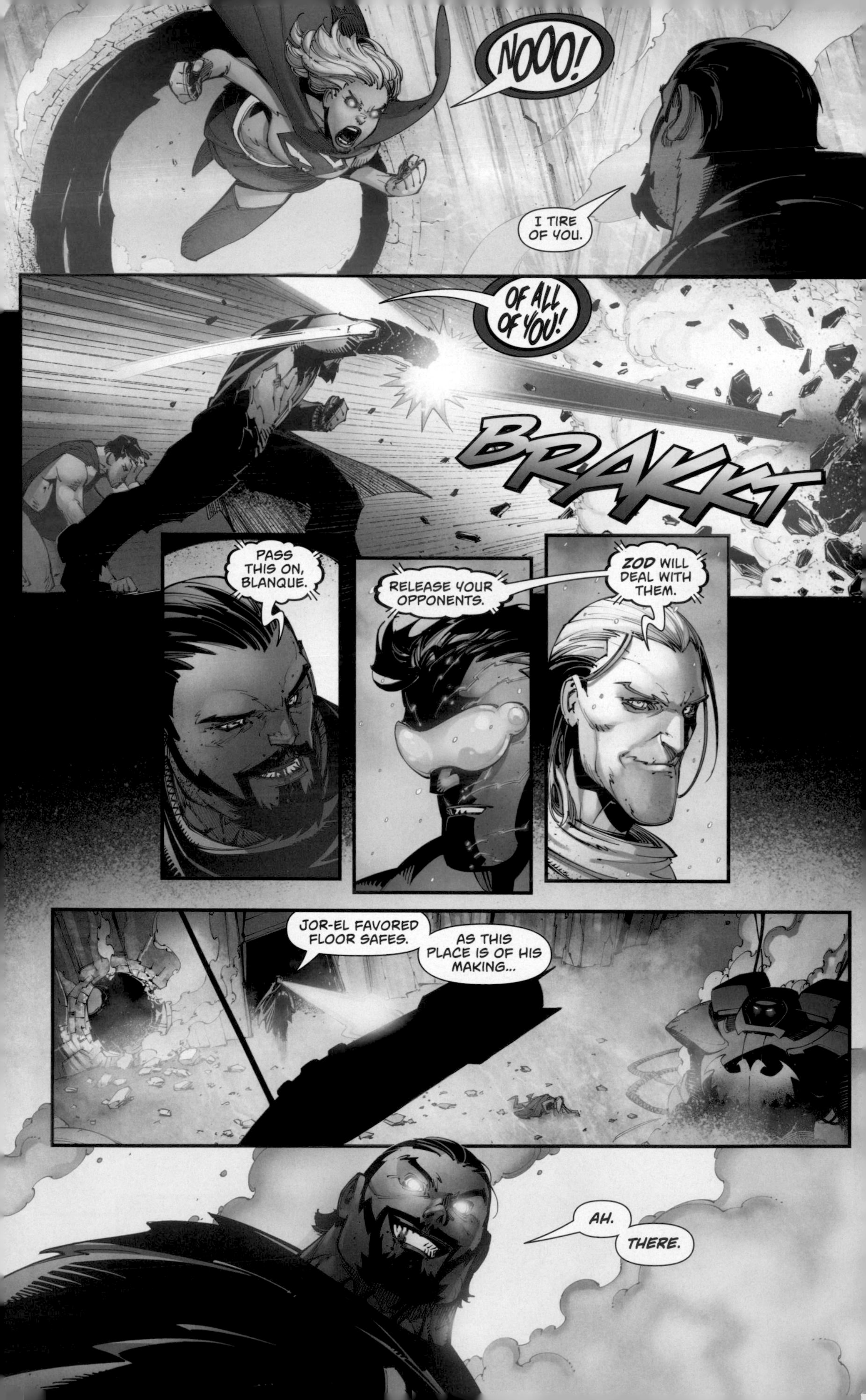
NOOO!
I TIRE OF YOU.
OF ALL OF YOU!
BRAKKT
PASS THIS ON, BLANQUE.
RELEASE YOUR OPPONENTS.
ZOD WILL DEAL WITH THEM.
JOR-EL FAVORED FLOOR SAFES.
AS THIS PLACE IS OF HIS MAKING...
AH.
THERE.

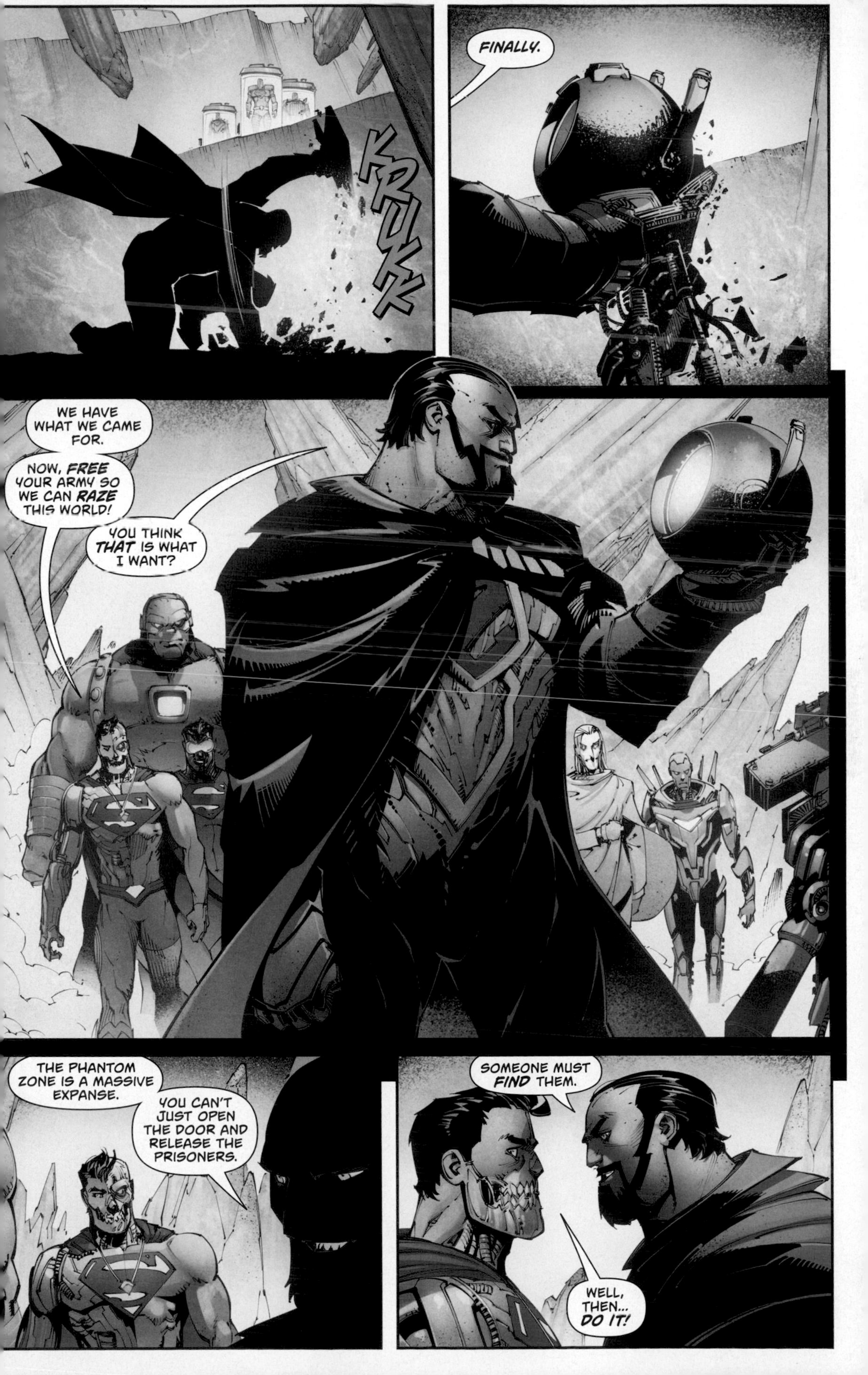
KRUKK
FINALLY.
WE HAVE WHAT WE CAME FOR.
NOW, FREE YOUR ARMY SO WE CAN RAZE THIS WORLD!
YOU THINK THAT IS WHAT I WANT?
THE PHANTOM ZONE IS A MASSIVE EXPANSE.
YOU CAN'T JUST OPEN THE DOOR AND RELEASE THE PRISONERS.
SOMEONE MUST FIND THEM.
WELL, THEN... DO IT!

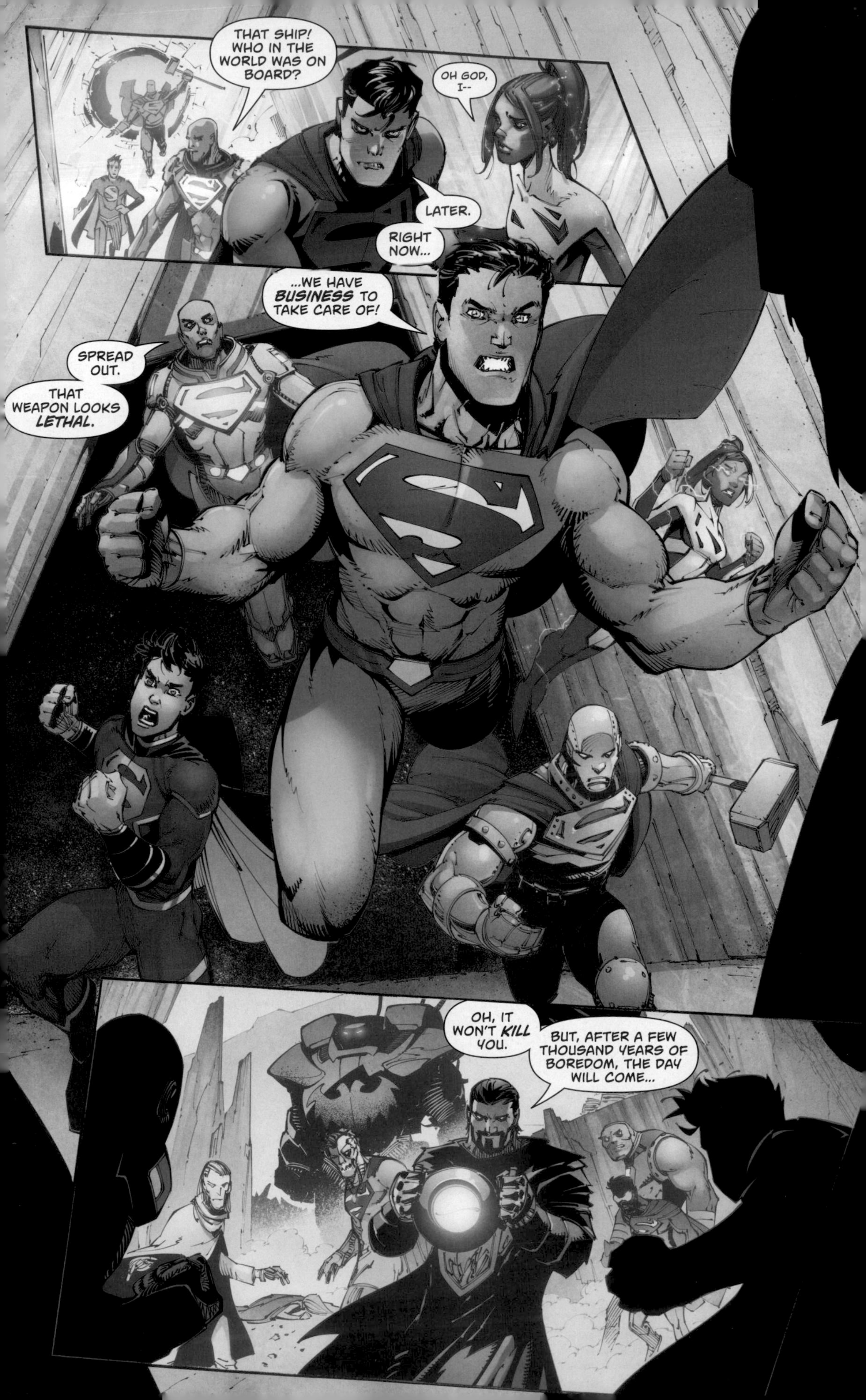
THAT SHIP! WHO IN THE WORLD WAS ON BOARD?
OH GOD, I--
LATER.
RIGHT NOW...
...WE HAVE BUSINESS TO TAKE CARE OF!
SPREAD OUT.
THAT WEAPON LOOKS LETHAL.
OH, IT WON'T KILL YOU.
BUT, AFTER A FEW THOUSAND YEARS OF BOREDOM, THE DAY WILL COME...

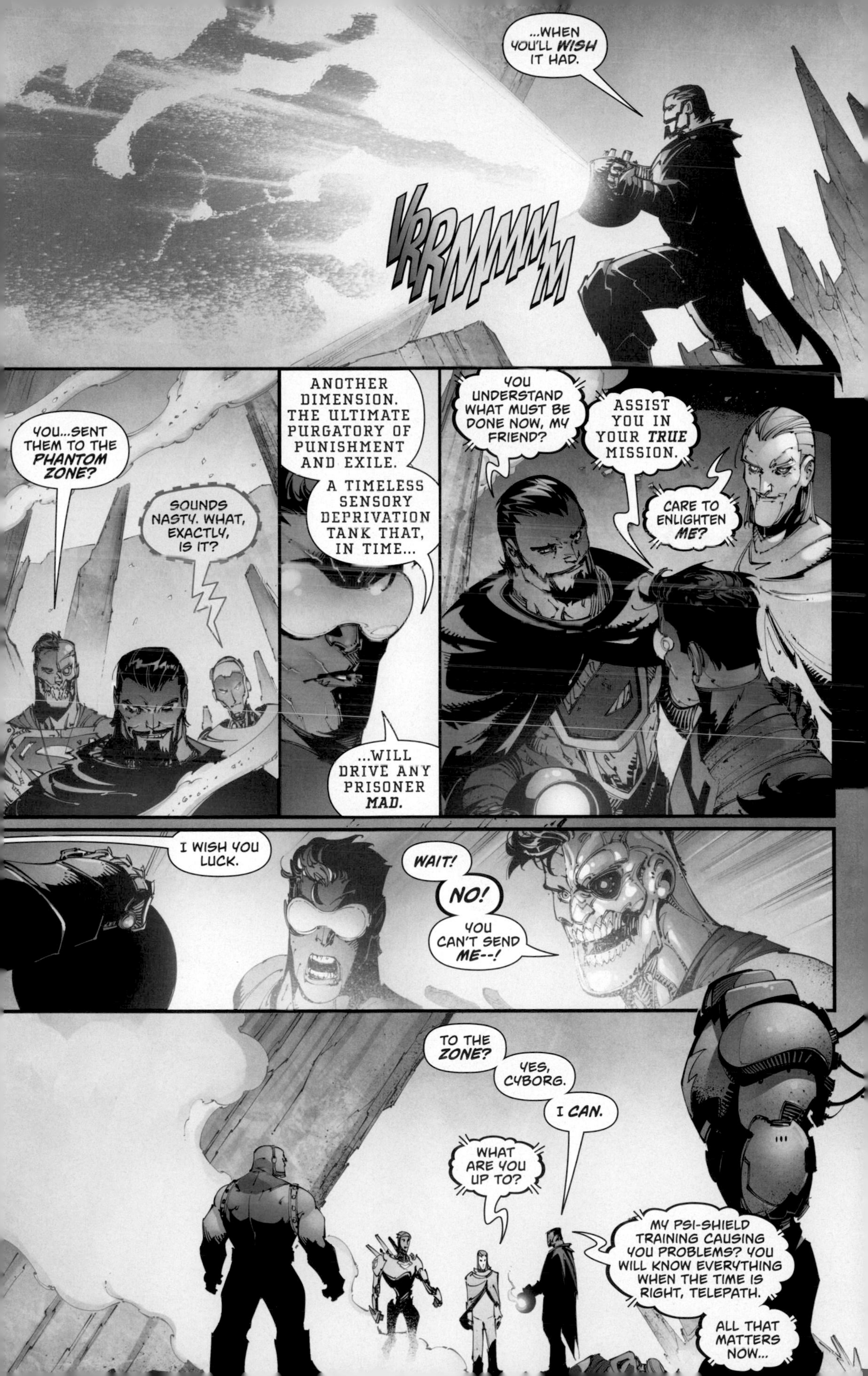
...WHEN YOU'LL WISH IT HAD.
VRRMMMMM
YOU...SENT THEM TO THE PHANTOM ZONE?
SOUNDS NASTY. WHAT, EXACTLY, IS IT?
ANOTHER DIMENSION. THE ULTIMATE PURGATORY OF PUNISHMENT AND EXILE.
A TIMELESS SENSORY DEPRIVATION TANK THAT, IN TIME...
...WILL DRIVE ANY PRISONER MAD.
YOU UNDERSTAND WHAT MUST BE DONE NOW, MY FRIEND?
ASSIST YOU IN YOUR TRUE MISSION.
CARE TO ENLIGHTEN ME?
I WISH YOU LUCK.
WAIT!
NO!
YOU CAN'T SEND ME--!
TO THE ZONE?
YES, CYBORG.
I CAN.
WHAT ARE YOU UP TO?
MY PSI-SHIELD TRAINING CAUSING YOU PROBLEMS? YOU WILL KNOW EVERYTHING WHEN THE TIME IS RIGHT, TELEPATH.
ALL THAT MATTERS NOW...

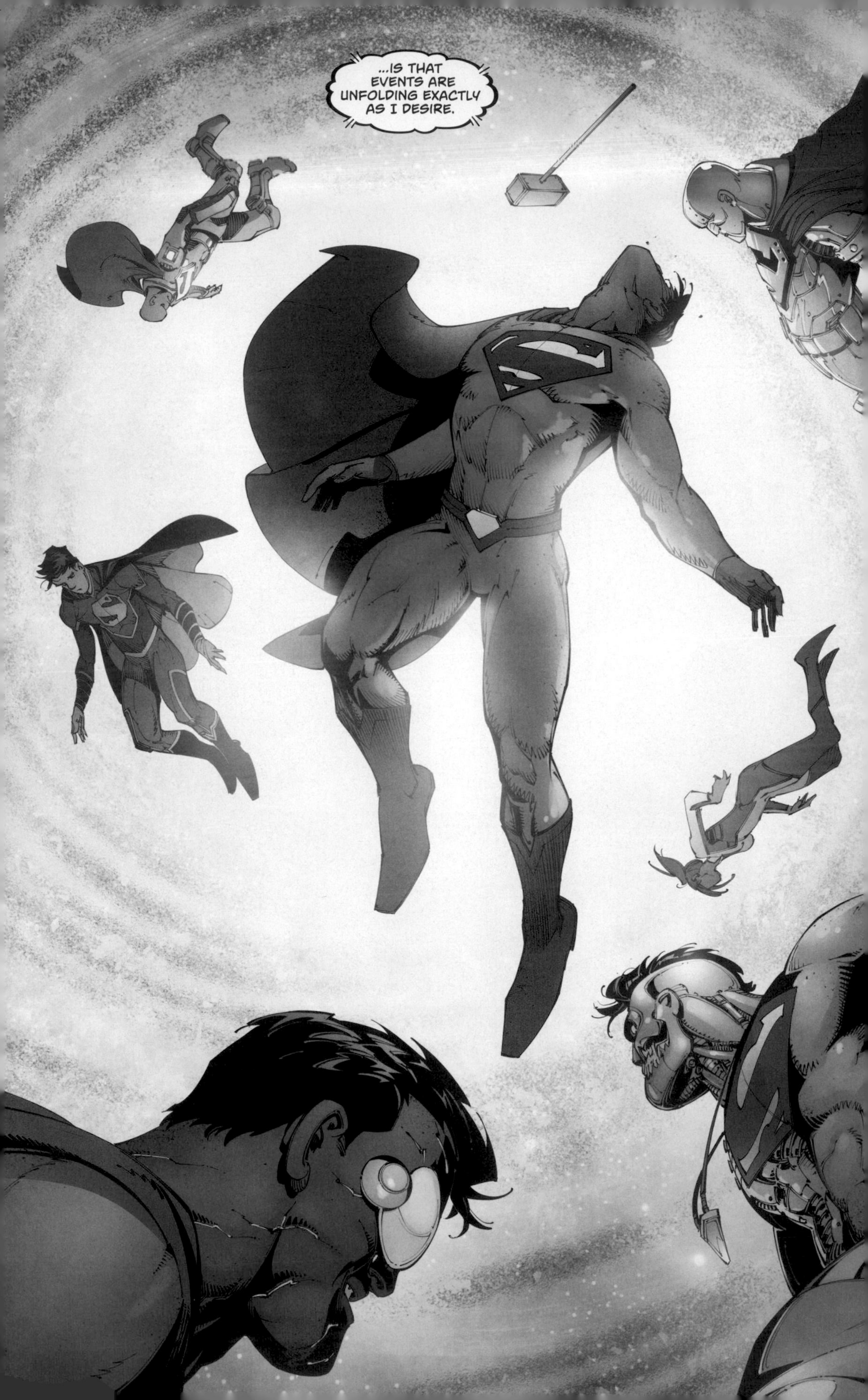
...IS THAT EVENTS ARE UNFOLDING EXACTLY AS I DESIRE.

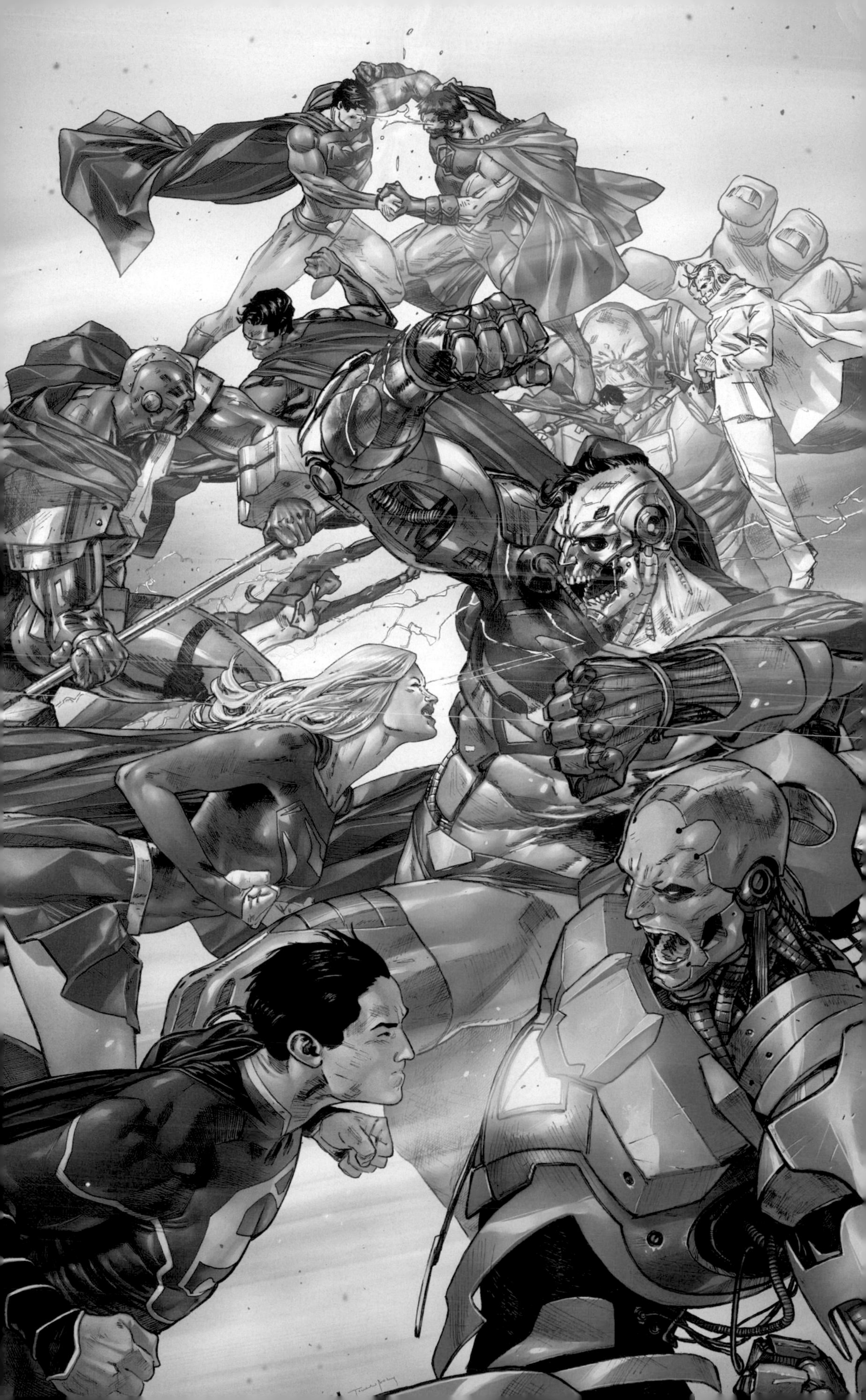

REVENGE CONCLUSION

PATCH ZIRCHER artist * HI-FI colorist

CLAY MANN TOMEU MOREY cover artists

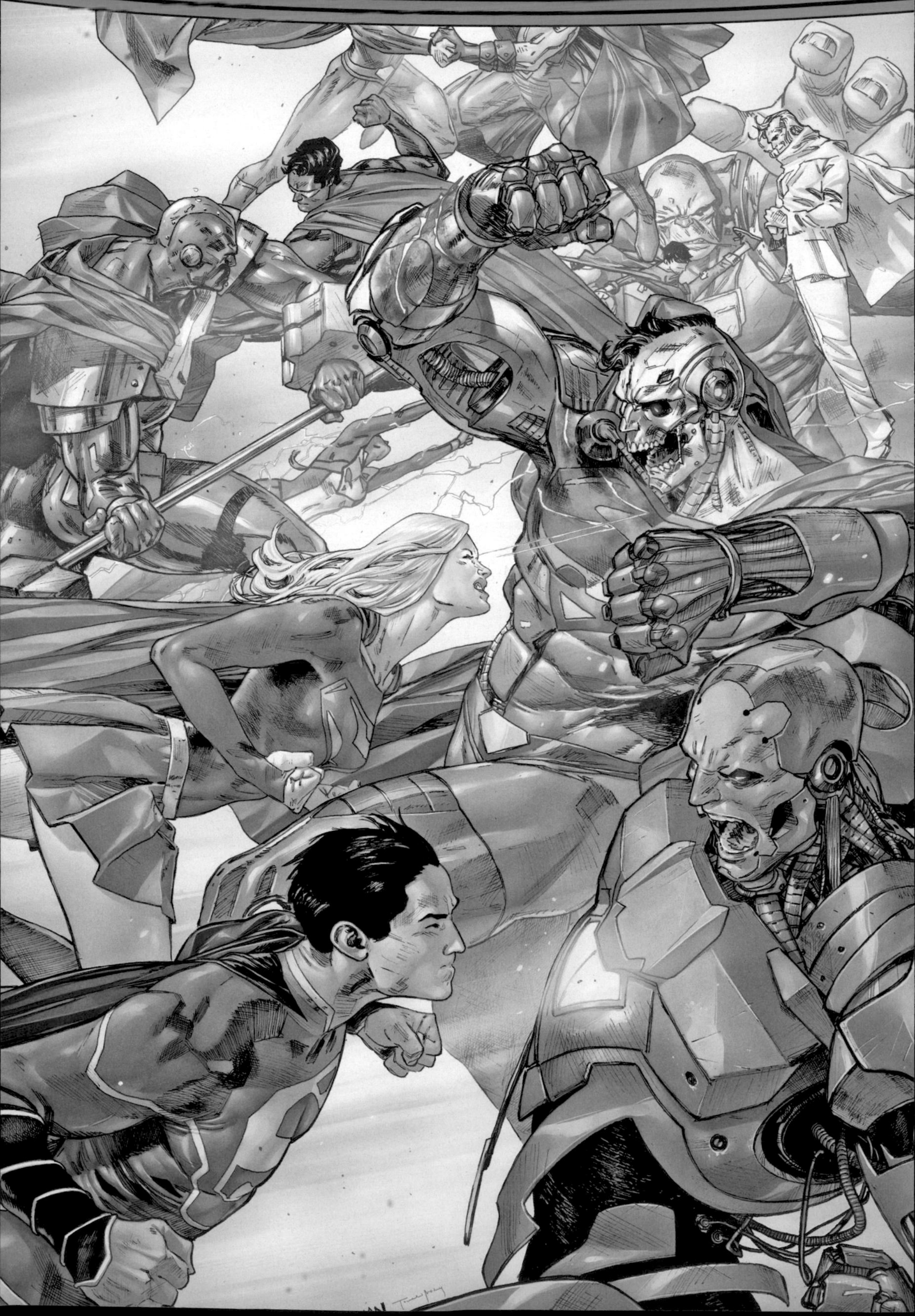

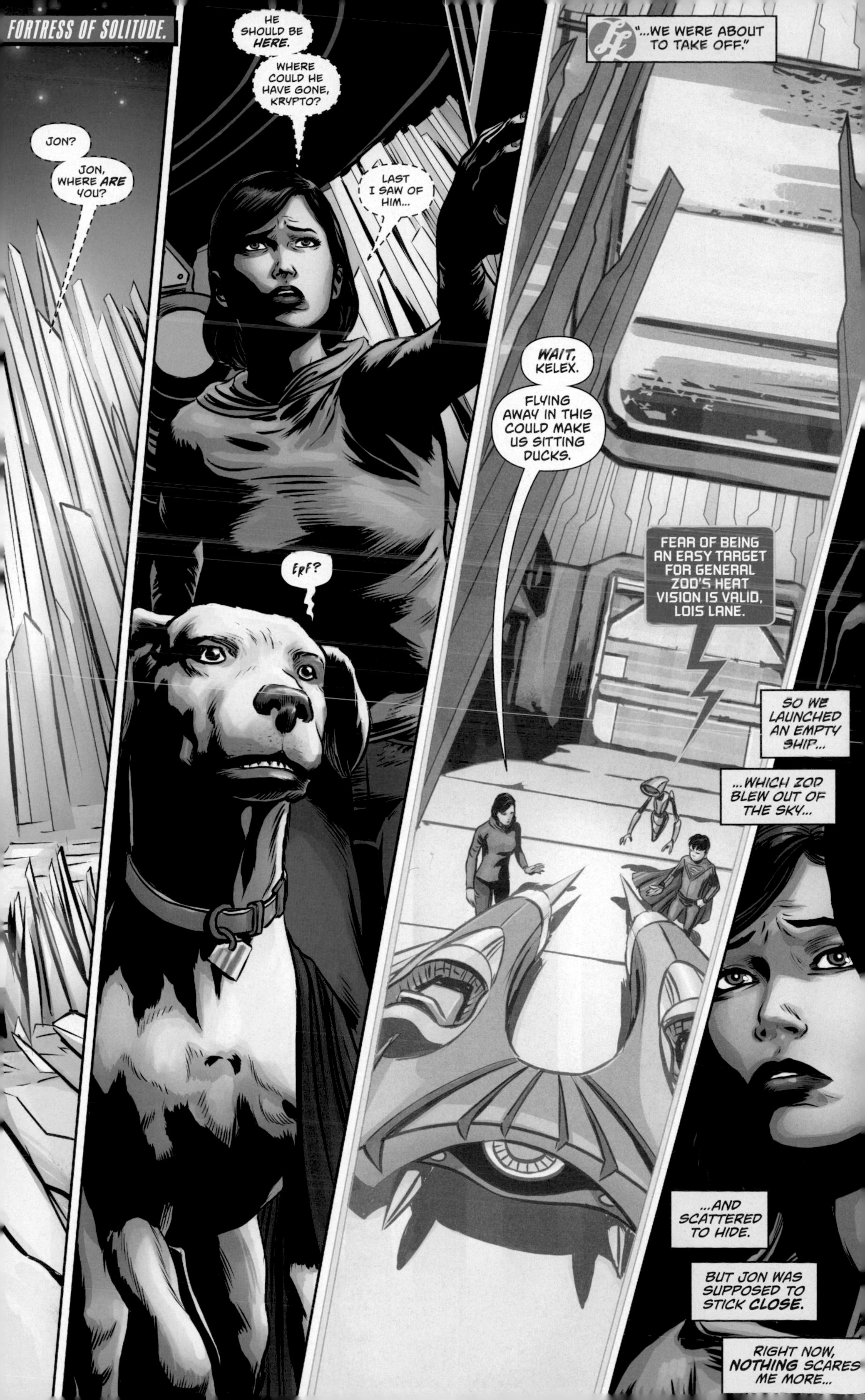
FORTRESS OF SOLITUDE.
JON?
JON, WHERE ARE YOU?
HE SHOULD BE HERE.
WHERE COULD HE HAVE GONE, KRYPTO?
LAST I SAW OF HIM...
ERF?
"...WE WERE ABOUT TO TAKE OFF."
WAIT, KELEX.
FLYING AWAY IN THIS COULD MAKE US SITTING DUCKS.
FEAR OF BEING AN EASY TARGET FOR GENERAL ZOD'S HEAT VISION IS VALID, LOIS LANE.
SO WE LAUNCHED AN EMPTY SHIP...
...WHICH ZOD BLEW OUT OF THE SKY...
...AND SCATTERED TO HIDE.
BUT JON WAS SUPPOSED TO STICK CLOSE.
RIGHT NOW, NOTHING SCARES ME MORE...

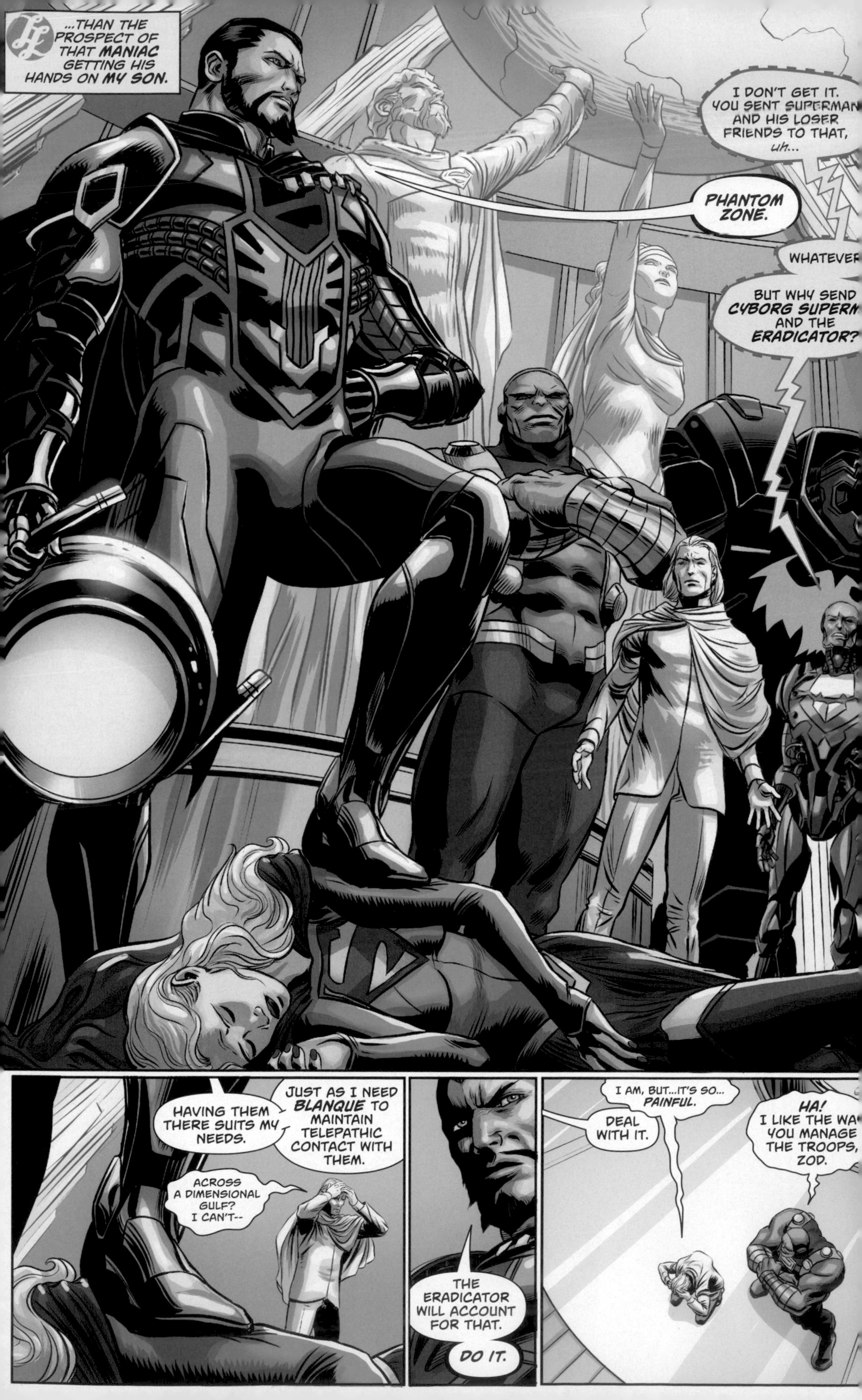

...THAN THE PROSPECT OF THAT MANIAC GETTING HIS HANDS ON MY SON.
I DON'T GET IT. YOU SENT SUPERMAN AND HIS LOSER FRIENDS TO THAT, uh...
PHANTOM ZONE.
WHATEVER
BUT WHY SEND CYBORG SUPERM AND THE ERADICATOR?
HAVING THEM THERE SUITS MY NEEDS.
JUST AS I NEED BLANQUE TO MAINTAIN TELEPATHIC CONTACT WITH THEM.
ACROSS A DIMENSIONAL GULF? I CAN'T--
THE ERADICATOR WILL ACCOUNT FOR THAT.
DO IT.
I AM, BUT...IT'S SO... PAINFUL.
DEAL WITH IT.
HA! I LIKE THE WA YOU MANAGE THE TROOPS, ZOD.

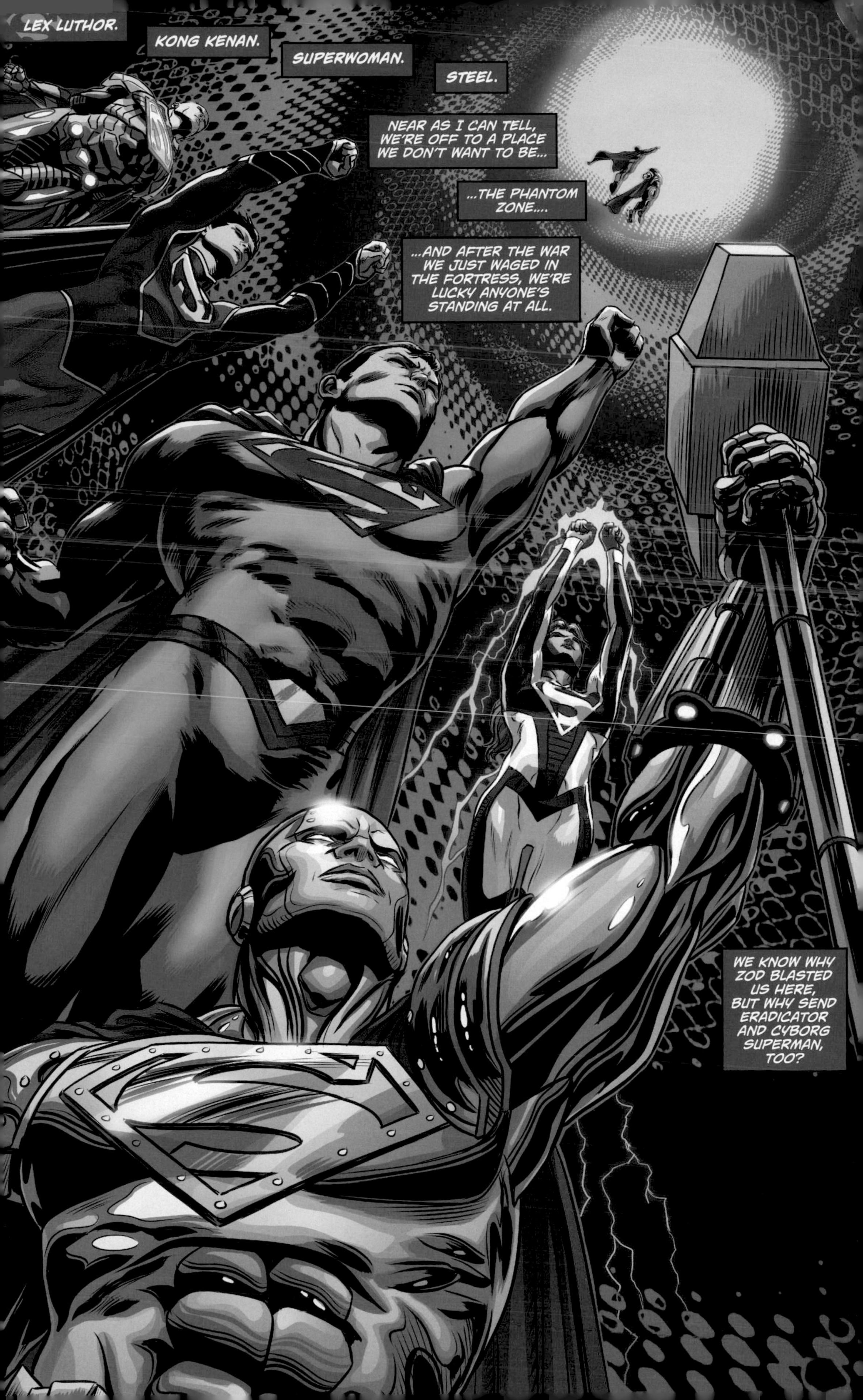
LEX LUTHOR.
KONG KENAN.
SUPERWOMAN.
STEEL.
NEAR AS I CAN TELL, WE'RE OFF TO A PLACE WE DON'T WANT TO BE...
...THE PHANTOM ZONE....
...AND AFTER THE WAR WE JUST WAGED IN THE FORTRESS, WE'RE LUCKY ANYONE'S STANDING AT ALL.
WE KNOW WHY ZOD BLASTED US HERE, BUT WHY SEND ERADICATOR AND CYBORG SUPERMAN, TOO?

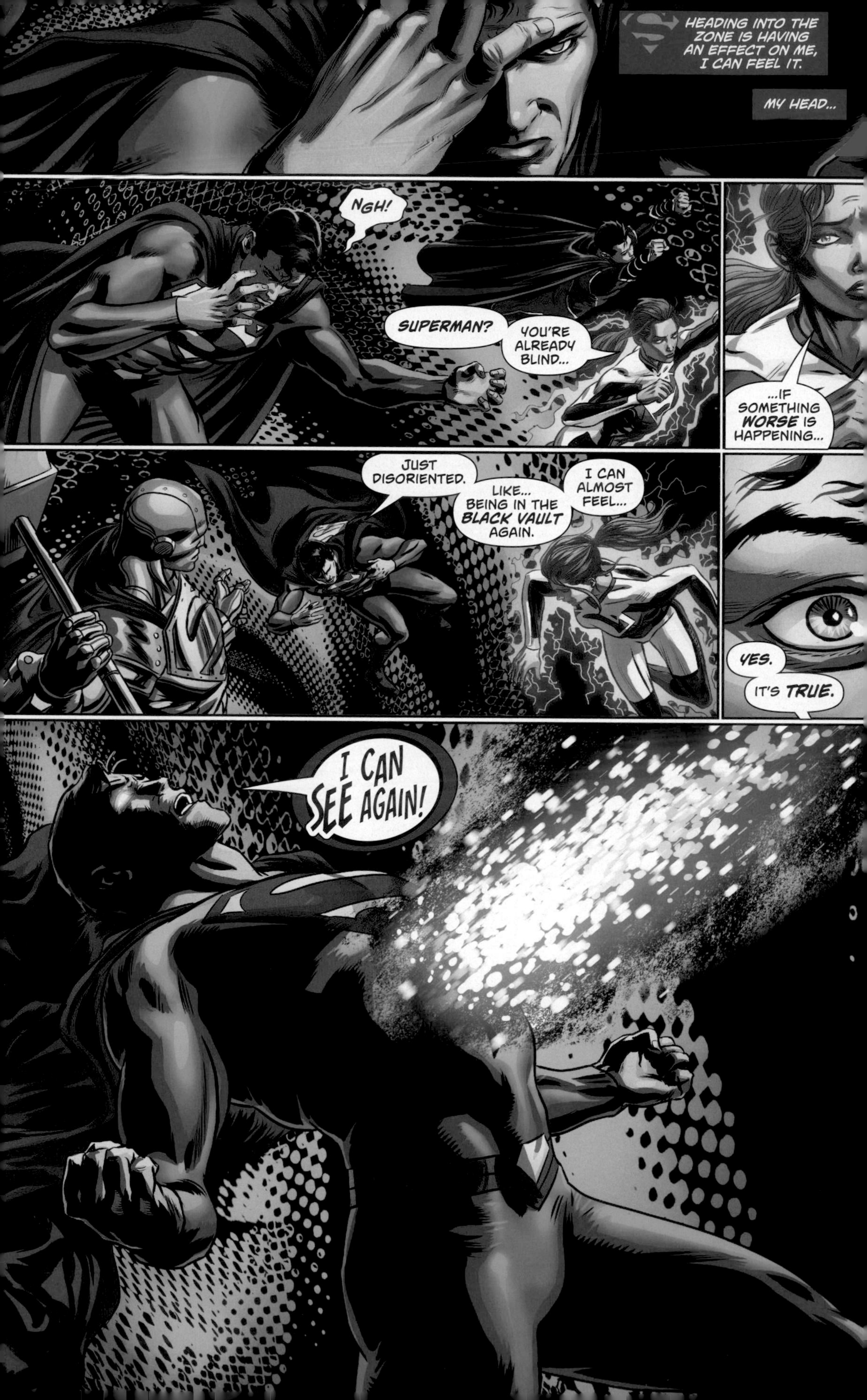
HEADING INTO THE ZONE IS HAVING AN EFFECT ON ME, I CAN FEEL IT.
MY HEAD...
NGH!
SUPERMAN?
YOU'RE ALREADY BLIND...
...IF SOMETHING WORSE IS HAPPENING...
JUST DISORIENTED.
LIKE... BEING IN THE BLACK VAULT AGAIN.
I CAN ALMOST FEEL...
YES.
IT'S TRUE.
I CAN SEE AGAIN!

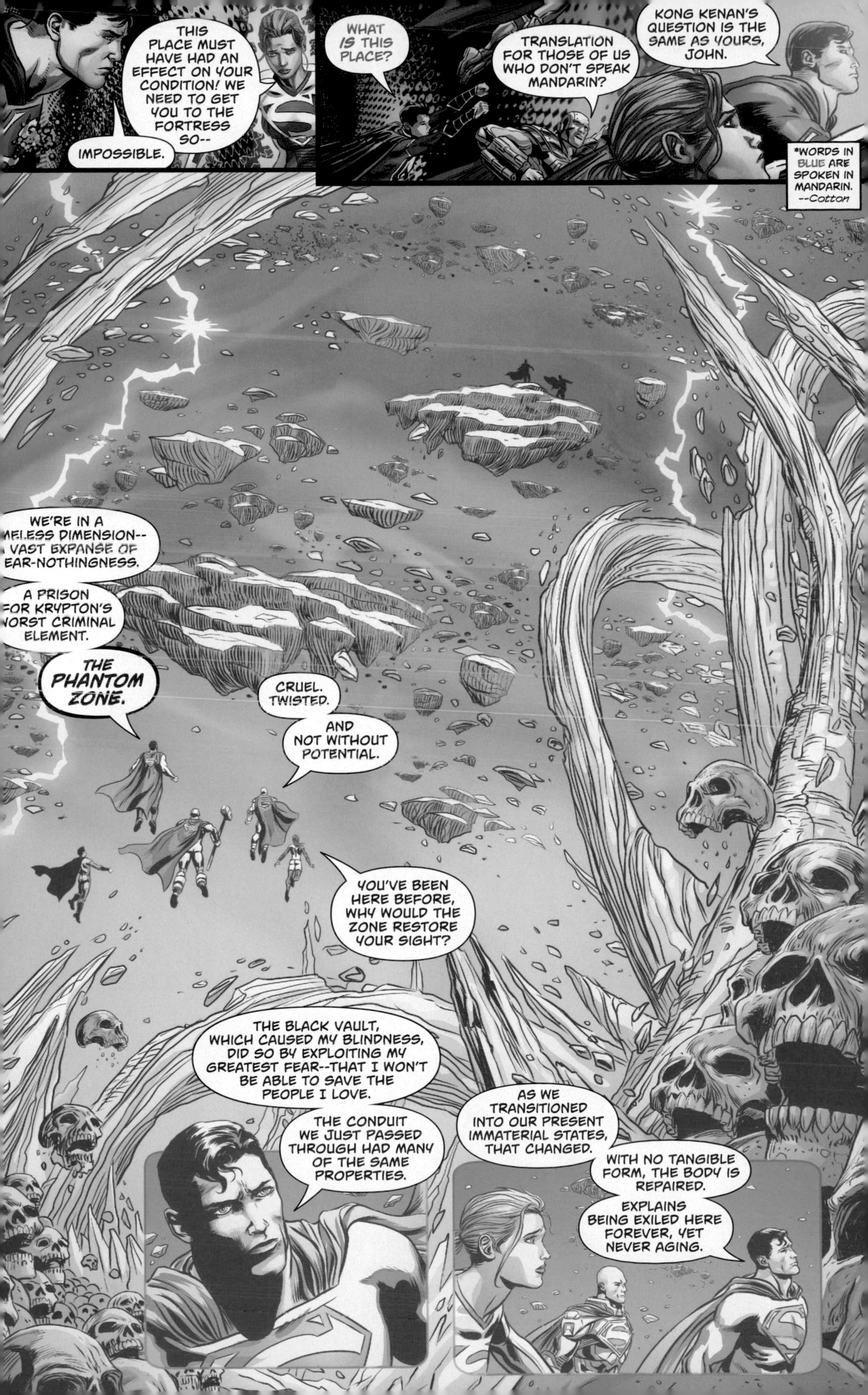
THIS PLACE MUST HAVE HAD AN EFFECT ON YOUR CONDITION! WE NEED TO GET YOU TO THE FORTRESS SO--
IMPOSSIBLE.
WHAT IS THIS PLACE?
TRANSLATION FOR THOSE OF US WHO DON'T SPEAK MANDARIN?
KONG KENAN'S QUESTION IS THE SAME AS YOURS, JOHN.
*WORDS IN BLUE ARE SPOKEN IN MANDARIN. --Cotton
WE'RE IN A MELESS DIMENSION-- VAST EXPANSE OF EAR-NOTHINGNESS.
A PRISON FOR KRYPTON'S WORST CRIMINAL ELEMENT.
THE PHANTOM ZONE.
CRUEL. TWISTED.
AND NOT WITHOUT POTENTIAL.
YOU'VE BEEN HERE BEFORE, WHY WOULD THE ZONE RESTORE YOUR SIGHT?
THE BLACK VAULT, WHICH CAUSED MY BLINDNESS, DID SO BY EXPLOITING MY GREATEST FEAR--THAT I WON'T BE ABLE TO SAVE THE PEOPLE I LOVE.
THE CONDUIT WE JUST PASSED THROUGH HAD MANY OF THE SAME PROPERTIES.
AS WE TRANSITIONED INTO OUR PRESENT IMMATERIAL STATES, THAT CHANGED.
WITH NO TANGIBLE FORM, THE BODY IS REPAIRED.
EXPLAINS BEING EXILED HERE FOREVER, YET NEVER AGING.

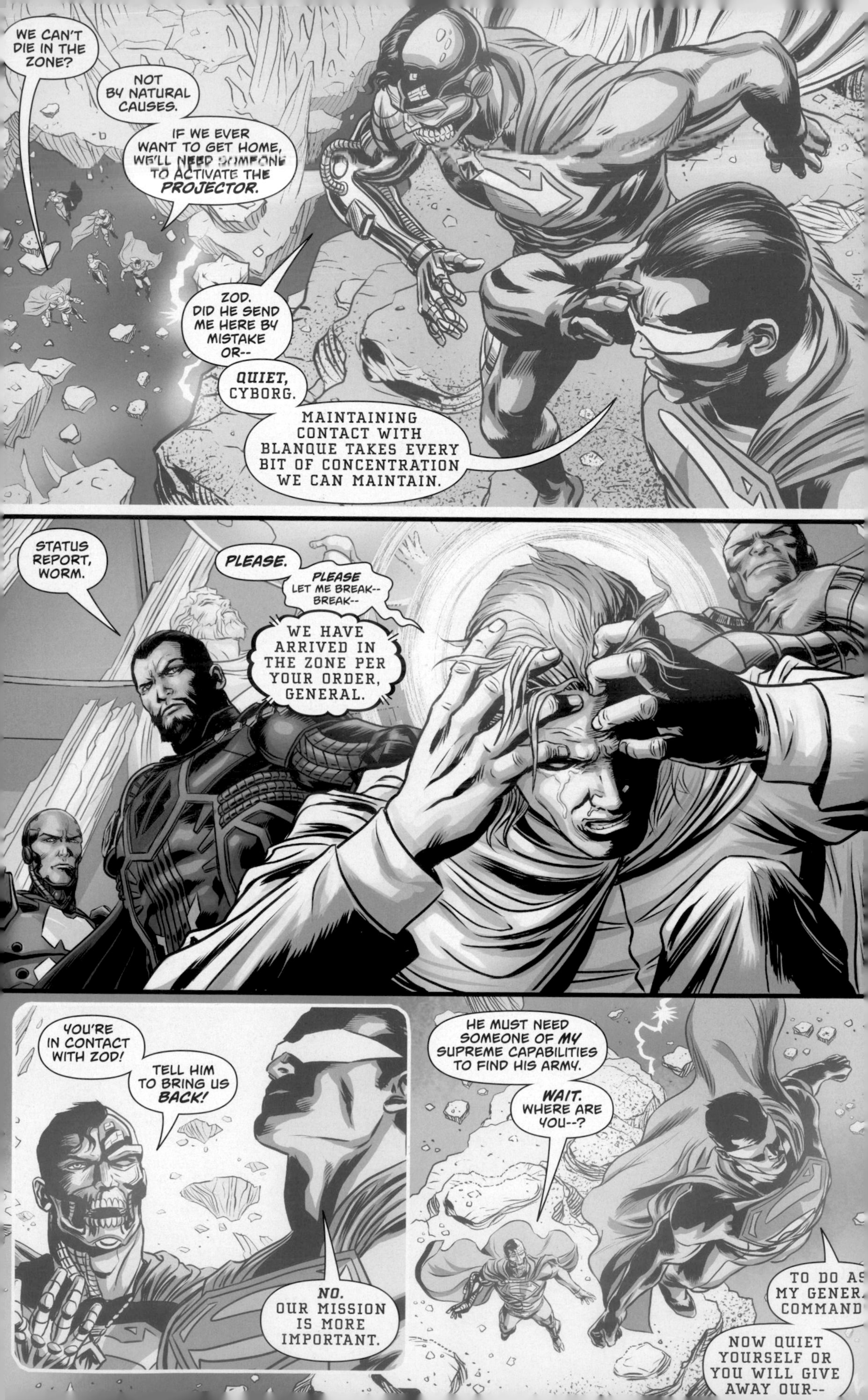
WE CAN'T DIE IN THE ZONE?
NOT BY NATURAL CAUSES.
IF WE EVER WANT TO GET HOME, WE'LL NEED SOMEONE TO ACTIVATE THE PROJECTOR.
ZOD. DID HE SEND ME HERE BY MISTAKE OR--
QUIET, CYBORG.
MAINTAINING CONTACT WITH BLANQUE TAKES EVERY BIT OF CONCENTRATION WE CAN MAINTAIN.
STATUS REPORT, WORM.
PLEASE.
PLEASE LET ME BREAK-- BREAK--
WE HAVE ARRIVED IN THE ZONE PER YOUR ORDER, GENERAL.
YOU'RE IN CONTACT WITH ZOD!
TELL HIM TO BRING US BACK!
NO. OUR MISSION IS MORE IMPORTANT.
HE MUST NEED SOMEONE OF MY SUPREME CAPABILITIES TO FIND HIS ARMY.
WAIT. WHERE ARE YOU--?
NOW QUIET YOURSELF OR YOU WILL GIVE AWAY OUR--

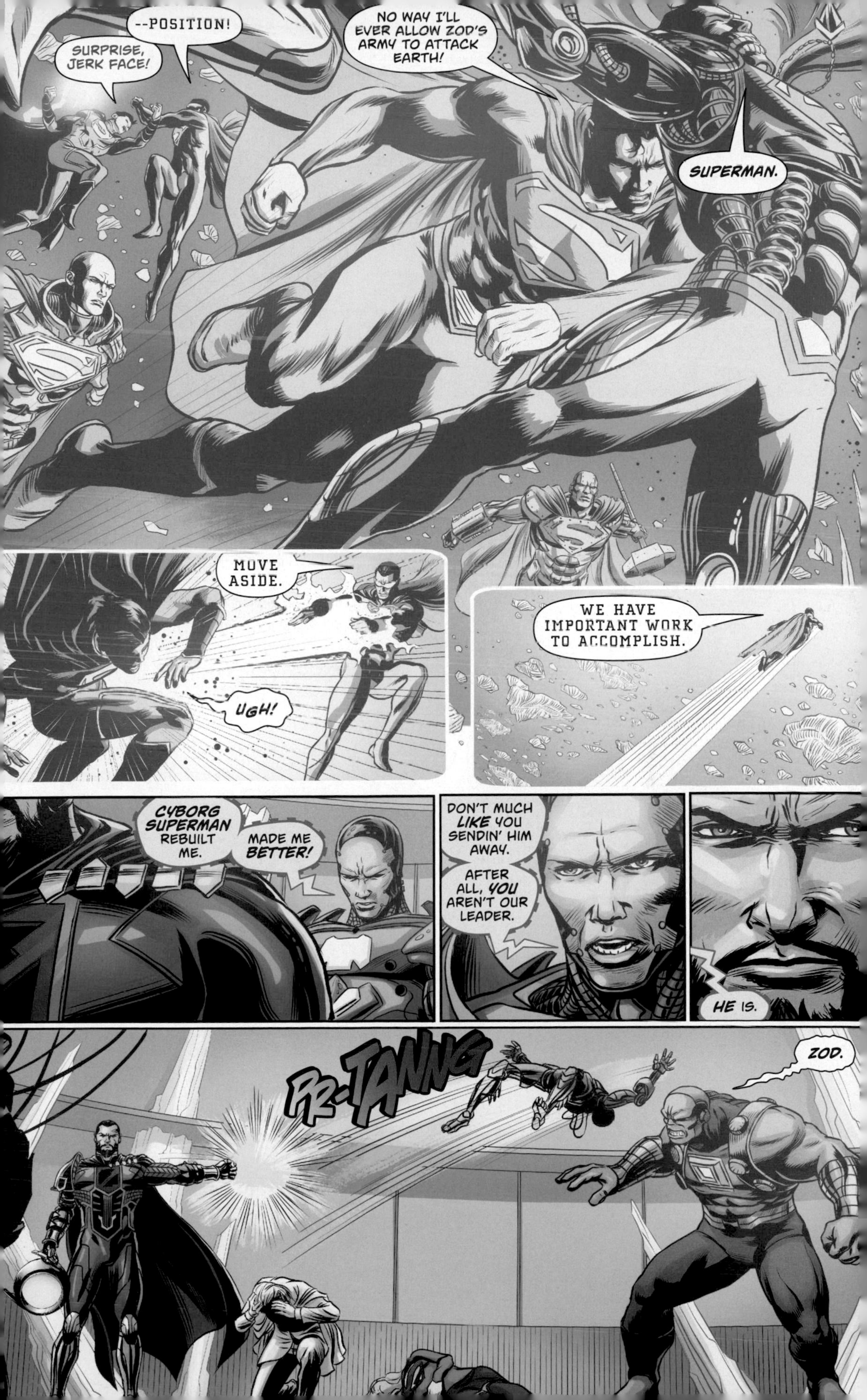
SURPRISE, JERK FACE!
--POSITION!
NO WAY I'LL EVER ALLOW ZOD'S ARMY TO ATTACK EARTH!
SUPERMAN.
MOVE ASIDE.
UGH!
WE HAVE IMPORTANT WORK TO ACCOMPLISH.
CYBORG SUPERMAN REBUILT ME.
MADE ME BETTER!
DON'T MUCH LIKE YOU SENDIN' HIM AWAY.
AFTER ALL, YOU AREN'T OUR LEADER.
HE IS.
PR-TANNG
ZOD.

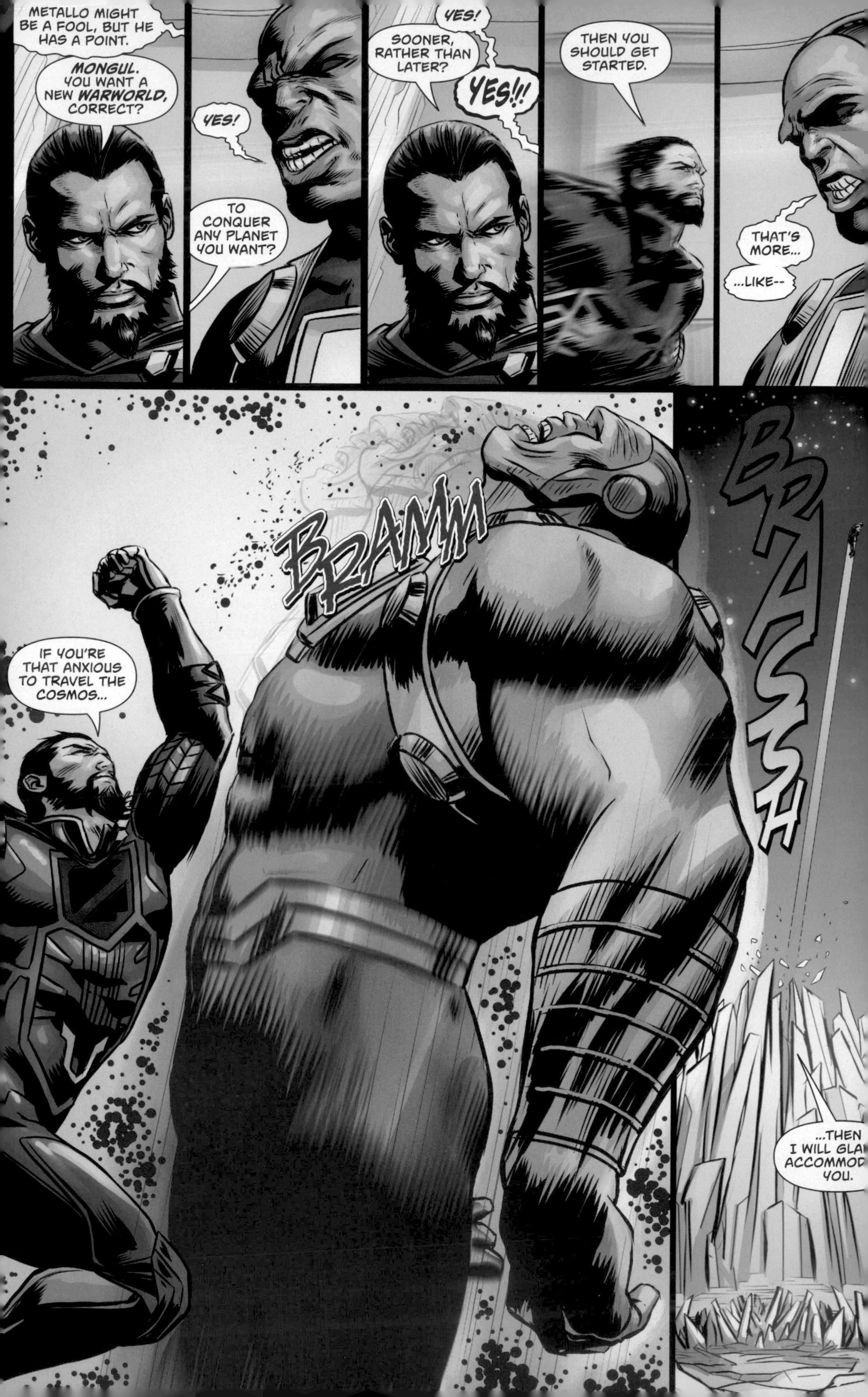

METALLO MIGHT BE A FOOL, BUT HE HAS A POINT.
MONGUL. YOU WANT A NEW WARWORLD, CORRECT?
YES!
TO CONQUER ANY PLANET YOU WANT?
YES!
SOONER, RATHER THAN LATER?
YES!!!
THEN YOU SHOULD GET STARTED.
THAT'S MORE...
...LIKE--
BRAMM
IF YOU'RE THAT ANXIOUS TO TRAVEL THE COSMOS...
BRASSH
...THEN I WILL GLA ACCOMMOD YOU.

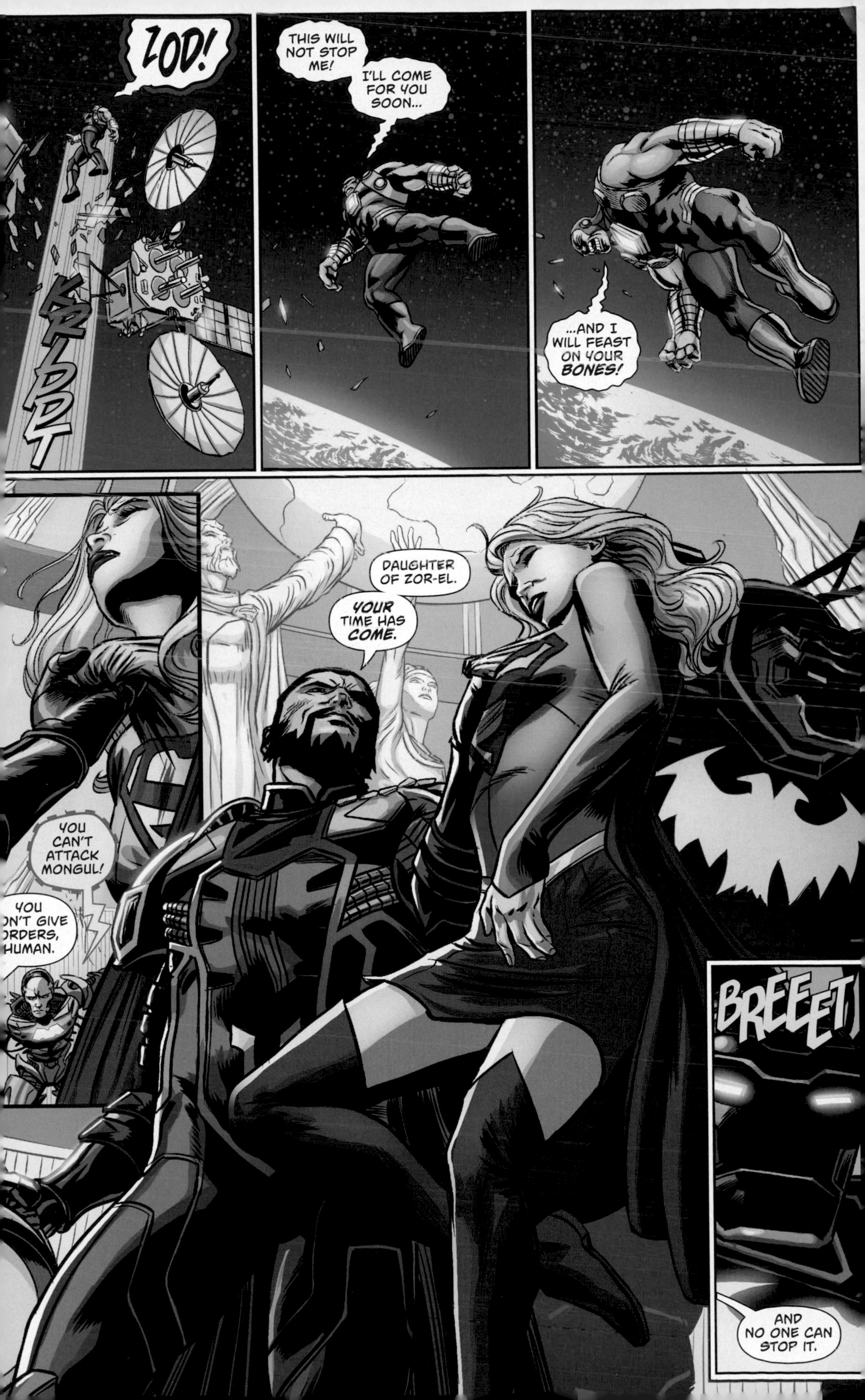
ZOD!
KRIDDT
THIS WILL NOT STOP ME!
I'LL COME FOR YOU SOON...
...AND I WILL FEAST ON YOUR BONES!
DAUGHTER OF ZOR-EL.
YOUR TIME HAS COME.
YOU CAN'T ATTACK MONGUL!
YOU N'T GIVE ORDERS, HUMAN.
BREEEET
AND NO ONE CAN STOP IT.

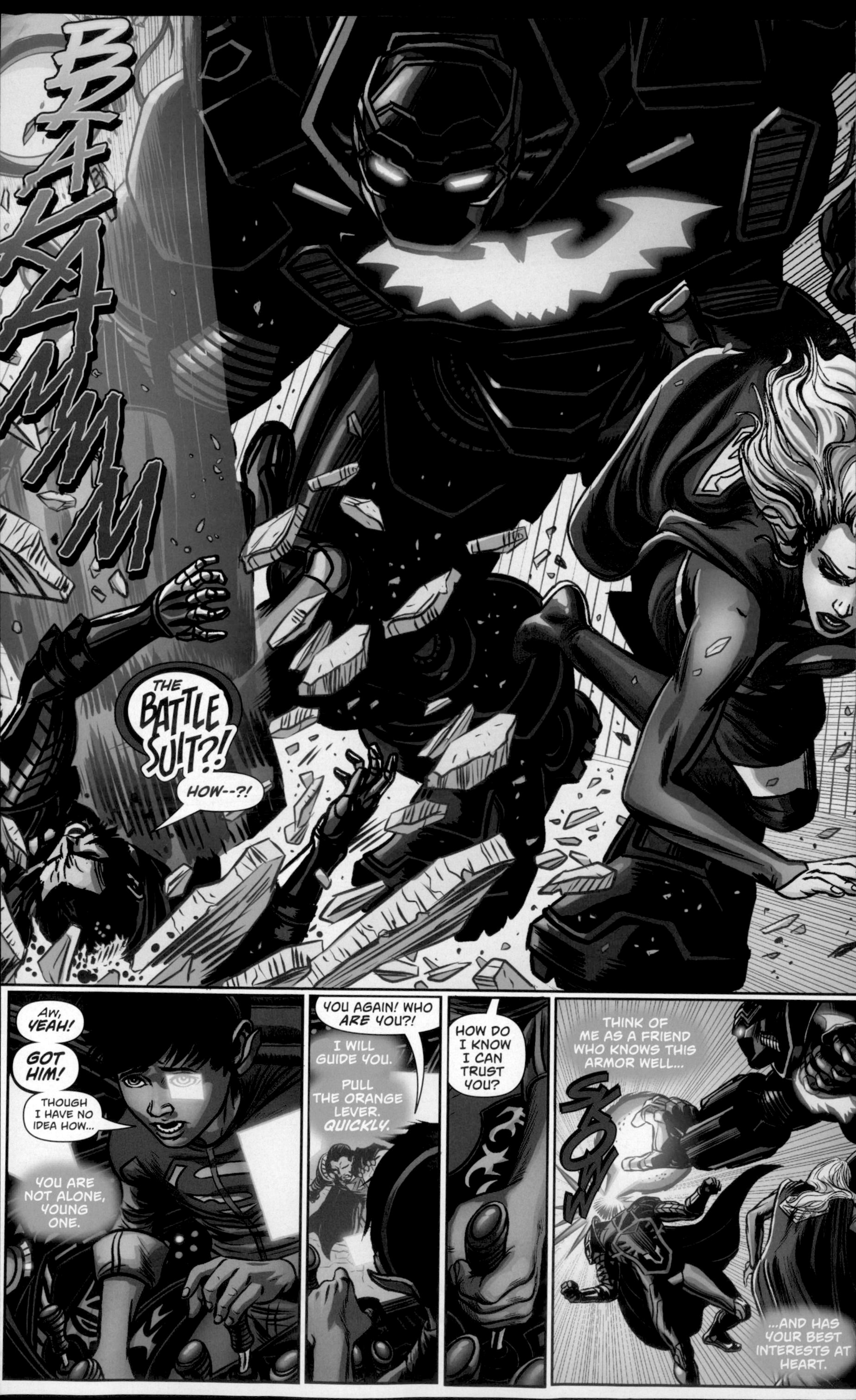
BRAKAMMM
THE BATTLE SUIT?!
HOW--?!
AW, YEAH!
GOT HIM!
THOUGH I HAVE NO IDEA HOW...
YOU ARE NOT ALONE, YOUNG ONE.
YOU AGAIN! WHO ARE YOU?!
I WILL GUIDE YOU.
PULL THE ORANGE LEVER. QUICKLY.
HOW DO I KNOW I CAN TRUST YOU?
THINK OF ME AS A FRIEND WHO KNOWS THIS ARMOR WELL...
...AND HAS YOUR BEST INTERESTS AT HEART.

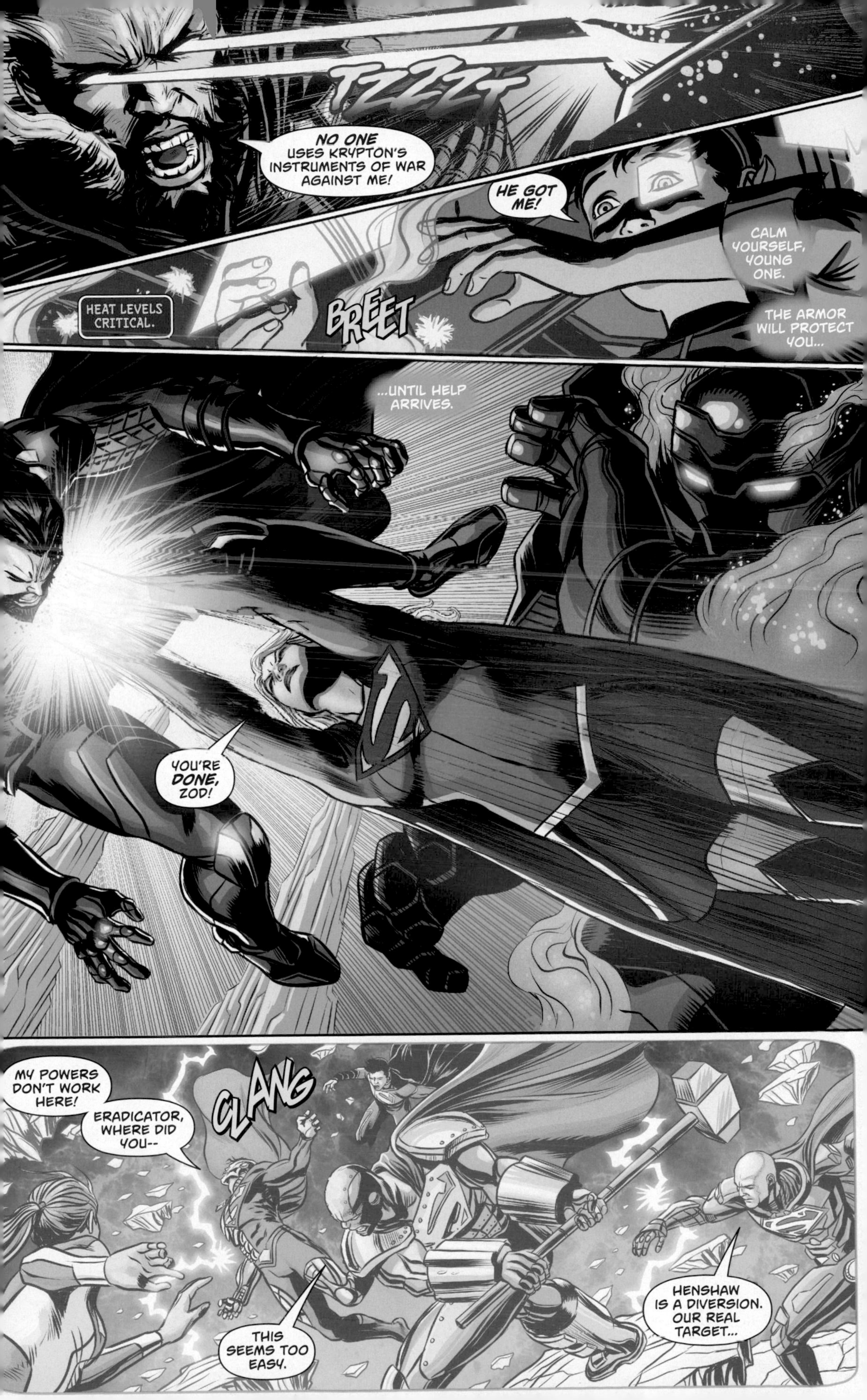
TZZZT
NO ONE USES KRYPTON'S INSTRUMENTS OF WAR AGAINST ME!
HE GOT ME!
CALM YOURSELF, YOUNG ONE.
HEAT LEVELS CRITICAL.
BREEET
THE ARMOR WILL PROTECT YOU...
...UNTIL HELP ARRIVES.
YOU'RE DONE, ZOD!
MY POWERS DON'T WORK HERE!
ERADICATOR, WHERE DID YOU--
CLANG
THIS SEEMS TOO EASY.
HENSHAW IS A DIVERSION. OUR REAL TARGET...

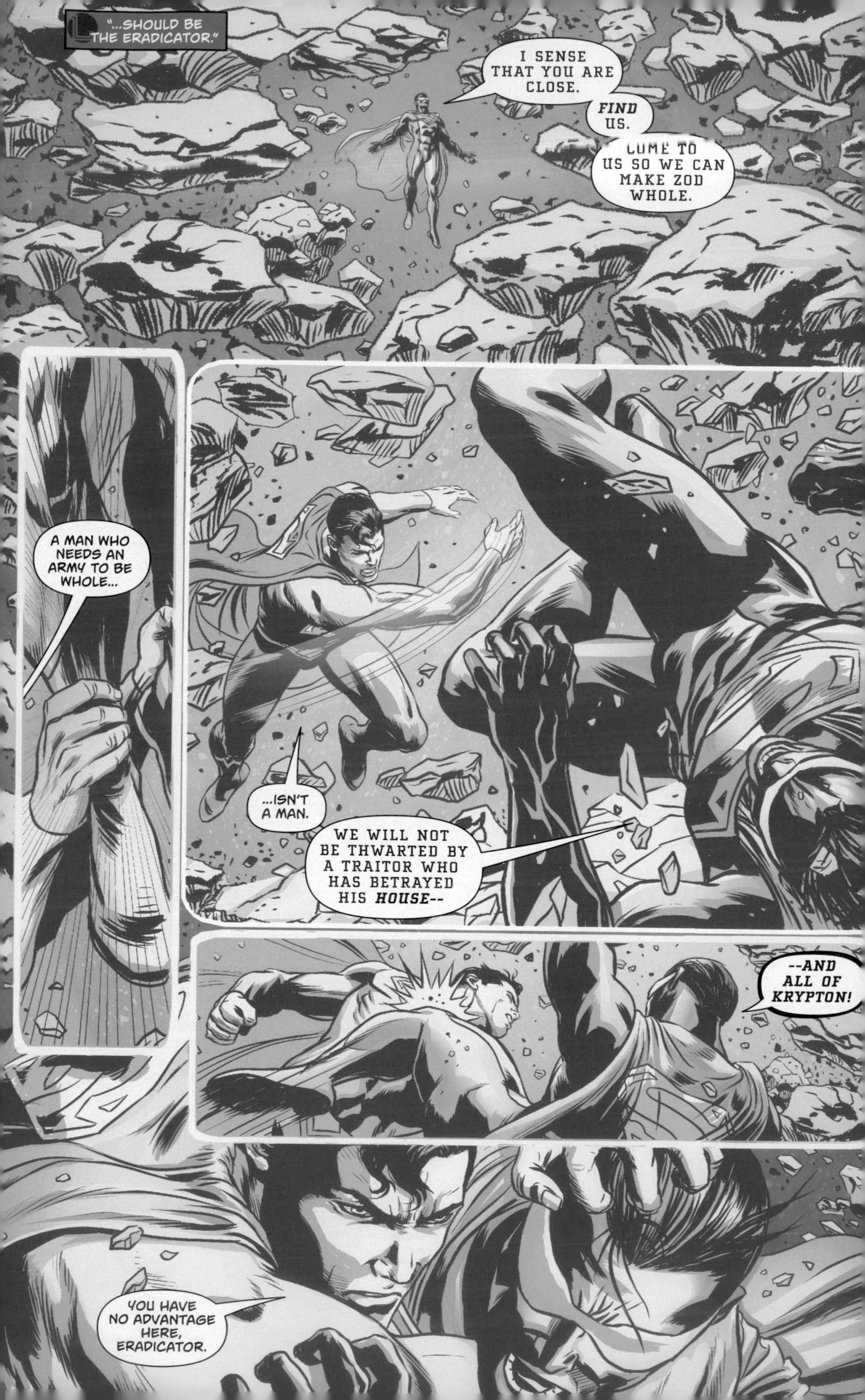
"...SHOULD BE THE ERADICATOR."
I SENSE THAT YOU ARE CLOSE.
FIND US.
COME TO US SO WE CAN MAKE ZOD WHOLE.
A MAN WHO NEEDS AN ARMY TO BE WHOLE...
...ISN'T A MAN.
WE WILL NOT BE THWARTED BY A TRAITOR WHO HAS BETRAYED HIS HOUSE--
--AND ALL OF KRYPTON!
YOU HAVE NO ADVANTAGE HERE, ERADICATOR.

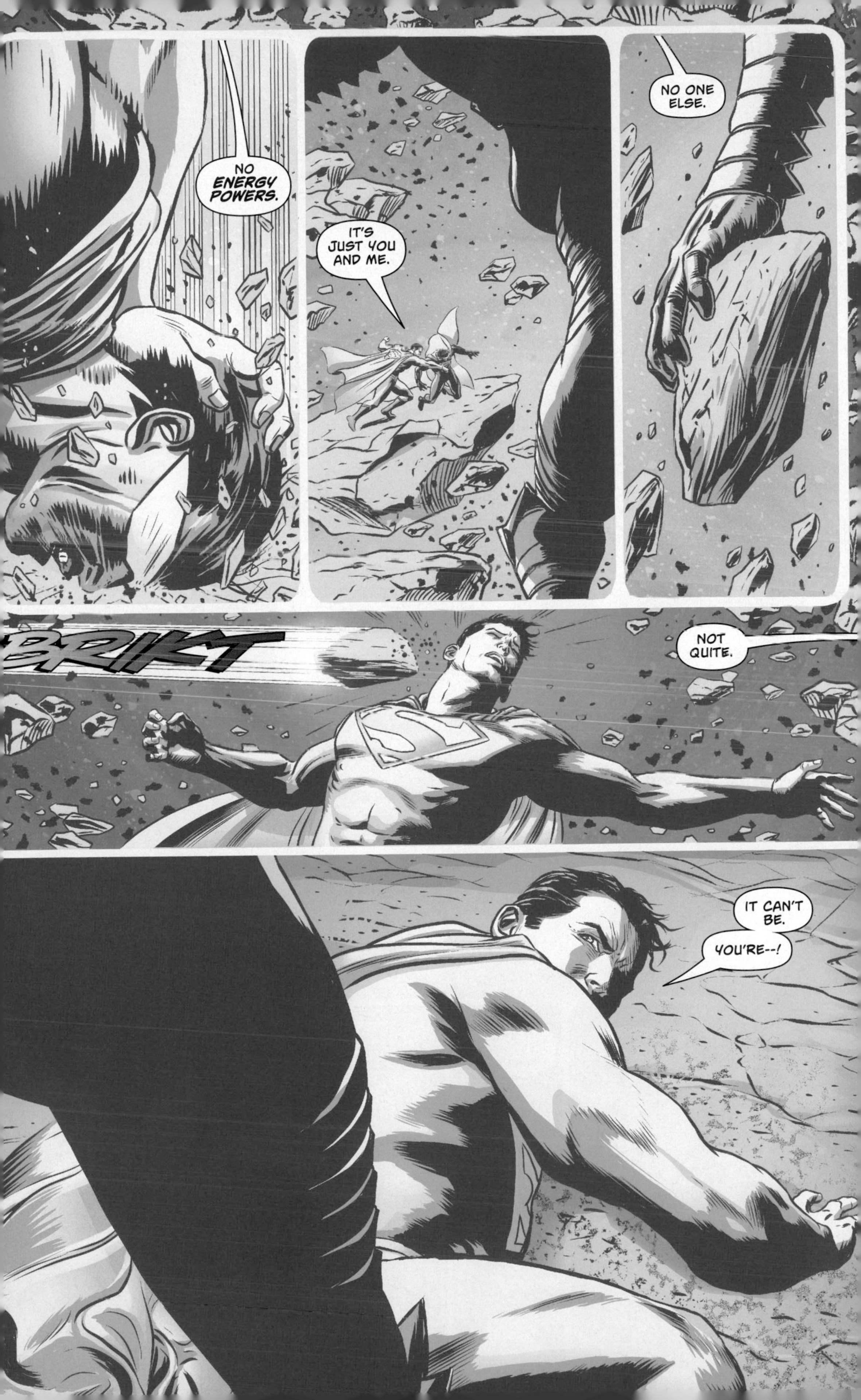
NO ENERGY POWERS.
IT'S JUST YOU AND ME.
NO ONE ELSE.
BRIKT
NOT QUITE.
IT CAN'T BE.
YOU'RE--!

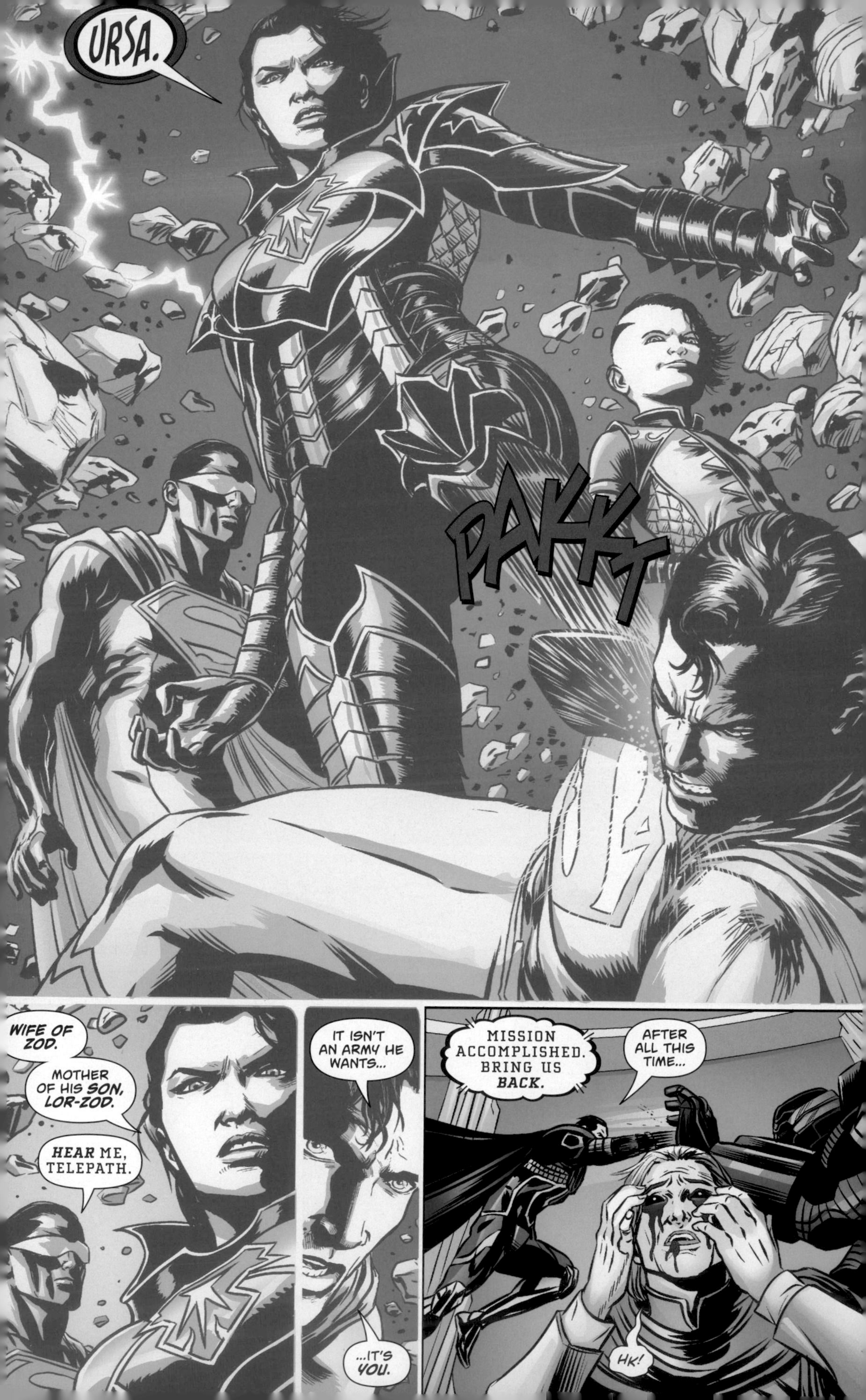
URSA.
PAKKT
WIFE OF ZOD.
MOTHER OF HIS SON, LOR-ZOD.
HEAR ME, TELEPATH.
IT ISN'T AN ARMY HE WANTS...
...IT'S YOU.
MISSION ACCOMPLISHED. BRING US BACK.
AFTER ALL THIS TIME...
HK!

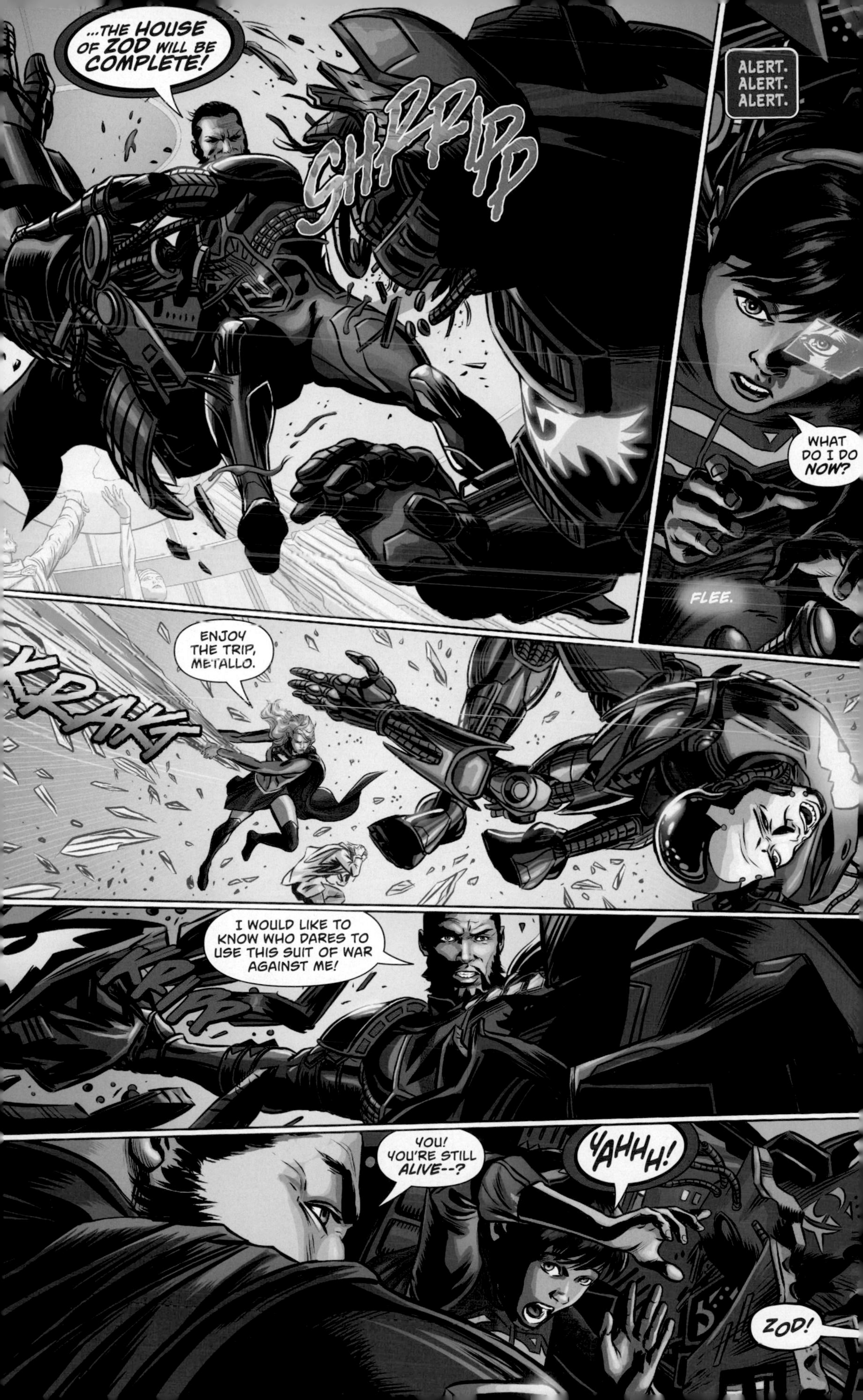
...THE HOUSE OF ZOD WILL BE COMPLETE!
SHDRIDD
ALERT. ALERT. ALERT.
WHAT DO I DO NOW?
FLEE.
KRAKK
ENJOY THE TRIP, METALLO.
KRIRR
I WOULD LIKE TO KNOW WHO DARES TO USE THIS SUIT OF WAR AGAINST ME!
YOU! YOU'RE STILL ALIVE--?
YAHHH!
ZOD!

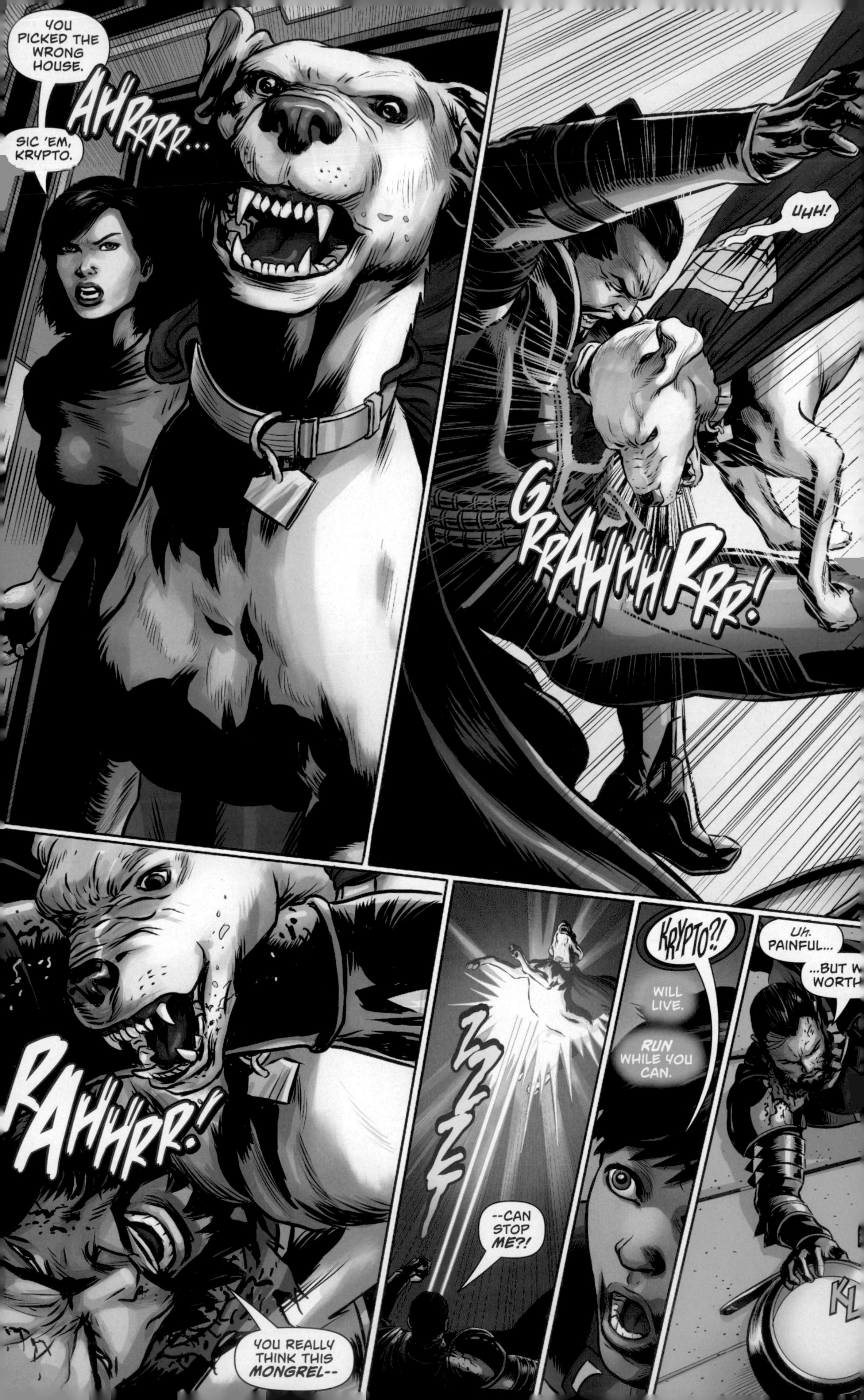
YOU PICKED THE WRONG HOUSE.
AHRRRR...
SIC 'EM, KRYPTO.
UHH!
GRRAHHHRRR!
RAHHRR!
YOU REALLY THINK THIS MONGREL--
--CAN STOP ME?!
KRYPTO?!
WILL LIVE.
RUN WHILE YOU CAN.
UH. PAINFUL...

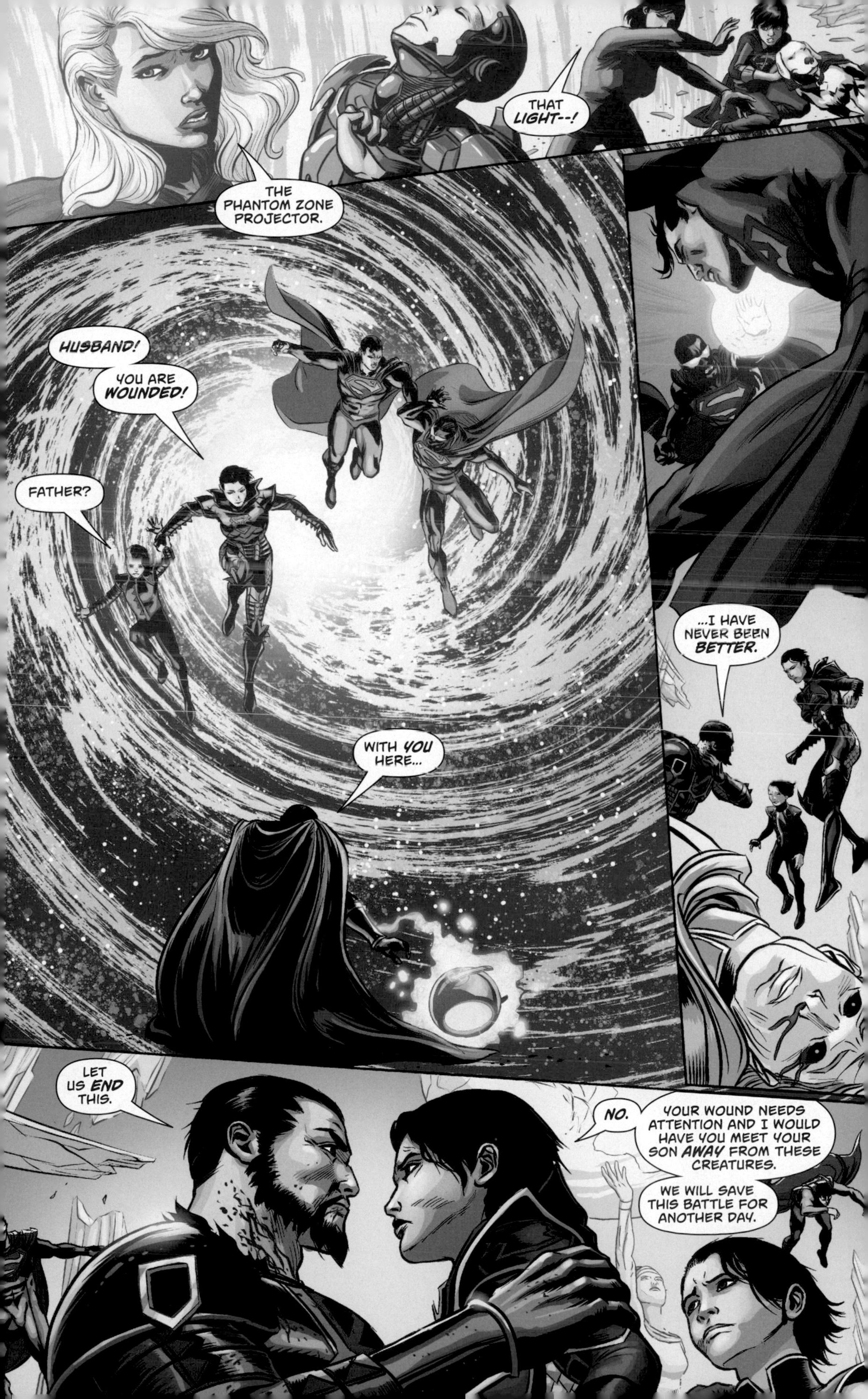

THAT LIGHT--!
THE PHANTOM ZONE PROJECTOR.
HUSBAND!
YOU ARE WOUNDED!
FATHER?
WITH YOU HERE...
...I HAVE NEVER BEEN BETTER.
LET US END THIS.
NO.
YOUR WOUND NEEDS ATTENTION AND I WOULD HAVE YOU MEET YOUR SON AWAY FROM THESE CREATURES.
WE WILL SAVE THIS BATTLE FOR ANOTHER DAY.

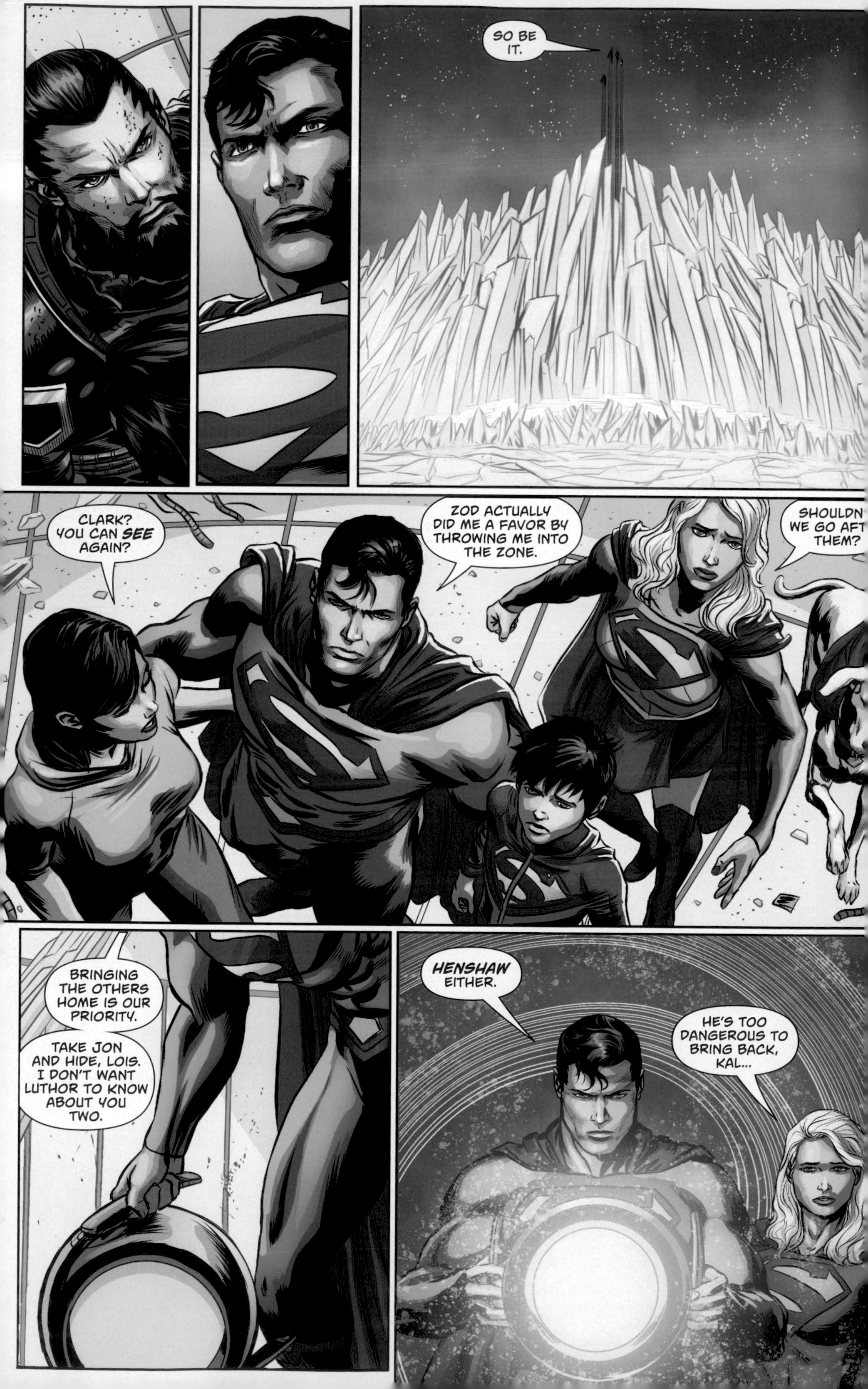
SO BE IT.
CLARK? YOU CAN SEE AGAIN?
ZOD ACTUALLY DID ME A FAVOR BY THROWING ME INTO THE ZONE.
SHOULDN WE GO AFT THEM?
BRINGING THE OTHERS HOME IS OUR PRIORITY.
TAKE JON AND HIDE, LOIS. I DON'T WANT LUTHOR TO KNOW ABOUT YOU TWO.
HENSHAW EITHER.
HE'S TOO DANGEROUS TO BRING BACK, KAL...

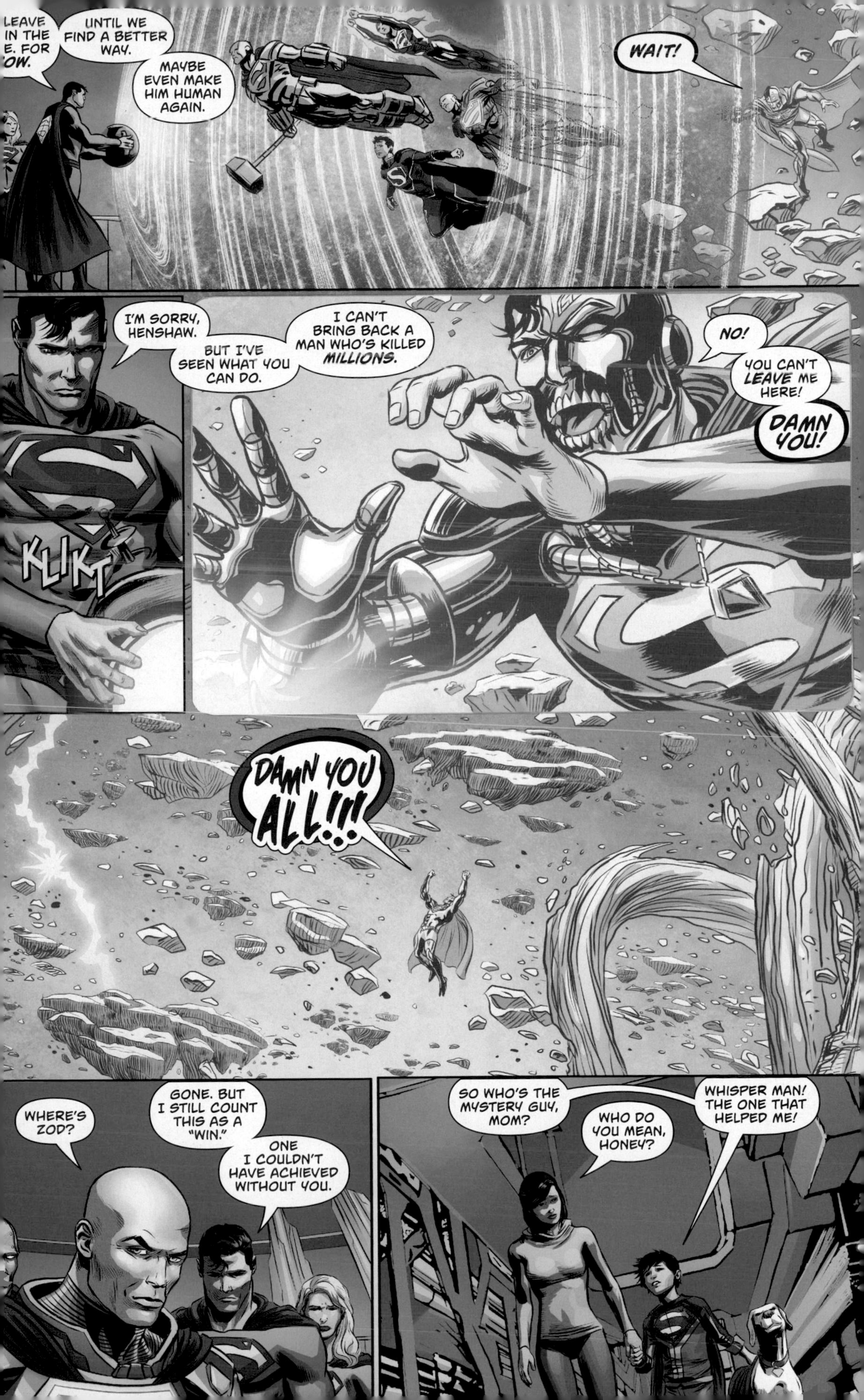
LEAVE IN THE E. FOR OW.
UNTIL WE FIND A BETTER WAY.
MAYBE EVEN MAKE HIM HUMAN AGAIN.
WAIT!
I'M SORRY, HENSHAW.
BUT I'VE SEEN WHAT YOU CAN DO.
I CAN'T BRING BACK A MAN WHO'S KILLED MILLIONS.
NO!
YOU CAN'T LEAVE ME HERE!
DAMN YOU!
KLIKT
DAMN YOU ALL!!!
WHERE'S ZOD?
GONE. BUT I STILL COUNT THIS AS A "WIN."
ONE I COULDN'T HAVE ACHIEVED WITHOUT YOU.
SO WHO'S THE MYSTERY GUY, MOM?
WHO DO YOU MEAN, HONEY?
WHISPER MAN! THE ONE THAT HELPED ME!

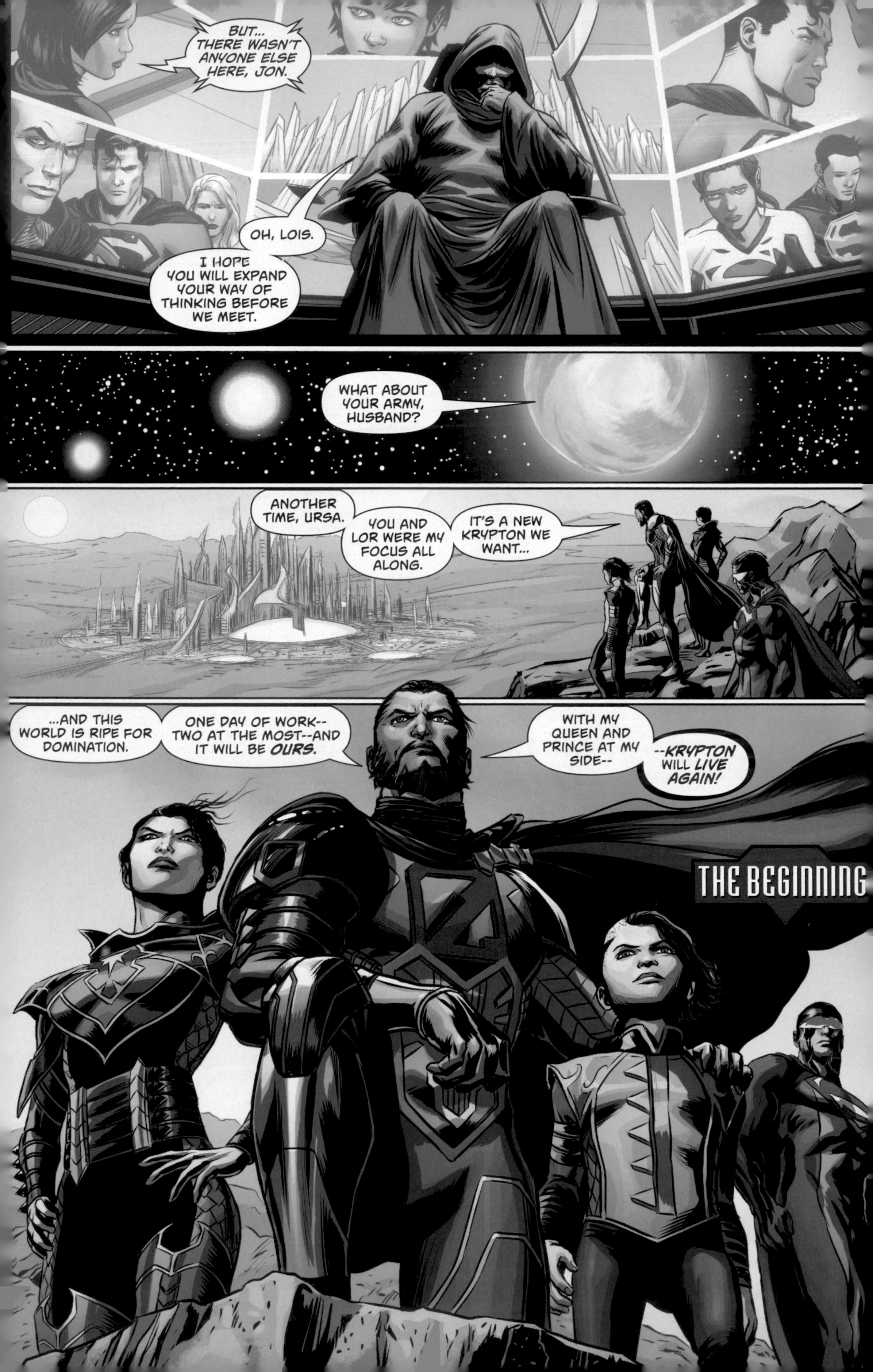
BUT... THERE WASN'T ANYONE ELSE HERE, JON.
OH, LOIS.
I HOPE YOU WILL EXPAND YOUR WAY OF THINKING BEFORE WE MEET.
WHAT ABOUT YOUR ARMY, HUSBAND?
ANOTHER TIME, URSA.
YOU AND LOR WERE MY FOCUS ALL ALONG.
IT'S A NEW KRYPTON WE WANT...
...AND THIS WORLD IS RIPE FOR DOMINATION.
ONE DAY OF WORK--TWO AT THE MOST--AND IT WILL BE OURS.
WITH MY QUEEN AND PRINCE AT MY SIDE--
--KRYPTON WILL LIVE AGAIN!
THE BEGINNING

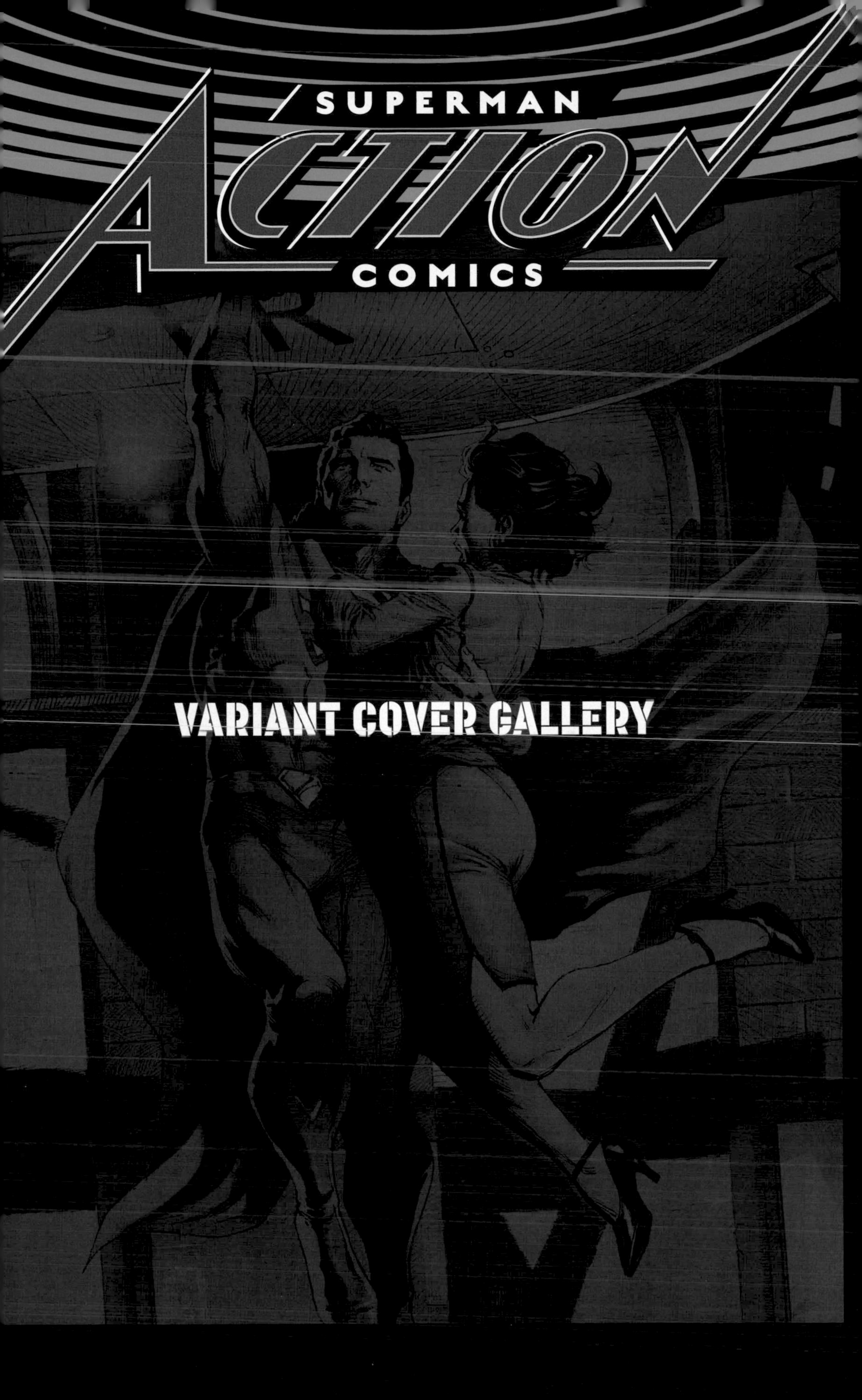
SUPERMAN
ACTION
COMICS

VARIANT COVER GALLERY

Variant cover art for ACTION COMICS #977 by GARY FRANK and BRAD ANDERSON

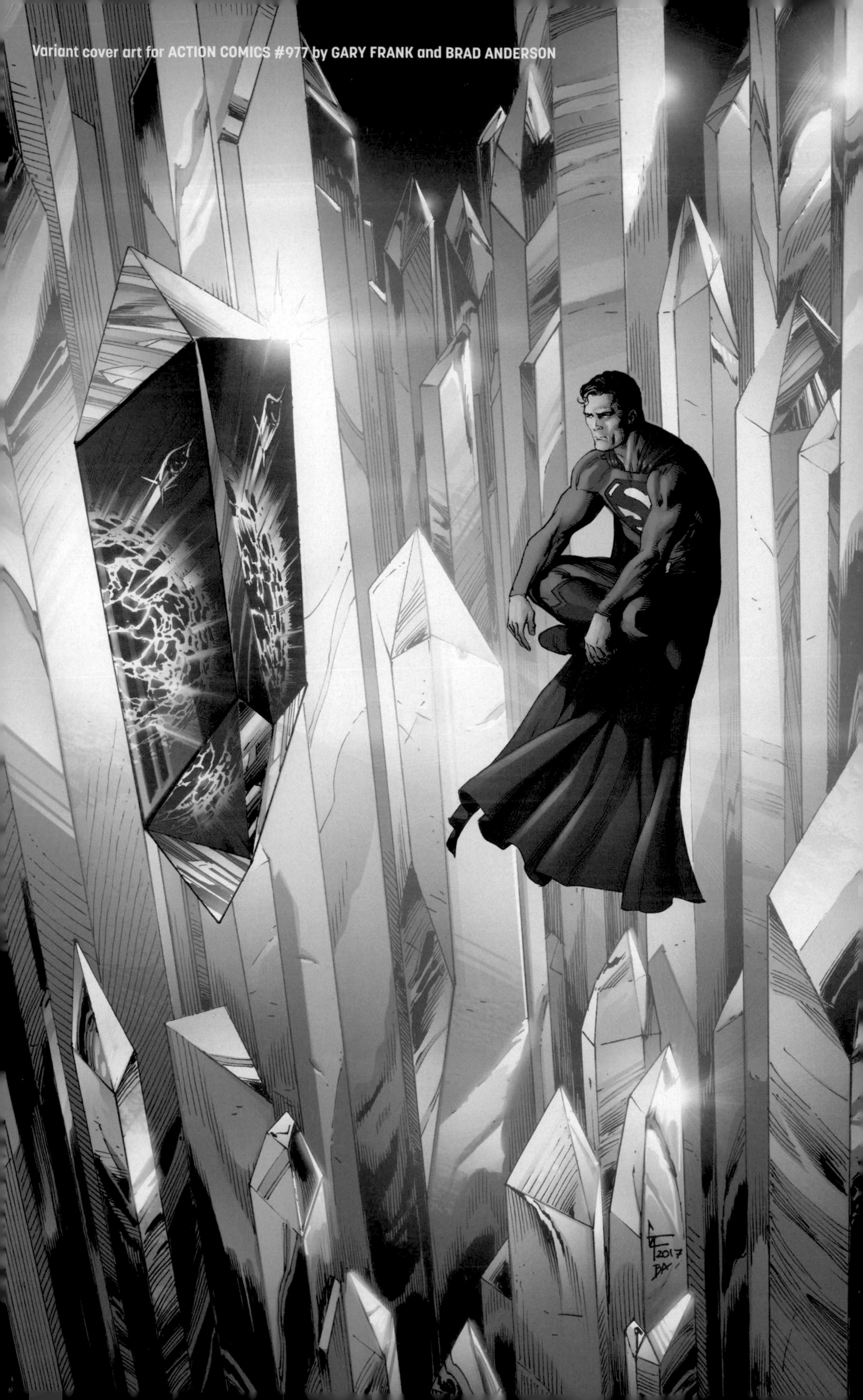

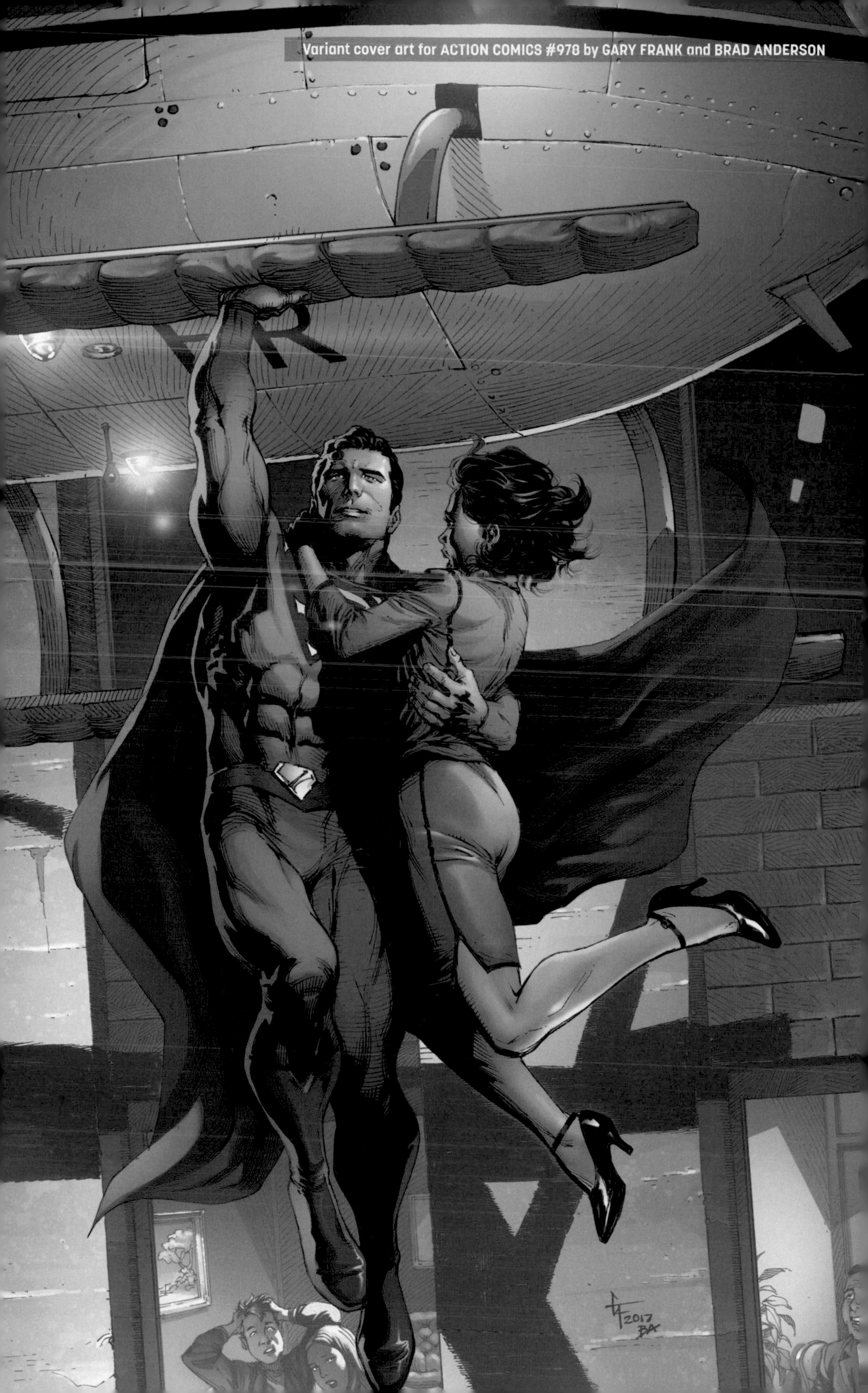

Variant cover art for ACTION COMICS #978 by GARY FRANK and BRAD ANDERSON

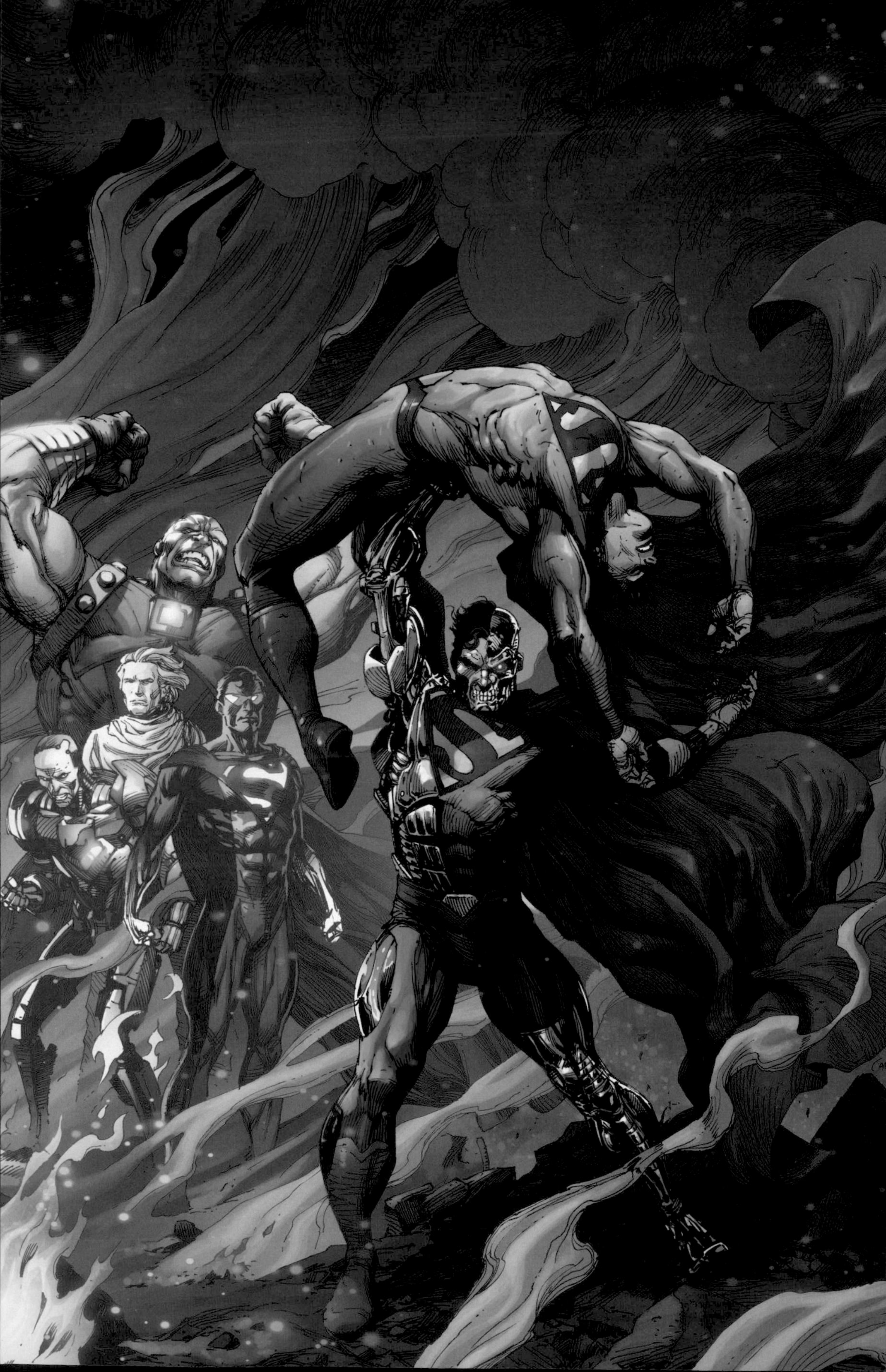

Variant cover art for ACTION COMICS #979 by GARY FRANK and BRAD ANDERSON

Variant cover art for ACTION COMICS #980 by GARY FRANK and BRAD ANDERSON

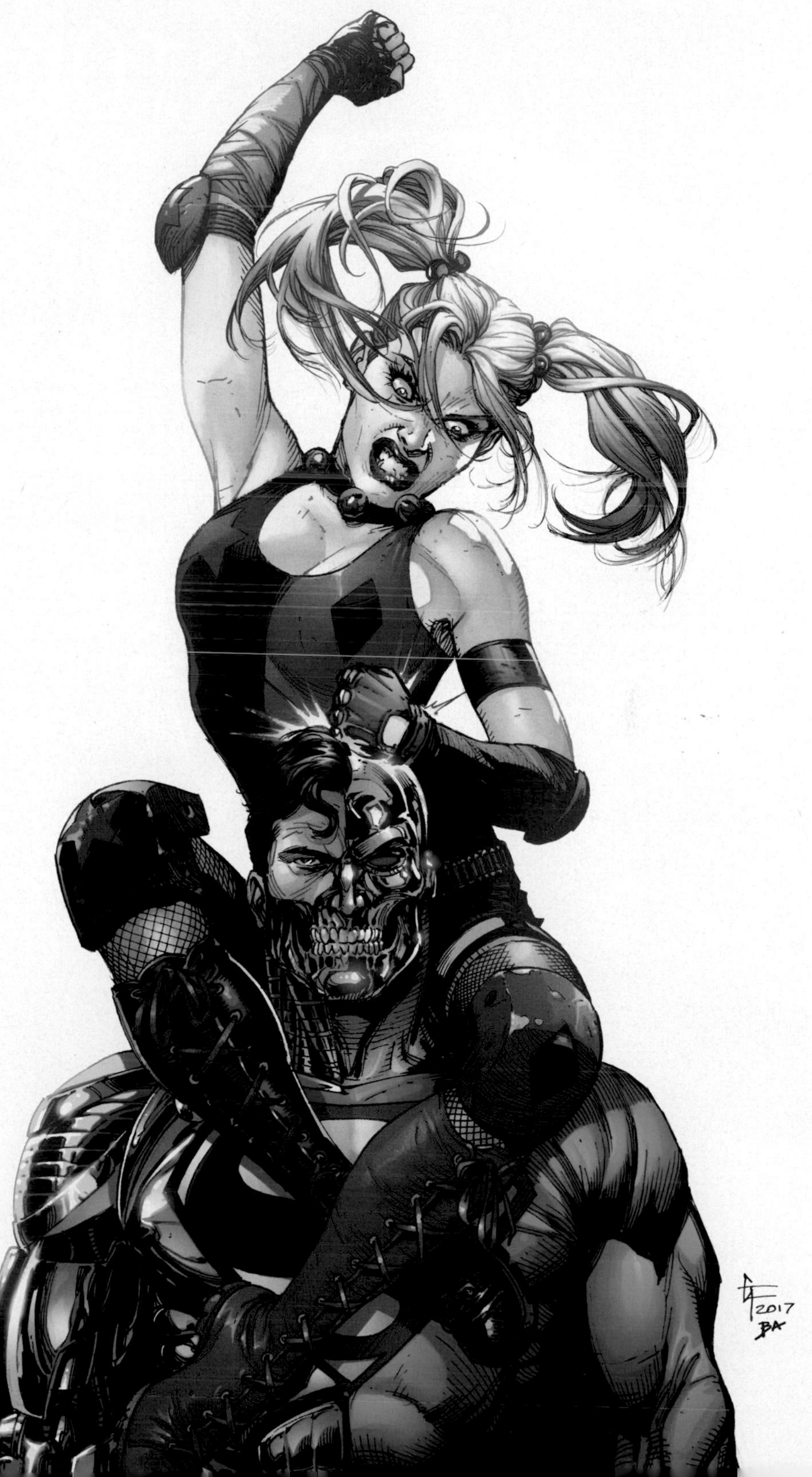
2017
BA

Variant cover art for ACTION COMICS #981 by GARY FRANK and BRAD ANDERSON

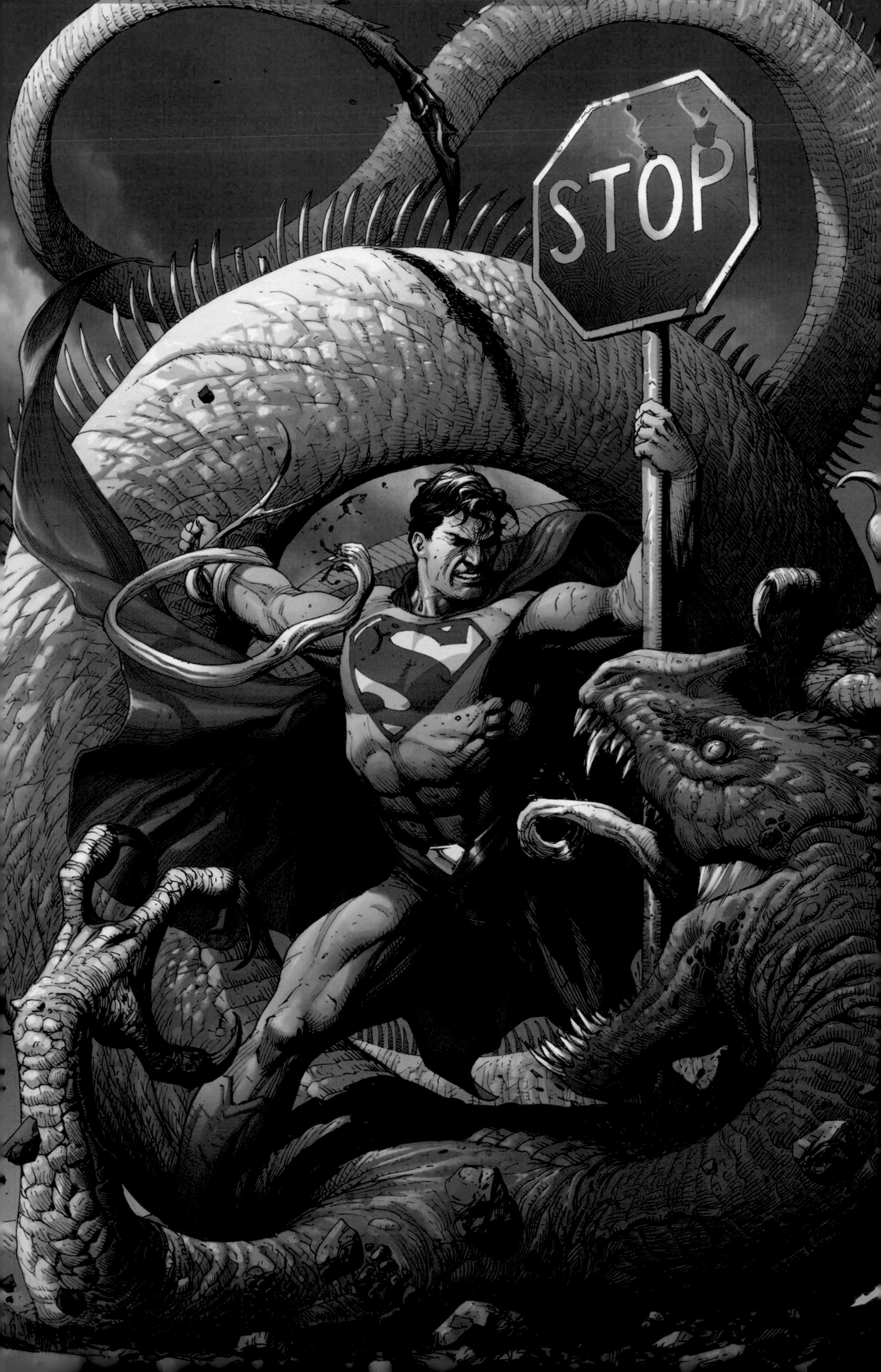
STOP

Variant cover art for ACTION COMICS #982 by MIKEL JANIN

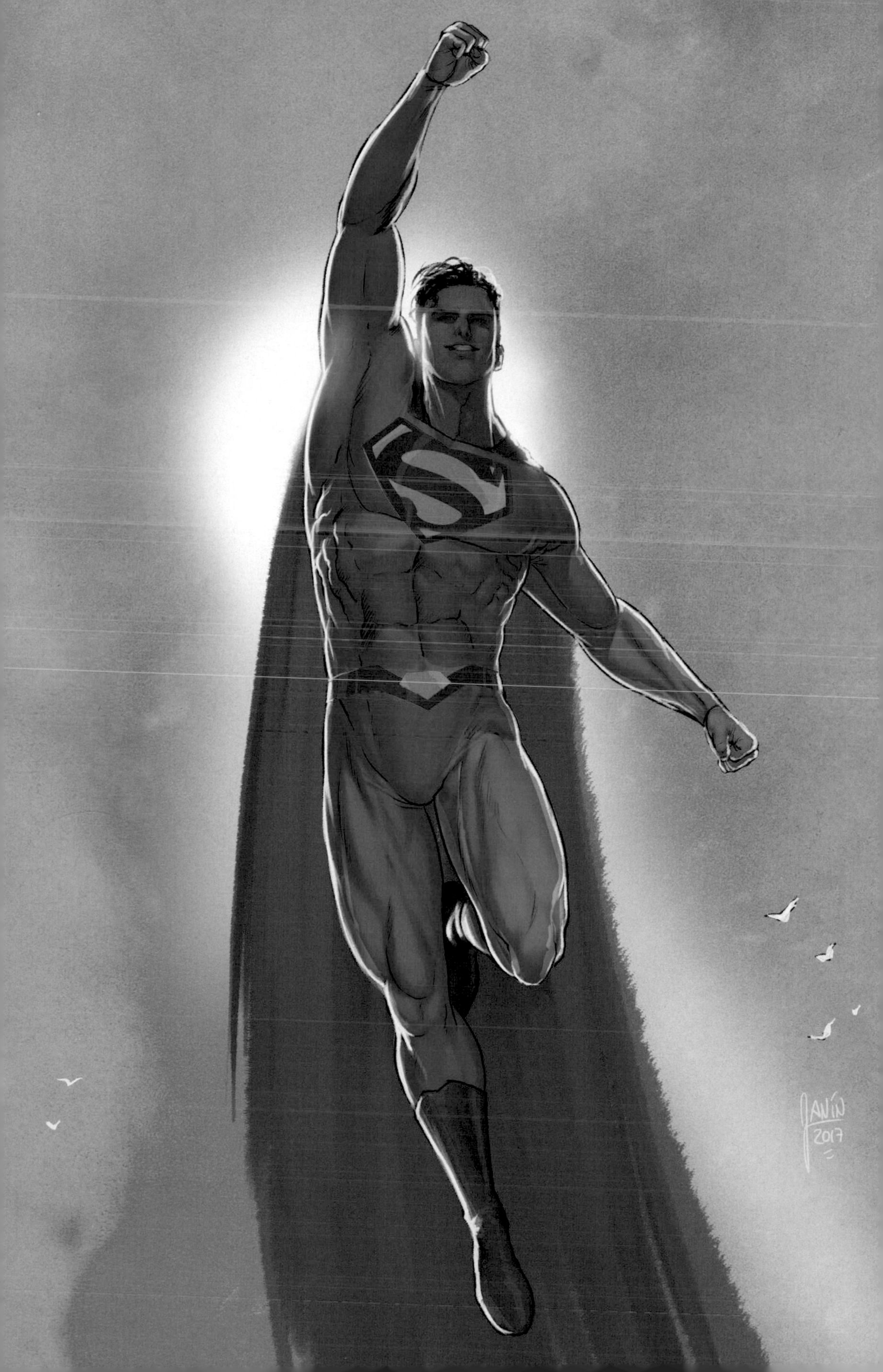
JANÍN
2017

Variant cover art for ACTION COMICS #983 by MIKEL JANIN

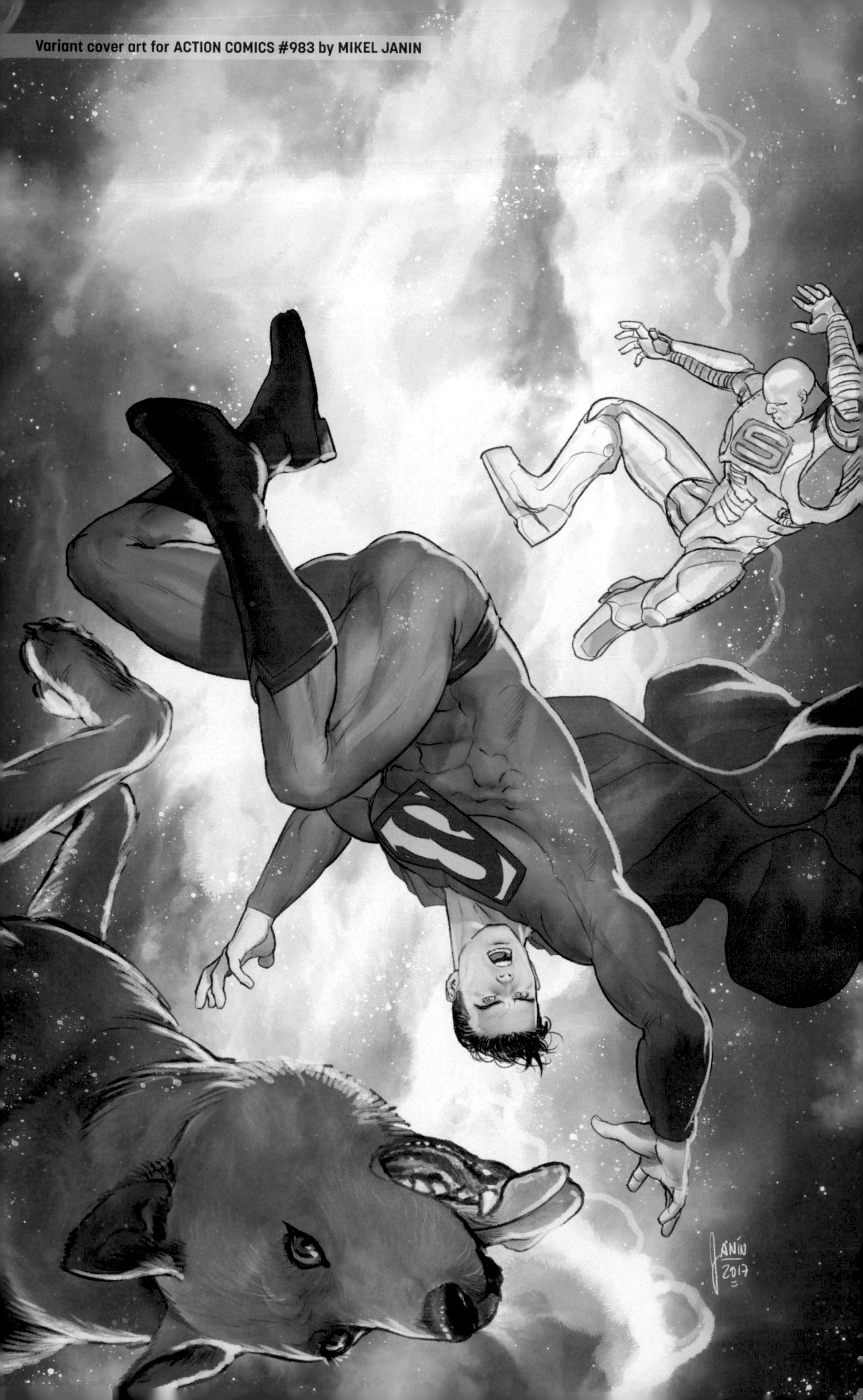
JANIN
2017

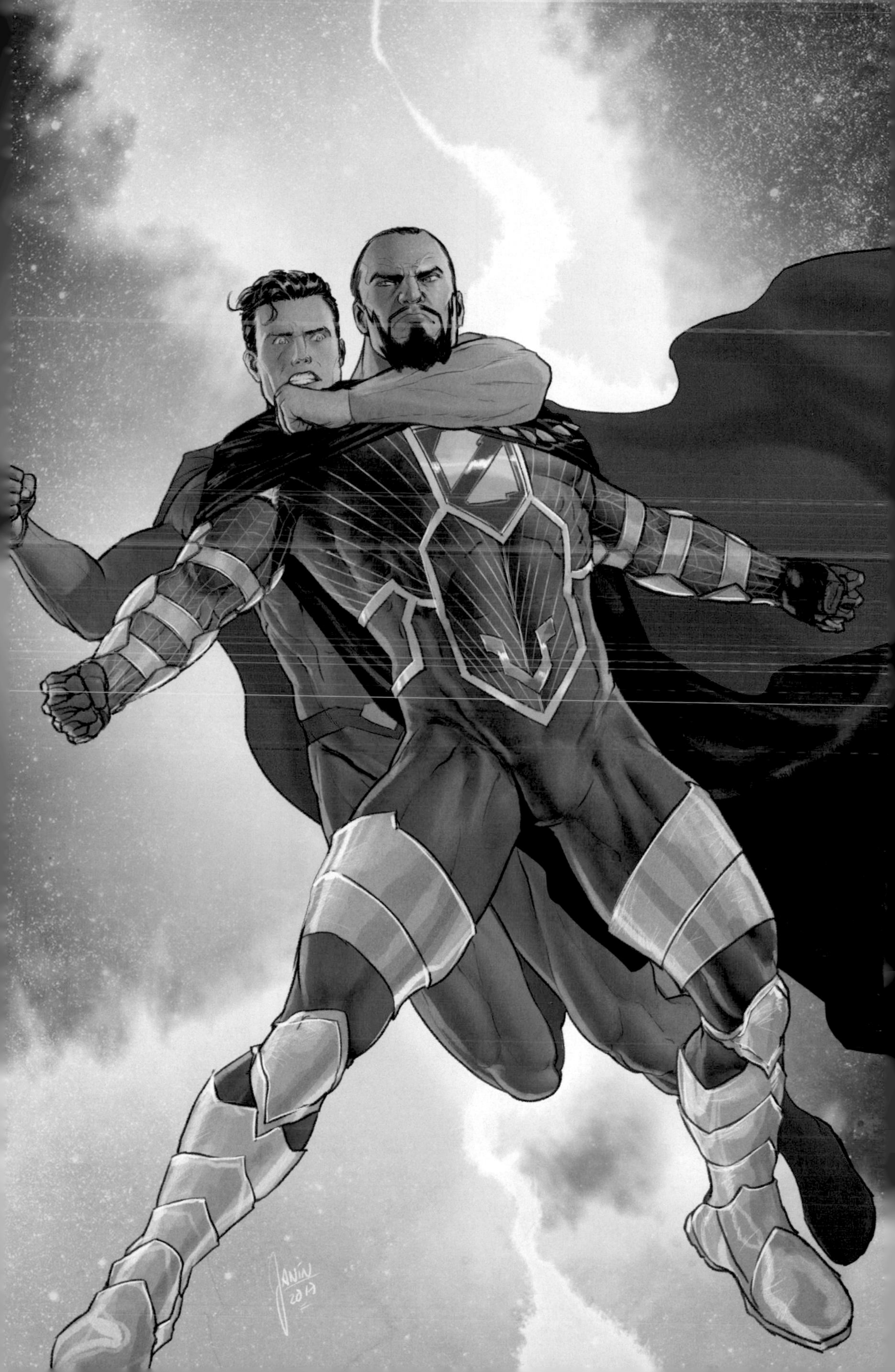
JANIN
2017

Variant cover art for ACTION COMICS #984 by MIKEL JANIN

"That gorgeous spectacle is an undeniable part of Superman's appeal, but the family dynamics are what make it such an engaging read."
– A.V. CLUB

"Head and shoulders above the rest."
– NEWSARAMA

DC UNIVERSE REBIRTH
SUPERMAN
VOL. 1: SON OF SUPERMAN
PETER J. TOMASI with PATRICK GLEASON,
DOUG MAHNKE & JORGE JIMENEZ

VOL. 1 SON OF SUPERMAN
PETER J. TOMASI • PATRICK GLEASON • DOUG MAHNKE • JORGE JIMENEZ • MICK GRAY

**SUPERGIRL VOL. 1:
REIGN OF THE SUPERMEN**

**ACTION COMICS VOL. 1:
PATH OF DOOM**

**BATMAN VOL. 1:
I AM GOTHAM**

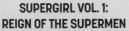
Get more DC graphic novels wherever comics and books are sold!

"Some really thrilling artwork that establishes
incredible scope and danger."
IGN

DC UNIVERSE REBIRTH

JUSTICE
LEAGUE

VOL. 1: The Extinction Machines

BRYAN HITCH
with **TONY S. DANIEL**

VOL. 1 THE EXTINCTION MACHINES
BRYAN HITCH • TONY S. DANIEL • SANDU FLOREA • TOMEU MOREY

VOL. 1 THE IMITATION OF LIFE
JOHN SEMPER JR. • PAUL PELLETIER • WILL CONRAD

**CYBORG VOL. 1:
THE IMITATION OF LIFE**

VOL. 1 RAGE PLANET
SAM HUMPHRIES • ROBSON ROCHA • ETHAN VAN SCIVER • ED BENES

**GREEN LANTERNS VOL. 1:
RAGE PLANET**

VOL. 1 THE DROWNING
DAN ABNETT • PHILIPPE BRIONES • SCOT EATON • BRAD WALKER

**AQUAMAN VOL. 1:
THE DROWNING**

Get more DC graphic novels wherever comics and books are sold!

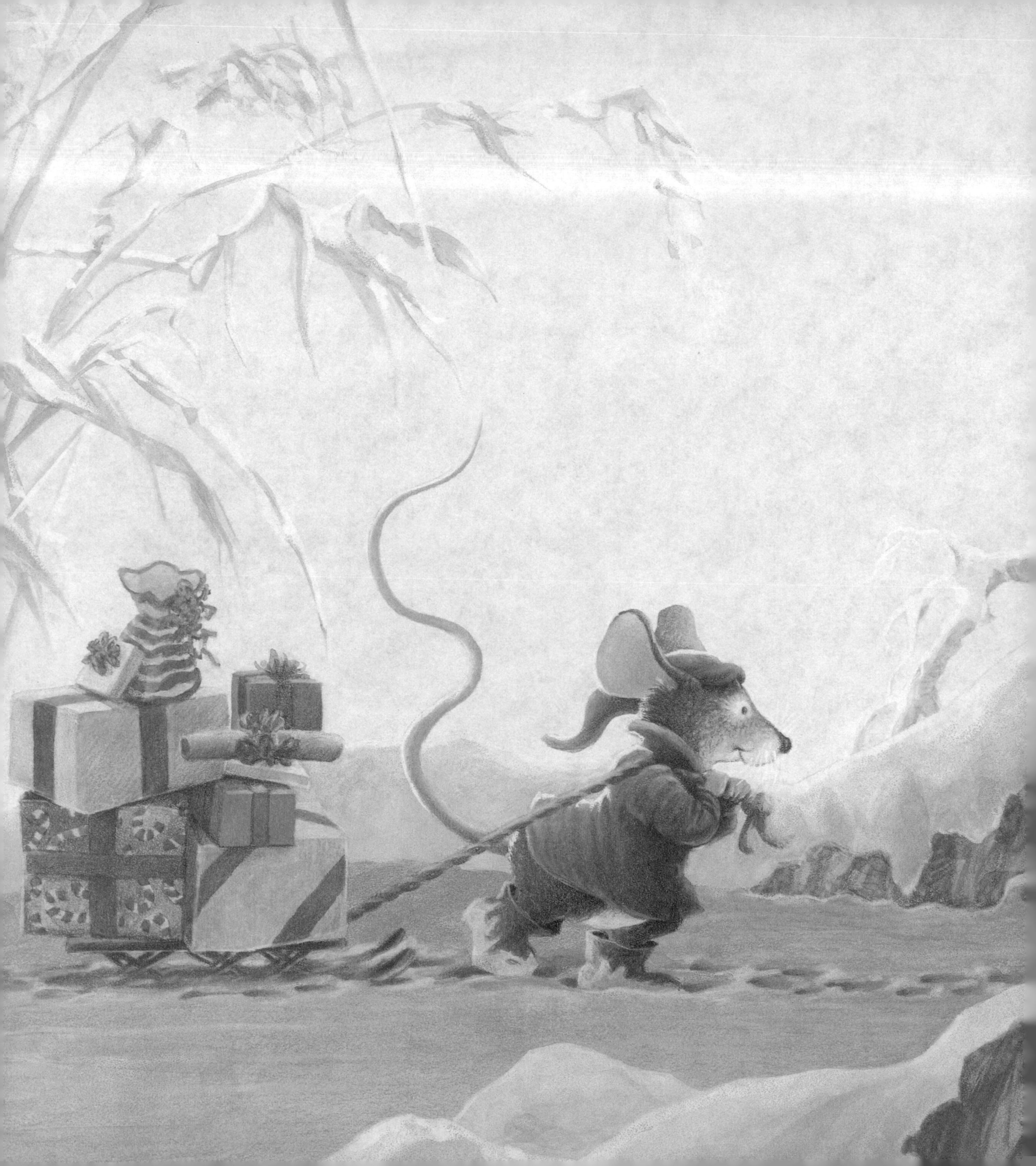

Merry Christmas, BIG HUNGRY BEAR!

by DON and AUDREY WOOD

illustrated by DON WOOD

Scholastic Inc.

New York Toronto London Auckland Sydney
Mexico City New Delhi Hong Kong Buenos Aires

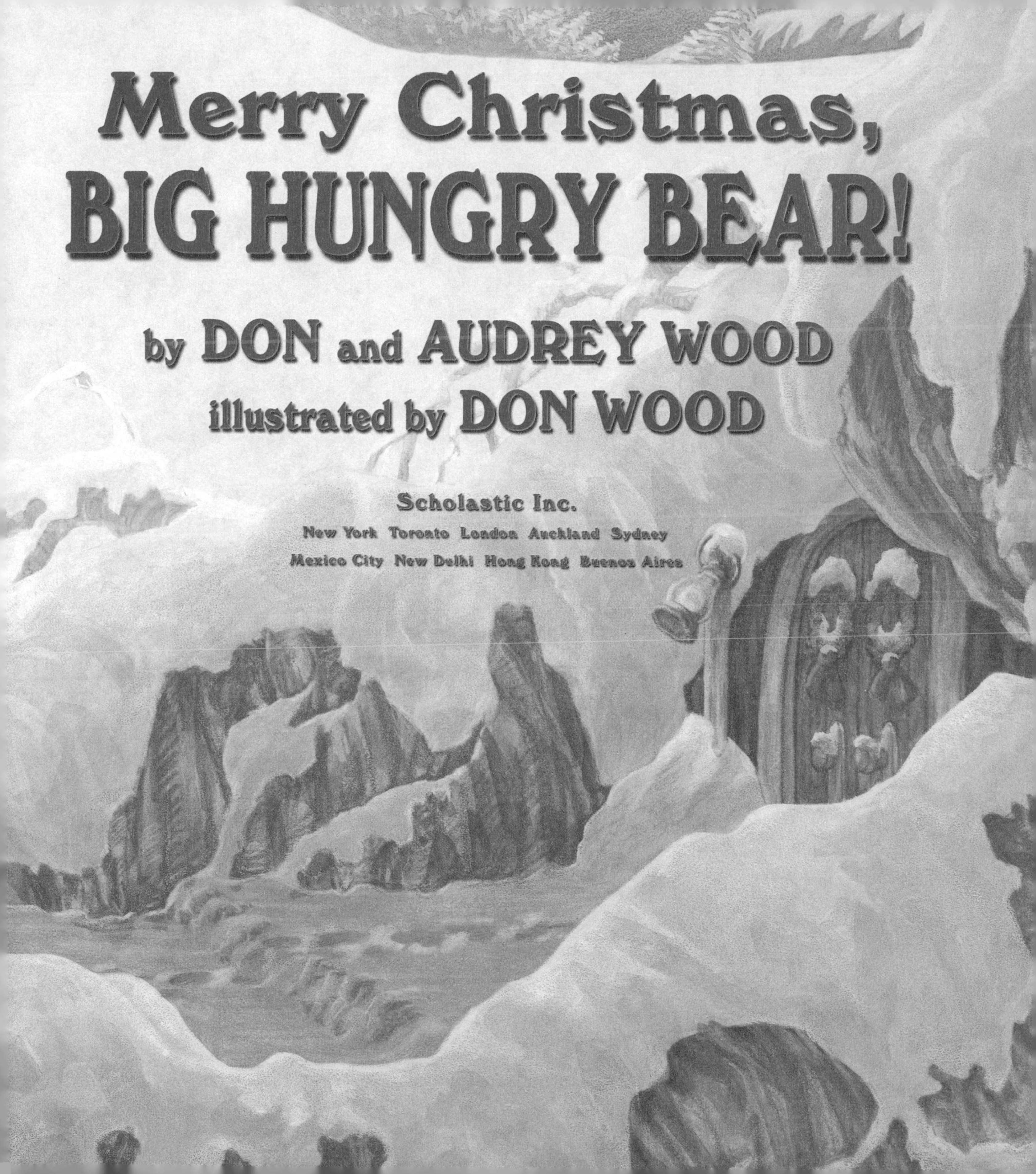

No part of this publication may be reproduced, stored in a retrieval system,
or transmitted in any form or by any means, electronic, mechanical, photocopying,
recording, or otherwise, without written permission of the publisher.
For information regarding permission, write to Scholastic Inc.,
Attention: Permissions Department, 557 Broadway, New York, NY 10012.

This book was originally published in hardcover by the Blue Sky Press in 2002.

ISBN 0-439-57458-7

Copyright © 2002 by A. Twinn. All rights reserved.
Published by Scholastic Inc., by arrangement with Child's Play (International) Ltd.
SCHOLASTIC and associated logos are trademarks and/or
registered trademarks of Scholastic Inc.

12   9 10/0

Printed in the U.S.A.   40

This edition first printing, November 2005

Dedicated to
Alejandra Demers

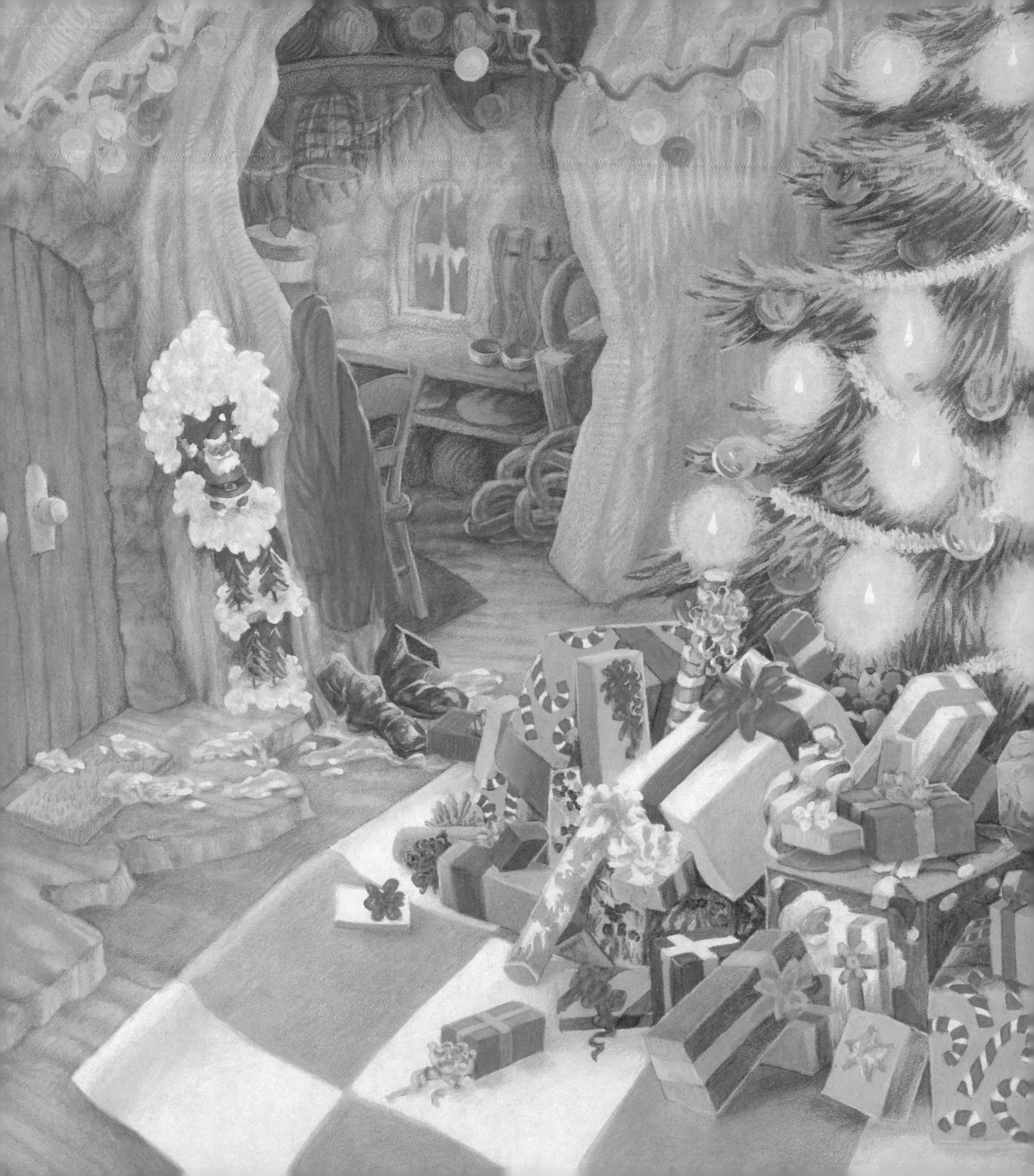

Hello, little Mouse.
I see you're ready
for Christmas.

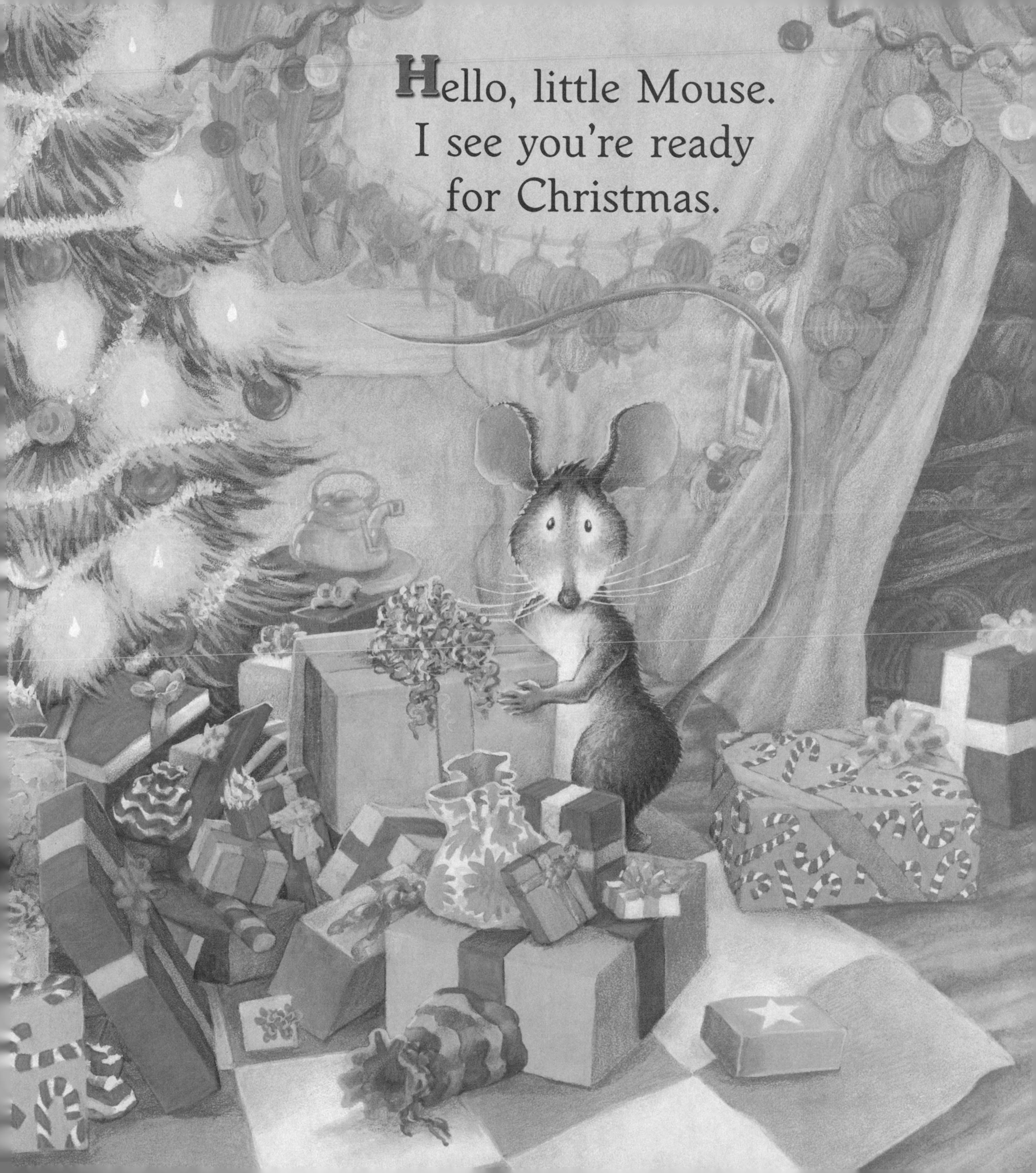

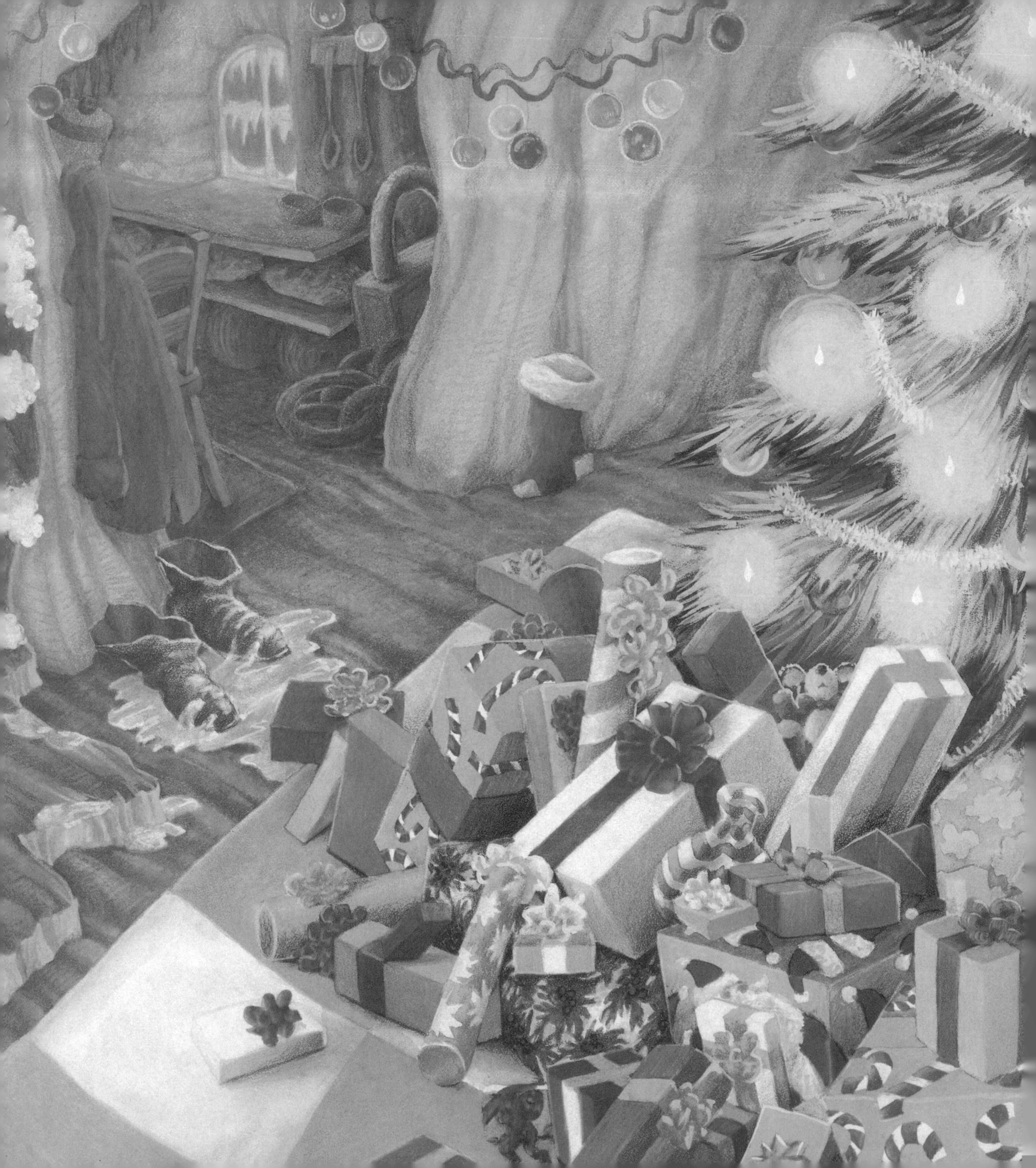

My goodness!
What a lot of presents.
Are they all for you?

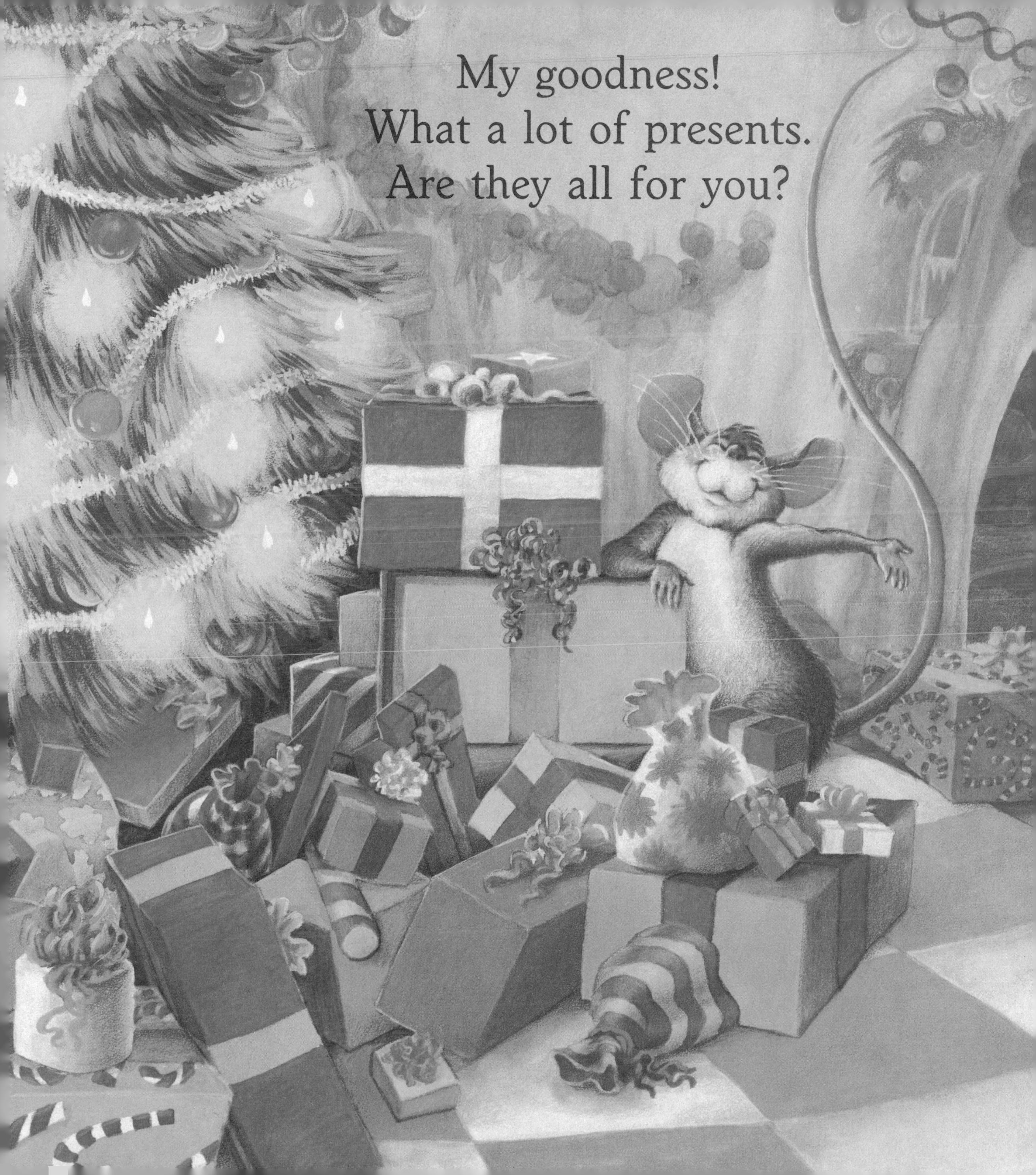

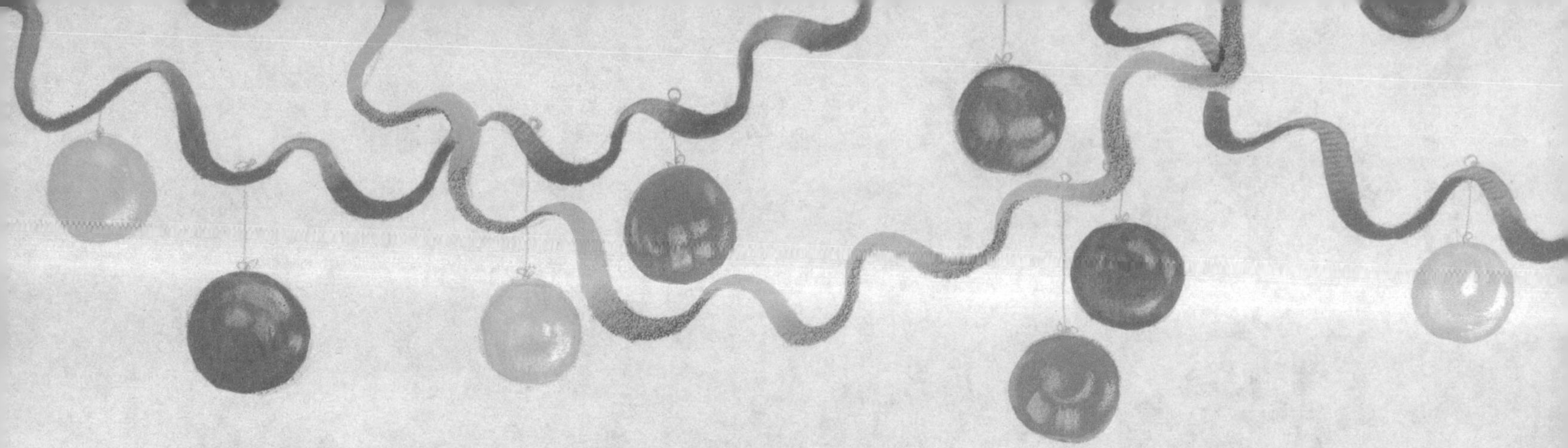

But, little Mouse,
what about the
big, hungry Bear
in the cold, dark
cave at the top
of the hill?

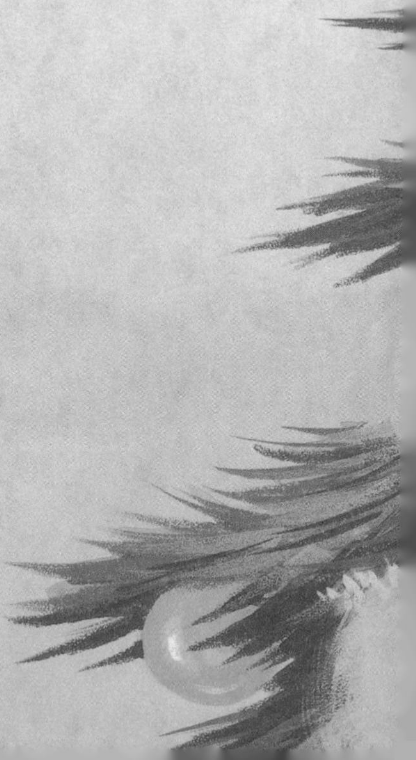

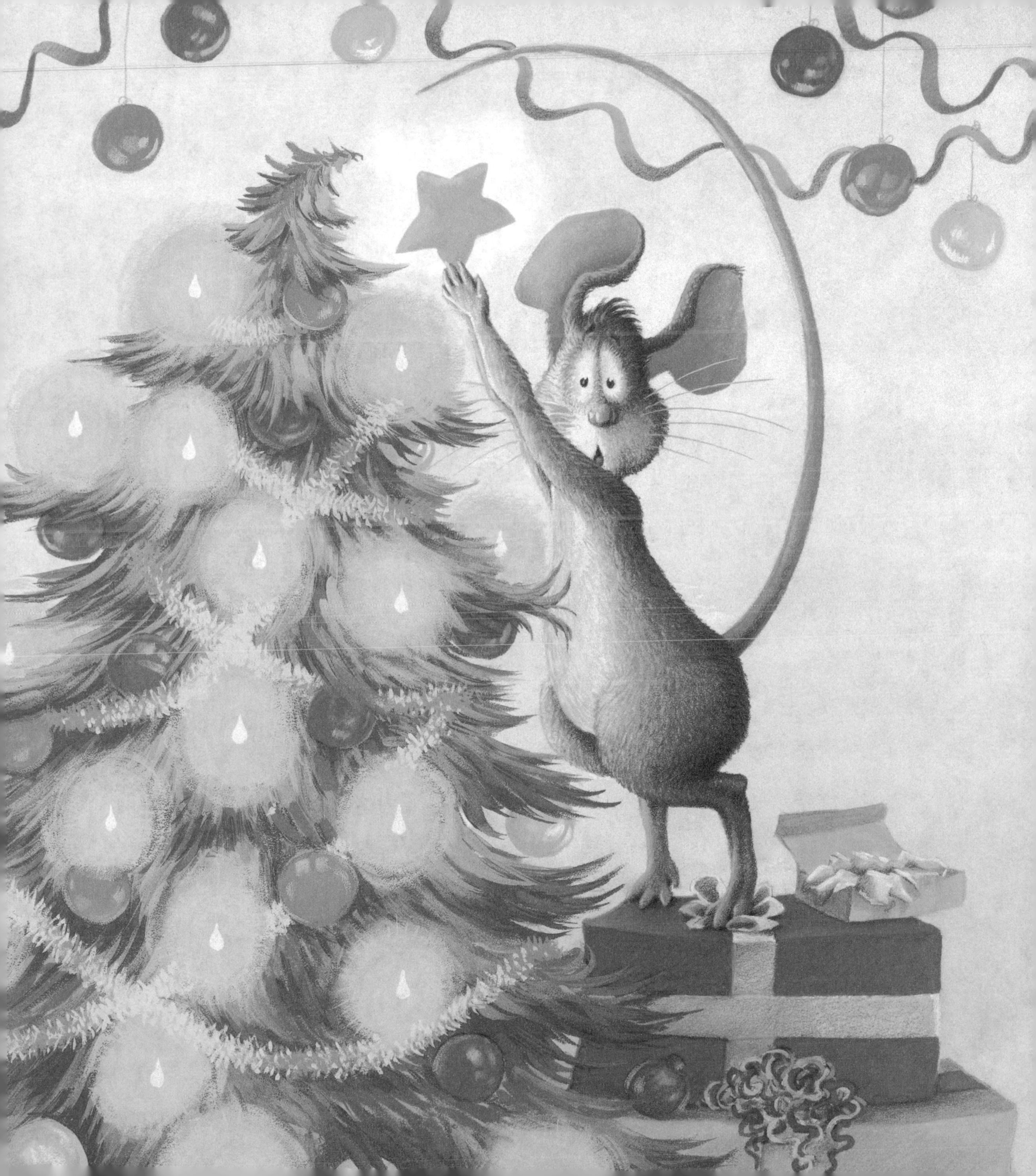

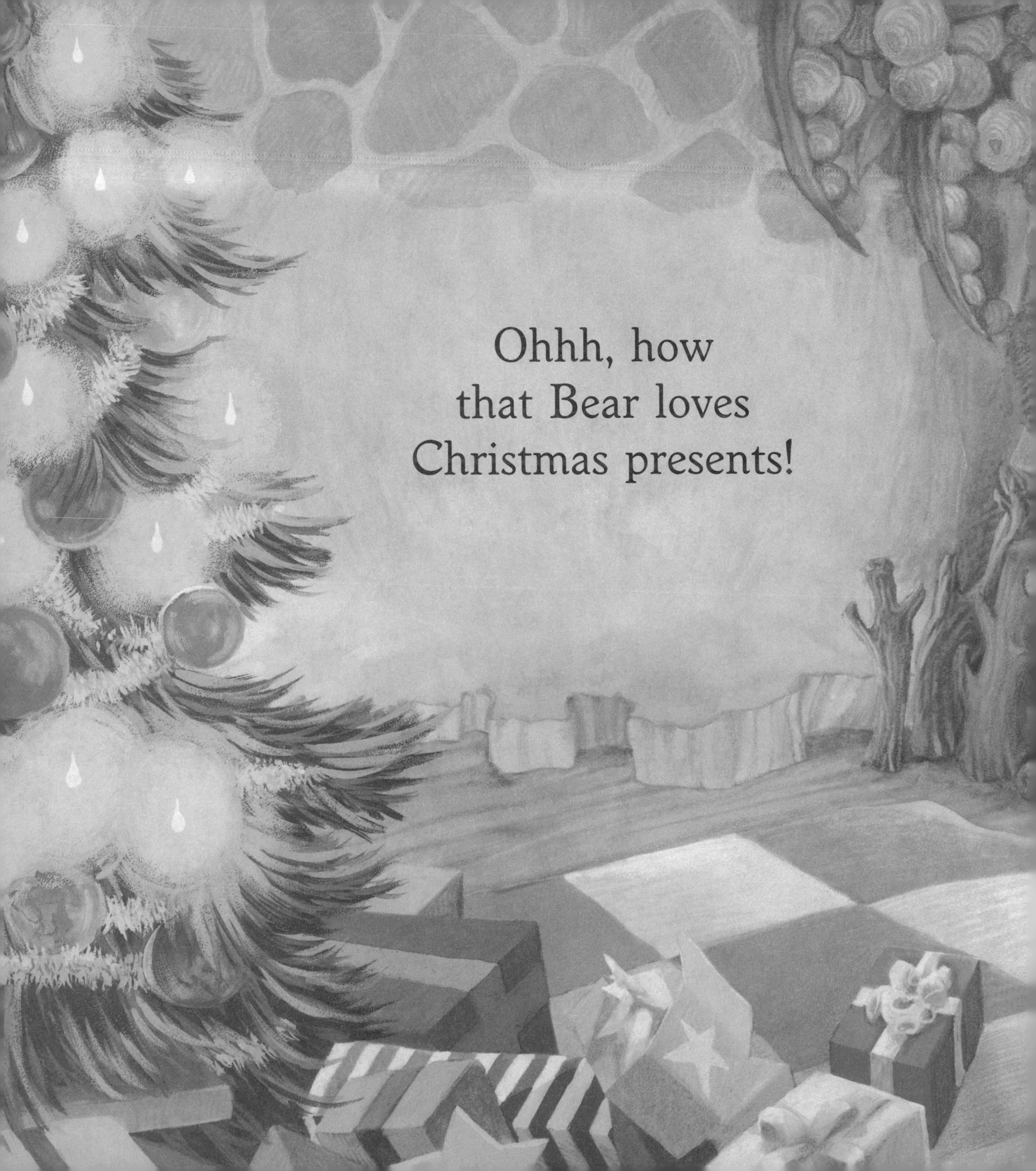

Ohhh, how
that Bear loves
Christmas presents!

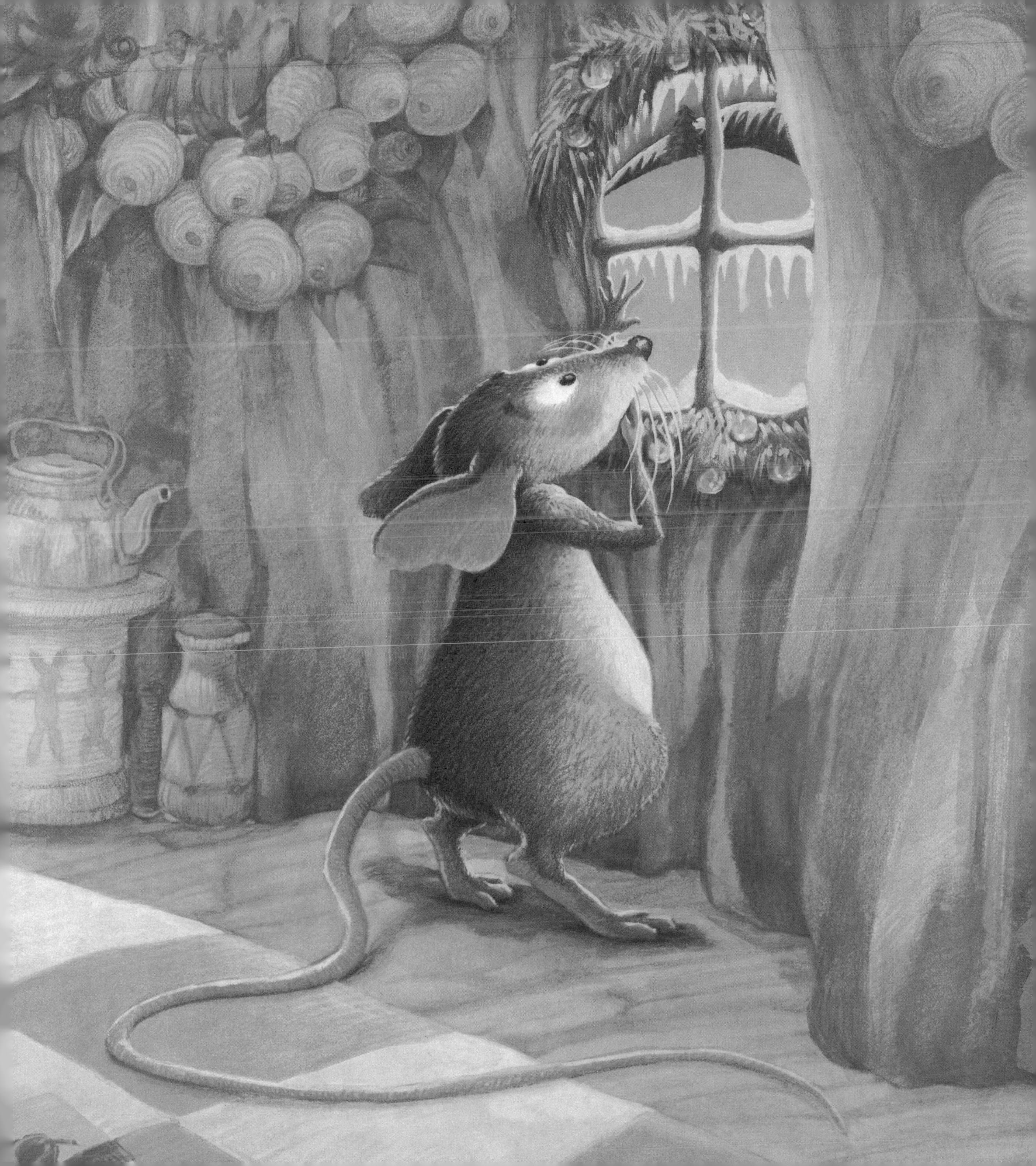

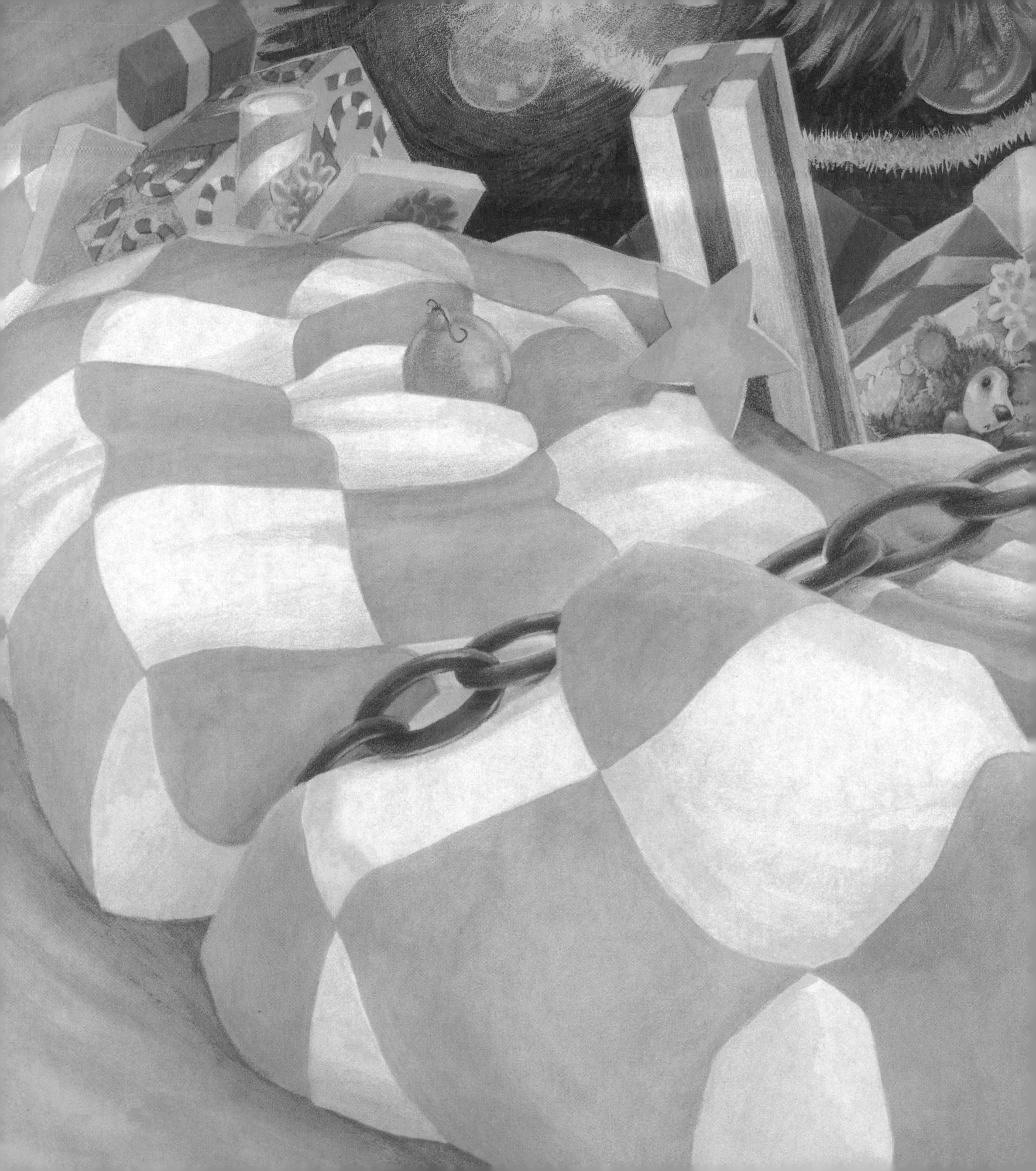

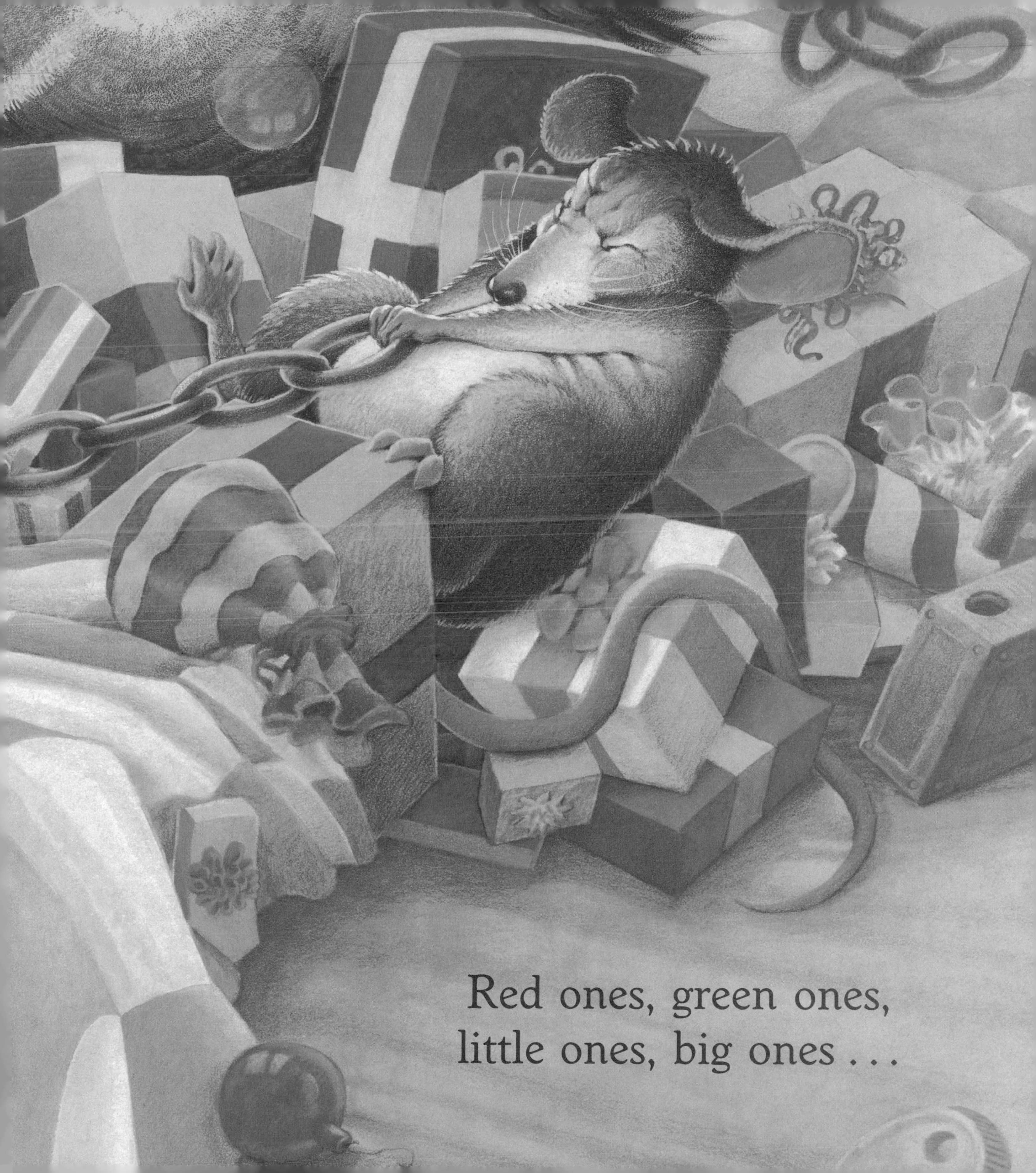

Red ones, green ones,
little ones, big ones . . .

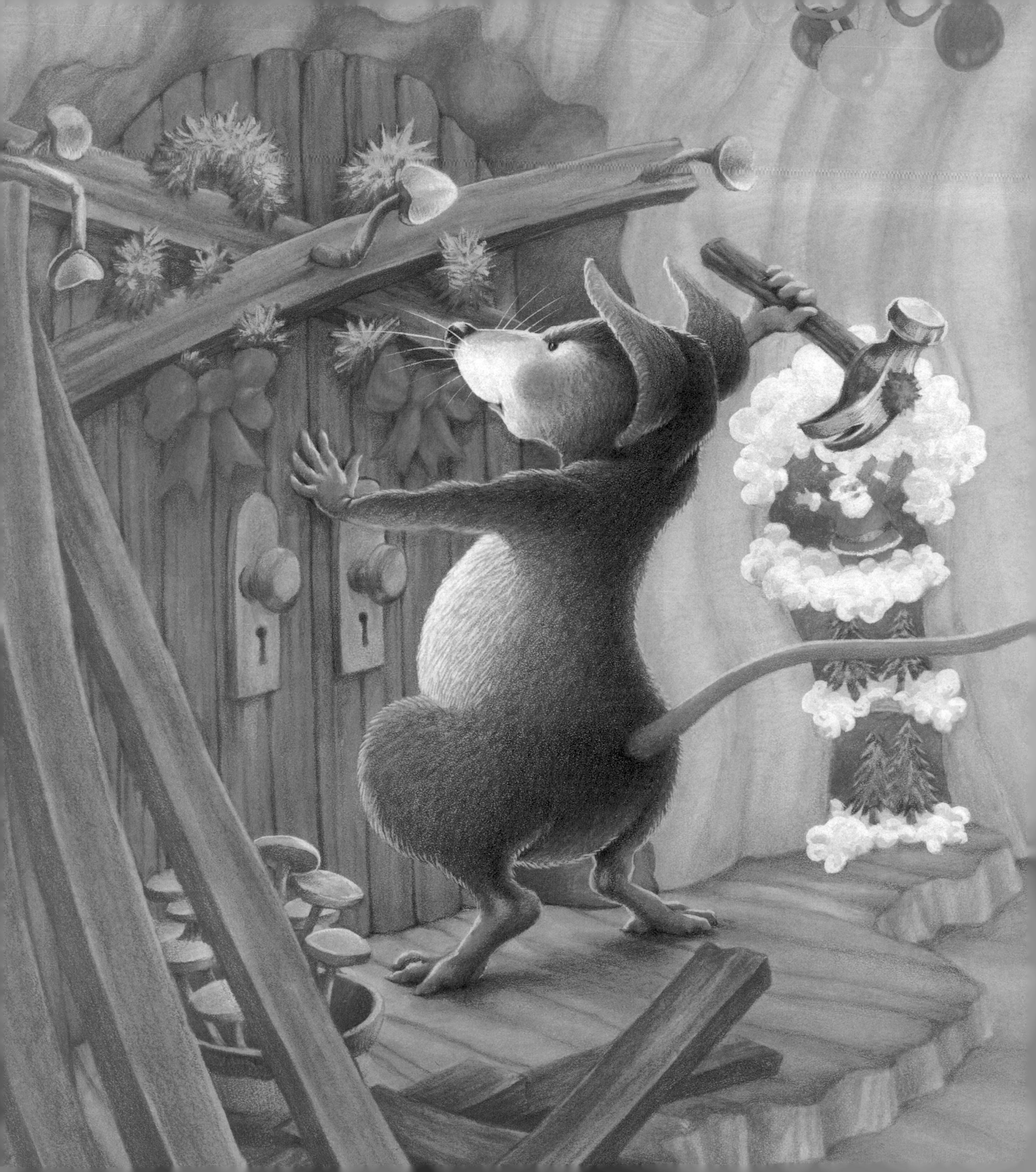

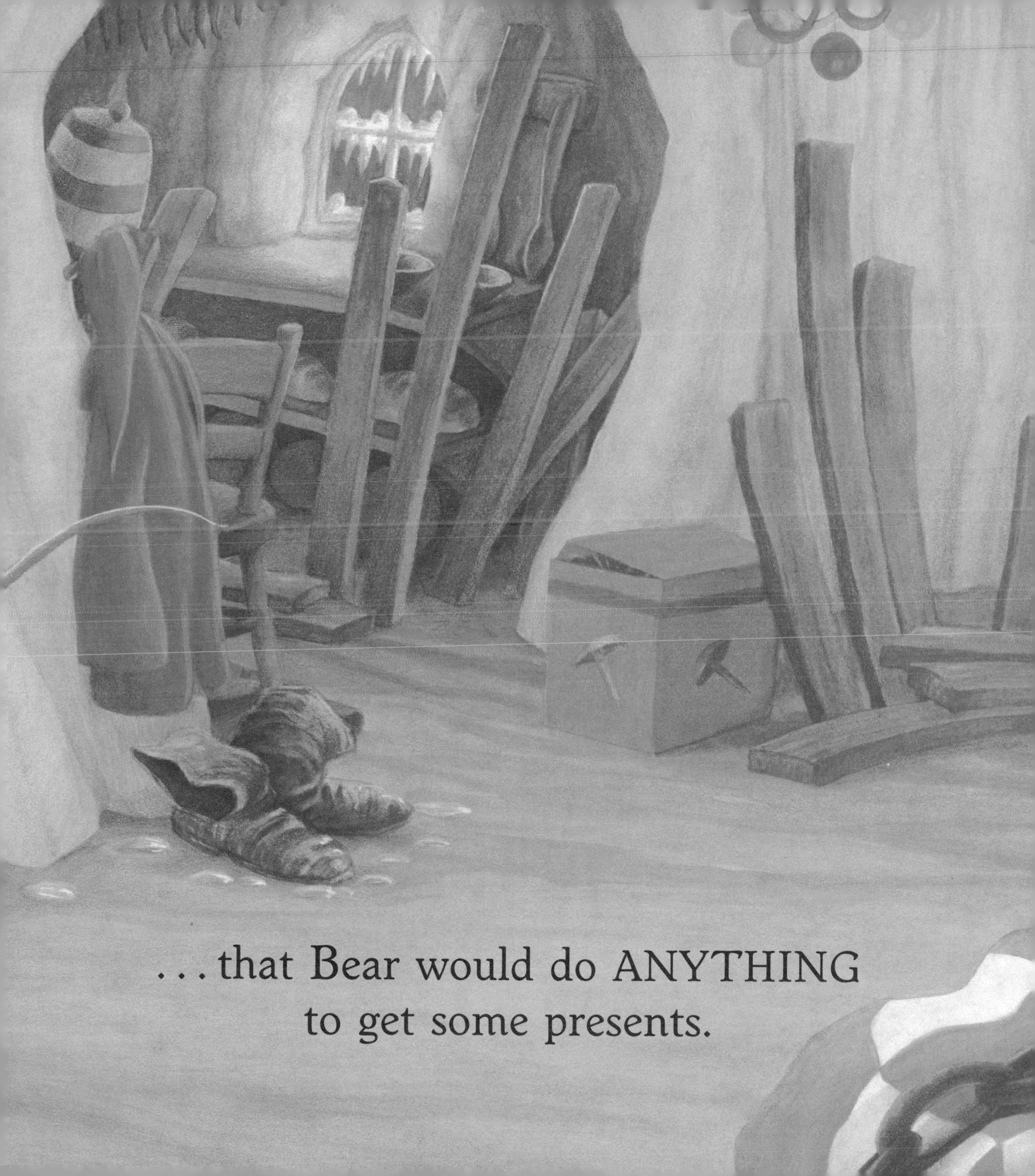

. . . that Bear would do ANYTHING
to get some presents.

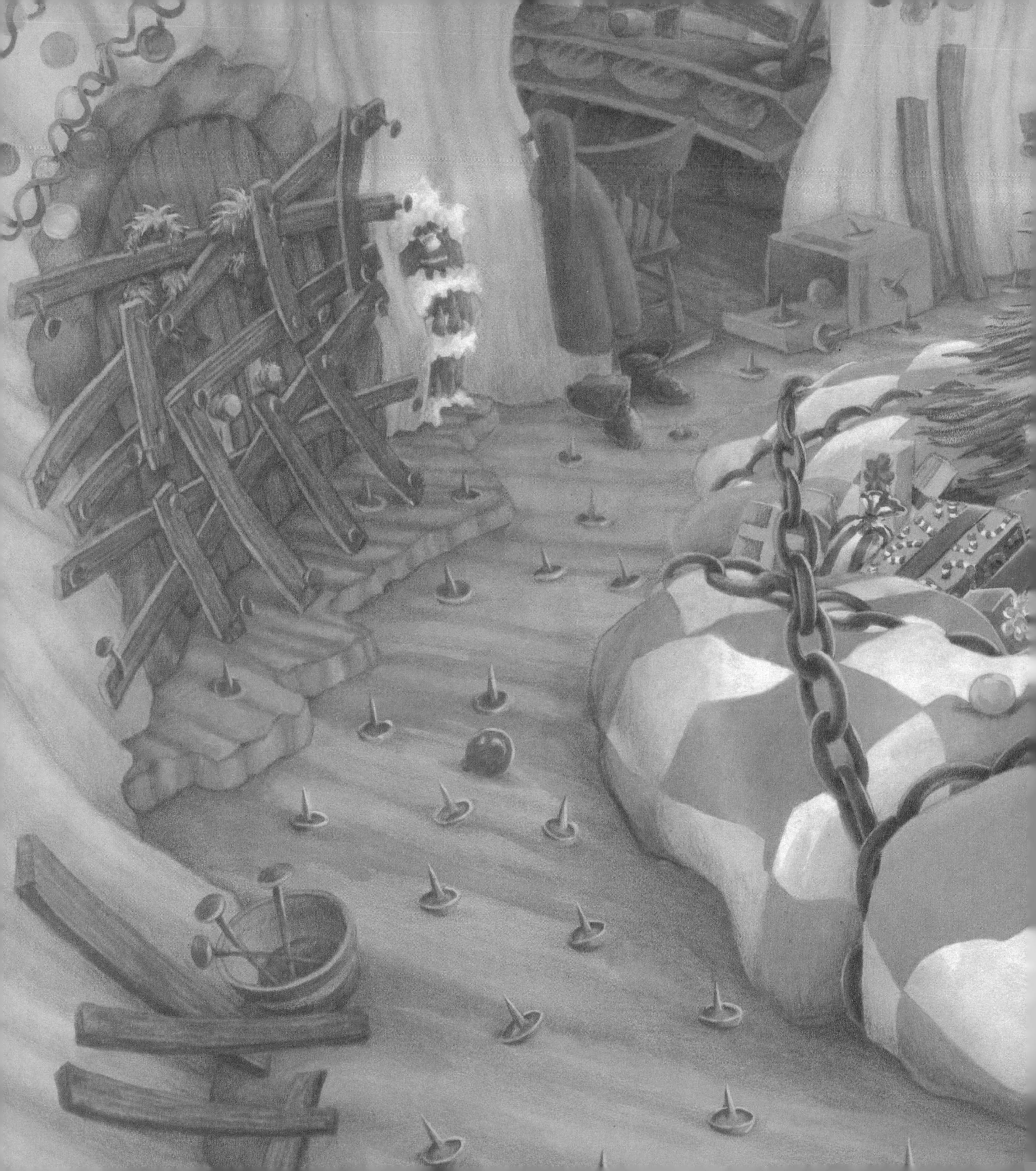

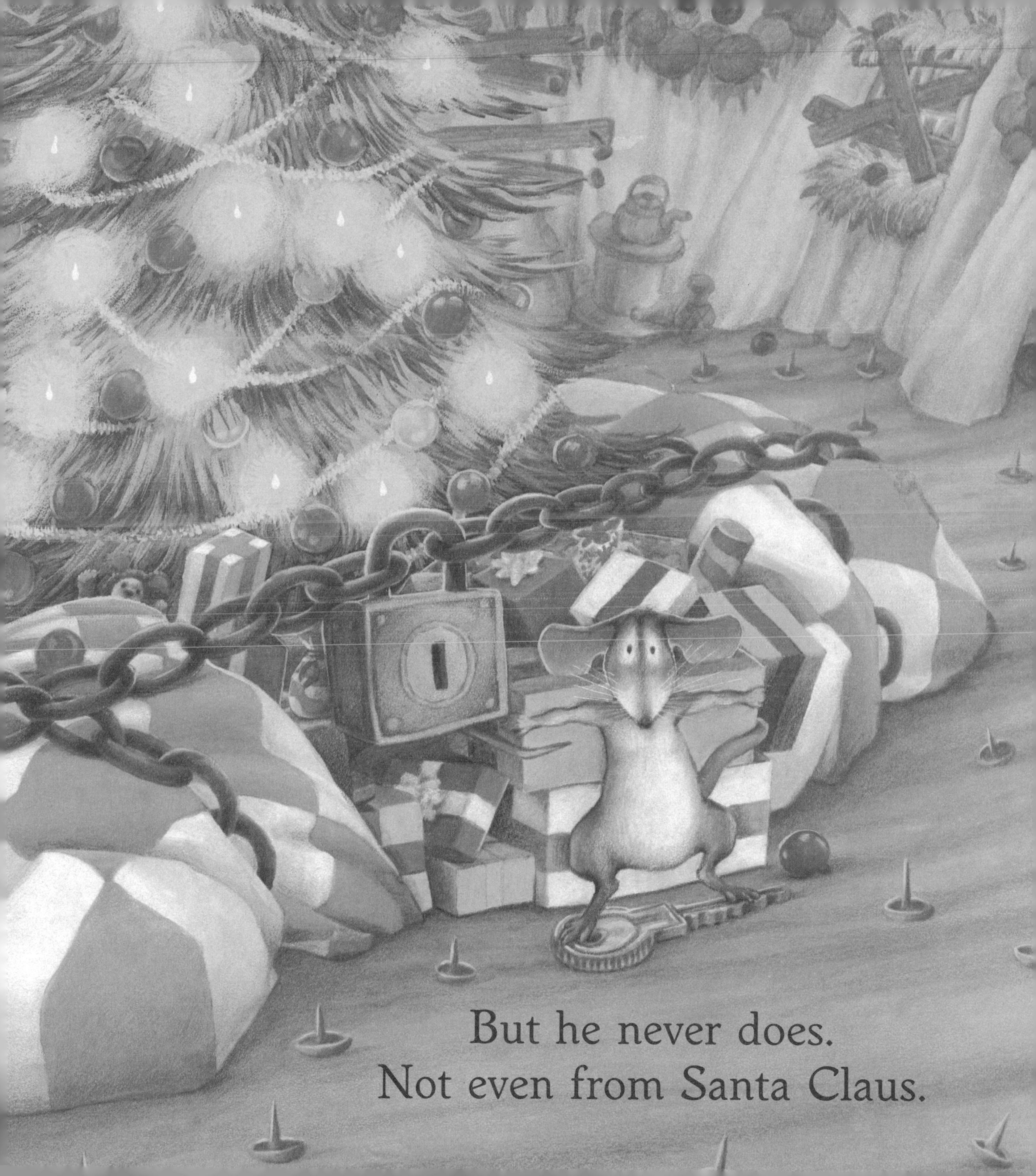

But he never does.
Not even from Santa Claus.

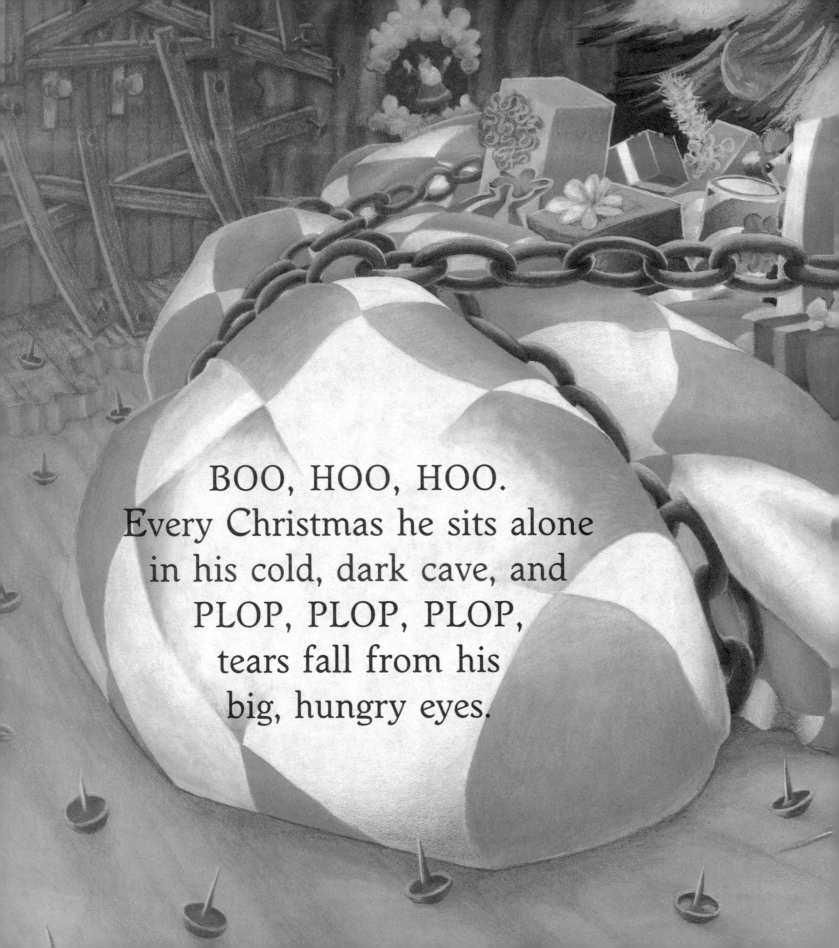

BOO, HOO, HOO.
Every Christmas he sits alone
in his cold, dark cave, and
PLOP, PLOP, PLOP,
tears fall from his
big, hungry eyes.

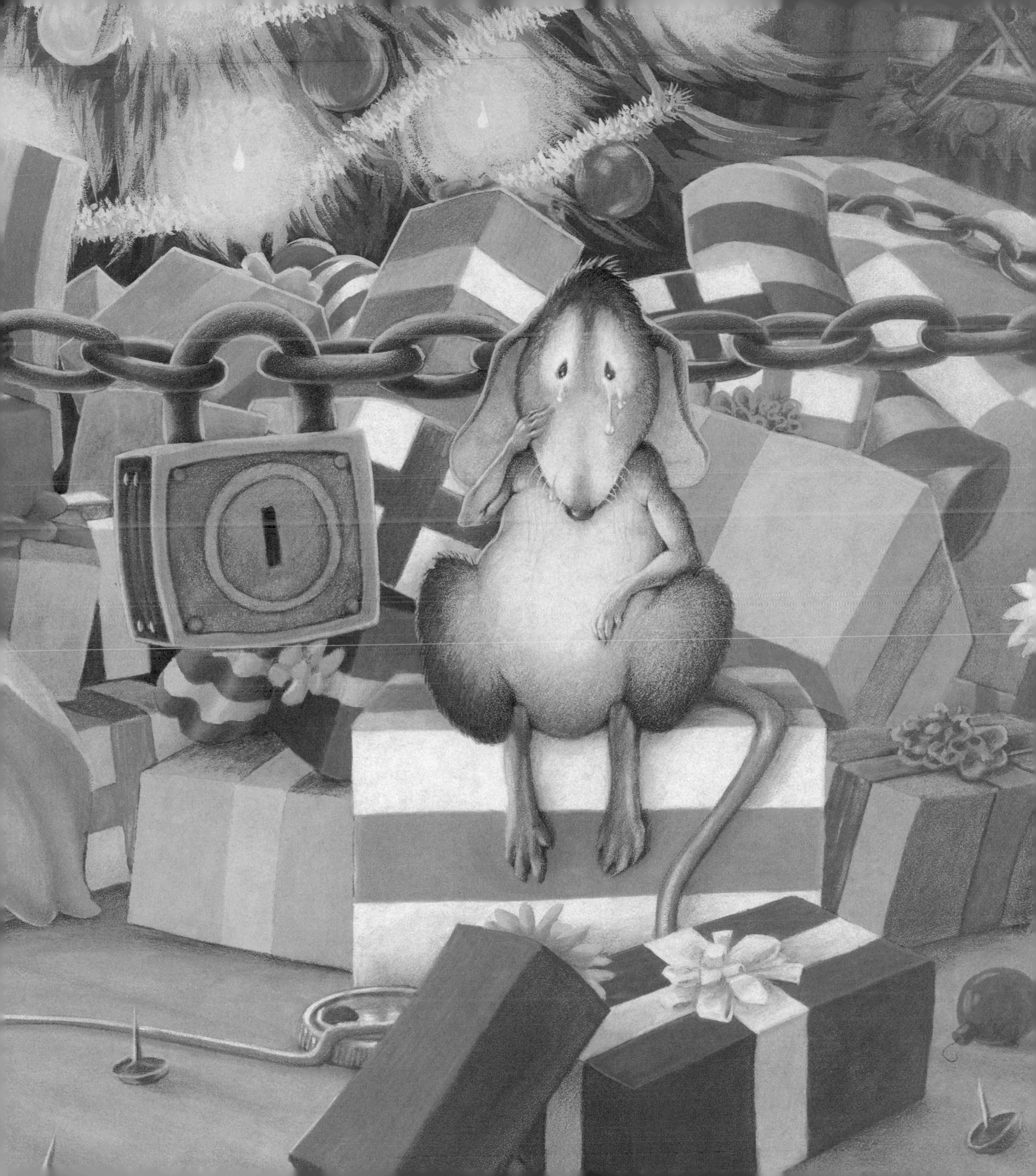

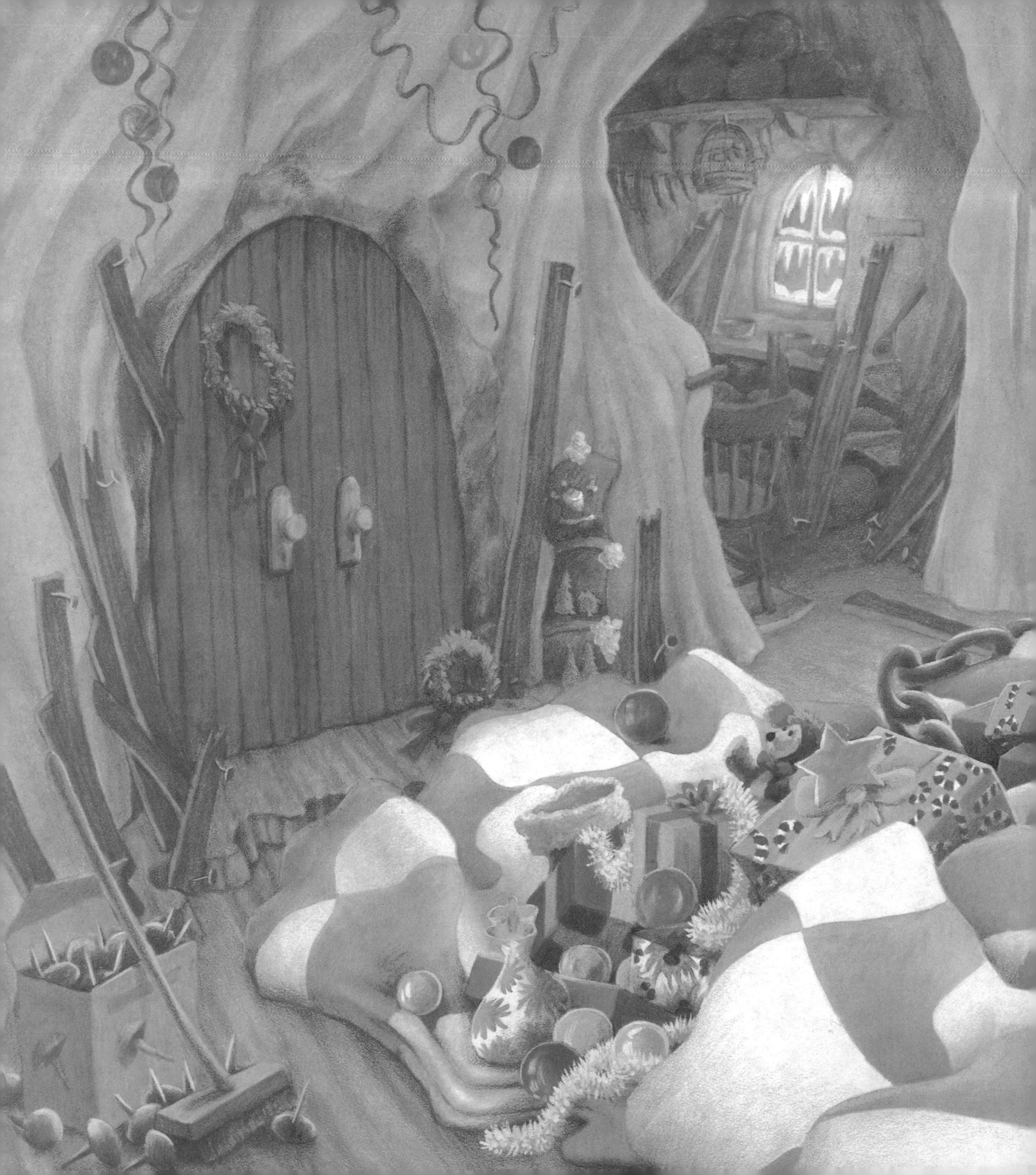

Little Mouse,
what are you doing?

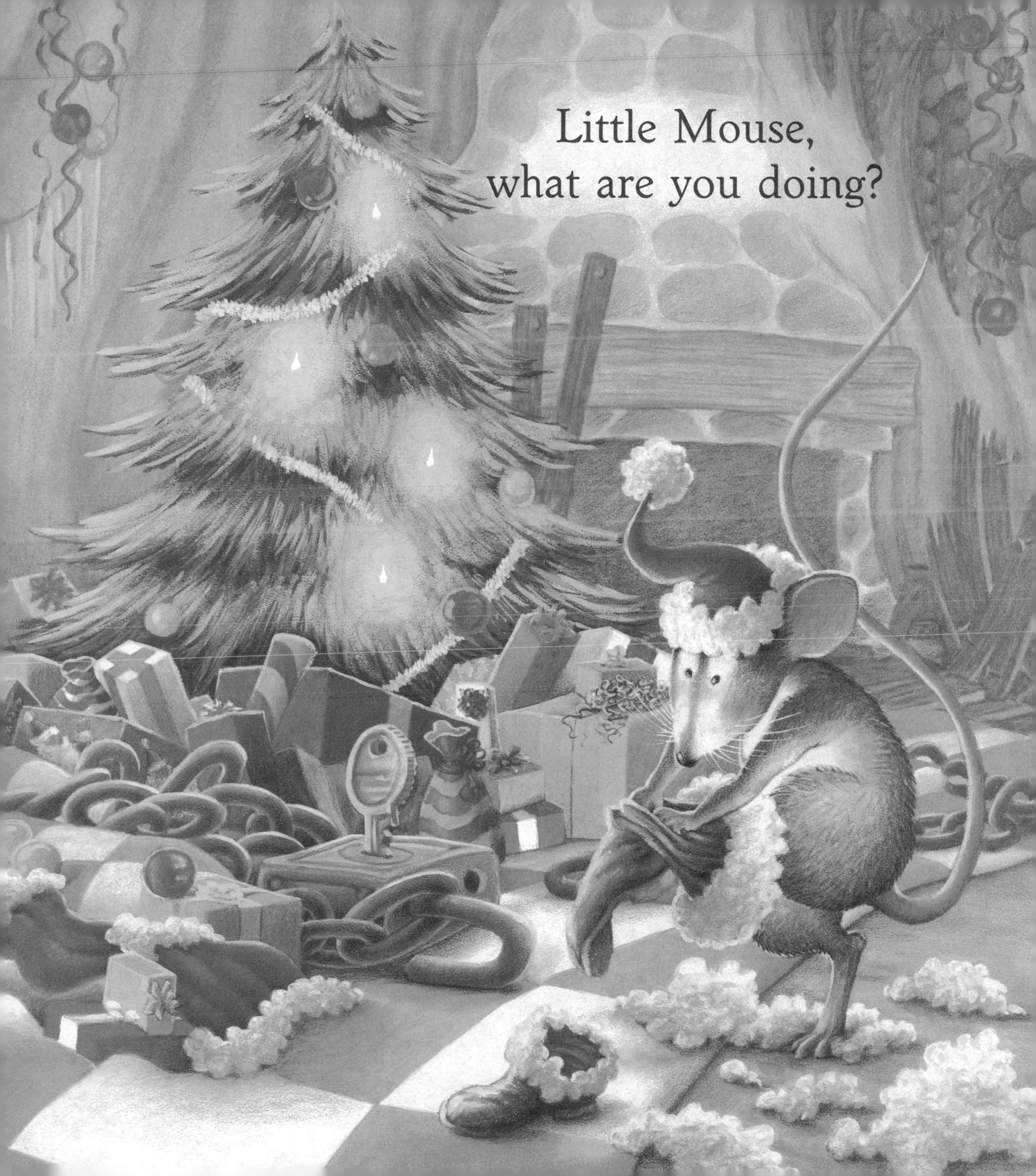

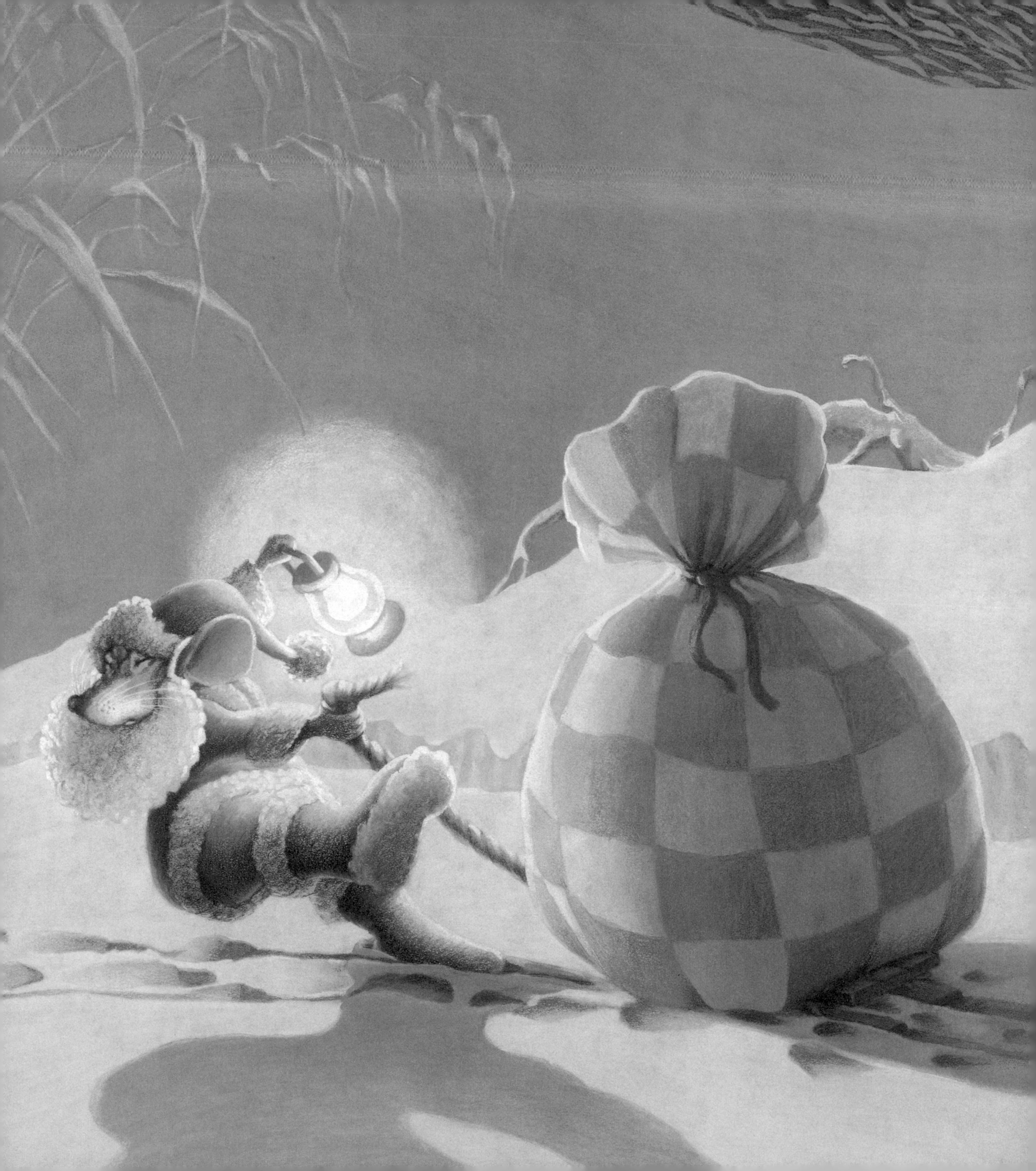

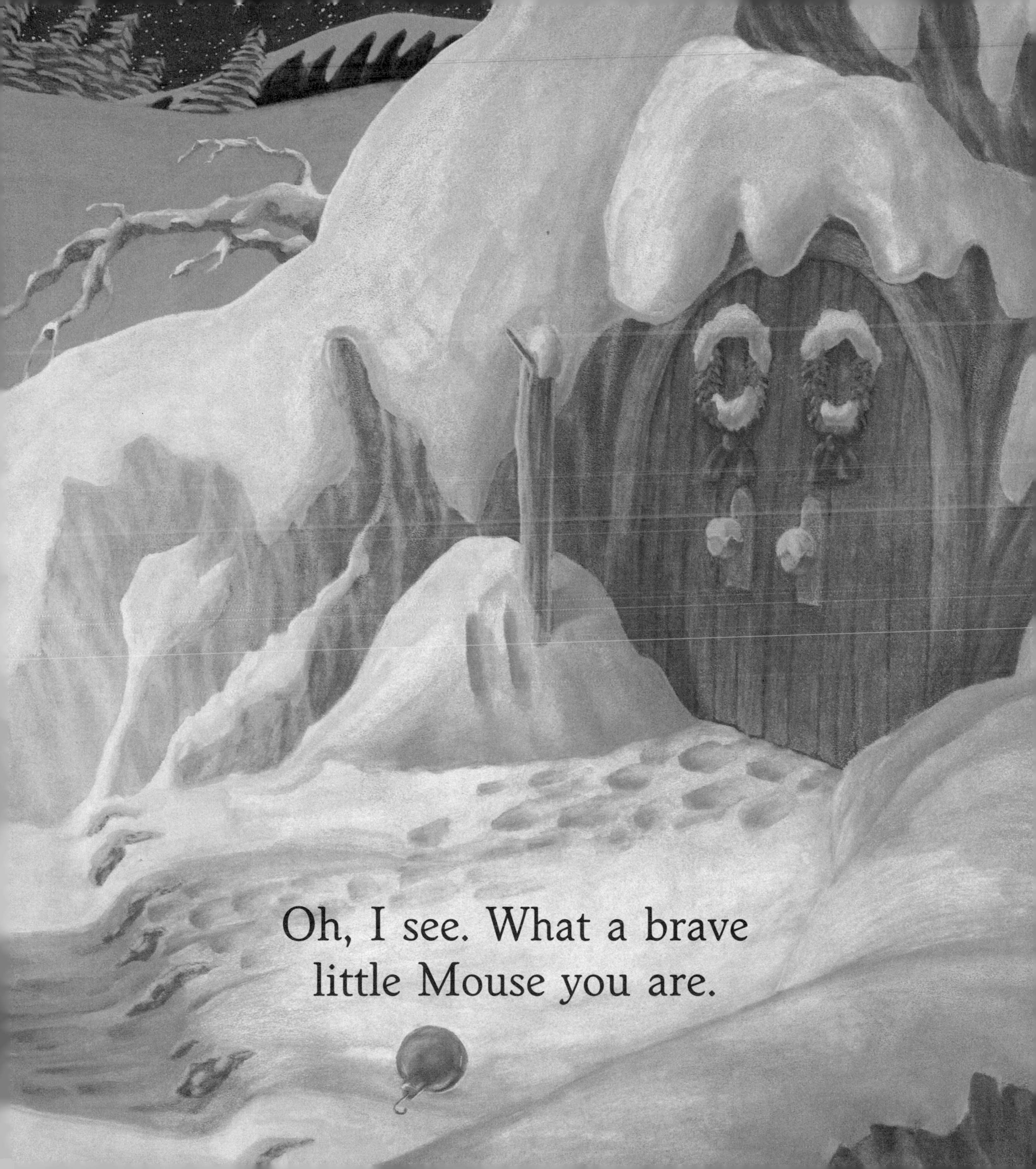

Oh, I see. What a brave
little Mouse you are.

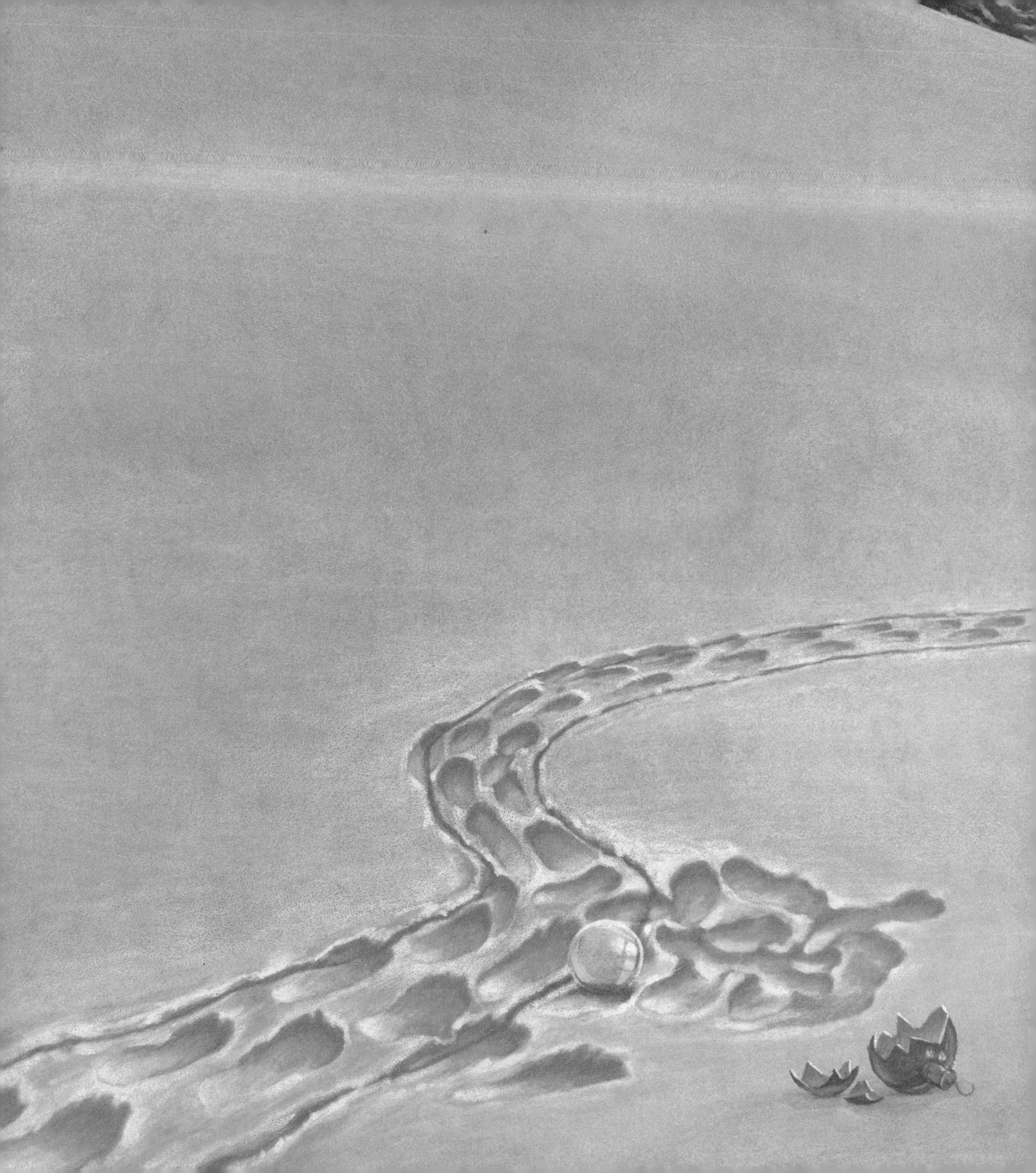

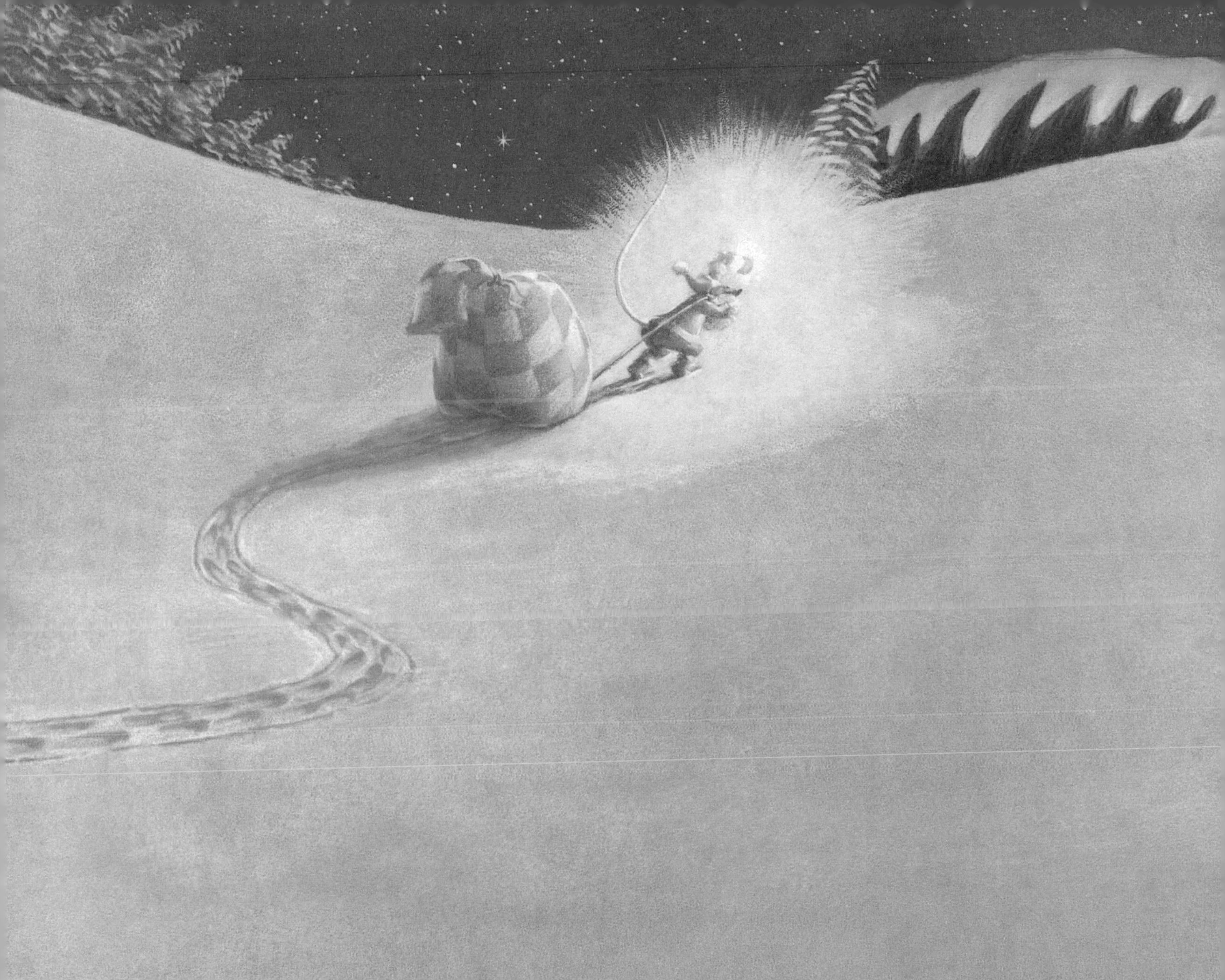

No one else in the whole wide world
would go to the cold, dark cave
of the big, hungry Bear . . .

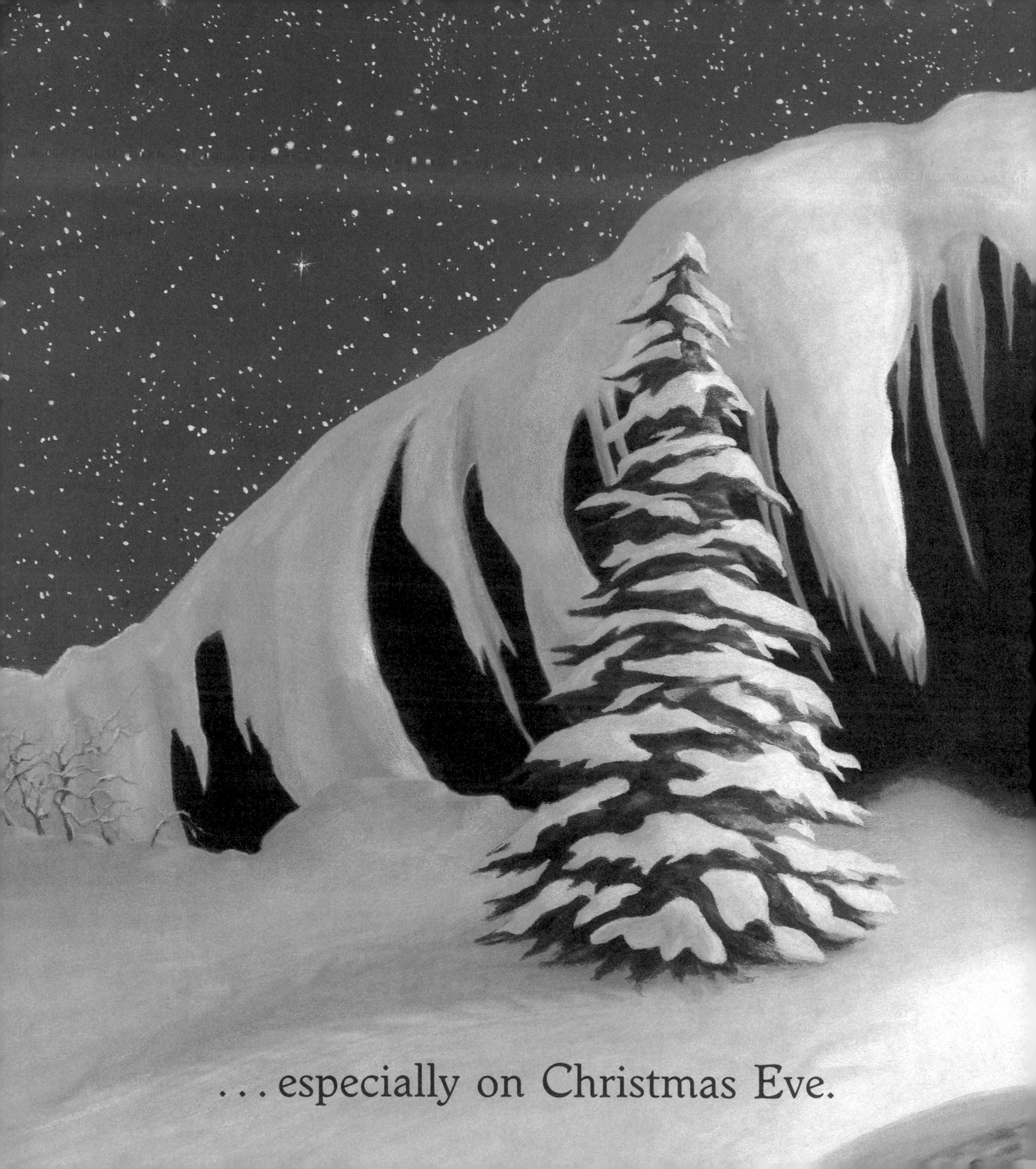

. . . especially on Christmas Eve.

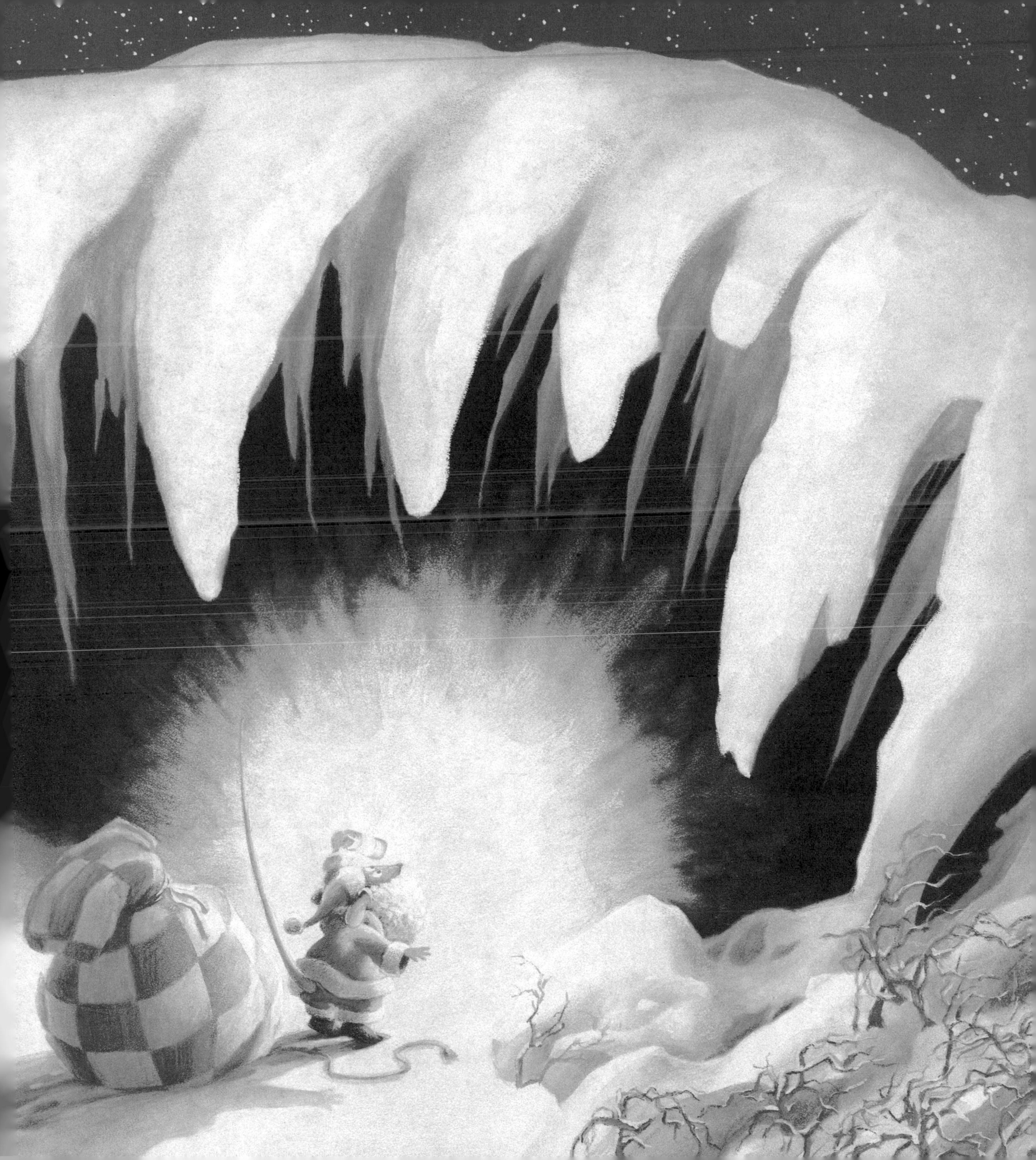

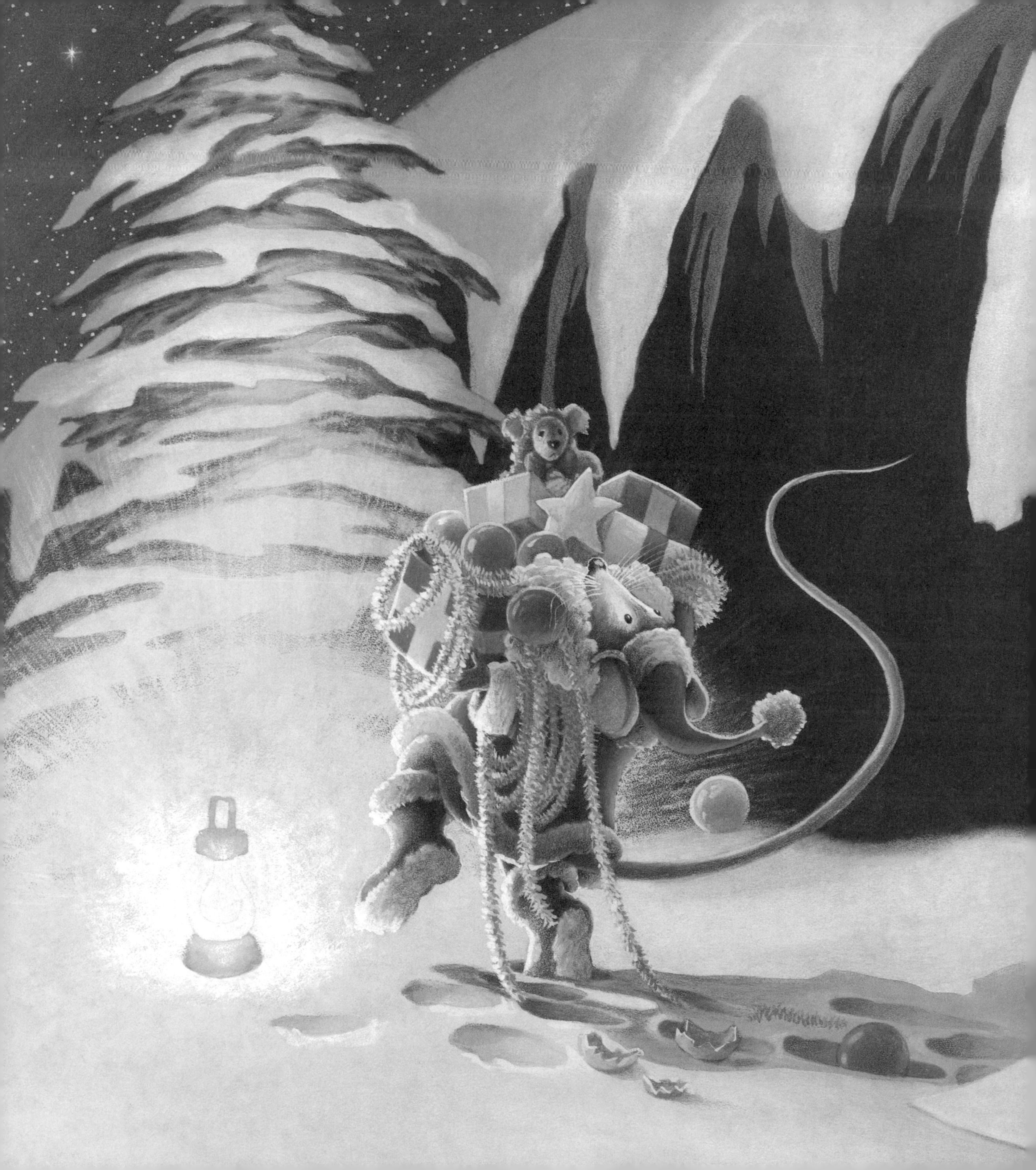

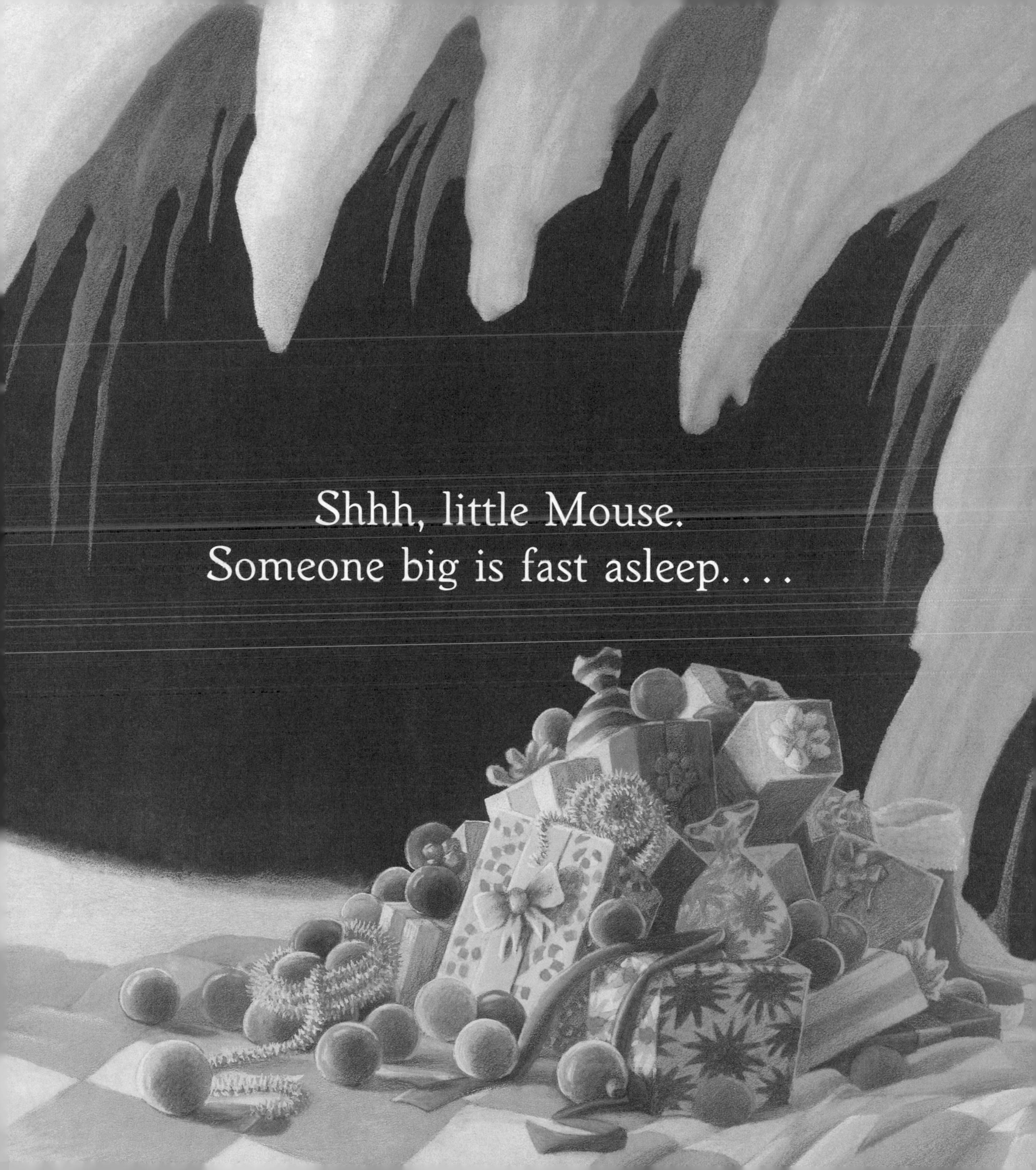

Shhh, little Mouse.
Someone big is fast asleep. . . .

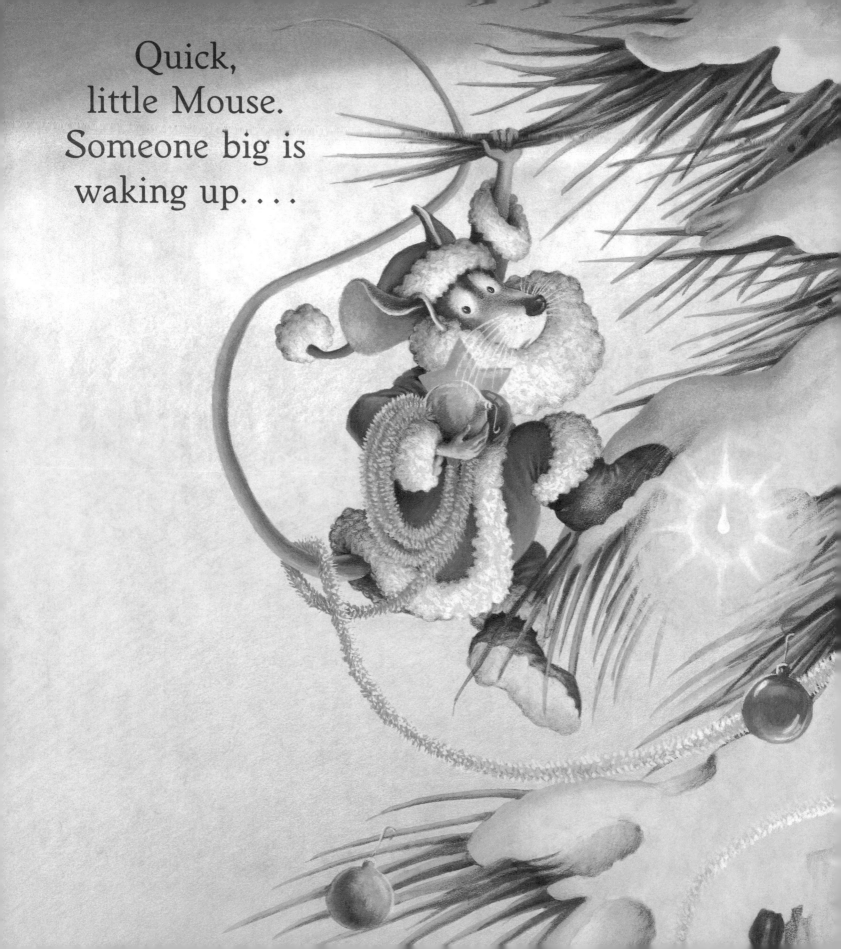

Quick,
little Mouse.
Someone big is
waking up. . . .

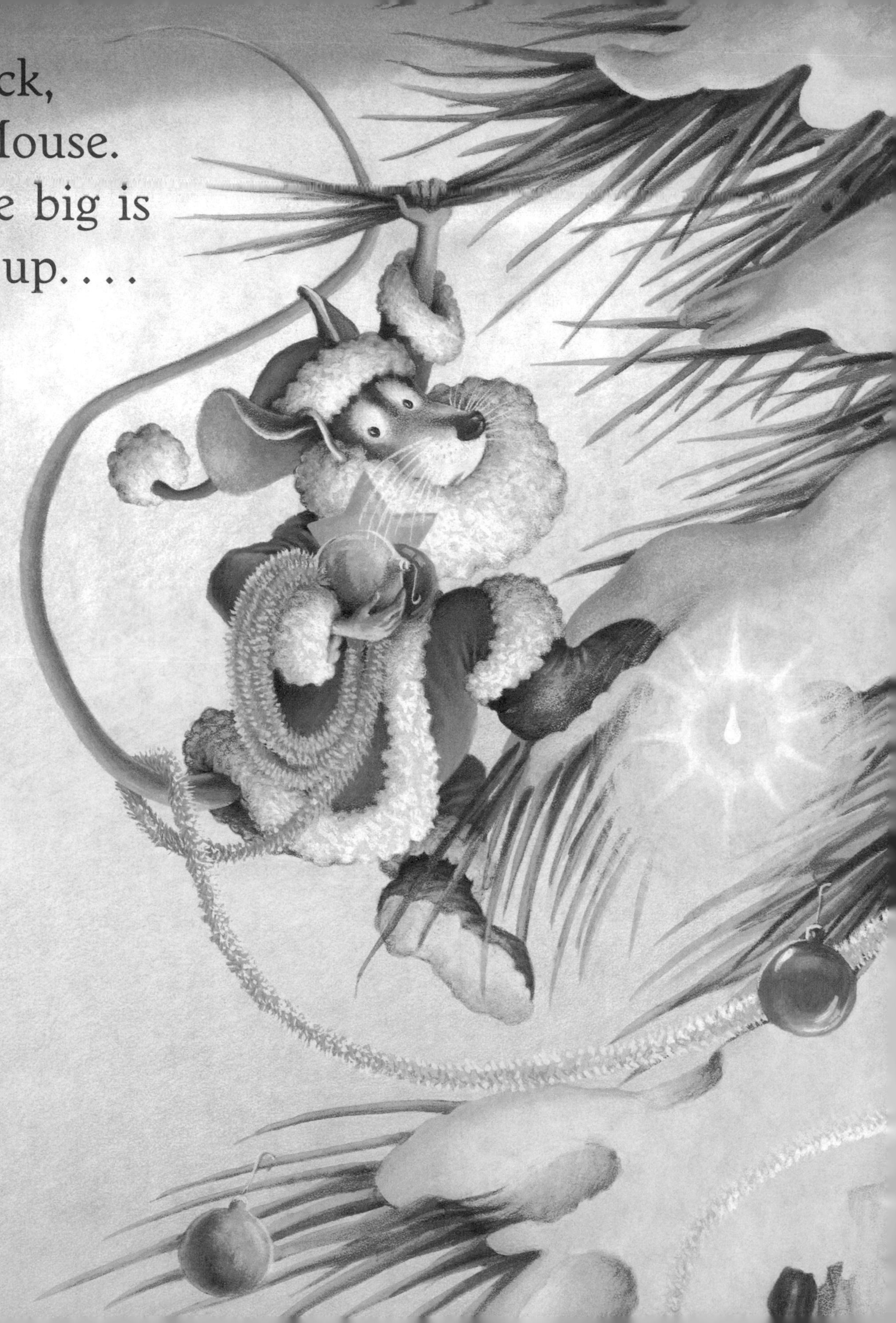

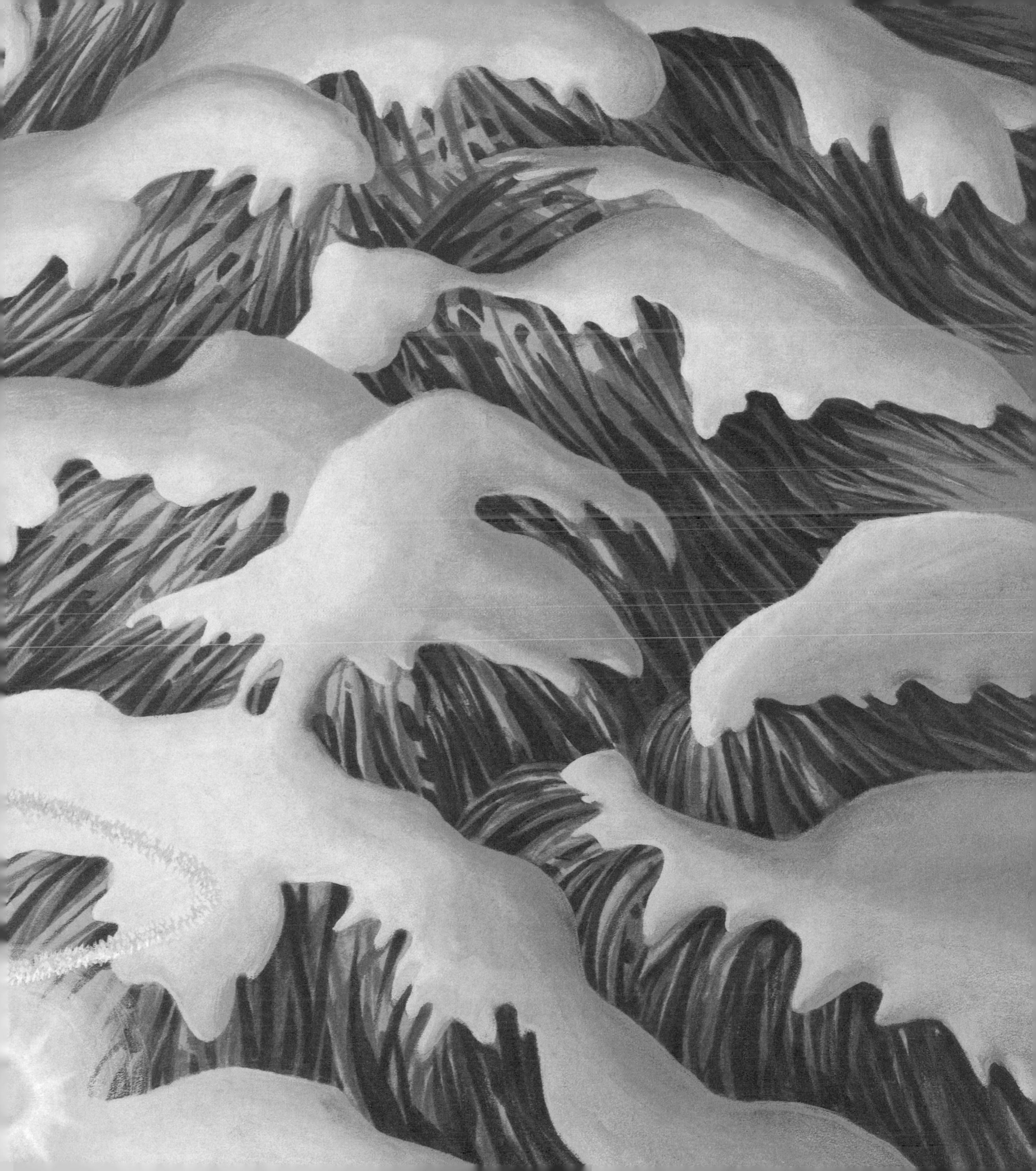

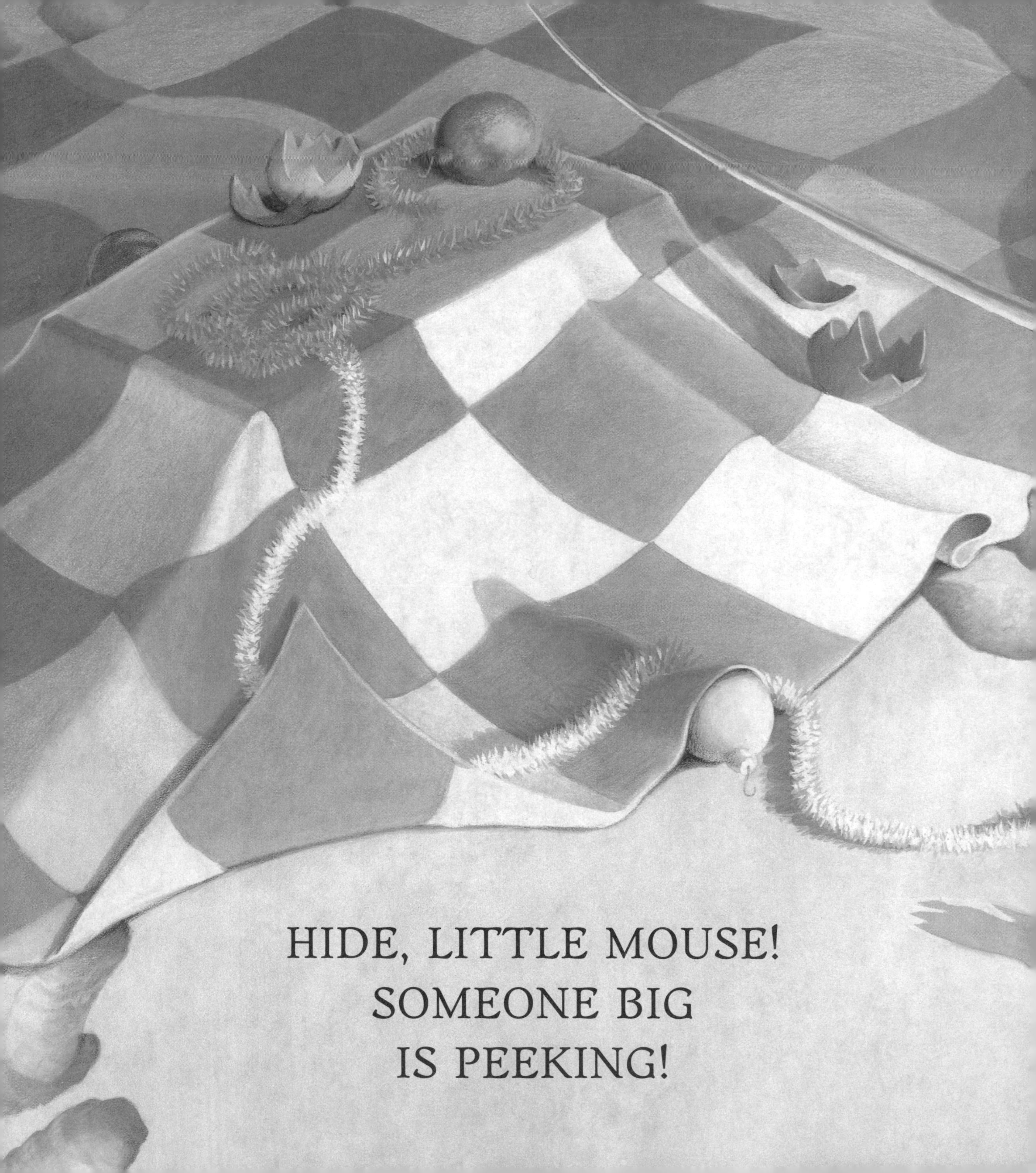

HIDE, LITTLE MOUSE!
SOMEONE BIG
IS PEEKING!

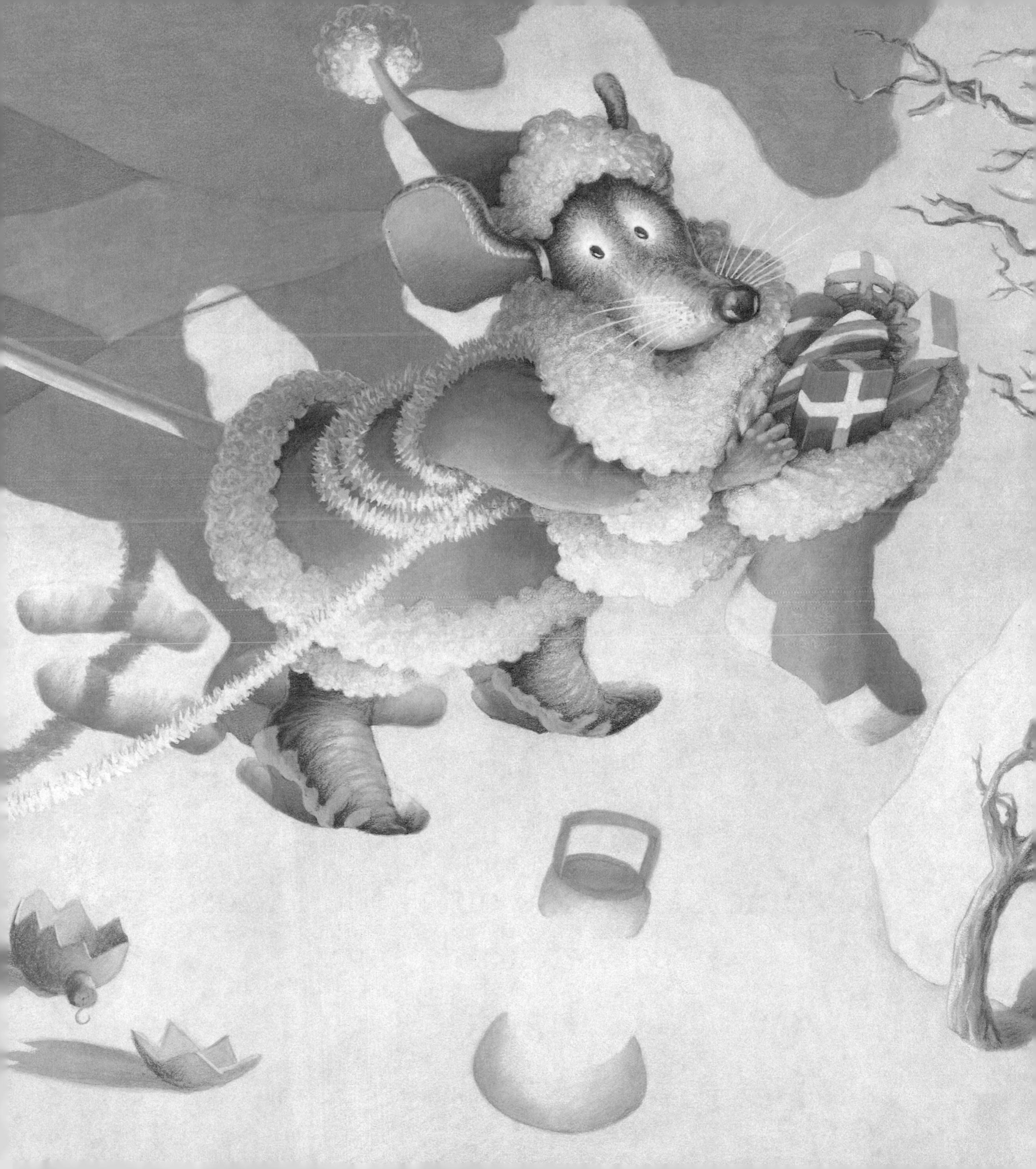

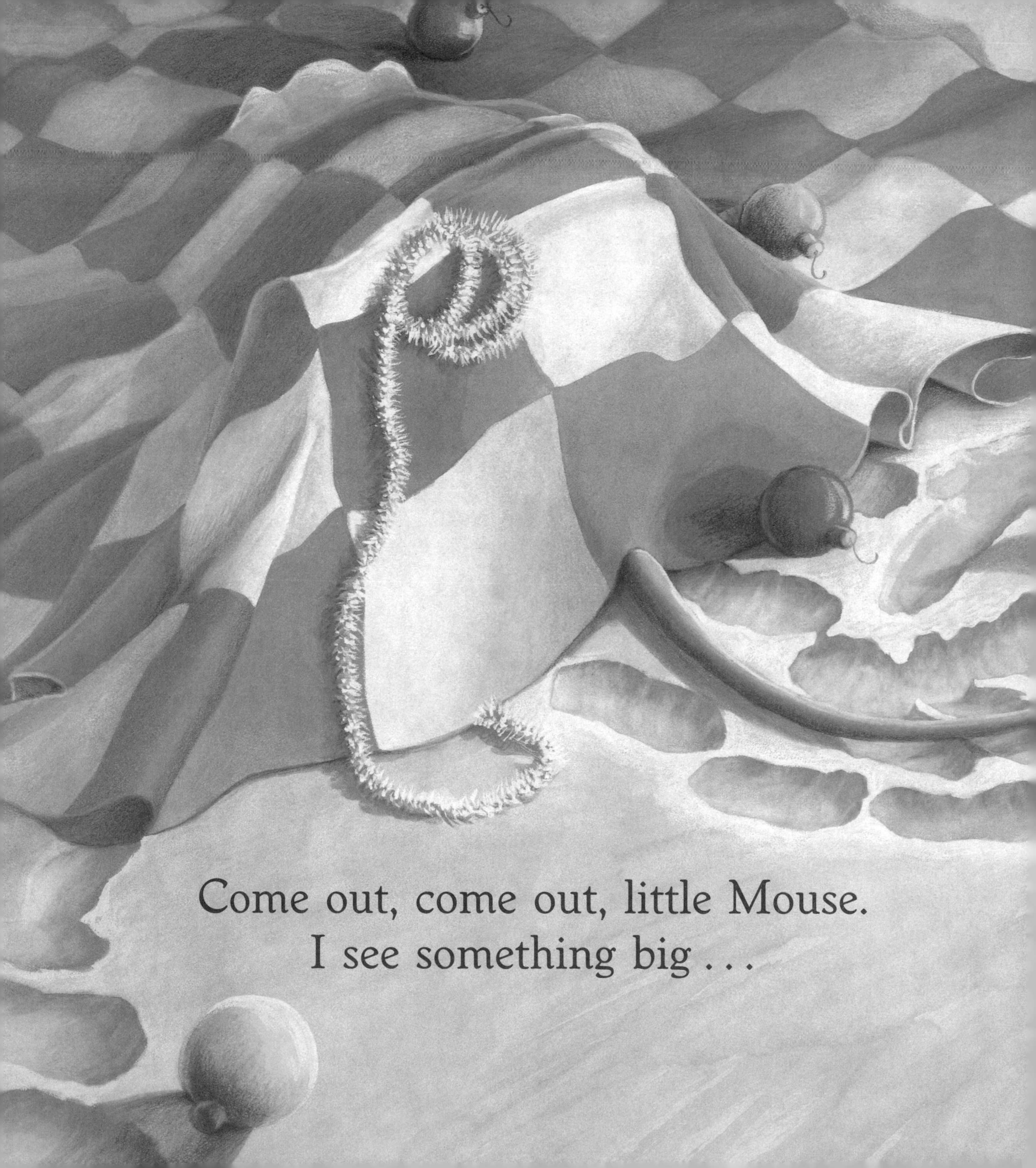

Come out, come out, little Mouse.
I see something big . . .

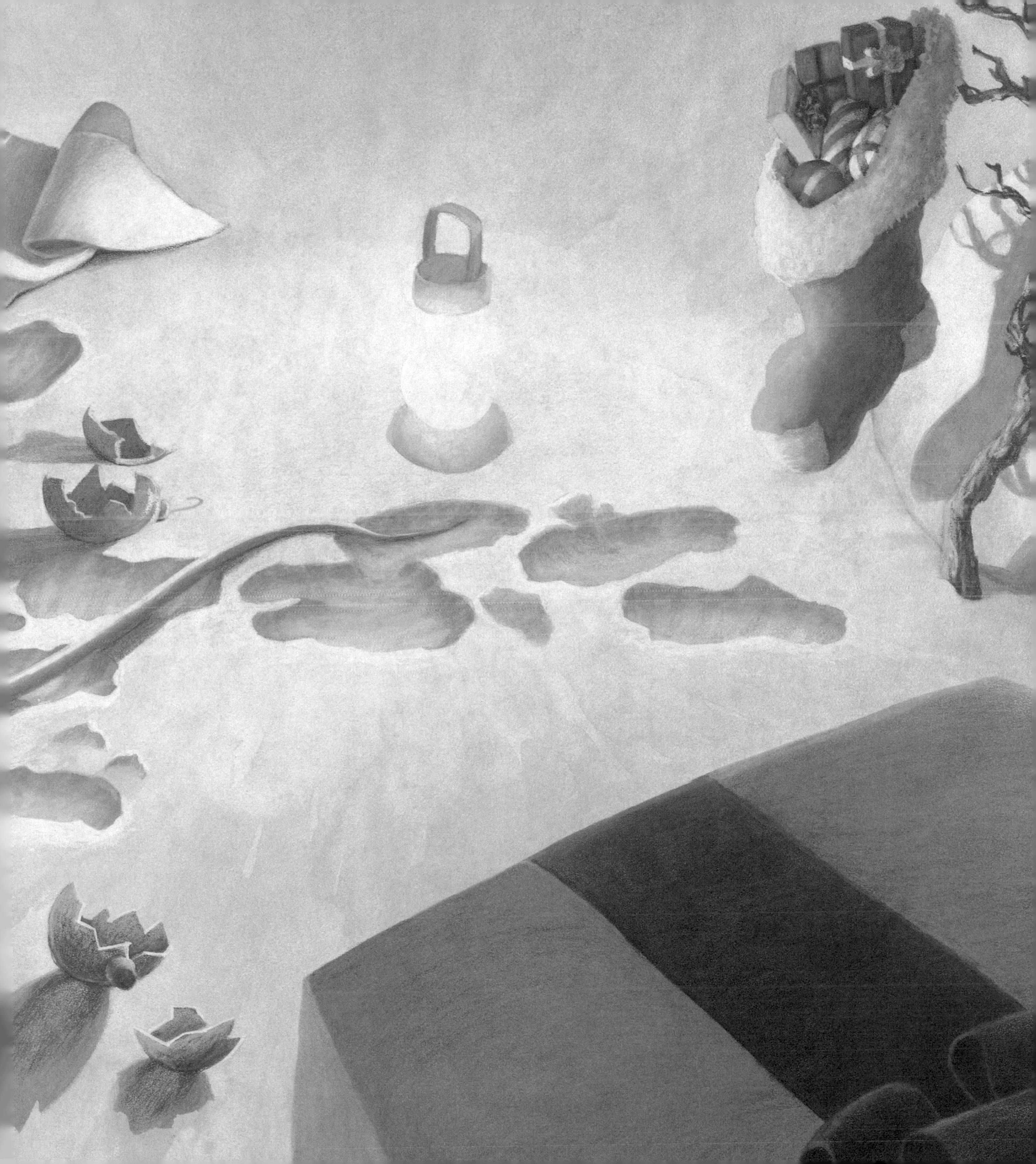

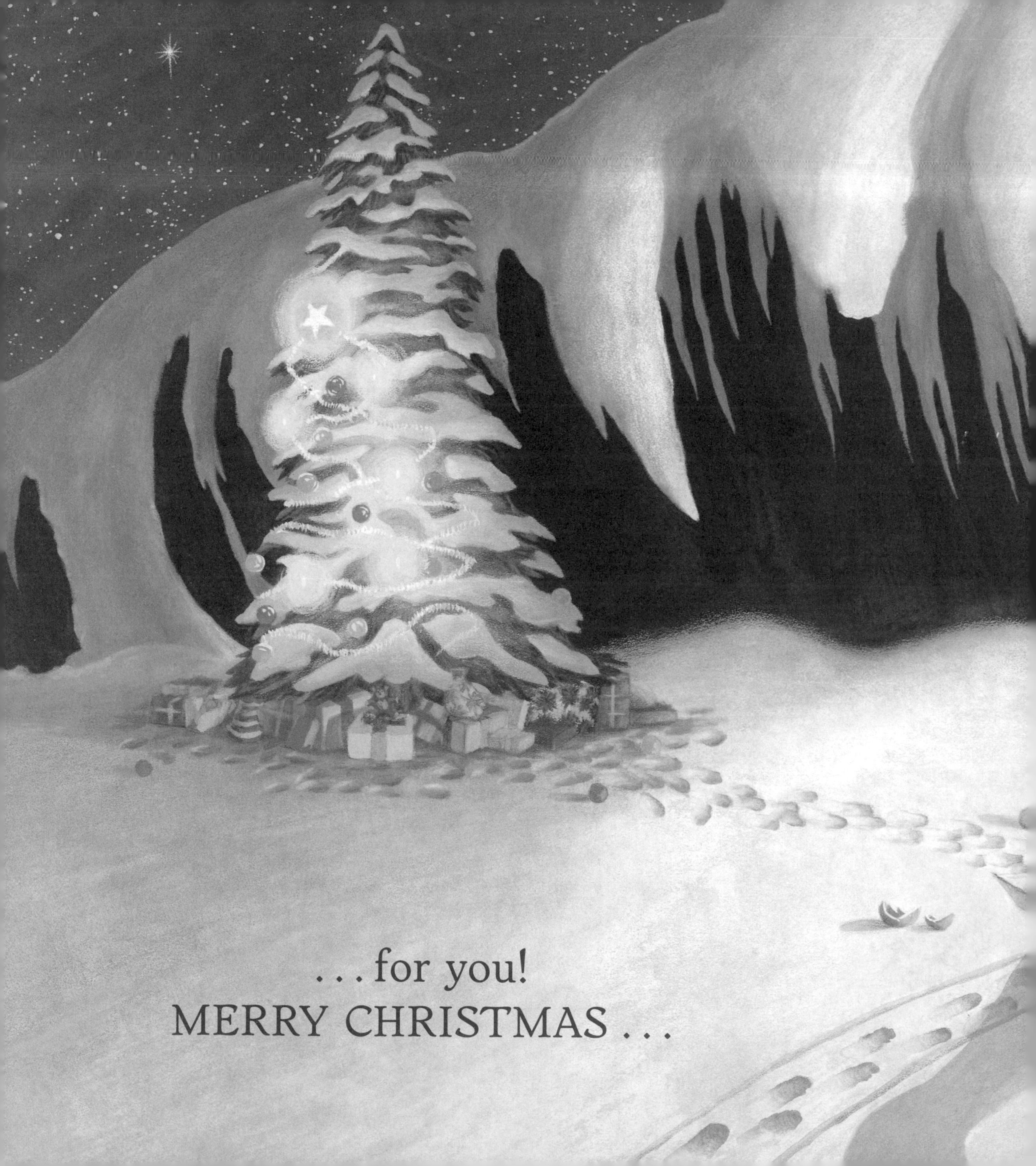

. . . for you!
MERRY CHRISTMAS . . .

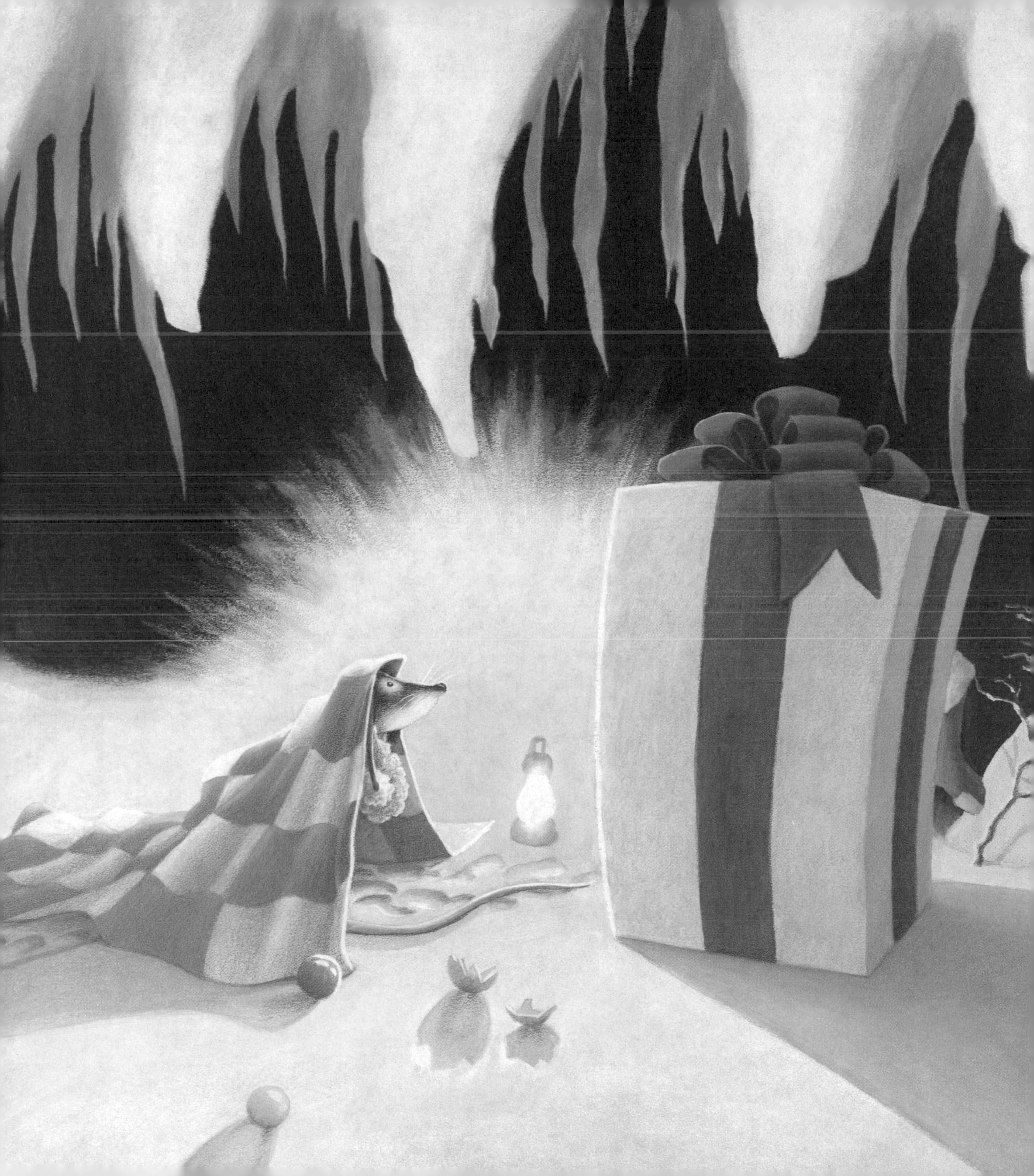

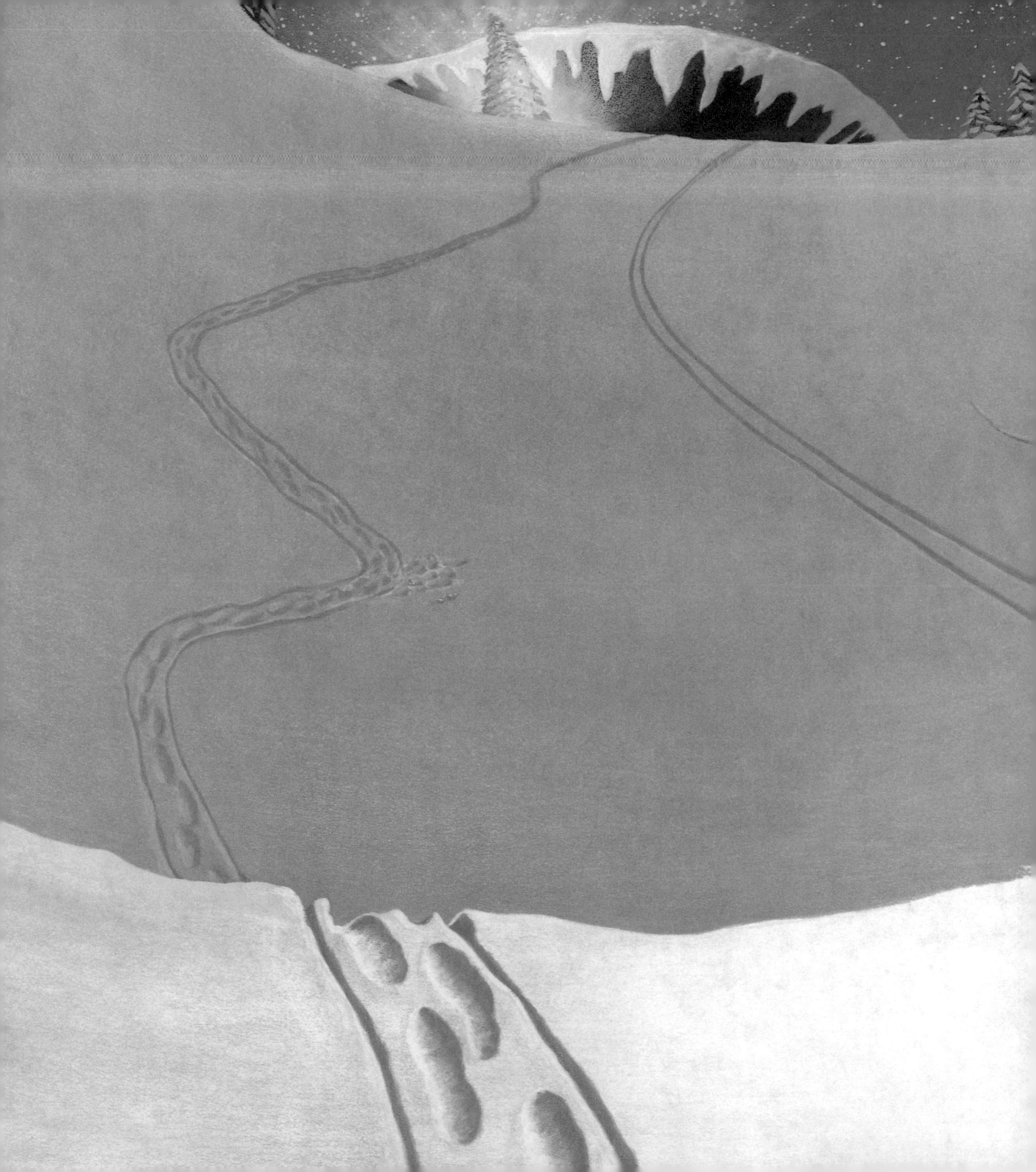

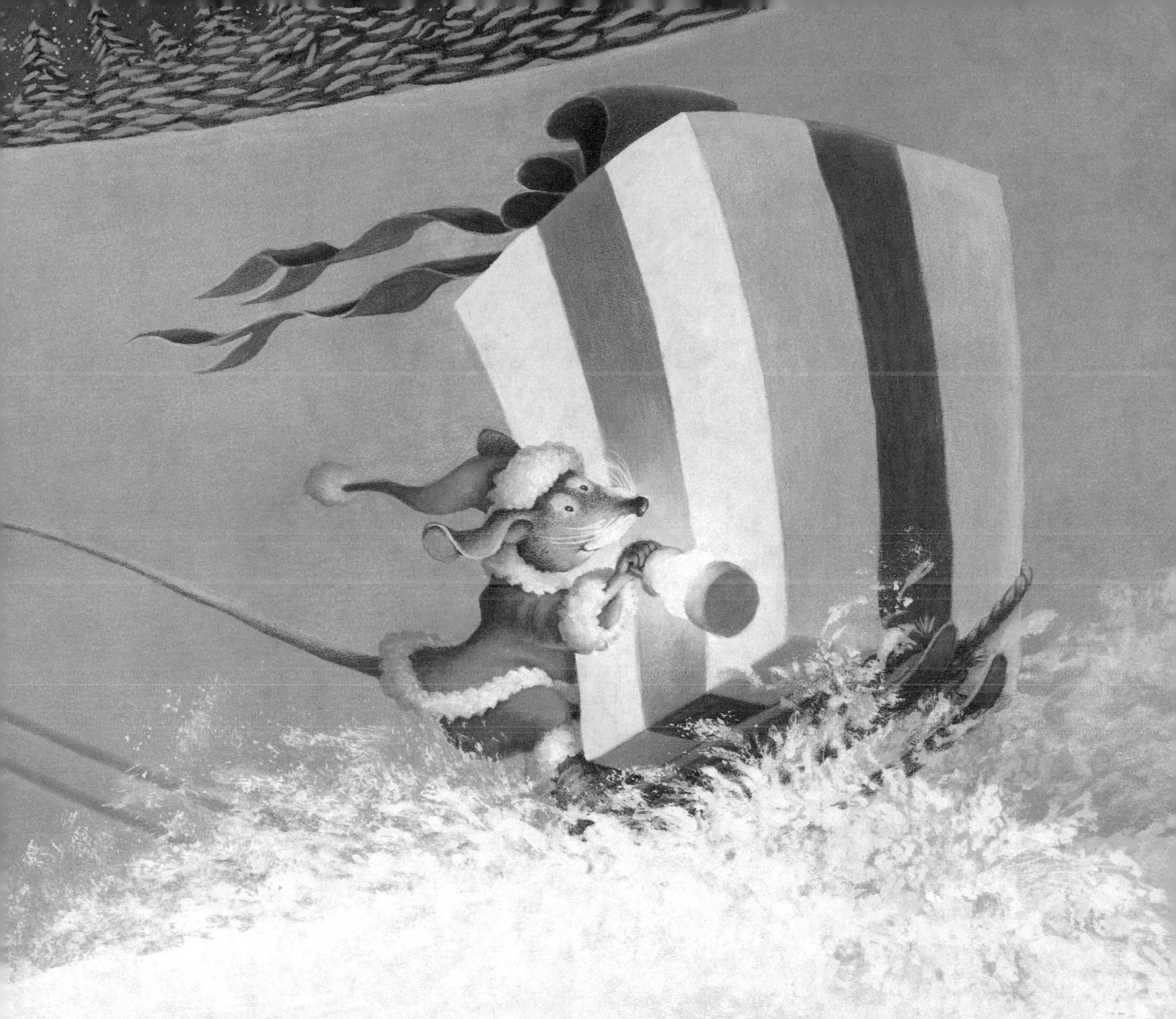

. . . FROM THE BIG, HUNGRY BEAR!

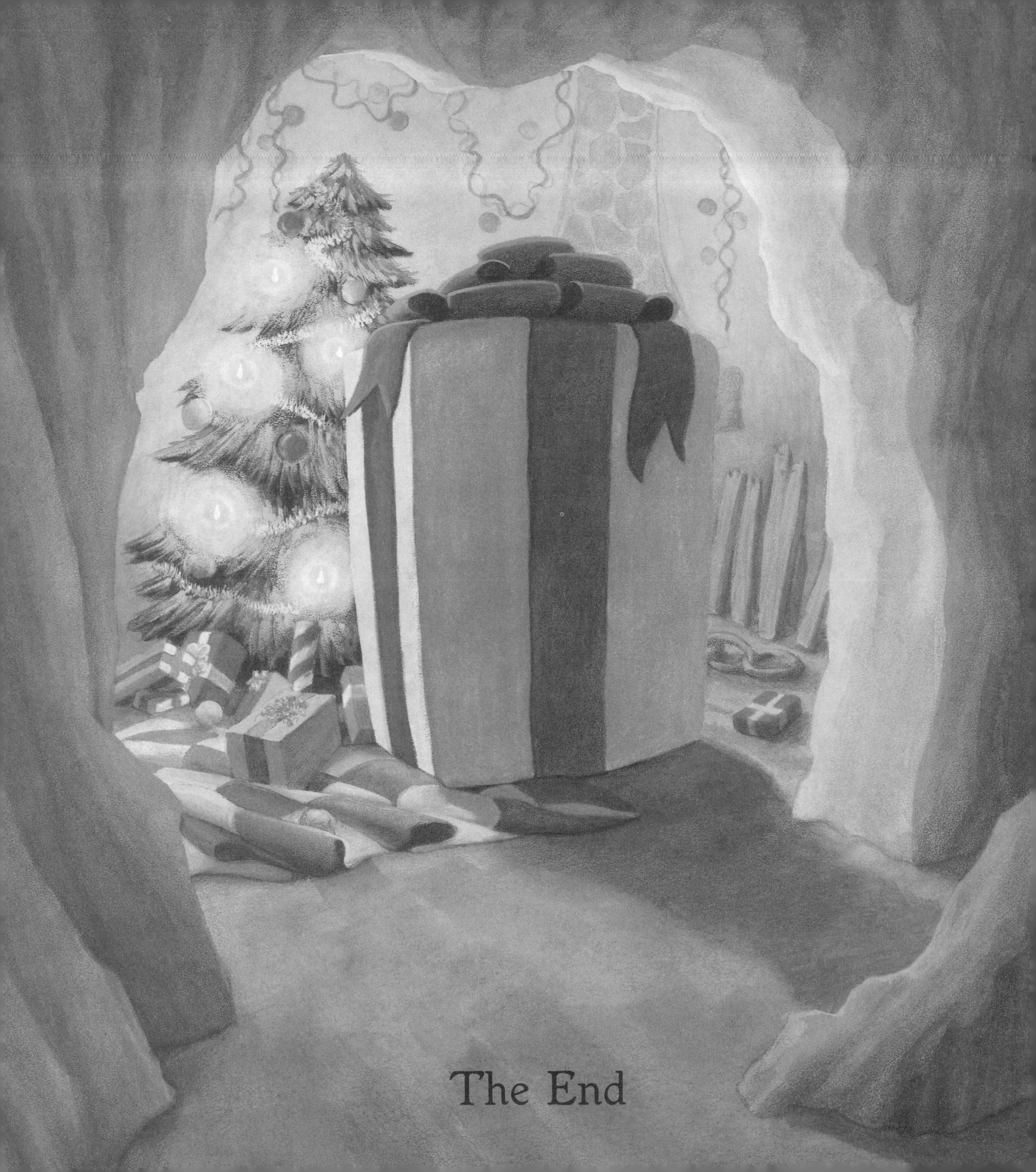

The End

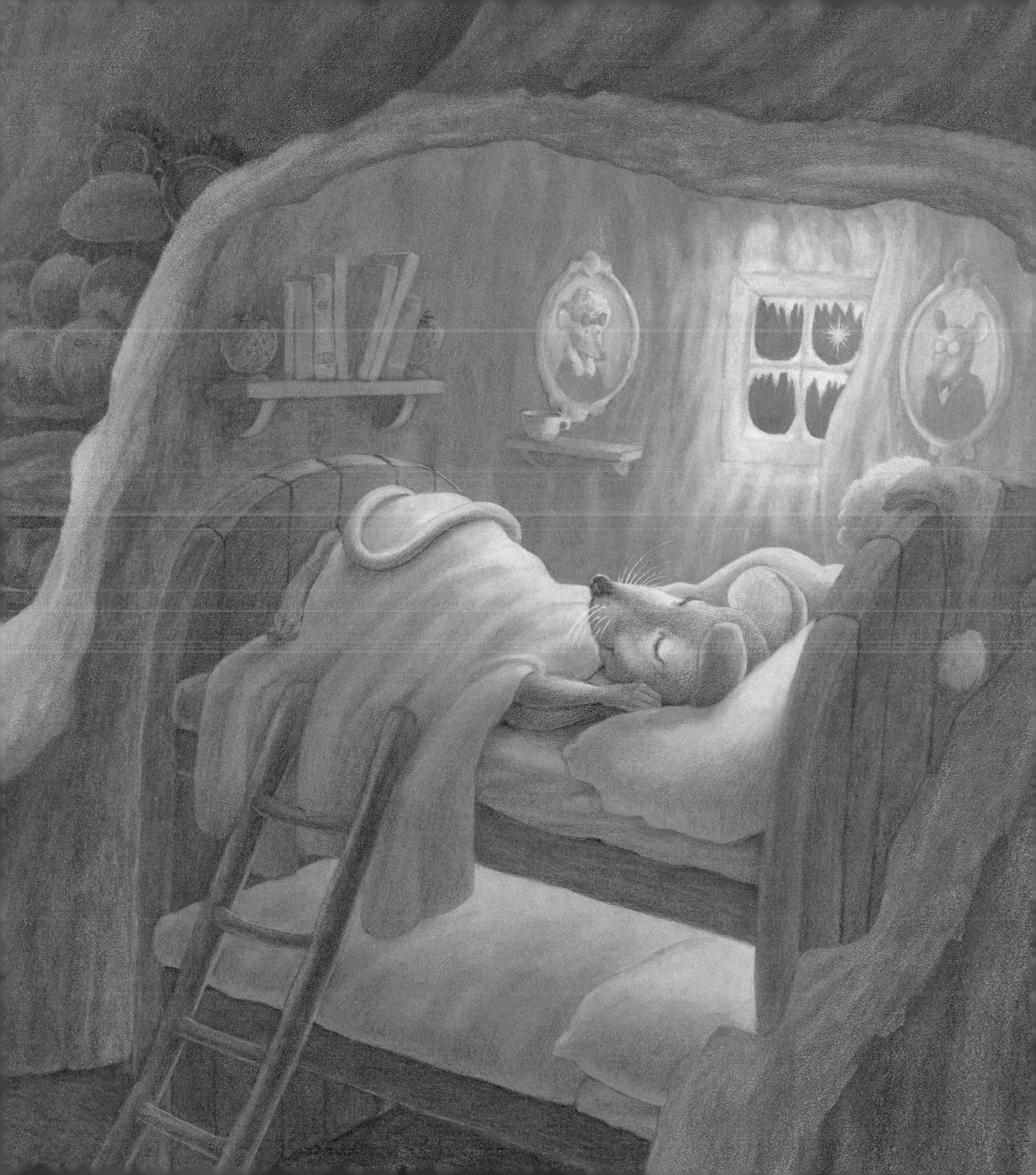